TALES OF TWO CITIES

TALES OF
TWO CITIES

Race and Economic Culture

in Early Republican North

and South America:

Guayaquil, Ecuador, and

Baltimore, Maryland

CAMILLA TOWNSEND

UNIVERSITY OF TEXAS PRESS, AUSTIN

Requests for permission to reproduce material from this
work should be sent to Permissions, University of Texas
Press, P.O. Box 7819, Austin, TX 78713-7819.

∞ The paper used in this book meets the minimum requirements of A N S I / N I S O Z 39.48-1992 (R 1997) (Permanence of
Paper).

Library of Congress Cataloging-in-Publication Data

Townsend, Camilla, 1965–
    Tales of two cities : race and economic culture in early
republican North and South America : Guayaquil, Ecuador,
and Baltimore, Maryland / by Camilla Townsend.
        p.   cm.
    Includes bibliographical references and index.
    ISBN 0-292-78167-9 (alk. paper). — ISBN 0-292-78169-5
(pbk. : alk. paper)
        1. Social classes—Ecuador—Guayaquil—History—19th
century.   2. Social classes—Maryland—Baltimore—History—19th century.   3. Guayaquil (Ecuador)—Economic
conditions—19th century.   4. Baltimore (Maryland)—Economic conditions—19th century.   I. Title.
HN320.Z9S67   2000
305.5′09752′6—dc21   99-36415

To Carmen and Edwin
and to John

CONTENTS

List of Maps and Tables *viii*
Acknowledgments *ix*
Prologue: First Impressions *xiii*
Introduction *1*

PART I

1. IN THE STREETS OF THE CITIES *23*

2. CONQUEST AND COLONY *47*

PART II

3. A MERRY PARTY AND SERIOUS BUSINESS:
The Elite of Guayaquil *71*

4. STRAWBERRY PARTIES AND HABITS OF INDUSTRY:
The Elite of Baltimore *100*

PART III

5. THE QUEST OF THE "PERSONAS DECENTES":
The Middling Ranks of Guayaquil *137*

6. THE QUEST OF THE CONTRIBUTING CITIZENS:
The Middling Ranks of Baltimore *154*

PART IV

7. WORKING ON DEAD MAN'S ROCK:
The Poor of Guayaquil *183*

8. "TO BECOME THE UNFORTUNATE TENANTS OF YOUR
ALMS HOUSE": The Poor of Baltimore *205*

Conclusion *233*
Notes *241*
Bibliography *289*
Index *313*

Maps and Tables

Maps

1. Guayaquil 22
2. Baltimore 48

Tables

1. Occupational Profiles of Early Nineteenth Century Baltimore and Guayaquil 66
2. Wealth Distribution among Taxable Households, Baltimore and Guayaquil c. 1830 67

ACKNOWLEDGMENTS

I have long looked forward to writing a thank you letter to everyone in-volved with this project. As one who has not left materialist questions behind, I thank those who paid me for doing the work I like best. At the dissertation stage, I received generous fellowships from Rutgers University, the Fulbright Commission, and the American Association of University Women, as well as a grant-in-aid from the Costume Society of America. As I have rewritten and rethought, the Research Council of Colgate University has been most helpful.

I owe an enormous debt to archivists and librarians in three countries and at least nine cities. In London the staff of the Public Record Office bore with me patiently. In the United States I received help from the University of Pennsylvania's Van Pelt Library Rare Book Room, Princeton University's Firestone Library Special Collections, Yale University's Latin American Collection, the Winterthur Museum and Library, the New York Public Library, the Library Company of Philadelphia, and the Maryland State Archives in Annapolis, as well as—in Baltimore itself—the Maryland Room of the Enoch Pratt Free Library, the Maryland Historical Society, and the Baltimore City Archives. When the Archives temporarily became my home away from home, Rebecca Gunby and Tony Roberts were especially kind to me. In Quito the staff of three archives aided my search: the National Historical Archives, the Archives of the

National Legislature, and the Archives of the Central Bank. I was also graciously received by the Jesuit Library Aureliano Espinosa Polit in Cotocallao and the Azuay provincial branch of the National Historical Archives in Cuenca. The Guayaquileño archivists outdid themselves in making me welcome: I thank especially Mariana Suárez and Nancy Palacio of the Municipal Library of Guayaquil, Carmen Aguilar Rendón of the Archive of the Municipal Secretariat, and the staff of the Historical Archive of Guayas, including Susana Loor, Lidia Quiñonez, Hector Peñaranda, and Diego Balarezo.

My former teachers and advisors have given me their time, their energy, their very selves. I owe the ultimate decision to embark upon this project to those who inspired me in early years—Jean Johnson of Friends Seminary, the late Jack Irgang of Stuyvesant High School for Math and Science, and Jane Caplan of Bryn Mawr College. But I owe most of all to my dissertation committee. As outside reader, Ronn Pineo led me through the maze of Ecuadorian archives. Paul Clemens guided me in my readings on Maryland and U.S. economic history. Tom Slaughter asked me not to be afraid to tell stories, while Mark Wasserman reminded me to keep track of reality. Sam Baily, my director, gave thoughtful advice at every stage: he is one of the finest teachers I can ever hope to know.

Others have had an impact on this study in numerous ways. Scholars who took time out of their busy schedules to talk to me and made trenchant comments include Enrique Ayala, Maria Eugenia Chaves, the late Julio Estrada, Stephen Innes, Ann Lane, Ed Papenfuse, and Stanley Stein. Others went an extra mile and read parts of the manuscript: Michael Adas, Marshall Eakin, Piedad Gutiérrez, Lyman Johnson, and Anne Rubenstein. The anonymous readers for the University of Texas Press gave key advice. The staff of the Press were all unfailingly helpful. Theresa May was a wise, kind, and efficient editor, and Kathy Lewis as a copy editor was a dream come true. Russ Shallieu beautifully digitized the otherwise unreproducible illustrations. I am eternally in your debt.

Without my friends and family, I could never have finished. I thank my mother, Carolynn Erickson Townsend; my father, J. Kenneth Townsend; my sister, Cynthia Townsend; and my friend Rebecca Davis, for loving me without reservation. My parents also provided more concrete aid, my father by proofreading and my mother by allowing me to invade her apartment periodically. In Baltimore Stephanie Seipp made room for me in her house. In Ecuador the García family made me welcome in their home for a whole academic year, and the Aguilar family treated me like a daughter. Alba Alfaro reached out her hand to me when I was most lonely, and Olivia Codaccioni used her keen intelligence and knowledge of Ecuadorian historiography to challenge my thinking. Guillermo Bustos and his colleagues at the History Workshop in Quito gave me food for thought to last a long time. Back in the United States, Richard Dunn and the seminar members of the McNeil Center for Early American Studies welcomed a Latin Americanist into their midst and improved my work immensely. In the final stages, my colleagues at Colgate University have been warm and funny, smart and demanding. I am lucky to work with them.

Most of all, I want to thank John Nolan, who drafted the maps, and Carmen Ortiz, who organized my files. You both did much more than this. You waited for me while I literally wandered the globe and then shut myself away for weeks at a time. Thirteen years ago, unblindfolded, we came together as three people from two generations, two classes, two races, two genders, two religions, and at least three different political persuasions and family and cultural backgrounds. I believe we should be proud of the bridges we have built and forgive each other where the chasms were too wide. I owe this project to you because you loved me and let me love you, reminding me daily why people and their history matter at all.

PROLOGUE

First Impressions

One day as Spain's colonies sat poised on the edge of their independence, the Indian woman María Magdalena decided to leave her home of many years and head for the city of Guayaquil with her young daughter, Ana Yagual. Together they departed from the coastal fishing village where they had lived in great hardship and began a sixty-mile journey up the River Guayas.[1] They went partway on foot and partway by raft. Along both sides of the river, leafy plants touched the gray water. Wherever mangrove bushes grew, they were perfectly reflected in the calm of the *río*, making it almost impossible to tell where the water began and ended.

To avoid answering questions, many newcomers waited until after dark to approach the city. Perched on rafts and boats, they stared at the populous riverbank, for at night the town appeared almost magical. Two horizontal rows of lights glittered for half a mile, the bottom row cast by street lamps and the top by lights in the upper floors of the stately white houses lining the shore. Giant palm trees grew along the river's edge. Those who waited on the water could hear strains of music clearly. To the right, at the foot of green hills, people who lived on *balsas* or small boats had lit fires aboard their crafts, and the sound of their laughing and talking floated across the surface of the water. Canoes darted in and out expertly, as if the darkness were no obstacle. The sight even made an impression on wealthy and well-traveled foreigners standing on the decks of big ships. "It was late in the evening when we came to anchor off the city, and I never beheld a more brilliant view than the one before us."[2]

But the lights shimmered almost too brightly. Another visitor later warned: "And when you finally reach the end of your voyage and stop before the vision of an enchanted city looking in from the outside, then if you want to keep your illusion unbroken and your poetic memories intact, you must not enter."[3] Either María Magdalena had never been to this world before or she did know something of it yet felt prepared to negotiate its pitfalls. She chose to enter, heading up one of the estuaries toward the outskirts of town, where she would make her home, with Ana Yagual right behind her.

Only a few years later in the 1820s, but thousands of miles to the north, another child entered another port. Frederick Bailey was about ten when his Talbot County master sent him to live in Baltimore. He could barely contain his excitement. "My cousin Tom had been there," he would later write, ". . . and when he came from Baltimore, he was always a sort of hero amongst us . . . I could never tell him anything that struck me as beautiful or powerful, but that he had seen something in Baltimore far surpassing it." Now Frederick himself had been sent to live with one of his owner's urban relations, to work as an errand boy and domestic servant.[4]

The wide waters of the Chesapeake formed the main approach to town. From a ship or a boat the city's appearance could be breathtaking, and travelers remembered the sight. "Baltimore, with its white buildings rising to our view on the sides of the hills as we approached it, had a most exhilarating effect."[5] But first contact with the actual wharves indicated to some that life in this city would hardly prove to be idyllic. The shallow waters were dumping grounds for refuse and, especially in summer, became "reservoirs of putrefaction." "We came along the wharf sides, under the red dingy-looking warehouses, between which the water ran in narrow dark-looking canals."[6]

Frederick Bailey's boat docked at Smith's Wharf on a summer Sunday morning. Some of the passengers drove a large flock of sheep they had on board to a nearby slaughterhouse. The boy's initial enthusiasm waned quickly, as his early impressions of the city were not very favorable after all. For a while he wanted to leave, "with hard brick pavements under my feet, which almost raised blisters by their very heat, . . . walled in on all sides by towering brick buildings; with troops of boys ready to pounce upon me at every street corner . . . ; and with startling sounds reaching my ears from all directions."[7] Not long after, the child also came to understand the full meaning of the word "slave," increasing his sense of entrapment as he got to know the city better. Yet as the years passed, Frederick became convinced that city life was to be his salvation, his path out of slavery and then out of poverty.

As Frederick in Baltimore and Ana Yagual in Guayaquil grew and neared adulthood, they learned to negotiate the daily workings of their respective worlds and became familiar with the opportunities open and closed to them. They learned to what extent their optimism was misplaced and to what extent well founded. Then they made decisions and took action based upon their sense of themselves and their knowledge of the societies in which they lived. In the coming chapters I ask the reader to follow them through the streets of their cities and let the details of their lives illuminate both the potential and the constraints of the worlds they inhabited.

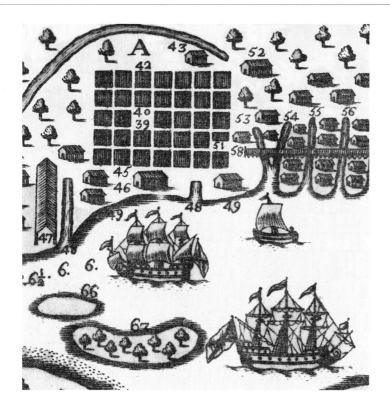

The town grew from a simple colonial village, shared by whites and Indians, into a city whose neighborhoods were densely packed and impressive to newcomers.

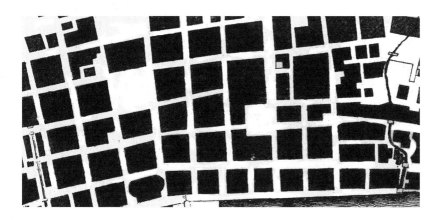

The port was always busy, especially after the war for independence.

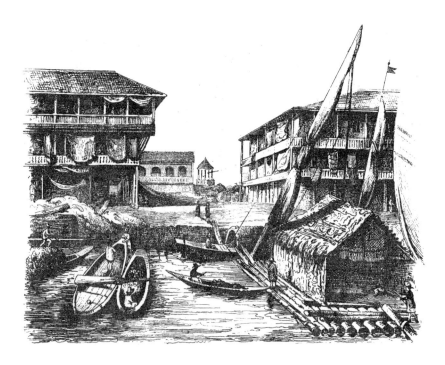

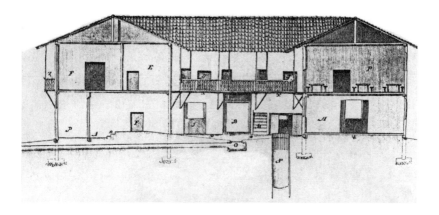

With their famous enthusiasm, the people designed factories,

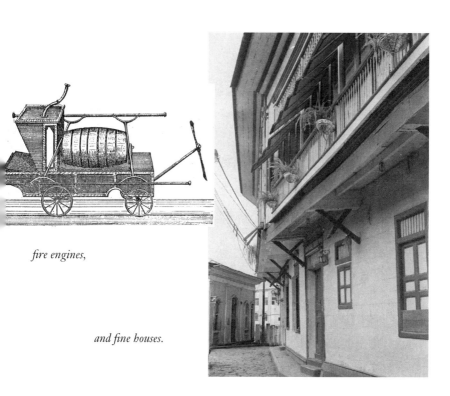

fire engines,

and fine houses.

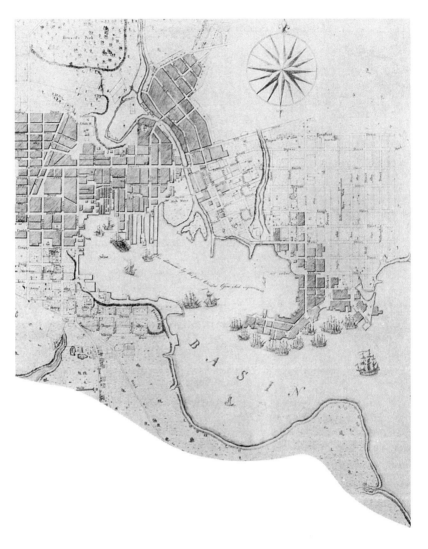

Thousands of miles away, after its own war for independence, another city grew out away from its river and into the surrounding countryside.

In the busy markets, crowds thronged and hawkers shouted.

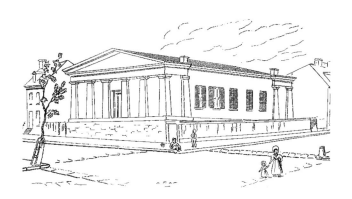

People came from all over to see the first public school

and to marvel at the aqueducts that brought water to town.

The people also loved to rest in the park and to dream of winning the lottery so that they would never have to work again.

Illustration Credits

Page xvii

Top: Fragment of a map published in Dionysio de Alfredo y Herrera, *Compendio Histórico de la Provincia, Partidos, Ciudad, Astilleros, Ríos y Puerto de Guayaquil,* Madrid, 1741.
Bottom: Fragment of a map published in Manuel de Villavicencio, Geografía de la República del Ecuador, New York, 1858.

Page xviii

Top: "El Malecón," reproduced in Guayaquil de Ayer. *Centro de Investigaciones y Cultura: Colección de Imagenes, Volumen 6.* Quito: Archivo del Banco Central, 1985.
Bottom: "Primeros Edificios en la Ciudad Nueva," from an unidentified nineteenth-century engraving reproduced in Modesto Chavez Franco, *Crónicas del Guayaquil Antiquo.* Guayaquil: Imprenta y Talleres Municipales, 1930.

Page xix

Top: "Fábrica de Tabacos de Guayaquil," Archivo General de Indias, Sevilla, reproduced in Julio Estrada Ycaza, "La Economía de 1800 a 1830," *Historia del Ecuador,* Tomo V. Quito: Salvat Editores, 1980.
Middle: Original model from Spain, from a 1779 engraving owned by Chavez Franco and reproduced in his *Crónicas del Guayaquil Antiquo.*
Bottom: Barrio las Peñas, Guayaquil. Photograph by the author.

Page xx

Fragment of map "Baltimore in 1792" courtesy of the Maryland Historical Society.

Page xxi

Top: "Centre Market" from John Latrobe, *Picture of Baltimore.* Baltimore: Feilding Lucas, 1832. Courtesy of Winterthur Museum and Library.
Middle: "Public School No. 1" from Latrobe, *Picture of Baltimore.* Courtesy of Winterthur Museum and Library.
Bottom: "Carrolton Viaduct" from Latrobe, *Picture of Baltimore.* Courtesy of Winterthur Museum and Library.

Page xii

Top: "City Spring, Calvert Street" from Latrobe, *Picture of Baltimore.* Courtesy of Winterthur Museum and Library.
Bottom: From the Baltimore Biennial Advertiser, 1832.

INTRODUCTION

In this book Ana Yagual, Frederick Bailey, and others who lived in their cities interrogate their world for the modern reader. They speak to us through word and deed about what they experienced as they tried their hands at making their lives and fortunes. They talk about the opportunities they imagined, the ambitions they cherished, and the frustrations they felt in the fledgling republics of the northern and southern hemispheres once the wars of independence were won. They help us to understand the relevance of the nebulous concept of "economic culture."

Why should we be interested in this concept? Clearly the constant comparisons—implicit and explicit—between the United States and Latin America that pepper our lives stem from the striking contrast between the United States' relative wealth and Latin America's comparative impoverishment. The northern Anglo world grew rich while the southern Hispanic world grew poor. If, then, in most of our minds, the ultimate point is an *economic* one, why study culture? Do I begin this work with the assumption that once we understand differences in "attitudes," we will have the final word on the different economic trajectories of the northern and southern worlds? Certainly not. In my mind, culture is only one element of the explanation for poverty. It is an important one to grapple with, however, because we are currently living in a world that prioritizes it as a variable and because it is probably the most mutually misunderstood and even abused term in the debate on poverty. Thus we need to study it both much more carefully and more creatively than we have tended to do. If we live in an era in which the concept is bandied about with some frequency, then we lay ourselves open to error and miscommunication if we do not question self-consciously what we mean by the term.

In the pages that follow the reader will walk through two comparable towns, becoming intimately acquainted with the people's economic lives between 1820 and 1835 when both societies were for the first time free of European domination and were making their own decisions. Moving beyond assumptions and assertions about attitudes to a study of the nitty-gritty details of daily life offers the possibility of rethinking our most common understanding of "economic culture." We see places where attitudes may affect the economy not only in terms of the more commonly considered issues like work ethic, business savvy, rationality, and individualistic willingness to take risks, but also in terms of consumer desires, popular beliefs about banks, joint stock companies, and taxes, and conceptions of workers. "Culture" is one of the most malleable of terms. *Webster's* calls it "the total pattern of human behavior and its products embodied in thought, speech, action, and artifacts and dependent upon man's capacity for learning and transmitting knowledge to succeeding generations." Rather than becoming embroiled in the academic debates as to its nature, choosing sides, and then searching for examples to fit, I prefer to let the details of people's lives suggest widely varying ways in which mental constructs and human behavior may impact the economy.

I am well aware that there are those who see understanding the social imagination as the key to knowledge and others who see its study as irrelevant. We live today with battles between "culturalists" and "structuralists." (Anyone who follows the debate on welfare knows this, for example, as analysts argue about the relative importance of the culturally inherited attitudes and values of aid recipients versus the lack of effective education and decent-paying jobs.) Scholars have in fact participated in several incarnations of this discussion. Generations of economic historians have developed increasingly complex understandings of what has happened over the course of the past few centuries in international and regional trade. In the last twenty years, however, the historical discipline as a whole has tended to ignore the often valuable contributions of materialists, rejecting as first order of business any purely structuralist explanations for change and emphasizing cultural variables instead. Occasionally the materialist scholars, who study what they see as the realities of power, wealth, and resources, scoff at others who insist on studying what they themselves understand as the superficial effects of change, rather than its underlying causes. At other moments the culturalists are equally dismissive of those who insist that there is a social reality somehow distinct from its formulation within human minds. Readers undoubtedly recognize the debate and can locate themselves somewhere between the caricatures of the two extremes.

In probing the meaning of "economic culture," I think there is in fact great value in bringing to bear the insights of both schools of thought, the culturalists and the structural economists. Of course, the goals of the two kinds of scholarship remain—and probably always will remain—inherently different. Thus participants in such a joint discussion stand to benefit for different reasons. What, for example, might a person who is a believer in the ultimate importance of economics notice in the discussion that follows? One might consider the possibility of defining economic culture so as to include the roots in human imagination of such institutions as coerced labor, credit networks, military arms in the hands of a few, etc., which even the most materialist scholars agree do matter to economic development. Some hesitancy is evident when Peter Temin asks, "Is It Kosher to Talk about Culture?"[1] There are good reasons to take this step, though. We might do so for tactical reasons—so that those of us who care about real people living in real poverty will not be eclipsed in a profession dominated more and more by those analyzing the social imagination as if its comprehension were an end in itself. And we might do so for intellectual reasons, refusing to accept "institutions" as a category of analysis without asking the question "Whence the institutions?"

What, on the other hand, might a person notice who is already a believer in the importance of cultural constructs? One might assess the ways in which, despite our best intentions to remain relativistic, we are all affected to some degree by the economic theories to which we have been exposed. Different studies focus on certain aspects of culture and ignore others, or even seek out examples of behavior that seem to indicate the presence of an expected cultural paradigm, often depending on what the author has consciously or unconsciously accepted as the driving force behind economic development or historical change. We should consider this possibility if we are to remain true to our goal of attempting to enter into any cultural world on its own terms.

A Preliminary Note on Cultural History

It is worth pausing to remind ourselves that the revolutionary breakthrough offered by students of culture in recent decades lies in the fact that "culture" is no longer conceived of as a shared and static set of symbol systems that a group of people uses to relate to the objects in the environment. Instead, "culture" is now understood as a constantly contested and gradually shifting terrain that is understood differently by various groups of people in any time and place. "Culture" ultimately consists of humans' relationships with each other. A cross, for example, isn't just a symbol of the divine; it has different meanings for different people as they interact with each other in their varied assertions about the divine and its relationship to themselves and others. In this concept of culture, power becomes a central issue. Interaction and conflict must by definition involve power imbalances. Where once the potential imposition of one group's will on another group was considered the subject of study for scholars who looked at law, government, and politics, it is now recognized that the theme concerns us all in different ways. Even manifestations of the "cross," to use the same example, are no longer exempt from what might once have been called "political" styles of analysis in that they concern power.

The key is that no human being exists as an inherent or autonomous "self." Rather we all learn to understand and define ourselves in relation to those around us. The same holds true for groups of people. The boundaries of any category are determined by who is present in a social universe. (Put simply, what would it mean to be "male" if there were no "female"? How could you be a "child" if there were no "adults"?) Thus the possibility of revolutionizing our concept of "economic culture" will lie in our ability to keep these ideas in mind as effectively as we are learning to do in analyzing other aspects of culture.[2]

It is in this regard that race is a particularly important category of analysis in a study of culture in the Americas. A discussion of race and economic culture does not have to imply a static connection between certain races and certain beliefs about money or behavior patterns regarding work. Rather we might use the terms to study relationships between racial groups working within one economy. Who is expected to work for whom and why? How is the "right to a decent living" a contested idea having different meanings for different groups? Who blames whom for economic woes and why?

Comparative Studies of New World Economies and Economic Culture

It is my assertion that scholars' views of economics influence what they observe about economic culture. In some cases, the connections are overt and explicit; in others, unconscious or implicit. It is important that we lay out on the table what the most widely available economic theories are before we discuss their impact on our beliefs about culture. I promise to do so in plain language. Directness, always a good quality in my opinion, is all the more necessary in this case as I am asking readers to bear in mind various economic theories at the same time as they engage in cultural analysis in two geographically divergent arenas.

Current paradigms in the field of economic history exist in response to the dominant perspective of the 1960s and 1970s: dependency theory. The latter held that not all parts of the world approach international trade with equal power and that, as a result, such trade can impoverish some regions (usually those exporting raw materials) even as it enriches others (usually those exporting manufactured goods). Broadly speaking, critics of the dependency perspective generally fall into one of two groups. According to the first school of thought, which is most common in the United States, international trade was more beneficial than harmful to those who engaged in it, but large portions of Latin America never really were fully integrated into the world trade system, or at least not in the best possible way: it remains for them to accomplish that goal in order to attain healthier economies. Members of the other group insist that relations between center and peripheral nations did in fact impoverish the latter, but they add that in order to understand *why* this was allowed to happen we have to look at relationships *inside* the peripheral nations. They argue that a society's relations of production are as important as international commodity exchange in dictating future patterns of development. That is, commodities take on their economic significance for a region in the context of local class relations. If wealth is distributed extremely unevenly, retarding the growth of a domestic market, incipient industrialization will be stymied no matter how rich the exportable resources are.

Both groups sometimes rely on the concept of "economic culture" at key junctures in their arguments, but they do so in dramatically different ways, as they envision the "motor" of history differently. Members of the first group are focused on trade or total production, so when they consider culture, they consider attitudes toward the act of producing, toward work. They say that certain values and styles of doing business—a strong work ethic, an emphasis on efficiency, the individualistic and rationalistic pursuit of profit, an opposition to traditionalism and protectionism—are more conducive than others to increasing production and thus to economic success. Members of the second group, on the other hand, are focused on internal relations of production and the growth of the domestic market, so when they deal with cultural practices at all, they tend to deal with institutions and societal assumptions concerning the labor force or the envisioning of relationships between rich and poor. In shorthand, one can say that they study cultural beliefs concerning workers, rather than work.

The first school of thought on the meaning and relevance of "economic culture" has a long and distinguished academic tradition behind it. Its inheritance is distinctly Weberian. At the turn of the twentieth century appeared Max Weber's *The Protestant Ethic and the Spirit of Capitalism:*

> It is a fact that the Protestants . . . both as ruling classes and as ruled, have shown a special tendency to develop economic rationalism which cannot be observed to the same extent among Catholics . . . Thus the principal explanation for this difference must be sought in the permanent intrinsic character of their religious beliefs, and not only in their temporary external historico-political situations.[3]

Weber's ideas struck responsive chords in many people and led to a warring exchange among scholars that lasted for most of the century. He argued that the rationalistic pursuit of profit encompassed the separation of home and worksite, the development of efficient systems of bookkeeping and exchange of money on paper, and the organization of free labor. These phenomena, he said, developed due to the Protestant values of hard work and thrift. Although by now historians have largely rejected any simplistic and easily disprovable view that Catholicism is always embedded in superstition and the irrational or that the rise of Protestantism is always accompanied by increasing business acumen, many scholars still adhere to the idea that Protestantism does transform a society in ways that are good for economic development.[4] Certainly the latter view is widely accepted among nonscholars in the United States. To many a young person growing up in this country, frequent jokes and subtle comments, the messages of home, school, church, and media, suggest that the ideals of hard work, thrift, and responsibility for self are Protestant ideals and that they are the reasons for the nation's success.

These attitudes peaked in the 1950s and 1960s, when they were still explicit and remained largely unquestioned. They had a direct influence on U.S. foreign policy. Puerto Rico was to be the "showcase of the Americas," demonstrating to the world the positive effect that exposure to U.S. values would have, while the Alliance for Progress—in theory—would aid countries further removed in learning to reshape cultural norms and institutions.[5] Many Latin American academics, interacting with U.S. scholars, also embraced this perspective. Tomás Fillól, for example, educated at the Massachusetts Institute of Technology, wrote that an Argentine believes "great success is obtained by waiting, by hoping, by the favor of the saints . . ."[6] He implied that when Latin Americans learned to replace their irresponsibility and superstition with rationality and responsibility for self, they would succeed.

Today politicians and academics avoid resorting to the once popular phrase "national character," but many of the patterns of thought developed in the earlier era retain their currency, especially in the United States. In the mid-1980s Harvard's Center for International Affairs published Lawrence Harrison's *Underdevelopment Is a State of Mind: The Latin American Case*. Harrison, whose career abroad in the 1960s and 1970s rendered him a direct product of the Alliance for Progress mentality, concludes that "it is culture [by which he means work ethic] that principally explains, in most cases, why some countries develop more rapidly and equitably than others." Even after recounting, for example, some of the historical differences in the situations faced by the relatively wealthy Costa Rica and the relatively impoverished Nicaragua, he ends by saying, "Costa Rica is different from Nicaragua *because Costa Ricans are different from Nicaraguans*" (emphasis his).[7] By extension, Harrison implies, most Latin Americans—although not Costa Ricans—have the wrong culture for promoting economic success, while North Americans have the right one.

Likewise, these ideas are present in the work of scholars whose primary focus is on the northern world rather than the southern. In his comparative study of French Canada, New England, and the U.S. South between 1750 and 1850, Marc Egnal opens with the following question and answer: "Why are some countries or regions economic success stories, while others languish in the doldrums of slow growth? The role of culture and institutions must be placed near the top of any list of reasons." Through the book, he explains his concept of "culture," including work ethic, attitudes toward the salability of land, and willingness to move households and otherwise break with tradition. In keeping with common expectations, he finds anecdotal evidence that people in the northern United States had more "get up and go" than people in French Canada or the South—or, he adds in his preface, than in Latin America and certain other regions. "To summarize, while the North displayed the bright colors of the entrepreneurial spirit, the South was brushed by only the palest tones."[8]

In his most recent study, *The Wealth and Poverty of Nations: Why Some Are So Rich and Some So Poor*, economic historian David Landes works with these ideas. Emphasizing cultural differences, he cites Weber and says succinctly: "The heart of the matter lay indeed in the making of a new kind of man—rational, ordered, diligent, productive. These virtues, while not new, were hardly commonplace. Protestantism generalized them."[9] Elsewhere in the book he does acknowledge that unusual and liberating attitudes may have taken root in England and northern Europe because these areas experienced a greater than typical number of invasions and a higher level of chaos in the Middle Ages, thus preventing lords from establishing strangleholds over local serfs.[10] This idea, however, is not emphasized, as it stems from a second school of thought, which is not his favorite.

The second school of thought concerning the meaning and relevance of "economic culture" is less familiar to most of us. Most people who have studied the importance of internal relations of production originally came from a materialist (Marxist) background, and until recently they shied away from using the term "culture" even though they often did discuss the formation of institutions in the minds of human beings. Their tradition, too, had its academic forerunners. By the late 1960s Ernesto Laclau, for example, had already formulated a subtle critique of the dependency perspective that in some ways allowed for a human dimension. Without rejecting the relevance of international power imbalances, he reminded readers that local forms of production are as important as processes of commodity exchange in determining development and that the former are not necessarily dictated by the latter in a given pattern. He asserted that what he called "feudal" relations of production can exist within a capitalist world trade system. Indeed, by separating the two issues, Laclau implicitly argued that even if the Latin American periphery had been allowed to keep a larger share of the profits in the international trade exchange dominated by the European center, the critical damage would still have been accomplished by the center's "fixing [Latin American] relations of production in an archaic mould of extra-economic coercion, which retarded any process of social differentiation and diminished the size of their internal markets." [11]

During the 1980s and early 1990s discussion of the importance of local relationships—as opposed to international trade—increased in subtlety. In a much-discussed public exchange with Immanuel Wallerstein, Steve Stern asserted the need for a paradigm that counts as relevant three factors—the European-dominated world system of trade, the agency of local Latin American elites, and the resistance of working people. [12] Stern's first factor (the world system) is essentially the older category of analysis called "commodity exchange," and in his following factors (the influences of local elites and working people) he is renaming "local relations of production." As a historian he is giving these processes human faces, acknowledging that the "European center" existed due to the activities of powerful Europeans and that the relations of production in the periphery existed by virtue of the efforts of powerful local elites in the context of the reactions of laboring people.

Currently a number of historians are drawing theoretical conclusions about the different trajectories followed by North and South America which rely on an understanding of the relationship between elites and commoners at the time of conquest and through the early years of colonial development. [13] Labor historian Charles Bergquist has pointed out that the productivity and wealth of various regions of the Americas today are often inversely proportional to the concentration of wealth and degree of coercion of labor experienced in the colonial years. Whether in British or Spanish territory, South Carolina or Bolivia, the decision to rely on an enslaved majority to produce great wealth for a few ended up inhibiting a general belief that people have a right to better themselves and created an impoverished majority who could demand few goods even when freed:

> These labor systems created or hardened class and racial attitudes which gravely compromised the potential for industrial and democratic development. Among these cultural attitudes was widespread disdain for manual labor and the people who performed it, and the idea that people of African, Indian or mixed descent were congenitally inferior to whites, if not subhuman. [14]

9

Here race has appeared in the discussion most explicitly. Lest anyone should willfully misconstrue his statement as some form of support for the traditional argument that people of the southern climes did not succeed because they were not white Protestants, Bergquist adds trenchantly: "These societies failed to develop in the post-independence era in the way their once-poor, predominantly white, northern neighbors did not because they had too many blacks, but because they had too many slaves."

Economic historians Stanley Engerman and Kenneth Sokoloff agree, although they use different language—the terms of their trade. They point out that U.S. economic historians have long created neat theories connecting the nation's success to early abundance of land and other resources. "Puzzles arise, however, when scholars of the United States turn to the experiences of Latin American economies." If ever there was a world of abundant land, fertile soils, precious metals, and other resources, Latin America was it. "Those seeking to account for the divergent paths of the United States and Latin America have usually made reference to differences in institutions, where the concept is interpreted broadly to encompass not only formal political and legal structures but culture as well." These "cultural" attitudes, they say, are usually identified with certain European groups and pertain largely to work ethic and entrepreneurialism. Engerman and Sokoloff, however, would like to return attention to factor endowments, defining them not only in terms of soil and resources, but in terms of "density of native populations," and arguing that the latter especially influenced "institutional developments." Wherever colonizers were able to dominate a large number of indigenous people or replace them with African imports, they accrued great wealth but left a legacy of poverty to their nations in later centuries. "The initial conditions had long, lingering effects" in that "government policies and other institutions tended generally to reproduce the sorts of factor endowments that gave rise to them." The resulting impoverishment of the majority ultimately curtailed development of markets and thus of trade: "There are reasons for expecting regions with more equal circumstances and rights to be more likely to realize sustained economic growth and . . . the breadth of evidence provided by the experiences of New World colonies supports this view."[15]

What Bergquist, Engerman, Sokoloff, and their kind are talking about *is* an aspect of culture, although it has little to do with work ethic and entrepreneurialism. Elites anywhere will extract as much as they can get away with extracting and will attempt to maximize that capability in times of flux and change. What specifically determines how much they can get away with is a set of factors which in today's language would be called "cultural" in that they stem from people's identity vis-à-vis others: people's relationships with others in their communities and outside of them, their very understanding of "community" or of "citizen," their beliefs about themselves and each other, their concepts of having or losing power. Power is certainly at the center of the picture. But at the critical juncture, we find that power can no longer be interpreted in a purely materialist fashion. Yes, an elite group's ability to coerce fellow humans as laborers depends on who has the guns, who knows someone in the government, who has access to loans, and other concrete realities. *Yet how was it decided who would have the guns?* To what extent is the decision accepted by the majority and why? In other words, *whence these institutions?* Only the new concept of culture, encompassing people's visions of themselves in relation to others, can offer us answers.

It might be tempting to decide that northern and southern Europeans were profoundly different in the ways in which they interacted with others, just as it has been tempting to see Spanish people as somehow inherently less efficient or hardworking than English people. The Puritans, after all, were idealistic and egalitarian, we are told, while the *conquistadores*, most of us have learned, treated their Indian servants brutally. But we would be mistaken to make such a summary judgment. Matters depended not so much on the colonists' country of origin as on the kind of indigenous civilization that existed in the area they settled and the ways the Indians therefore chose to interact with the colonizers. Settled, tribute-paying Indians whose societies were too complex to endure a flight to the forest and who were accustomed to class hierarchy accepted—to a certain extent—living under the Spanish, who in turn conceived of themselves as superior beings who would dominate the majority.[16] Despite the desire of John Smith and others like him to reduce Indians to laboring tributaries, interactions with the Native Americans in the northern world did not turn out similarly, as we know. Many years ago Stanley and Barbara Stein wrote in a path-breaking book, "One might surmise that had Englishmen found a dense and highly organized Amerindian population, the history of what is today called the United States would record the development of a stratified, bi-racial, very different society."[17] Only recently Engerman and Sokoloff turned this conjecture around and said, "Other New World economies might have been able to realize growth in much the same way as the United States if not for their initial factor endowments [of valuable export products and dense Indian settlement] and the government policies that upheld their influence."[18]

If these suggestions seem too much like speculations, then we can consider concrete examples. Where the Spanish did not find valuable export products or densely settled Indians who became their laborers, they came closest to establishing egalitarian societies of smallholders that later prospered—as in Costa Rica, for example.[19] And the English did not behave as we like to remember them behaving when their circumstances were different. Although our history books have chosen to forget this, a large group of Puritans went to an island off the coast of Nicaragua in the same year Massachusetts Bay Colony was founded. There, with lush fertile soils at their disposal and surrounded by other colonists who relied on coerced Indian and African laborers, the Puritans eagerly became slaveholders and operated large plantations. The original owners absolutely refused to sell off the land to colonists in plots for family farms.[20]

Both worlds' historiographies stand to gain from this style of comparison, not only that of Latin America. Work on the United States is improved by putting it in context, even if only implicitly. U.S. historians have tended to study U.S. history in isolation. Thus even the most brilliant of the explanations for the Market Revolution that occurred in the early nineteenth century have sometimes fallen flat. Gordon Wood has written that we must look beyond business transactions to more broad-based transformations in economic culture:

America did not become a prosperous, scrambling, money-making society because a few leaders like Hamilton created a bank or because a few rich merchants sent ships to China. America developed the way it did because hundreds of thousands of ordinary people began working harder than ever before to make money to "get ahead." No constitution, no institution, could have created or restrained these popular energies.[21]

But many of the peoples of Latin America also worked hard after their own wars of independence. Why did the policy not work for them? Seeking an explanation for his nation's exceptionalism, Wood offers: "As ordinary [North] Americans, they brought their ordinary interests and tastes into play as never before, including not only a rather scrambling propensity for money-making, but also their popular beliefs in evangelical Christianity." Here we are, still well within the confines of Weberian analysis nearly a century after its original presentation. Ethnic differences, bordering on traditional racial distinctions, are still at the heart of the matter.

Stephen Innes, in a very different kind of work, also studies the economic culture of New England, but rather than depending on traditional assumptions, he asks himself what the Puritan forebears actually did differently from others of their era. Although working hard was not unique to them, he finds something that was: their "civic ecology"—a belief in the importance of the social and human capital of community members, in the right of all men to own land, in a shared prosperity being good for the future.[22] They could create such a culture, I might add, in a world populated only by themselves, in which the Other, the enemy race, the Indians, were being pushed to the outer fringes.

To avoid stereotypes and learn something new, we need to look more closely at economic culture than we often have. We must look at the evidence without prejudice, allowing for the possibility of surprise. This book's contribution is to bring the daily economic lives of two comparable early republican towns into as full a view as possible. It shows people working, buying, innovating, and investing. Specifically, for ordinary folk, I ask how and when they worked and what they wanted to buy. For the more elite people, I ask how and when they worked and how they invested. Why did owners choose to expand artisan shops into manufactories more often in one place than in another? Why were they more in favor of making a public investment in infrastructure in one place than in another? Answering these questions will allow us to explore differences in attitudes toward work as well as divergent concepts of workers, of people. On one level, we can consider which of our assumptions about differences in economic culture have been right and which wrong; on another level, we can consider shifting our understanding of what economic culture might mean.

Methodology

The theoretical power of this study of minute aspects of daily life lies in the fact that it is comparative. Comparison allows us to determine which aspects of people's lives really differed and which did not. It also allows us to explore causation: if these sets of characters had exchanged places, would their new contexts have changed their economic decisions? Did their choices stem from a *mentalité* that they had learned at their mother's knee and would carry with them everywhere or from the experience of interacting with the others who lived in their world? *Why*, in short, did the people of Guayaquil or Baltimore invest or not invest, try to invent or not try, work longer hours or close down the shop, insist on shoes or go without? We need to become intimately acquainted with more than one set of people and circumstances to answer this kind of question effectively.

The task of getting to know people who are long dead is not an easy one. Because most of them did not leave for posterity summaries of their economic decisions—together with explanations as to their reasoning, conscious and subconscious—I take a "circumstantial evidence" approach. I explore the fabric of daily life not simply to communicate its "flavor" but also to account for the actions people took every day. I believe it is not only the novelist's but also the historian's task to help us stretch our minds to the point of understanding other people's experiences. Only in researching carefully the lives of ordinary people will we be in a position to say with fairness: "These were their circumstances. How can we make sense of their behavior in such circumstances?"

In writing this history, I analyze subjective experiences using the same techniques historians generally employ in studying more concrete events: I do not always use a document in the way that its maker intended, and I often compare two or more documents in order to arrive at a whole thought. For the opening paragraphs of the Prologue, for example, I do not have any memoirs by Ana Yagual or her mother concerning their journey to the city. But I do have court testimony that they arrived from the coast; I have learned what the terrain looked like from the accounts written by wealthy travelers as they passed along the same stretch of land. In this way I am trying to create a holistic picture that is as faithful to the sources as any other historical writing. Some will say that subjective experiences cannot be recreated in this way, that I will never know what Ana Yagual saw as she approached the city of Guayaquil, because she has no way of speaking directly to me. To a certain extent, those people are right. If, however, we take that argument to its logical extreme, then we will study only those who leave articulate records—usually a rather small percentage of human beings. We cannot let our sense of the infinitely variable nature of social experience become yet another reason to study only the powerful. We can but do our best in our efforts to study Ana Yagual.

Others will say that I may indeed effectively gain insight into Ana Yagual's experiences on the way to town and her reasons for not buying shoes—but that this knowledge remains only anecdotal, as I have no way of proving that nine out of ten people thought as this young woman thought. Yet I would argue that if we can prove that a sizable migration was occurring from Ana Yagual's natal province to the city of Guayaquil and we know something about the material conditions in which these new urbanites lived, then Ana's experiences are likely to be relevant to more than just herself. We can loosely tie interpretations to situations.

An additional issue that emerges in any comparative study is the question of equivalent sources. Two different cultural worlds will leave two different kinds of written records. In this case, the answer lay in widespread reading—a year in each place—of almost anything I could find from the period. Both cities kept useful municipal records, but the human dimension is not always found here; we need far more. Literacy, like other forms of cultural capital, was much more evenly distributed in the northern world than in the southern. Thus in the Baltimorean world I am able to rely on diaries and memoirs not only of merchants but also of artisans and even of former slaves. In the Guayaquileño universe such testimony is indeed scarce. However, the people of colonial South America kept official notes on almost every recordable act; their assiduity and eagerness in this regard would have impressed even the Victorians. The usual format of these notarial documents included several sworn statements, often of a very personal and chatty nature. A woman in Guayaquil who operated a bar, for example, was not likely to leave any letters or diaries when she died, but she was very likely to leave at least one court case or will or record of sale that included a partial autobiography and several emphatic opinions.

The fact that Baltimore was long finished with the wars of independence and Guayaquil only emerging from them affects the nature of government documents available. In Baltimore, for example, we have a relatively accurate census, but in Guayaquil no such thing—not, that is, until we turn to church records. Parish priests often knew where people were when the government did not. The fact that exactly equivalent records are not always available does not mean that we must give up on gaining insight into comparable aspects of life. Instead I chose to submerge myself in multiple kinds of records in both worlds, reading with my eyes open for unexpected strains of information. Sometimes I could not help but close my eyes and think about what the words I read once meant in someone else's life; I ask my readers to do the same. I believe that this habit improves our understanding of what happened "in the big picture," rather than distracting us from it.

The Two Cases: Guayaquil and Baltimore

A comparative study necessarily poses certain questions: why these two places, and why this period? In this case, why Guayaquil and Baltimore, and why 1820 to 1835? What is the issue to be explained, and what explanatory factors are under consideration? There are various ways to construct a comparative study: mine most closely resembles the "contrast of contexts" model described by historical sociologists, in which the two cases maintain their integrity in the account and are used to illuminate each other.[23] Typically, "contrast of contexts" studies are envisioned as being antithetical to theory, in that by their very nature they provide in-depth coverage of specific places for the purpose of underscoring the unique features of each. Yet I would ask why contextual and macrocausal studies need be entirely opposed. The two approaches may well fit together. This is especially true when a theoretical question is posed concerning cultural mindset and custom: an in-depth study of contrasting local detail must of necessity be done, and from the similarities and differences the conclusions must be drawn. In choosing the cases to study there must be enough constants to make a comparison worthwhile. I chose postindependence Guayaquil and Baltimore because they had enough in common in a structural sense to make a study of any differences between their people's behavior and economic thinking meaningful. I could study people in two places where they might be likely to behave and think somewhat similarly. If they did, the results would be logical from a materialist point of view. If they did not, I could scrutinize those aspects of their lives.

The structural similarities between the Baltimore and Guayaquil must be outlined. Urban historians classify both river ports in this era as "mercantile" cities, dependent on exports of grain (in Baltimore's case) and cacao, used to make the popular cocoa beverage (in Guayaquil's). The classic mercantile city has a heterogeneous central area with artisanal shops scattered throughout, a waterfront attracting active development, large or noxious manufacturing or processing plants (such as tanneries) on the periphery, and possibly mills on nearby rivers to process exports. During the late eighteenth and early nineteenth centuries, Guayaquil and Baltimore both experienced a boom period that brought almost euphoric hopes for the future, but they were in decline relative to their own expectations by the second decade of the century. Both cities were surrounded by hinterlands consisting of a mixture of family farms and large plantations. In each area, slavery played a role in the economy but was declining in importance. Each city was dependent upon international exports and shipbuilding, but only to a limited extent on manufacturing. They each had had a population of at least 20,000 a generation earlier, although Baltimore expanded at a dizzying pace and by 1820 had greatly outdistanced Guayaquil, with over 60,000 people.[24] Indeed, Baltimore, like a number of other urban areas in the United States, was about to enter the transitional phase on the way to becoming an industrial city.[25] Guayaquil, like most other South American cities, did no such thing. Beyond the period considered here, it would be impossible to analyze Baltimore within a preindustrial framework. This book, however, looks at the moment before the divergence became clearly defined.

I could have elected to study a Latin American port on the Atlantic Coast. Such a choice would have been useful in eliminating the remaining structural variable of easy geographic access to international trade as a factor that might produce differences in people's economic behavior. I specifically avoided cities such as Havana or Cartagena, however. The high level of involvement in foreign trade of the Hispanic ports on the Atlantic coasts was unusual by the standards of most regions in Latin America. While there may not be any city that is "most typical," it is certainly possible to avoid choosing those that are overtly atypical. In other words, I chose to sacrifice "perfect" structural equivalence for the sake of accuracy or relevance in a wider sense. The economic cultures of the Americas should not in fairness be studied without connection to geography: access to the Atlantic *did* affect people's behavior. Thus eliminating that variable by choosing to study an Atlantic-oriented town would be in some ways dishonest, as I would be choosing a town that was by definition exceptional. Baltimore, likewise, cannot be dismissed as either a model northern or model southern port within the U.S. context, sharing as it does the features of each.[26]

Time is a separate issue. I wanted to begin when the residents of both ports were free to make their own rules without regard to colonial policymakers, thus escaping an assumption of persistence. Baltimore had long been free when Guayaquil first declared its own independence in 1820. The next fifteen years were important ones; Jacksonianism was triumphing in the United States when the Ecuadorian presidency, after much struggle, passed to the enlightened Vicente Rocafuerte in 1835. I could have looked at each port during its own earliest republican years, comparing the 1790s in Baltimore to the 1820s in Guayaquil, much as revolutions or slave systems have previously been compared. The problem of such an approach for this study is that it assumes each case can be effectively studied in isolation, when in fact economic attitudes and decisions must be placed in international context. Guayaquileño and other South American merchants of the 1820s, for example, did their thinking with reference to the actions of Baltimoreans and Liverpudlians of the 1820s, not those of the 1790s. Beliefs in economic possibilities and constraints depend to some extent on an area's relationship with the rest of the world in "real time." Baltimoreans already had established advantages by the time Guayaquileños freed themselves; knowledge of this would affect both parties' behavior, as we shall see. It is not my goal to prove that particularly momentous changes occurred within these fifteen years. In fact, what follows is essentially not a motion picture. Instead I have sought to take two snapshots, as it were, that are especially illuminating when viewed next to each other.

Overview

The following study is divided into four sections of two chapters each. Part I provides a general overview. In Chapter 1 Ana Yagual and Frederick Bailey walk about the towns. The impressions they glean stem from my use of "visible sources"—architecture and material culture, descriptions of parades and festivals, newspaper advertisements, etc. Such observations, we all know from our own travels, give us fascinating insight into new places, but cannot answer all our questions. So Chapter 2 takes the reader where our travelers could not go—back in time to view the origins and evolution of each city. This chapter is based largely on previous studies. It culminates in a statistical overview of the cities—in terms of professions and wealth distribution—as they were in the time of Ana Yagual and Frederick Bailey.

Parts II, III, and IV form the core of the book, on the economic ideas and behavior of the elites, the middling sectors, and the very poor, respectively. Each part contains two chapters, the first on Guayaquil, the second on Baltimore. At the end of each chapter on Baltimore I make explicit comparisons and analyses. I also offer the hope that readers will be able to draw their own conclusions: the chapters have parallel structures and provide numerous details that others may choose to interpret differently than I do.

My categories deserve comment. The three groups of "elite," "middling," and "poor" certainly were not equivalent in the two places in terms of relative proportion, permeability, or racial composition. Nor did the people of the time necessarily divide themselves in this way or consistently think about three groups or give power only to the elite. Indeed, these very kinds of differences are what the chapters demonstrate. My categorization in fact is based on a very simple idea: material wealth alone. Those people with the most material goods make their appearance in the first part, those with the least, in the last.

In each chapter I rely on familiar sources for historians—legislation, court cases, charity records, letters, diaries, account books, government correspondence, pamphlets, probate records, petitions. I ask similar kinds of questions about each group: how they thought about their work, their investments, and their buying, how they imagined their futures, and how these factors affected their strategies and decision-making. In the Conclusion I suggest that the lives of Ana Yagual, Frederick Bailey, and others like them illuminate larger questions concerning the predicaments that their regions faced and the solutions that their peoples forged. At the very least, the details of their lives should raise questions worthy of our consideration.

PART I

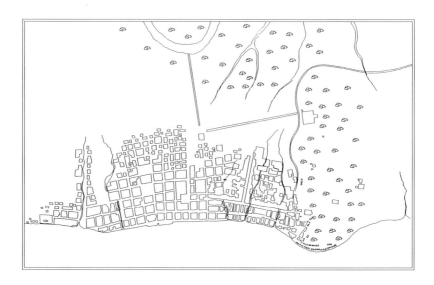

Map of Guayaquil. Based on a map published by Manuel Villavicencio in Geografía de la República del Ecuador *(1858) with correctives made for the late date.*

CHAPTER 1

IN THE STREETS OF THE CITIES

In the 1820s María Magdalena and her daughter Ana Yagual found themselves living in Guayaquil at a tense but optimistic moment. Times were changing rapidly, and many residents believed their city would be able to benefit. British merchants who visited the city during the independence period and explored the possibilities were full of enthusiasm. Consul Henry Wood reported to George Canning:

> As a commercial station there are few ports which possess such vast natural advantages as Guayaquil. [It is] situated on the bank of a magnificent river of the most easy and secure navigation, surrounded by a country capable of producing an immense quantity of exportable produce, and intersected by numerous minor rivers which serve to facilitate its transportation . . . Guayaquil further offers every facility for the repairing and building of ships. Although there are no docks, ships of very considerable burthen may with security be "hove down" at the river's side and thoroughly repaired. The timber used at Guayaquil for the purposes of ship building is in point of durability perhaps superior to any in the world.[1]

María Magdalena and Ana Yagual had to wend their way through the market's profusion of trade goods. Newcomers were usually overwhelmed.

"Everything is recommended to you, and your ears are saluted with the cry of 'Barrato, muy barrato [cheap, very cheap],' at every step."[2] The local ships from Guayaquil and from Chile and Peru and elsewhere along the coast came and went with butter, lard, soap, sleeping mats, mattresses, quilts, carved boxes, fruit, wine, flour, tanned goatskins, sea lion pelts, tobacco, cigars, raw fibers, cordage, cotton, and straw hats.[3] The smelliest crates contained oil: the best was from the sperm whale, but the oil of the giant Galápagos tortoises that once swarmed the islands named for them was cheaper. Other goods came from the hinterland for the cityfolk to eat: rice, beef, pork, poultry, and fish from upriver. Most plentiful of all were the fruits and vegetables brought by Indians on rafts, especially the bunches of plantains, the staple of all the townfolk, rich and poor. Bright Andean textiles and animal skins came in on smaller river boats and mule trains from the mountains. In exchange for these, Guayaquil's merchants sent back to the highlands local products and luxurious European goods: wax, crystal, china, paper, razors, knives, silk stockings and breeches, cashmeres, satins, fine cottons, ink, wine and other liquors. They also received the more mundane bars of iron, tea, boots and shoes, and a few manufactured shirts and pants.[4] The foreign ships always left again with cacao beans, used to make cocoa powder for the popular beverage. Sometimes they also left with specie in gold or silver, or with lumber or unprocessed cotton or other raw materials, but they always took some cacao.

Everyone in the city knew that cacao was Guayaquil's trump card. The racks of the drying beans were among the most common sights in town. The fruit, which grew on trees and was as big as a melon and bright pink when ripe, came from plantations for miles around. No one left the precious fruit out to spoil in the heat. People cracked it open and dug out the brown beans (each one as big as a cat's foot) and left them to dry in the sun. The smell was delicious, reminding some passersby that there were fortunes to be made here. The energy that the import-export trade brought to the port reverberated in all the streets of the city, past the port and the markets in four directions, extending down long streets and up neighboring hills. The focus, however, remained the river that brought the ships.

The city really began in the river, in a floating neighborhood borne on rafts. If the newly arrived María Magdalena and Ana Yagual knew someone who lived in the aquatic *barrio*, they might well have gone there first. Despite all the efforts of the authorities to reduce the size of this warren, the river-borne village had existed for years. Some people built little houses on their rafts, and others operated taverns. Some guided their crafts away from the city in times of war troubles. The raft dwellers said proudly that at least they never had the problem of the foundations of their dwellings rotting away in the rainy season. During the day, the river dwellers were joined by other city folk, who came to wash clothes or to bathe. They shared an exhilarating fear of the alligators that sometimes prowled the area, and occasionally they enlivened the day by trying to catch one alive and then taunt and kill it.[5]

This riverbank was the gateway to the world; here faraway places did not seem so far away. The water was deep, and big ships could approach the city fully loaded: there were fifteen to twenty in the port on an ordinary day. People stepping off them had been in Lima or Callao in Peru only a week ago, or two weeks ago in Panama, where they had seen the Caribbean Sea. Sometimes they came from much further, from the United States or England, and the big, sunburnt men aboard shouted words in English that made the children laugh. As soon as the first load of passengers or cargo was put in a *balsa* and sent ashore, excitement broke forth in the port. Arrivals averaged one every other day, and each new arrival brought news and work. Indians who lived on the anchored *balsas* or who came from just outside the city rushed toward the ship with their small boats. The docks were not well developed: no one had bothered to invest much money in them because there was no need. The *indígenas* were always there to cart goods in their boats and on their backs for little money. Since long before the arrival of the Spaniards they had been navigating expertly with a twist of a sail or a rudder in their *balsas* made of tree trunks, bark, or sea lion skins. Individuals could maneuver on a single trunk, "maintaining so exact a balance, that although the log is round they very seldom fall off."[6]

Near this neighborhood of boats, the shipyard came into view. Here the men working on the boats were not Indians. They were black. So were some of the men shouting orders. These were the children or grandchildren of Africans, some of whom also had Indian and white forebears. They worked amidst piles of timber brought from nearby parts. The tools and other materials they used were familiar to any observant foreigner, for they were nearly all imported from Europe. People here spoke with pride about the fine quality of their timber and craftsmanship. They pointed to one boat and claimed it had lasted almost one hundred years. In 1828 the men here converted the sailboat *Felicia* into a steamer, albeit a fragile one.[7]

The *malecón*, the wide street that ran along the river, charmed newcomers when they first saw it. It was paved with rock and crushed oyster shells. The stonework edging the water was quite new. Construction had begun at the end of the colonial era and would continue intermittently until the local government began to push in the early 1830s to finish the job. The city officials even started a lottery to raise money for the work. Tickets cost four reales, at least a day's wage for a laboring man. A "child of the multitude" was randomly chosen to draw the numbered balls from the bin.[8] The roadway was lined with 102 crystal lamps, lit nightly by city workers. The stately wooden houses were impressive. All of them were white, with tiled roofs and balconies extending the width of the building or recessed ground floors. They were built close together, so that someone walking below was always protected from the sun or the rain. Here lived eminent citizens. Gauzy curtains fluttered from the upstairs windows, and sometimes fine ladies stepped outside, talking and laughing. Many of the lower floors housed elegant shops or inviting cafes. Someone with money could stop to rest and order sweet bread and a glass of fresh fruit mixed with the crushed ice that was transported down from the mountains.[9]

This part of the city, called the Ciudad Nueva, was the most modern, cosmopolitan neighborhood. One block in from the *malecón*, and parallel to it, ran the Calle Comercial. Here were many shops, from ordinary textile sellers to fine chocolate makers and watch repairers. The streets which led inland, perpendicular to the main thoroughfares, bore the names of well-known landmarks: Street of the Church of San Francisco, Street of the Theater, Street of the Prison, Street of the Shipyards . . . Between the *malecón* and the Calle Comercial loomed the large, modern Casa Consistorial or government office building, the first floor of which was lined with small shops. At the corner there were weekly newspapers for sale, although few people bought them, as they were expensive and most people could not read them anyway. Interspersed along the inner streets were well-known artisans' shops, including an especially large shoemaking establishment, bakery, master blacksmith, and several rum distilleries.

In giving directions, however, people did not usually locate themselves in relation to such edifices and only rarely used the names of the streets. They said instead, "Across from the house of las Señoras Rocafuertes . . ." They knew where the principal houses were, interspersed throughout the city, for no neighborhood was entirely reserved for the wealthy.[10] Different social classes often shared the same building, as the lower floor frequently housed servants or was rented to the family of an artisan or shop-keeper. The Elizalde family was one of the most elite in Guayaquil, and even Juan Bautista Elizalde rented his ground floor to a tailor (albeit a French one) and then to the owner of a cafe who advertised in the news-paper. Other houses had floors divided into *cuartos* or apartments rented to families. In such cases, there might be more than one kitchen built in the rear or in the courtyard. Everyone in the Ciudad Nueva, rich and poor, shared these conditions. Each morning they shooed the same wan-dering pigs and dogs. They all heard peddlers crying their wares, water carriers selling their precious commodity, and passing herds of goats bleating. Church bells rang, and somewhere on the street a musician played.

Whatever the pleasures of life in Ciudad Nueva, however, Ana Yagual and María Magdalena found no shelter there. They continued on to the poorer part of town. To get to the Ciudad Vieja they had to cross a bridge over a small estuary leading into the river. Past the bakery near the bridge, at the base of Santa Ana Hill, two ferocious-looking cannons were trained on the river. Looking up over the warren of houses, they could see the Iglesia Santo Domingo, built of heavy stone. Everybody knew it was the oldest church in the city, the first the Spanish had built. For in the beginning everyone had lived here on this hill, using the cannons to de-fend themselves against angry Indians or pirates. Then the city began to grow lengthwise, hugging the riverbank. When the city was about a hun-dred years old, the wealthy began to invest in the shipyards, building them away from the crowded hill where the people lived. Tiny rivulets cut into the land perpendicular to the river, creating a series of small peninsulas that made it difficult to walk to work. So the owners of the shipyards built bridges over the rivulets; suddenly it became possible for the city to be-come much bigger. Those who had the resources moved off the hill and across the bridges, until eventually there were only poor families left there. The Dominicans from the church had complained as early as 1768 that they were hardly able to collect rent anymore from the houses built on their property. There were only "poor black people" remaining. On the stiflingly populated Santa Ana Hill, smoke from the cooking fires hov-ered in the houses, filth ran down the narrow alleys and stone steps, and disease spread rapidly.[11]

Ana Yagual and her mother crossed the hill and headed for the plain that wrapped around the town on both sides, the "savanna" as it was called. Between May and December it was hot and dry, but pleasant and cool when the sun went down. Between January and April it was steamy hot, and either was raining or had just rained. Then the streets beyond the paved ones close to the *malecón* ran with mud and made it useless for anyone to attempt to use a carriage or a cart. There was a decent road to the cemetery on the edge of town, but if people's way lay toward the slaughterhouse or the tannery instead, then they had a difficult walk. Recently, more people had been building bamboo houses here. To cope with the rainy seasons, they built them on stilts, as the indigenous peoples of the coast had long been accustomed to doing. In the sheltered areas beneath they cooked and kept their animals. When they were ready to go inside, they climbed up a ladder. Those who were better off partitioned their one room into two; usually the only furniture consisted of a hammock.[12]

Here the people shared many of the problems of the inhabitants of the Ciudad Vieja.[13] Water had to be carried for a long distance or up a steep incline or bought at high prices from the *aguateros*. The entire city swarmed with mosquitoes, but the people in this part of town could not afford mosquito netting. It was difficult to keep the dirt floors free of snakes, scorpions, and the dangerous *niguas*, insects which laid their eggs in bare feet. When an army of ants carried off the bread, it was often impossible to find the money to buy more. Sometimes fifteen people lived in one room; even with so many contributing, it usually required all their resources to survive from day to day. There was rarely anything left over. The cost of living had doubled in the last thirty years. An influx of people into the city had brought wages down. Less food was available, as war had interrupted production and more landowners were growing the valuable cacao instead of food crops. More people and less food meant higher prices: one chicken could cost as much as three reales, and an ordinary *jornalero* or day worker earned only three or four in a day. Renting a room cost at least three pesos (or twenty-four reales) a month. To raise revenue, the government had imposed monopolies on tobacco, salt, and even flour, which rendered bread more expensive. There seemed to be taxes on everything, including marriage. Priests were only supposed to charge three or four pesos for a ceremony, but they often charged thirteen or fourteen instead.[14]

Who were these people crowding onto Santa Ana Hill and building more and more houses on stilts despite the conditions? Ana Yagual's mother clearly was not the first to have the idea to come here; many had responded to the optimism of the era, if only to end up disappointed.

They had skin some shade of brown; they wore loose-fitting cotton pants or skirts and usually no shoes. The men, women, and children worked busily or walked quickly. It was common for a foreign visitor to notice their energy, even if he generally felt condescending toward South America. "The lower classes are more industrious than the people generally are in other colonies; indeed everything here bears the marks of exertion and activity."[15] A Spanish traveler later reflected that in his understanding of Guayaquileño society the whites were merchants and landowners and the blacks and mestizos everything else, "menestrales y jornaleros [craftsmen and day laborers]."[16] Most people would have agreed with him. The words these people used to describe themselves and each other—at least in court—were *negro* and *indígena*, or *mulato* and *mestizo* if they had any white ancestry. Quite often now they said *zambo*, meaning a mixture of indigenous and African. They had various social origins. Some who were of African descent were still slaves; others had been allowed to buy their freedom in the last thirty years, as their masters turned to growing more cacao, which required attention only at certain seasons, while slaves required food year-round. Some of the people were indigenous and came to the city in hopes of finding employment or avoiding the steep tribute payments levied against them in their home parishes.

It was not always clear to Ana Yagual or to anyone else exactly who was who. In the city, Indians and Africans met and formed friendships and had children with whomever they liked. The patterns of their lives became almost indistinguishable, except that they described themselves before judges as *mulato* or *zambo*.[17] Any stranger could see that more than half of these *jornaleros* were women. Men could look for agricultural work.[18] The city offered women their own opportunities: they worked as cooks, maids, peddlers, bakers, laundresses, seamstresses, dancers, barkeepers, wetnurses, and, if need be, as prostitutes. Without property, it was difficult to set up a business rather than offer a service, but some tried. They might buy a vat to make soap or sit under an old parasol and sell garden produce or even used clothing. María Magdalena convinced someone else to play a guitar while she and her daughter sold drinks, probably from their own hidden distillery.

When she was exhausted by her new life, Ana Yagual could retreat to one of the churches. Outside, the surrounding plaza buzzed with the noise of traders and peddlers and people who had arranged to meet there or who had just stopped to talk. When one stepped inside, the sound suddenly receded and the light gave way to dimness. The wide wooden floor

29

boards creaked, and women's voices whispered in the confessionals. Parts of the wooden walls were painted bright colors, and the roof was made of glazed tiles. The saints and the Virgin gazed down from their recesses, their wooden faces serene, their clothes more beautiful than any other clothes for miles around. The smell of the incense permeated the room. Older people could tell Ana that not long ago they had come to the church *cofradías* for help in paying for funerals and meeting other life emergencies. These mutual aid groups were disappearing, however, for it cost a family one real weekly to belong; in this time of transience and flux, loans were generally awarded only to the most established families, rather than the neediest.[19]

Ana Yagual's new neighbors brought their own energy with them, and it was to their own inner resources rather than to the church that they tended to turn for rejuvenation. They rarely attended the city's theater, for tickets cost too large a share of what they had to spend, but there were other, cheaper sources of amusement. Dances formed, formally and informally, on the street and in the houses, wherever someone wanted to play a guitar or violin or harp. Those who were not shy pounded the floor and swept the air in brusque motions. People visited the *chinganas* or bars that dotted the city, not only to drink, but also to talk and to gamble. These establishments were ordered to close at 10 or 11 o'clock, but they did not always do so, and some patrons stayed laughing far into the night. Periodically, bullfighting tournaments took place in the big bullring. They were always announced ahead of time and might last a day or several days. Part of the money made in the associated betting always went toward the building of a charity hospital or chapel or some other project that was sure to have God's blessing.[20]

On festival days men climbed up the church steeples and called people to mass by playing drums and trumpets. There was general excitement in preparing for a *fiesta cívica*. For the celebration of Guayaquil's independence day—with October 9, 1820, still in recent memory—working women cleaned and scrubbed, and wealthier ones hung colored bunting from windows and balconies and pillars. In the morning all the church bells rang, followed by a triple salvo of artillery, and each church celebrated a high mass with *Te Deum*. Then the dancing began, in the breezy second- and third-floor parlors of the rich and in the streets and the open air. At night there was a "general illumination": everyone who had candles put them in the windows.[21]

Carnaval was the wildest time of the year. It came at Lent, in the middle of the hot, humid season when tempers were short. The object was to throw as much water as possible on other people without getting thoroughly drenched oneself. The more genteel bought the pretty colored eggshells that had been filled with water and sealed with wax. Ladies might toss them from balconies; children might hurl them as they ran by. But if a young man were bolder and more efficient in wetting others, he might join with friends and throw someone directly into the river. Many wealthy people could not abide Carnaval. "Work stops at midday, and a general craziness takes control of everybody; . . . there is no corner where civility presides, nor law, for complete disorder is allowed to grow in those days." Every year the police issued edicts forbidding certain activities (such as tossing someone bodily into the Guayas River), but to no avail.[22] Carnaval did not change much.

Perhaps most people needed the cool water. It was, after all, a momentary diversion from the undercurrents of poverty and rage that sometimes flashed out visibly, despite people's efforts both to work hard and to enjoy life rather than suffer through it. A man was not simply murdered, but propped in the church doorway in the Ciudad Vieja, to be found the next morning in a most lifelike position.[23] A day could begin like any other and end in an inferno if sparks flew from a kitchen or even from a frigate anchored in the port. Sometimes whole city blocks exploded in flames. People came to stare, then tried to hurry away, for the troops called in to fight the disaster hurled insults and abuse as they worked. Afterward, the wreckage smoldered; the rich wrung their hands at the "extraordinary expense" of rebuilding, unless they had bought shares in the new mutual insurance company.[24] The poor sometimes did not even try to rebuild.

Most frightening of all, every person on every street was subject to the epidemic diseases that struck with deadly effect. Poverty made some neighborhoods more dangerous than others. In early colonial days the Guayas River had been considered healing water, but in recent times, as more and more migrants poured down from the Andes, the river's reputation had deteriorated: these migrants were used to cooler, drier air and had never been exposed to these tropical maladies before, so they succumbed easily and painfully. By 1813 the shipyard neighborhood on the edge of the savanna and Santa Ana Hill were so famous for being unhealthy that some doctors would not even go there. Most political leaders made a connection between filth and standing water and disease. They spoke publicly of the need to release plugged-up water in the streets, to clean and drain one of the estuaries, to pave the inner streets and squares, to repair wells, and to construct the cemetery in such a way that drinking water would never end up being filtered through dead bodies. The difficulty was that residents were supposed to be responsible for improvements made on or near their property, but the vast majority did not have one single peso to spare to give to these projects. The few who did have the silver did not want to spend it on streets that belonged to everybody. So, except in the wealthiest parts of town, they waited for the money to come from the city's coffers. In the case of most projects, they were still waiting.[25]

Still, the political leaders made strong efforts. Yellow fever, cholera, and smallpox were perhaps the greatest enemies of all. There was nothing to be done about the first two, except to check incoming ships for signs of disease, but people could fight against smallpox. The local government ordered vials of the "best-quality" vaccinating serum from Bogotá, where it had been sent from London. These officials were not afraid of the miracles of modern science. They hung a flag to advertise the vaccine from the windows of the government house and wrote articles for the newspaper to try to bring people in. Few came. The authorities stormed against "the indolence of parents" who did not look out for their children. But still few came. The people seemed to be more afraid of the vaccine than they were of the disease. Maybe they thought they would be forced to pay a great deal of money for it—and perhaps they were right.[26] After all, the government was short of money, certainly for hospitals. Those who were better-off brought nurses and doctors into their own homes, but the poor needed somewhere to go for help. In some years there were such places, but their doors opened and closed, depending on the availability of resources. There was a women's hospital, for example, for those who were pregnant and indigent, but it was transformed into a military hospital in 1826, despite protests. There was a Charity Hospital, rebuilt each time it burned down, but a person could not enter without legal proof of poverty and slaves could not receive attention at all, as their masters were supposed to care for them. The City Council wanted to put the hospital in the area where María Magdalena and Ana Yagual now lived, on the edge of town behind the reeking slaughterhouse, "the most appropriate place for such a thing." In 1829 the clinic temporarily shut down, in grave need of repairs and reorganization. When it still had not opened the next year, a doctor wrote an anguished letter to the city government. He spoke of "the many poor who wander without shelter," warning that if they died in the streets the souls of the rich would answer for it.[27]

Other elite figures, however, were becoming tired of dwelling on the pain and the poverty in their dynamic port and wanted to return to their early republican optimism. This was, after all, a city of opportunity and accomplishment. Were all these to be lost in a torrent of self-incrimination? After several years of debate, some anonymous contributors to a newspaper wrote succinctly: "[If we think this way] then the most miserable and lowly neighborhood in Liverpool or Baltimore is worth more than any of the Republics that have been born on the American soil that was Spain's!"[28] Surely, they said, their people were doing better than those in the worst neighborhoods of such a city as Baltimore.

When Frederick Bailey arrived in the narrow, stinking streets of Baltimore's Fell's Point in the 1830s, he did not consider himself doomed, but rather blessed. After he had attained adolescence, his master had taken him from the city where he had grown up and rented him out to different rural plantation masters in need of laborers. Recently Frederick had been caught trying to escape. His owner had left him in prison for a while and then decided not to deal with the problem himself. Instead, he sent the seventeen-year-old troublemaker to a different master in Baltimore to work as an apprentice—which was exactly the punishment Frederick would have selected, had he been allowed to choose.[29]

For Frederick liked Baltimore. He knew it well and believed that it offered him a future. In these years he was not the only one to have such an idea. Hundreds and even thousands of people were pouring into Baltimore equally full of hope. They came almost every day: as runaway slaves, as apprenticed slaves and servants, as German and Irish and English immigrants, as free wanderers from rural Maryland and Pennsylvania, and as businessmen. Many were at first at least a bit put off by all the bustle, but often they made positive assessments anyway.[30] The population grew fast. Budding "internal improvements" brought the wheat-growing hinterland closer to the port, creating a need for builders, millers, wagoners, barrel-makers, and others.

Baltimore's traditional shipping industry was in something of a slump, now that Britain was done with the eighteenth-century wars and its commercial fleet was free to sail. The port was not moribund by any means, however. Approximately 550 boats still arrived every year. The energy of the docks was as attractive as it was overwhelming. People ran everywhere, shouting to be heard above the noise of others. The water was deep enough to let large ships approach, and news of the world came down the planks with the passengers and goods. There was always the possibility that something interesting would happen here. Once in 1827 considerable excitement had been added to everybody's week when a shark lost his way and ended up near the Ferry Bar. On an average spring or summer day in 1835 there might be 150 boats bobbing in the water. At least one new one would arrive almost every day. This was not the case in the winter months, when travel could slow to a standstill. "The river is completely locked up in ice, . . . arrival and departure of vessels having been now suspended for upwards of a fortnight." In the warm months there were far too many for even the local people to keep track of them without advertising. "For New Orleans, the fine fast sailing cooper," or "a good vessel is wanted to load for an Eastern port." The new steamship lines tried to keep to a schedule, but sometimes they did not and apologized after the fact for delays and sudden changes which may have inconvenienced their irate clients. Generally there might be one or two boats in port from such faraway places as Liverpool or Ireland, the Caribbean, or the Pacific coast of South America, but the majority came from Boston or Charleston or Richmond or towns even closer.[31]

Of course, the decline in the city's share of international trade did mean that the dockyards and docks had lost something of their stature, but they were still the city's focal point. On Bowly's Wharf and Spear's Wharf—depending on the season—there were dealers in brandy, clover seed, coal, apples, flour, salt, mackerel, rice, codfish, molasses, potatoes, cotton, tallow, sperm whale oil, pig iron from England, and hides from South America. Charles Pearce had a major business on Bowly's Wharf, specializing in goods from South America and the Caribbean: chocolate and spices, Puerto Rican and Brazilian coffee, Cuban sugar, Guatemalan indigo. Finer imports were not left out to be sold in the midst of chaos, but were carefully removed to more genteel streets deeper in the city. Water Street, one block in from the wharves, was something of a misnomer, judging by the number of crates of wine, champagne, port, madeira, and sherry.

Daily newspapers advertised the goods for sale. Boys hawked the papers, and people lounging on corners read them. As a child, Frederick Bailey had watched people reading and wondered what the words said. As he thought, they advertised apples and raisins, but other "goods" were available, too. Some of the people walking on the street—including Frederick himself at one point—were for sale, listed in notices between those for flour and sweets. "At auction, . . . at 10 o'clock, on Bowly's Wharf . . .

trinidad molasses," and then: "I will sell at public auction [out in Baltimore County] one young Negro woman, to serve till 1841, two female Negro children, slaves for life, also horses, cows, sheep and hogs together with farming utensils." Or in the city: "I will at all times give higher prices for slaves than any other purchaser who . . . may be in the market." Looking around, it was impossible to tell which black men and women were free and which might be picked up and sold at any moment. "Ran away from the Subscriber, a Negro Man by the name of Henry . . . Whoever will arrest the fellow, and secure him in jail, will receive the above reward [of $5]. Captains of vessels and all others are forewarned not to harbour him at their own peril." "For sale or hire—an excellent black waiter or coachman; he can come well recommended." [32]

Frederick Bailey grew up in this chaotic world of seaborne commerce called Fell's Point, in which blacks and whites rushed everywhere and free blacks mingled with the enslaved. As a child, he lived with relatives of his master; when he returned to the city as a young man, he was allowed to live with free blacks in exchange for making weekly payments to his owner. He knew the neighborhood intimately. The streets first seen approaching from the wharves were pleasant enough. Thames Street was home to sea captains and doctors and merchants, and some of the main thoroughfares leading deeper into Fell's Point looked similar. But the back streets were different: they gave Fell's Point its reputation that reached even as far as Guayaquil. Men threw bales from upper-story windows, and boards leaning against buildings slid down with a bang. A workman was gradually putting up painted signs to mark the streets, most of which were unpaved in this section of town. Even Market Street, the main thoroughfare, was graveled rather than paved. Some streets became so "washed into gullies" that the residents complained it was "no longer possible to use . . . wagons, and the houses are in danger of soon falling down." The gutters and water courses running down the middle of the streets reeked of whiskey and chewing tobacco and garbage. The refuse piled high, as households had to pay to have it carried off. "The quantity of water which falls down that alley leaves those holes full of stinking mud which very soon stagnates after the hogs have wallowed in it." The land here was low and damp, and basements often filled with water. In 1820 yellow fever landed and took its toll, even while the rest of the city remained relatively healthy, and in 1832 cholera passed through with all its terrors. To make matters worse, despite the presence of so much groundwater, there was never enough of the precious liquid available for drinking and cleaning. The local springs frequently ran dry; residents signed petitions begging that the city organize the carting of fresh water.[33]

A number of the area's problems stood to be corrected through paving and piping and building wells. Other sections of town were already in much better condition in this regard. Such projects were accomplished when a majority of a block's property holders decided to make a joint venture: at their request the city conducted an assessment, and each one paid a contribution proportionate to his or her assets. Needless to say, this procedure worked best in the better-off neighborhoods. Still, it could work even in Fell's Point. At Strawberry Alley and Lancaster, for example, the block's property holders decided in 1830 that they had managed without enough water long enough. They wanted a well, pump, and pipes. The two wealthiest men bore the largest burden, and eighteen others were charged approximately five dollars each. Many residents, who were tenants and not house owners, paid nothing, though their rent undoubtedly increased in some cases. The system worked well as long as there were enough property owners in residence who wanted the changes so that the project became a communal responsibility: occasionally tempers would flare if a small number of property holders felt that they were being abused by a larger population of poorer people who would benefit from the improvements without having to pay for them.[34]

Some houses in Fell's Point were brick, narrow fronted and close together, while others were wooden. The majority had two stories. Half the width of a house was sometimes taken up on the street side by the slanted entrance to the cellar. If the first floor was a store or workshop or tavern, the owner and the family usually lived above, but most of the houses simply contained apartments for laborers who rented. Inside, the houses shared similar features—small rooms, wood floors, a table and chairs, possibly a few other pieces of furniture, and, usually, a metal stove. "Hardly a poor family in Baltimore but has one or more [stoves], at which the cooking is all done in winter." The quality of construction was poor: once at a funeral on the first floor of a house the boards gave way and dumped everyone into the cellar.[35]

Blacks and whites lived together on some of these blocks, but blacks alone congregated in certain narrow streets called "alleys," where all the problems of the Point were at their worst. It was becoming harder for them to earn a living. As more white immigrants arrived, they took the available positions as apprentices. Men became day laborers looking for whatever work they could get on the wharves or in stores. Most women worked as domestic servants or as laundresses, but even some of that work was being taken by the immigrants. If they had to, they did what desperate white women also did: they walked the docks as prostitutes, sometimes even before dark fell.[36] As Frederick Bailey soon found, a person needed to earn at least three dollars a week. This would cover room and board, laundering one's only clothes, and some of the expenses involved in doing any job. Laborers with regular work usually earned at least seventy-five cents a day, totaling more than a living wage. But many, especially many black citizens, had only irregular work.[37]

Any black man or woman could turn for help to at least five black churches in the area, which sometimes offered night or weekend classes. In desperation they could turn to the walled Almshouse or even to crime. A high proportion of the faces looking back at visitors of the two penal institutions were black, staring impassively at white interrogators. They must have felt they were surrounded. There were more free blacks in Baltimore than in almost any other place in the country, yet they were only a minority, less than a quarter of the population. They could not live where they chose or work where they chose or speak as they chose, and they stood accused of their own poverty.[38]

It did not take the young Frederick long to discover that Baltimore offered a far pleasanter life than this less than a mile away. A person could take a small boat from Fell's Point over to the other side of the basin, in the main part of town, or hire a carriage, or walk the mile. The stream called Jones' Falls divided Fell's Point from the rest of town as it made its way down to the harbor. Only thirty years before, the entire area had been a marshy bog, but the marsh had been drained and houses built. Now only a walled-in stream remained, although it last overflowed in 1820.[39]

The 80-foot-wide Market Street (recently renamed Baltimore Street) stretched westward away from Jones' Falls. It was dominated by the courthouse and, just to the west of it, the jail. The street was lit by lamps, which in 1832 were changed from oil to gas, and lined by elegant shops. The first store after the falls, "adjoining the bridge," was a paper shop, where you could buy writing and blotting paper and school slates. You could pay cash or trade in old paper. Walking farther along the street, you could find an artificial flower maker, imported raisins and teas, Parisian paper wall hangings and flower vases, English cut-glass dishes and umbrellas, South American straw bonnets, Venetian blinds, and even a "caleidorama."[40] Around the corners, on the smaller cross-streets clustered artisan shops, some of them growing into small manufactories. In a short walk you could pass a machinery manufactory (cotton and wool cards, reels, etc.), tinware manufactory (tea trays, knives, frying pans), looking glass manufactory, locksmith and brass founder, iron dealer, boot and shoe manufactory, millinery establishment, cabinetmaker, stockings and suspenders manufacturer, upholsterer, gunpowder manufacturing company, saddlery and coach furniture maker, instrument warehouse, Spanish cigar factory, stove factory, draper and tailor, and gun maker. Interspersed amongst the craftsmen's shops were the stores of petty merchants, whose goods were meant for the well-to-do as well as the poorer sorts. Here was a "patented rotary cooking stove," there an "antisyphilitic specific" or a "roach and bed bug bane." This was a city of walkers who had money for shoes: "Snow shoes for children to keep their feet dry," "Indian moccasins for school-going children," or "Gum elastic overshoes available at $1 a pair."[41]

The houses here were mostly of brick, some plain red and some painted, often with brass knockers and door handles and white marble steps. In places the sidewalks were paved with matching red brick as well. The dwellings were full of windows, though they were kept carefully curtained and blinded so no one could see what went on inside. Some were row houses, but generally there was space between the buildings in this part of town, referred to as "ground lying waste" or "gaps of meadow," depending on one's perspective. In these spaces occasionally wandered lost cows, roving hogs, and loose dogs, all innocently marring the sense of perfect order. But tranquillity always seemed to reign supreme at one spot: at Calvert and Saratoga Streets, the city spring bubbled cheerfully over a marble floor, and passersby stopped to rest.[42]

The brick and wooden churches fit unobtrusively into the city blocks. A newcomer looking at these unassuming buildings would not at first have guessed that in this town, as in others up and down the coast, people were talking about faith more than they had been in the habit of doing only a few years before. The ministers of the Protestant churches were eagerly trying to enlarge their flocks in this great awakening of the spirit. Only the new Catholic cathedral was a noticeably massive building, dark and square. Baltimore, indeed, was known for its large Catholic presence: Maryland had been a haven for people of that faith in the colonial period. Hostile observers went so far as to refer to it as the "headquarters of popery."[43] Other commentators were more positive: guidebook writers, travelers, and city recordkeepers noted the extensive and inclusive network of charity organizations supported by the church—relief funds, medical establishments, schools, and orphanages.

Yet it was not the churches that formed the spatial frame of reference here. The "landmark" buildings were always large and grandiose, offering excellent views that came well recommended; but, according to those who wrote about them, the structures were not always handsome and certainly often in need of attention. It was easier to make extravagant plans than to actually gather money for projects that did not seem absolutely necessary. Years ago, carvings for the Battle Monument (dedicated to those who had fallen at the Battle of North Point in the War of 1812) had been ordered from Italy and then sat in their packing crates for months on end due to a shortage of funds. Baltimore's Washington Monument had been designed to be taller than it was and then scaled back. It remained unfinished for years until the end of 1829, when the statue of Washington was placed atop the column, and in 1832 the carvings for the base still had not been completed. The Merchants' Exchange had been built in 1825, an impressive building on the outside, with huge marble columns. But the merchants and lawyers who had been expected to rent space had not done so, and now it, too, had an abandoned, forlorn appearance. "A few shabby strangers in an immense hall," said one woman.[44]

On the edge of the city the Infirmary of the College of Medicine tried to keep illness at bay. The gated grounds were thick with foliage, and in the brick buildings lodged sick sailors and local people who had come for help. Three doctors, four barber-surgeons, eight Sisters of Charity, and several servants worked hard at their jobs. Patients paid for their keep (if they could afford nothing, they might go to the Almshouse), and tourists were even willing to pay twelve cents to visit the impressive establishment. The maintenance of a healthy city was considered by most elite citizens to be a worthy public project. To this end, the city council budgeted money every year for carting garbage and cleaning the streets and harbor, as noxious odors were associated with disease. The council members also organized several house-to-house vaccination campaigns against small-pox, which were greeted with varying degrees of welcome in different neighborhoods. A group of private citizens sponsored a new Dispensary in Fell's Point, but it foundered without the support of public monies as well. Motivations for these projects were mixed: to some extent the wealthy wanted to keep the majority healthy so that their own families would be less subject to contagion, but they also saw that to keep most people healthy would lessen economic losses in the long run. Baltimore's consulting physician wrote the council that "a general vaccination, once every year or two, not only would lessen the mortality from small pox, but would be less expensive to the city . . ."[45]

Thus far, a person wandering through the town had not yet seen the city's back door, a hub as important as the port and the downtown area. At its western extremity, Baltimore Street ran into Howard Street, which connected to Pennsylvania Avenue leading out of the city to the northwest. Here heavy wagons, sometimes connected to two or even three teams of horses, unloaded the produce they brought from farms and plantations: "Great numbers of wagons from distant parts of the country [come] every day, with barrels of flour for the merchants, and fat hogs, dead, for the market."[46] In the worst of winter sleighs replaced wagons and carriages. There were so many of them that they were required to use bells on cold, dark evenings to avoid accidents. Harvest time in August brought the greatest traffic, however, when the wheat poured in from the hinterland. If it had not already been ground into flour, then the wagons carried it to one of the mills along the falls.

Increased internal trade meant that there were more travelers on the road: not only wagoners, but also vendors, businessmen planning ventures, and people whose families had spread out as they followed opportunities. Where the turnpikes were ungraveled, wheel tracks cut deep into them; after a rainstorm they could be impassable for a brief period, but they generally were kept in good repair. It was now possible to travel to Philadelphia in eleven hours, by steamer, stagecoach, and boat. Most travelers complained that the going was rough, but they never stopped traveling. Inns and stage lines multiplied and competed for the business available: on the front pages of newspapers stagecoach companies accused each other of causing blood-curdling accidents. Sometimes they tried other tactics: "Opposition!" cried one ad. "A People's Line . . . wishing to carry Passengers at a fair rate, whatever others may do . . ." Baltimore was a hub, and two large hotels prospered where mere inns had sufficed before. "Mr. Barnum" himself presided over the meals in his establishment. Downstairs there was a large public reading room dotted with tobacco spittle, and upstairs his guests shared rooms cleaned by slaves, unless they wished to pay more for a private room. Stagecoach company offices were located in the two hotel lobbies.[47]

Frederick Bailey watched vehicles come and go with interest. He knew he was not allowed to board a stagecoach. Even free blacks could only do so if they could prove that they were legally free and had special business. The coaches were called "republican" because they were not divided into first- and second-class compartments, but were available only to those allowed to participate in the democracy. Occasionally they were also available to the "Red Men" who were allowed to pass through, but had ceased to participate in society on the shores of the Chesapeake. Most of the Native Americans who traveled in stagecoaches and put up at hotels were on missions to the United States government, to plead for their people's rights. Some came "dressed most fantastically," with white men "gone native" to act as interpreters; some wore suits and spoke the King's English to the other travelers. None came to stay; that era was gone.[48]

In this culture of transience and transport, some business leaders thought it most appropriate to develop Baltimore's first railroad. The Baltimore & Ohio was begun in 1828, with the first stage to consist of cars dragged by horses until the system could be replaced by steam. By 1830 newspapers explained where to buy the tickets for this fascinating ride.

Two horses were placed in a kind of heavy wagon in the rear of our carriage, and, by the motion of their feet in walking over a revolving platform, put into action a variety of springs that were fixed underneath it; and these again operating on the wheels of this curious piece of mechanism, pushed forward our vehicle, which was attached to it, at the rate of ten miles an hour. Thus, the horses . . . by walking only four miles an hour, though without advancing a single inch on the platform, caused us and themselves to be conveyed ten.[49]

Of course, there were other amusements available to Baltimoreans as well, which had little to do with changes in technology or the current mania for internal improvements. One visitor who was familiar with the peoples of many climes, northern and southern, spoke disparagingly of the "desultory and improvident habits of the majority." Sales of whiskey and playing cards were indeed impressive, and holidays were popular. On Whit Monday, for example, which fell in May, nobody went to work. "Horse racing and county parties were the order of the day." Here there was a social division. Carriages filled with well-to-do young people rolled out of town toward streams and country estates, while day laborers, young apprentices, and their lady friends made their way to the race-ground, where they would find a tavern, bowling, shooting at marks, and gambling booths. They took their gambling seriously: for the big races back in April on Easter Sunday, they had begun taking bets as early as the middle of March.[50]

Some entertainment was free and spontaneous. "Bull-baiting" was popular, for example: men would tie up a bull and let loose a few ferocious dogs. But almost everybody was accustomed to being able to spend some part of the week's income in search of pleasure, so people also enthusiastically attended shows for which they had to pay admission. At most of these events, you might see people of all classes—though people of color were confined to separate galleries. "A one-horned rhinoceros . . . taken at the foot of the Himalaya Mountains" was on view in the city from 9 A.M. to 9 P.M., costing twenty-five cents a look, half price for children. Another time it might be "the largest anaconda ever exhibited alive" or an entire New York visiting menagerie, with musicians playing "the most popular composers of the present day," including "Rossini, Runnell, and Mozart."[51]

There were two—and sometimes three—operating theaters or "Play Houses," although some actors complained that the city could not support that many. Certainly they had to compete to present ever more exciting plays. The melodrama *Paul Jones* promised an unforgettable evening of special effects: "a SHIP completely armed with her crew on board—men at their quarters beating to and from among rocks and currents . . . the blowing of the wind, the orders of the Pilot, the shrill whistle of the boatswain, the raging Ocean, all conspire to . . . impress the mind with the horrors of a dreadful storm." Peale's Museum, operated by the brother of the famous Philadelphian, was often criticized for its disorder and rotting stuffed animals, but it tried to compete by hosting fireworks and "comic songs and scenes from a comic play."[52] For fifty cents (children half price, as usual) many people took a day trip by boat to Annapolis with a live band playing aboard. At Christmas people fired guns, threw firecrackers, and drank "egg-mogg [*sic*]." Stores advertised "books for Christmas and New Year's," "family porks," "Christmas presents— Toys, Toys, Toys, at very low prices"; one promised that out of consideration for the customers, "The store will remain open the best part of Christmas Day."[53]

In September a military review annually commemorated the defense of the town in the War of 1812, and the various local volunteer militia groups staged other reviews whenever possible—for a funeral or in honor of visiting dignitaries. Foreigners often wondered at the thrill which the generally unused bayonets seemed to inspire in most people. Men also organized themselves in volunteer fire companies, making themselves an active presence in the newspapers and on the streets. Others went to political rallies, usually called in each ward in favor of a certain candidate—in 1827 you were "an Adams man" or "a Jackson man"—but sometimes organized by trade and class, as, for example, in an advertised "Meeting of Mechanics."[54]

Walking by a review or a rally, it was striking to think what an optimistic, inclusive place this was. There were several libraries open to the public, public schools available to all the white children, and a wide variety of books advertised in all the papers. One paper promoted itself by saying, "If you subscribe to a paper, your children will succeed better in life."[55] Many young men believed this and hoped to improve their own chances in life through book learning: they enrolled in night school or intensive week-long writing courses and advertised hopefully in papers that they "wrote a good hand" and were "industrious." They believed luck might smile on them, visiting fortunetellers enthusiastically and buying lottery tickets in such numbers that other cities' lotteries sent representatives to try to sell them their tickets, too. Sometimes, on the way home, they stopped in a tavern to have a glass of whiskey or of "switchel"—vinegar and molasses in water. They laughed and talked.

Frederick Bailey sometimes stopped by, too. He, however, had stopped believing that Baltimore was a hopeful or inclusive place. He was more familiar with the city than he had been as a child, and he knew there was a small minority of citizens who were not citizens, who could not taste the city's opportunities. He was a slave, prevented from deciding where to live or with whom and from keeping his earnings. "I contracted for [the salary]; I earned it; it was paid to me; it was rightfully my own; yet upon each returning Saturday night, I was compelled to deliver every cent of that money to Master Hugh."[56] Even if he were freed, as a black man he was excluded from the schools, stagecoaches, hotels, militia. The yoke grew heavier every day. He could not accept this state of affairs: he began to lay his plans.

The visible commonalities and differences between the cities of Baltimore and Guayaquil provide food for thought. If we are looking for evidence of disorganization, irrationality, or sloth, there is plenty to be found in Baltimore. The shipping lines published their schedules only to publish retractions, delays, and apologies. Stores sold liquor of every description.

The garbage piled in the streets for the pigs to roll in while Jones' Falls overflowed its streambed. Monuments were begun and left unfinished. Workers took every possible holiday and used the time for racing, gambling, and bull-baiting. People of all kinds bought tickets to events whose sponsors made patently false boasts; indeed the general credulity and optimism made lotteries and fortunetelling profitable businesses. On the other hand, if we are looking for evidence of industry, ingenuity, and entrepreneurial risk-taking, there is plenty to be found in Guayaquil. People dispersed according to gender where work was to be found. They were willing to do any kind of job and creatively thought of ways to start businesses—such as opening informal restaurants or carting ice to the tropical city to sell to the rich. If flooding was a problem they put their establishments on stilts or on boats. They made calculated risks and kept their businesses open when the authorities demanded that they close at a certain hour.

The point is not that Guayaquileños had a more developed work ethic and greater aptitude for business than did Baltimoreans. The point is simply that the two groups of humans seem to have been roughly similar in this regard if we do not approach them with preconceived notions. In neither place did religious institutions seem to dominate. Certainly neither group embedded its behavior in religious practices or beliefs in any easily visible way. Thus far we cannot look at such factors to find clear differences between the two places.

There *is*, on the other hand, evidence of strikingly different patterns of consumption. Even the poorest houses in Fell's Point had a stove and basic furniture. Ordinary folk bought tickets to shows and boat trips, and advertisers targeted them for such goods as bedbug bane and shoes for schoolchildren. It was assumed that even people without much money would want to participate in buying: a store made the offer to exchange recyclable paper scraps for a school slate. In Guayaquil, on the other hand, playhouses couldn't survive because so few bought tickets, and there were almost no advertisements, either creative or dull.

We might of course conclude that the people had different culturally constructed desires. But such a conclusion would be premature: it assumes a lack of flexibility in the Guayaquileño imagination for which we have no evidence. Guayaquileño servants responded immediately to European finery and gathered it whence they could, although they also continued to wear traditional clothing. Consumers in general showed a preference neither for the cottons brought down the mountains nor for the foreign ones bought off ships, but bought whichever was cheaper and wore both together. They learned foreign melodies and dances brought by sailors almost instantly, but also continued to play their own. Indeed, they generally responded positively to creative entertainment schemes—but only when they were free of charge. Sellers were not averse to drumming up business: hucksters advertised market foods aggressively and appealingly. It was worth their time, for they were selling goods people had to have to live, and publicizing them in a way that might work with an illiterate audience as a newspaper never could.

Here perhaps we have the difference: the majority of Guayaquileños had no discretionary income; the majority of Baltimoreans did. The lowest wages paid to workers in Baltimore—where they had steady work—provided a living; the lowest wages paid in Guayaquil did not. We cannot simply say that this is a matter of "market forces" alone. What people pay others, and what they are willing to work for, is at least in part a matter of cultural expectations. In Baltimore the Indians had been forcibly removed and slaves were too small a minority to perform all the work; it was impossible for some whites to extract nearly unpaid labor from other whites. In Guayaquil the tradition of coercing the dark-skinned majority was apparently very old. Although ideas about work—what should be undertaken, what accomplished in a day—seem to have been remarkably similar in the two places, ideas about workers—different groups of people and their relative expectations—seem to have been notably different.

These different conceptions ultimately had an impact on everyone. There were material ramifications. In Baltimore streets were paved and bridges and roads built because it was assumed that there were enough neighbors to share the cost; in Guayaquil such projects waited, as a few individuals did not want to shoulder the entire burden. In Baltimore processing plants and factories were appearing in response to the popular markets for their goods; in Guayaquil such large shops remained rare. There were also psychological reverberations that were far from simple. Life can hardly be said to have been "better" in one place than in another. In Guayaquil people of varying non-Spanish racial categorizations intermingled and formed the majority: they worked together, argued, called each other names, and had children together. In Baltimore a comparatively simple bifurcation between black and white existed. In Guayaquil there were no voluntary associations among peers, and the common people did not voice a sense of being in control of their destinies. In Baltimore such organizations proliferated, making loud displays and demanding statements, specifically excluding only African Americans. If in Guayaquil the poor majority could carve their own space in the interstices of a less controlling or specifically rejecting system, they still lacked any opportunity to make their own futures. If in Baltimore a smaller group of oppressed experienced the greater psychological strain of being more tightly controlled and expressly rejected, they often still believed in the possibility of opportunity. According to Frederick Douglass, the place they inhabited was subject to their critical judgment, for they knew that it offered hope to the majority surrounding them, rather than only to a tiny minority, as was the case in Guayaquil.

These aspects of their lives our sojourners could see and feel. They could not, however, have explained the origins of the differences between their worlds so easily. An explanation rather than a description requires more than our two travelers could take in as they walked the city streets. It requires that we move back in time.

Chapter 2

CONQUEST AND COLONY

There was much that explained Baltimore and Guayaquil that neither Frederick nor Ana Yagual could ever see with their own eyes, however keenly they observed. Differences between their adopted homes lay partly buried in the past and in statistics recorded by governments and later deposited in archives—so that posterity could read what was hidden from the view of our wanderers. Ironically, Baltimore would soon be considered a "failed" city, the town that never became New York or Philadelphia, while Guayaquil would be portrayed as emblematic of Latin American dynamism and potential.[1] Yet when the two cities are placed next to each other, it becomes evident that proportionately more Baltimoreans than Guayaquileños approached their dream of living a little better. "Success" is a relative term, entirely dependent on context. Thus we should start by moving back many generations before our adventurers were born and present a structural view of the world of each city as it unfolded over time.

Conquest

In some ways the Andean region had remained unchanged for millennia. The coastal flatlands lining the Pacific, lush in some places and desertlike in others, gave way to the famous craggy peaks with their highland valleys.

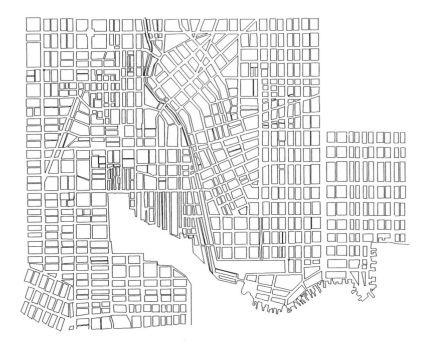

Map of Baltimore. Based on a map commissioned by the City Council of Baltimore in 1822 and currently housed in the Maryland Historical Society.

As the mountains sloped down to the east, they ran into the rain forest that sheltered the sources of the Amazon. The inhabitants of this world, however, had not remained unchanged. They migrated and made war and influenced one another and created kingdoms. In the century before the Spanish arrived, the Inkas from central Peru had made themselves mighty, conquering much of the highlands from Quito in the north to the Maule River in Chile, ruling over as many as nine million, building the network of roads and edifices that is still visible today.

The coastal peoples of the area that is now Ecuador lived at the edges of this empire. They were of the Puruhá-Mochica language family: scores of villages spoke somewhat different languages, but in a continuum of variation such that neighboring villages could always understand each other.[2] The Spanish later called them the Manta people, after one of their settlements; scholars now call them the "People of the Merchant League." There were three discernible groups, each containing several chieftainships. The Manta proper lived furthest north in a fertile area crisscrossed with rivers and streams. The Huancavilca lived just to the south, on the dry Santa Elena peninsula. The Puná lived on the great island in the gulf of the Guayas River that still bears their name. All were expert producers of cotton, from which they made the lively colored shifts they wore as well as durable cloaks and bedding sheets. They used gold, emeralds, and red shell beads to make jewelry; important people wore gold teeth. None of the emeralds and only some of the gold and shells were available locally: they obtained what they needed through trade, building unique ships with cotton sails that could carry twenty people and thirty tons of goods. In these ships they may have gone as far as Mexico. They also hunted and fished and were active farmers of corn and plantains.[3]

Further inland, along the Guayas River basin, lived the Chono, now called the Milagro-Quevedo by archaeologists, of the same language family. They had fine craftsmen of their own, both in weaving and in metallurgy, and they, too, were active traders, linking highland and coast. The Chono used beads and a kind of copper ax money, as a permanent medium of exchange. Near today's Guayaquil they maintained 50,000 hectares of "raised fields." Farmers created artificial ridges and hollows, so that they might plant on the ridges in the rainy season and in the furrows in the dry season. Labor had to be carefully organized. It is estimated that the chief of the settlement of Daule received tribute from 5,000 vassals.[4]

The Inka soldiers never conquered this region, but they loomed large on the horizon and made brief appearances. The empire's extraordinary successes in so many arenas (agricultural techniques, freeze-dried food production, food distribution, architecture, water projects, military development, goldwork, textiles, music, surgery, etc.) were due largely to the fact that its people acted as talented resource brokers, bringing the knowledge and discoveries of each region of the Andes to the attention of others. Whether they used their expanding power and influence to gain a stranglehold over those they conquered or to create an improved world in which hunger was diminished and peace strengthened is an argument that can never be finally settled, as the answer is a function of one's perspective. It is, however, certain that in exchange for the many cultural gifts they offered (as well as material gifts to the local chiefs) they demanded tribute in the form of material goods, labor time, and young brides for the king (to bring each village into the emperor's family). It is equally certain that different areas responded with varying degrees of enthusiasm to the "offer" to become part of the empire. The Chono's neighbors to the east, the Cañari of the mountains, fought tenaciously to maintain their independence and were only completely broken just prior to the Spaniards' arrival. The Inka, however, proved unable to permanently conquer lowland peoples whose climate and terrain were so unlike their own. The closest they came to control of the Ecuadorian coast was at the island of Puná. They attempted to isolate the chieftains there and turn the valuable trading hub to their own profit. By the time the Spanish arrived, the Puná warriors had a fearsome reputation, yet the island had been induced to pay tribute to the emperor. The more peaceful Huancavilca had apparently come to some arrangement with the Inka's emissaries, as there is evidence of interaction but none of outright conquest.[5]

Whatever political arrangements existed at the start of the sixteenth century crumbled at the arrival of the Spanish. News of what happened in the Caribbean after 1492 did not come to the Manta or the Chono; nor, apparently, did they know about the Aztec empire and its fall to Hernán Cortés in 1521. But by 1522 the Spanish were sailing down the Pacific coast of Central America and northern South America. How their explorations progressed is not known with any exactness. The Spanish chroniclers often did not write until years after the events and, without any previous knowledge of the area, often were not sure where they had landed.[6] We know that between 1524 and 1526 Francisco Pizarro and his right-hand man Diego de Almagro made an unsuccessful foray down the coast from Panama. They returned to the isthmus to replace both their supplies and the men who had died, and then started out again for another two years. This time they came across one of the impressive Manta boats. It carried valuable Inka goods, and they saw more when they made landfall. So in 1528 a more hopeful Pizarro returned again to Panama and thence to Spain to obtain a contract from the Crown. In late December of 1530 a well-supplied convoy sailed south from Panama in search of the fabled empire of which they had seen traces. They spent some confused months on the coast of Ecuador before making their way inland to Cajamarca, Peru, there to defeat the emperor Atahualpa in one of the most famous scenes in South American history.[7]

The Manta and the Chono may have breathed some relief when Pizarro passed on, full of his hopes of bringing low the Inka. Any joy was short-lived, however, for in 1534 Pedro de Alvarado arrived from Nicaragua with the intention of continuing the slaving operations that had begun in Central America. He met with resistance. Some claim he slaughtered as many as 20,000 Chono within the year. In 1535, with the area apparently pacified, and the Inka defeated in the highlands, the conquistador Sebastián de Benalcázar founded the city of Santiago de Guayaquil. In a legal sense he merely moved the city of Santiago, which had been officially founded in the highlands the year before, as the Crown had decided a port should be established instead. The next year Chono warriors avenged their dead and killed most of the new town's seventy inhabitants; those who lived fled. It was not until 1547 that the city was established on its present site.[8]

The Spanish considered an area truly settled not merely when it had been claimed in the name of the king, but when encomiendas had been established. These were granted to the original conquistadors, as well as to other leading citizens who petitioned the Crown. An encomienda gave its recipient the right to demand tribute of a certain Indian village and was usually offered with a land grant. The tribute was to be paid in a specified combination of precious metals (in some cases) and goods and services (in all cases). Needless to say, to enforce the system the Spanish were at first dependent on the native lords who had traditional authority over the villages. Indeed, a number of Atahualpa's sisters and children and other Inka nobles married into the Spanish elite. The fact that in South America the Spanish conquest spread outward from the Inka heartland was critical. There a rigid hierarchy of tribute-payers and collectors was already established; the Spanish simply took over the reins of government, and the idea became planted in their minds that this was how the system ought to work everywhere. Even those Indians technically outside of the

Inka empire were familiar enough with the idea that this was how power worked. The Puná chieftains, for example, had paid tribute to the Inka, and their own vassals had paid tribute to them.[9]

The goods that the coastal Indians were required to pay to the encomienda holders have been calculated as worth roughly the equivalent of four months' earnings every year. Unlike the Inka government, the Spanish did not use the money to build roads and schools in temples or to supply armies and feed the disabled. At first, the Indians were even required to pay quantities of gold and emeralds, but the Spanish were grudgingly convinced that these items were not native to the area and had traditionally been obtained through trade. Then the tributes were paid in cotton cloth, corn, beans, chickens, and salt fish. The labor tax was another matter. Indians provided labor time first and foremost in that they farmed for the newcomers and built their new towns. By the time the project of searching for gold gave out, the Spanish had discovered that some Indians knew how to dive for pearls. They put so many to work under such dangerous conditions that the enterprise was eventually forbidden by the Crown. But no brakes were ever put on the practice of sending labor gangs long distances to harvest sarsaparilla (used in curing syphilis) and valuable timber.[10] Ironically, these coastal people probably considered themselves lucky that they were not shut into workshops and forced to produce cloth, as were their neighbors in the highlands, and many of those who worked in such shops considered themselves lucky to have been given such an assignment rather than being sent down into a mine for a shift of several weeks.[11]

Except for mining, however, it was the raising of coastal products like sugar and cacao that was, of all Spanish businesses, the most detrimental to the Native American population. The coastal peoples were disappearing before each other's eyes. Crops that could be farmed in small amounts and harvested slowly, like tobacco or indigo, did the villages little harm, but the necessarily large and intensely demanding sugar and chocolate fields drained them of their energy and time so they could not feed themselves. One Spanish observer claimed that the disorientation and depression caused by the cataclysms they had suffered caused the women of the town of Puerto Viejo to commit infanticide regularly. And disease was as large a factor here as it was everywhere in the Americas. The people had no immunities to the European and African microbes brought by the twenty-five to thirty ships that stopped at Guayaquil every year. Scholars estimate that over 90 percent of the coastal people disappeared during that century.[12]

It is wrong, even foolish, to argue that the Indians accepted their lot passively: they resisted as much as their limited power allowed in each situation. They delayed Guayaquil's taking root by attacking the city aggressively; when that was no longer possible, hundreds of them withdrew to the unconquered wildlands of a small chain of mountains near Colonche. They lived there until the end of the century, when they were finally forced to enter the Hispanic world. Other Indians managed to profit from the new commerce, capturing escaped horses, for example, and breeding them so that they could hire them out to the Spanish.[13]

For a time Guayaquil failed to thrive. By the 1570s it had between thirteen and twenty-three encomenderos, over a hundred *vecinos* (elite heads of household of pure Spanish descent), and a total population of several hundred. It did not rise in stature, for its encomiendas steadily lost value due to Indian deaths. In 1556 the encomienda of Yaguachi consisted of 1,000 Indians, for example, but by 1574 there were only 110. Fewer Indians meant less tribute and decreased labor for farming. To make up for the losses, the white Guayaquileños began to import African slaves. By 1586, 13 percent of the population was non-Indian, and by 1605 more than half of these non-Indians were black or part-black, leaving about 5 percent of the population to call itself white and command the others.[14]

Even after the wars with the Spanish were over, the people of the coast lived in fear of the English, who in their envy of the Spanish sent pirates to prowl the seas and look for plunder. In 1579 Francis Drake was seen many times off the coast, engendering panic, though he never landed at Guayaquil. In 1587 Thomas Cavendish sacked the island of Puná. By that time, however, the English were becoming distracted by colonies they were attempting to establish far to the north, above the northernmost Spanish settlement of Saint Augustine in Florida; they did not return to the mouth of the Guayas.

Although the first English colony on the Carolina coast died, by the early 1600s others were surviving, beginning with Jamestown on the Chesapeake. Still, the English investors and settlers remained resentful of the Spanish. William Simmonds wrote in 1612:

It was the spaniards good hap to happen in those parts where were infinite numbers of people, whoe had manured the ground with that providence that it afforded victuall at all times; and time had brought them to that perfection [that] they had the use of gold and silver . . .

But we chanced in a lande, even as God made it. Where we found only an idle, improvident, scattered people, ignorant of the knowledge of gold, or silver, of any commodities.[15]

The people whom the Englishman condemned so bitterly had actually worked out a style of life in which hunger was rare and leisure relatively plentiful, a *modus operandi* that was effective for their thin population. Between 26,000 and 34,000 people of the Algonkian language family lived in the Chesapeake tidewater. From April through September they farmed, living in large villages that were relatively permanent, moving only once in many years when the lands around had become depleted. After the harvest of corn, beans, and squash, they followed the game for the fall hunting season. While the men were at the chase, the women gathered wild foods to supplement the crops. In the dead of winter they lived in dispersed camps, making clothes, moccasins, snowshoes, baskets, nets, weapons, and other necessaries. In March they sought the bodies of water that yielded the greatest abundance of fish. Then the "season's round" began again. The English spoke scornfully of their "flimsy" wigwams, but the layered dwellings were far cooler in summer and warmer in winter than the English wood-frame dwellings.[16]

It took years of experience before the English were willing to give up the dream of imposing an encomienda-like system over the Indians they settled among. The colonists repeatedly told the Indians that they should produce corn for them. John Smith was particularly smitten with the idea, for he said the Spanish "forced the treacherous and rebellious Infidels to doe all manner of drudgery worke and slavery for them, themselves living like Souldiers upon the fruits of their labours."[17] But the whites could not force compliance on the part of the Indians, despite having superior weaponry. The problem was not only that these people tended to be more mobile than the indigenous of Ecuador, but also that they had a different idea of political authority. The Algonkians did have a hierarchy, and even a class of nobles from whom their leaders were drawn, but theirs was a kinship state of face-to-face governance in which all men were warriors, not a far-flung empire of divided labor, even including professional soldiers. Sometimes certain chieftains became more powerful than others. The father of Pocahontas, for example, was a paramount chief. He could, however, extract loyalty and even tribute from vassals only as long as shifting alliances and population figures supported his demands. If one group made demands on another group that were too great, they could fight, or, if likely to be defeated, they might melt into the woods and temporarily disappear.

When in 1622 the Powhatan Indians decided they had suffered enough depredations and lost enough corn to the insatiable newcomers, they rose and killed one-quarter of the colonial population in Virginia. The event did indeed lead to innovations in the colonists' dealings with the Indians. They attempted to extract no more labor from them. Rather they sought other, more market-oriented ways of profiting, establishing a partnership with the powerful Susquehannocks who lived to the north and with London financiers interested in beaver pelts.[18] Little by little the Indians would find that the beaver population could not sustain itself in the face of such assault, that other game was dying off, that the colonists' pigs were laying waste to the land, and that they themselves were being fenced out of their old farmlands. It was a much more subtle attack than that experienced by the Manta and the Chono, but it was a process of displacement nonetheless.[19]

After 1632, feeling more secure in their environment because of the partnership with the Susquehannocks, the Virginia colonists focused their enmity on the English Catholics who had been granted the northern section of the Chesapeake. The first Lord Baltimore, Sir George Calvert, obtained the charter to "Maryland" and then passed it to the second Lord Baltimore, Cecil Calvert. The colony was conceived as a haven for Catholics. Five of the six initial investors were of that faith, and Jesuit priests shortly set about converting Indians. It was, perhaps, the Catholics' plan to profit from the beaver trade that so enraged the people of Jamestown that they asked the Susquehannocks to attack the newly arrived English. Vicious warfare between the two groups of whites ensued in 1637–1638 and again in 1642–1648, until finally Calvert was forced to appoint a Protestant governor to attain peace.[20]

Despite his predecessors' failure to reduce the Indians to peonage, Lord Baltimore had still hoped to introduce the English manorial system in the Chesapeake as effectively as the Spanish had brought their own form of feudalism to the southlands. If the Indians would not work for him, he could transplant British people of all classes and thus replicate the system at home. The plan failed. First, few English lords wanted to migrate after the Indian war of 1622, and, second, the men who came as servants soon learned how much land was available in the New World and how easily a man could grow and sell tobacco for himself. As the growing supplies of that plant caused its price to fall, a mass demand emerged in Europe. Merchants would buy straight from the farms that lined the waterways of the Chesapeake; no quantity was too small. Eventually certain plantations would rise to prominence and a patriarchal tradition of southern "gentility" would emerge, but that was years in the future. For now, a man and any servants he possessed labored together to grow as much tobacco as possible.[21] There were no obvious ruling families recognized as such by all settlers no matter where they were from. The lack of such made those who governed the colony quite nervous. "Injunctions and appeals to the past, to tradition, were intoned endlessly throughout the century," observes one historian.[22] But the stridency of their insistence only underscored the problem—if indeed it was a problem.

By the end of the century 400,000 English had moved to the New World, 120,000 to the Chesapeake. Lest anyone imagine yeoman citizens founding town councils together as equals, we should remind ourselves that at least 70 percent, and perhaps as many as 85 percent, came as servants. A typical ship arriving in 1636 brought wine, rum, sugar, cheese, clothing, shoes, candles, nails, and seventy-four men for sale for a term of several years.[23] Who were these people selling parts of their lives? Were they destitute and desperate, not sure where they were bound and subject to abuse? Or were they enthusiastic young people bent on gaining independence for themselves in the New World? The answer is a little of both, but scholarly opinion lends greater support to the second interpretation. At first recruiters concentrated on young men from middling families, meaning the younger sons of yeomen and artisans. However, as demand increased after the hard times that had existed in England in the first part of the century improved, recruiters were forced to turn as well to orphans, poor day laborers, displaced Irish, and women of those classes, who were also, after all, accustomed to working in the fields. Hunger, debt, and other imperatives may have driven the poor to sign contracts, the ramifications of which they did not fully understand, but the nature of the contracts themselves indicates that they were in fact bargaining and making choices. One study of servants who left London in the same decade, for example, shows that those who could write their names signed on for an average of seven months less than the illiterate, and those who agreed to go to Barbados rather than Maryland accepted an average of nine months less, probably because the Caribbean was known for its high mortality rates and limited opportunities for poor whites.[24]

If they lived to complete their terms—usually four to five years—the ex-servants were free to "establish headrights" themselves. Any free man could claim fifty acres of land per able-bodied hand who would be working it. (Thus wealthy men who had many servants claimed large tracts for themselves.) As the Virginia territory began to fill, Maryland was still a frontier, and many former servants from the Jamestown area headed north. Between 1634 and 1681 Maryland headright listings record about 32,000 arrivals. Such people pursued two goals: to form families and become landowners. The two agendas were linked, for women were scarce and would only choose men with land, and a man could only establish a successful farm with the help of a woman.[25]

It is possible to paint a bleak picture of the ex-servants' lot. Diseases like malaria that flourished in the unfamiliar environment killed them in droves, and it was only in the final years of the century that the white population became self-sustaining. Even then, one-third of the householders in southern Maryland were tenants. Only one-third of former servants became actual landowners, usually of small farms. Indeed, they were poorer in material goods than were comparable sectors in England at the time—due to the shortage in a frontier area both of time for producing domestic items and of channels for purchasing them.[26] This kind of interpretation, however, ignores the larger context. For only one-third of householders to be tenants was an extraordinarily good ratio; in no town in Europe or anywhere else could one-third of the servants expect to own their own farm in the near future. If their houses were smaller and less well built than the ones they would have had in England, they also ate much better.[27] Their descendants, as we know, would buy domestic goods in plenty as they became available.[28]

Baltimore County was established in 1659. Most of the settlers were not "great folk." The land grants were not large by the standards of Jamestown: there were a few for four and five hundred acres (indicating the presence of eight and ten men in the household), more for three, two, and one hundred, and even some for fifty.[29] There were only 12,000 white residents in all of Maryland when the county was founded; but more poured in over the course of the next generation, and the Indians were pushed back by the fencing, the pigs, and depletion of game. In 1675 tensions between the white settlers and the Susquehannocks exploded into open warfare. This time, the former enemies, colonists in Maryland and Virginia, sided together against the Indians, and by 1677 the latter had been militarily destroyed and driven from the land. To the south, in Virginia, those whites fighting in the Indian wars became involved in "Bacon's Rebellion": they rose against the elites who controlled the colony and who themselves had plenty of land far from the Indian frontiers. Edmund Morgan and others have argued that it is no accident that it was only after this point that African slaves began to be imported in large numbers. They were people who would serve for life, who could not go in search of land of their own after a few years or make demands on their betters. The disgruntled former indentured servants who were having trouble gaining land or profiting as they had hoped found a newer, lower class of people to distinguish themselves from, and they rebelled no more against their government.[30] It is certainly true that beginning in the 1680s Africans were imported to the Chesapeake by the thousands. Harsh laws were passed to keep the lives and expectations of blacks and whites entirely separate. At last the colonial authorities had found a way to impose the manorial system they had so long desired.

Still, the class of yeoman farmers that had already taken root in Maryland could not be done away with. They continued to flourish on family farms, many of them turning to growing grain rather than tobacco for export.[31] They needed a town, and in 1729 the colonial assembly passed "An Act for erecting a Town on the North Side of the Patapsco, in Baltimore County." Sixty acres were surveyed on land belonging to Daniel and Charles Carroll, who were paid by those who took up lots.[32] Baltimore had been born. The city's origins could not have been more different from those of Guayaquil. The lots of Guayaquil had been given as rewards to the original conquerors, who were to use the city as a base of operations from which to subjugate the Indians and make them tribute-paying peons. The lots of Baltimore were purchased by volunteers who wanted to live there with their families, fifty years after the Indians had been killed or driven away to make room for a new population. It had the makings of a different world indeed.

The Colony and Independence

For years Guayaquil remained a backwater, unspoken of in the world at large, until suddenly in the late eighteenth century it was catapulted into the position of one of the leading cities of America's Pacific coast. Baltimore likewise remained little more than a village with no more than twenty-five houses in 1752, until it experienced a meteoric rise and became the fourth largest city in the fledgling United States. Despite the similarity of their trajectories, however, their stories were profoundly different.

The cloth production workshops that once thrived in Ecuador's northern highlands declined in the 1700s, due partly to natural disasters and partly to misguided Crown policy. As a result, many Indians who could not meet their tribute payments in other ways migrated south, where some cottage industries still survived, or to the coast, where the shipyards were known for paying cash to workers. The population of the Guayas region began to swell; after the 1790s it grew dramatically, for at that point the cacao trade took off.[33] Even when Spanish lawmakers had forbidden its export—as part of an effort to protect Mexican trade—the coastal peoples had managed to sell it illegally. Then a limited trade had been legalized, and now the liberalized laws of the Bourbon monarchs had opened the doors to trade with any Spanish ship. The fruit had a reputation for being of lower quality than that of Colombia, but Guayaquil's merchants solved the problem by mixing more sugar with their cocoa powder, creating a cheaper and more popular drink for commoners in Spain and elsewhere.[34]

The Spanish Crown was quick to follow up on the success of its policy by collecting taxes on the burgeoning trade. It was not long before the coastal provinces were providing the lion's share of the Kingdom of Quito's revenues. In addition, as early as 1764, the internal trade that was inspired by the infusions of cash brought by cacao came to be increasingly taxed. Even small-time traders in fruits and vegetables came face to face more often with adamant local commissioners.[35] It comes as small surprise that a variety of coastal peoples harkened to the cries for independence when they were heard—or at least when they had been heard often enough. Guayaquil remained relatively unperturbed when early rebellions were staged in other cities in 1808 and 1810, but the leading citizens joined the bandwagon of northern South America in 1820 and declared independence from Spain. The royalist armies were otherwise engaged, and the province of Guayas rather easily became a small, sovereign nation, able to send troops to aid Simón Bolívar in his ventures. In 1822 the great generals Simón Bolívar and José de San Martín brought their troops together from north and south in a great pincerlike motion designed to drive the Spanish from the land. The two men met for the first time in the city of Guayaquil.

Guayaquil was made into the southernmost city of the nation of "Gran

Colombia," encompassing today's Venezuela, Colombia, and Ecuador. It seemed as though the stresses of war would shortly end, but it was not to be. The military campaign had to be continued against the Spanish troops holding out within the borders of their still Loyalist neighbor, Peru. In 1827, after the last Loyalists had been defeated, Guayaquil was invaded: the commercially valuable port became a prize sought by the warring armies of Gran Colombia and the newly liberated but still recalcitrant Peru. Gran Colombia won this battle; but the strains of war proved too much for its component states, and in 1830 they voted to become separate republics. The state of Ecuador then had further problems, for certain leading families now hoped to attain great regional power, given the enormous wealth that was at stake, and in 1833 they fought among themselves. By 1834 the leaders Juan José Flores of the highlands and Vicente Rocafuerte of Guayaquil had reached a peace accord and agreed to an alternating presidency.

The peace was to last for a period; but in the meantime damage had been done. War left its marks. Soldiers swarmed the city; they had to be fed every day and eventually paid. At one point the regional treasurer wrote to the governor in anguish that even if they could make every citizen pay three pesos, there still would not be enough money to satisfy all the soldiers owed back-pay. Generally the government resorted to loans from the wealthier classes in these emergencies. At critical moments during the wars, when battles raged dangerously near, people would close their shutters and stop doing business for up to a few days at a time. Foreigners described these periods in an agony of excitement: "The greater part of the [wealthy] townspeople have deserted the place and business is quite at a standstill."[36]

Clearly the continuing wars were a major factor impeding the area's development, yet they cannot be used to explain all ills. The business of living never really stopped. The population did tend to dip during the worst moments, as most men were anxious to avoid being drafted to fight. At such times, workers might be scarce, but the municipality's continuous records barely even noted these events. Most families, after all, could not leave town at the drop of a hat. And many men did not need to make themselves scarce, for they were excused from fighting if they were clergymen or slaves or students or skilled craftsmen or conductors of foodstuffs or invalids or the main supporters of families. Many who were impressed later deserted and made their way back to the city, although they and those who hid them risked punishment. A few businesses were actually inspired by the violent events: meat providers organized themselves to increase production in case of a siege, and delighted craftsmen sold the army boots and cartridge belts.[37] Even in 1834, at the peak of the fighting on the Guayas River, foreign ships came to do business. At first they had difficulty finding local pilots to guide them up the river, but eventually they all did; the pilots' hesitancy may have stemmed more from a desire to hold out for higher pay than from a determination not to go out in times of war.[38]

Trade was at first mostly local. Between the initial moment of independence in 1820 and 1825, the vast majority of imported goods came from Guayaquil's nearest neighbors, first Peru, then Chile, then Mexico. The sum of the values of all the products from Great Britain, the United States, and Panama (consisting of goods brought over the isthmus from the Caribbean, about three-fifths British and two-fifths North American) was less than the value of the goods brought from Peru alone.[39]

What European trade did exist came to be almost instantly dominated by the British. They brought iron, tea, boots, shoes, and a few manufactured shirts and pants; they took away cacao. Between 1820 and 1825 Guayaquil sold more cacao to Great Britain than to any other nation.[40] The English were not consuming more cups of chocolate than anyone else; rather, the English merchants were reselling it to other countries. They could afford to buy and ship it in large quantities and keep it until scarcity drove up its price. In his report the British consul encouraged the loan his government was negotiating with Gran Colombia: if the South Americans were under a primary obligation to pay off a debt in pounds, they would devalue their own currency to encourage exports to Britain. Then, in exchange for every pound's worth of china or tools they imported, the local merchants would have to pay a greater share of their own income to obtain it.[41]

Within fifteen years, by 1836, a great reversal had occurred: the value of imports from Britain and the United States was almost ten times greater than the value of goods coming from near neighbors. This was partly due to the general need to import iron and manufactured goods unavailable locally, which were especially expensive when their own currency was devalued in relation to the pound, and partly due to political pressure to buy specifically from Britain, as Ecuador was left to pay its share of England's loan to Gran Colombia when the nation broke into three parts. The value of Ecuador's own export products, like cacao, had declined, and merchants complained that they did not have the capi-

tal or political clout to bargain successfully in the international arena.[42]
Still it is not clear why some debt or increasing dependency on Britain for imported goods should necessarily spell disaster. Baltimoreans, as we shall see, had earlier made the decision to rely on the English for certain goods. After all, in exchange for the imports, the British were buying ever larger quantities of cacao, which, according to some theories, should have contributed to prosperity. Yet poverty seemed to be increasing all around Ana Yagual. One problem was that only a handful of men were gaining most of the profits of the chocolate windfall. At the end of the eighteenth century 15 percent of the landowners had planted 63 percent of the new trees; five men planted 40 percent of the total. There were seasonal jobs on these few plantations, it is true, but not nearly enough to absorb all the workers migrating from the highlands in the wake of the textile trade fiasco. In addition, because cacao only demanded attention at certain seasons of the year, several hundred slaves were allowed to buy their freedom during this era and work for wages in the periods when they were needed, so they would not have to be fed by their masters year-round. They sought other employment the rest of the year. Furthermore, many indigenous peasants who had been independent farmers were pushed off their land as the commercial estates expanded along the waterways. The province of Machala, for example, produced nearly a quarter of the cacao grown because of its ideal climate; by 1830 the workers of Machala lived in more visible desperation than any of their neighbors.[43] Members of all three groups—migrating highlanders, freed slaves, and dislocated locals—wandered to the city in search of employment. There they camped on the savanna and wondered where to turn next. For them, the chocolate prosperity had proved a chimera.

Baltimore, too, experienced major transformations in the eighteenth century, but its denizens met a different fate. Many of Maryland's farmers and planters had converted or were in the process of converting from tobacco to grain and livestock: tobacco exhausted the soil, and their European markets had shrunk dramatically, first when Maryland ceased to be a British colony and then when Europe was engulfed in war. Farmers on the bay brought wheat and other goods to town on rafts and boats. Those to the north brought their goods to the shores of the Susquehannah when the waters were high and let the river do the work. Labeled barrels and wooden "arks" bobbed southward by the hundreds. Most arrived battered at the mouth of the Chesapeake, and there were broken up to be sold as timber and firewood.[44] Slaves were not needed year-round to grow grain, so plantation owners considered options that had been previously unthinkable: they let many bondsmen free themselves through self-purchase, and they transferred many slaves to Baltimore, where they worked as domestics or artisan apprentices. Thus the number of slaves declined in the surrounding countryside and increased only in the city.[45]

With wheat an elite manufacturing class was born—not one that had any intention of competing with British manufactured goods, but one that profited by processing the agricultural products, such as flour millers, ship builders, sawmill owners, and large-scale coopers. The larger millers especially found it easy to expand into merchant trade. They arranged to ship their flour to neighboring ports, the Caribbean, and Europe. In exchange, they imported rum and other liquor, molasses, salt, French luxury products, and English manufactures. The European wars of the eighteenth century—as long as they were fought elsewhere—gave the merchants the power they most wanted: the ability to monopolize trade. While European ships could not sail due to the danger of attack, neutral American ships usually could. Even during the American Revolution, Baltimore had been the regional port farthest removed from the commotions of the Atlantic; the British navy patrolled the Chesapeake only intermittently. The city's shipbuilders had made fortunes by developing the speedy "clipper ships," which could not only outsail the enemy but also arrive at destinations experiencing the shortages of war while people were still willing to pay high prices.[46]

Baltimoreans had themselves briefly experienced the horrors of war. Still fresh in most adults' memory was the trauma of the War of 1812. The cityfolk felt they had suffered painfully when they repulsed the British invasion in 1814. They recorded their fears in diaries and letters:

> Nearly half past four in the Morning; our Alarm Guns were fired at twenty minutes past twelve, since then the Bells ringing drums beating the Houses generally lighted. We have all been up since that period, we know not the hour when we may be attacked . . . The City looks almost deserted. Some moments I feel very resolute, the next quite the reverse.[47]

Besides the temporary closure of businesses, other kinds of losses were suffered when working men met their deaths in the fray. Their widows and mothers were supported by the city for years afterward. In 1813 the city borrowed $75,000 from local merchants to put toward defense. After the war the municipality issued stock to the creditors at 6 percent interest, a drain on public coffers for years. When the British approached, the city sank all the ships which had the misfortune to be at home; though they were later raised, the sodden vessels suffered irreparable damage.[48]

When the war was over, however, the merchants missed it. The fighting had not been nearly as damaging as the contemporary conflagrations in South America were proving to be. Furthermore, it had been a part of the last great eighteenth-century European military conflict. Since then, Baltimore traders had faced the prospect of figuring out what to do now that the Europeans were no longer "at each other's throat." Indeed, Britain's peacetime capabilities spelled disaster for local merchants, who could not compete successfully against rivals with more capital. Within one generation, they learned to concentrate instead on domestic markets and infrastructure. Even at great cost, they would build roads, canals, and railways to funnel wheat from the west toward their port, rather than toward Philadelphia, and they would sell imported goods (cloth, clothing, tools, and crockery) to the smallholder farmers, many of whom could afford to buy. Baltimore in its own right formed a significant market.[49] On the strength of their reputations, the wealthiest merchants made use of the cargo system, under which they received shipments of goods from British merchants with the promise that they pay for them within a year. Then they sent the goods throughout the city and the hinterland. A wholesaler, in a typical advertisement, solicited "the favors of the public generally, but most especially the County Merchants." The country store had long been a primary distribution point for cloth, clothing, and other manufactured goods: most rural customers paid in cash; if they could not, it was still assumed that they could buy, paying with credit or in kind. It was, in fact, the existence of such people that made the system viable.[50]

Thus it was that "internal improvements" became the order of the day. Language waxed superlative:

> Among the various objects which have claimed the attention of the public for the interest and embellishment of Baltimore, there is none in usefulness which merits our attention more, than the contemplated bridge across the river Susquehannah . . . which will connect the fertile Country on the Eastern side of that River with the City of Baltimore, from whence we shall receive large and regular supplies to our markets.[51]

The new bridges, roads, canals, and railways were not always as individually profitable as their backers hoped in terms of profits from tolls, but taken as a whole they became the key to the region's prosperity. They employed workers in their construction and, once finished, allowed small farmers as well as great to sell their goods on the international market and receive shipments of other goods in return. But they did not work magic: there had to be a potential clientele to render their construction useful to more than a handful of families. It was this element that had been systematically destroyed in the hinterland and streets of Guayaquil, not only by war, but even more by the custom of accepting that the many should work toward the profit of the few.

Statistical Overview of the Cities

In the early nineteenth century Baltimore attracted new residents in greater numbers than did Guayaquil. Even after the tobacco trade and then the shipping industry faltered, the grain trade and new internal improvements kept Baltimoreans busy. The cities had been the same size a generation earlier, but by 1820 Baltimore's population was slightly over 60,000, while Guayaquil's was roughly 20,000.[52] Yet in many ways the cities still resembled each other, as they resembled other major mercantile centers, for Baltimore had not yet become an industrial city. Occupational statistics recorded at comparable moments—in 1815 in Baltimore after the War of 1812 was over and in 1831 in Guayaquil after independence from Gran Colombia had been declared—indicate that in this period the cities were still organized along similar lines (see Table 1). In neither case do we have an accurate sense of the proportion of unskilled day laborers in relation to the rest of the population. The Guayaquil statistics do not include them at all, and the historian who has analyzed the numbers for Baltimore tells us that it is impossible that the percentage of day laborers should have dropped from a recorded 19 percent in the 1790s to 11 percent in 1815; in fact, the 1815 city directory simply did not count black workers, nor most seamen and new immigrants.[53] Aside from the percentage of day laborers, however, we have good statistics for each city that show a remarkable similarity. Indeed, we cannot ascribe later divergences between the ports to dramatically different functions as represented by the occupational structures.[54] Yet in retrospect we know that the cities would soon cease to resemble each other, one becoming an early industrial city, the other not.

TABLE 1. OCCUPATIONAL PROFILES
OF EARLY NINETEENTH CENTURY BALTIMORE AND GUAYAQUIL

Category of Work	Baltimore (post–War of 1812)	Guayaquil (postindependence)
Artisan crafts	48%	58%
Trade/Commerce	26%	24%
Professional Services	15%	10%
Day Labor	11%	[not recorded]
Agriculture	[not recorded]	8%

Sources: Hamerly, *Historia social*, pp. 113–120; Andrien, *Kingdom of Quito*, p. 52; and Steffen, *Mechanics of Baltimore*, pp. 13–15.

If we want to see sources of the divergence encoded in socioeconomic statistics, we will have to look "behind" these occupational statistics, at the ways people were divided other than by profession. We can ask questions about divisions *within* occupational groups, for example. Ideally, we would ask questions like the following: among artisans, how many could hope to become masters, and how many would be permanently employed as assistants? Among traders, what proportion rented stalls, or were allowed credit to buy small shops, or were engaged in wholesale trade? Unfortunately, the sources do not allow us to answer these questions with any precision in the case of either city. It is, however, possible to observe the general distribution of wealth, and those numbers, combined with a more qualitative study of the numerically unanswerable questions, allow us to meet the goal of looking beneath the occupational profile.

To collect a comparable representative database for each city, I started at the busiest section of the waterfront and moved inland, capturing 500 households in 1830–1831.[55] Baltimore's neighborhood was Fell's Point, and Guayaquil's, the parish of the Matriz. In each case, interestingly, the total number of people living in the houses was just over 3,000 (3,284 in Baltimore and 3,059 in Guayaquil), indicating a roughly equal average household size. Five percent of the neighborhood's population was enslaved in Baltimore, and just above nine percent in Guayaquil, both figures very nearly approaching the wider city statistics.

At first glance, the similarity between the two samples is stunning: in each, just under 15 percent of the households had recognizable wealth that brought them onto the tax lists; in each case, wealth was defined to include land, house, furniture, plate, jewelry, and slaves. But the similar numbers are deceptive, for several reasons. First, the nature of the sources indicates that every last person with a recognizable income was desperately added to the combined census and tax register in Guayaquil, while in Baltimore the census and the extant notebook of a tax assessor are separated by three years, so the correlation between the two is lower than it would be if the lists had been composed at the same time. Second, although the percentage of property holders would remain relatively constant in Fell's Point if we moved beyond our 500 households, as similar streets continued many blocks northward, it would drop almost to zero in Guayaquil within the equivalent of one block. Finally, and most importantly, the excluded 85 percent were not equivalent, for in Baltimore only those who had amassed at least one hundred dollars' worth of property were included, while in Guayaquil households with any taxable property were counted. Thus, for example, the "excluded poor" in Baltimore included barbers with apprentices, while such men were taxed in Guayaquil.

Even among the 15 percent of households that were taxable, differences between the two cities are marked. Guayaquil's were far more weighted toward the lower categories than were Baltimore's. That is, if we divide the families into four groups, establishing rough correspondences according to their lifestyles, they are spread relatively evenly in Baltimore, while proportionately more of them are found in the less well-off categories in Guayaquil (see Table 2).

TABLE 2. WEALTH DISTRIBUTION AMONG TAXABLE
HOUSEHOLDS, BALTIMORE AND GUAYAQUIL C. 1830

Taxable Wealth Baltimore (dollars)	(Fell's Point)	Taxable Income (pesos)[1]	Guayaquil (Matriz)[2]
100–199	28%	200–299	47%
200–599	44%	499–999	37%
600–999	14%	1000–2999	9%
1000+	14%	3000+	7%

Sources: Guayaquil: Padrones of 1832, Biblioteca Municipal de Guayaquil. Baltimore: 1830 Federal Census; 1827 City Directory; 1827 tax assessor's notebook for Fell's Point, Baltimore City Archives, RG 4.

[1] The Ecuadorian peso was worth one dollar at this time.

[2] In Guayaquil income was assessed based on visible property, but I have not been able to locate the source that explains the conversion of property into income. By comparing the lifestyles of people in the different brackets in the two communities, I was able to create four roughly equivalent categories.

The most striking findings of all, however, appear when we move away from the standard method of calculating wealth by household and look *within* households. We can separate members of the householder's biological family from live-in servants, slaves, and other dependents, as these groups obviously did not have equal power to buy and participate in the economy in the same way. In Baltimore, when we subtract slaves and the few live-in domestics from the total number of people in the sample, we find that we are left with 92 percent of the people renting or owning their own houses and making their own consumer decisions. (The total is 95 percent if we do not subtract the free black live-in servants and assume that they had wages to save and spend.) If we go further and subtract white apprentices and live-in servants, who were temporarily excluded from most buying, both legally and for lack of means, we are still left with well over 80 percent. In Guayaquil, when we subtract comparable dependents from the population, we are left with 53 percent, so that even in the taxable households where people lived relatively well almost half the residents were penniless or nearly penniless dependents on people far more powerful than themselves. Another way to look at this phenomenon is that in Baltimore most households actually approached the average household size of 6.4 persons, of whom biological family members formed the largest number. In Guayaquil, on the other hand, the average of 6.2 persons was not usually reflected in reality. Households were often tiny, with one to three people renting a room, or else very large, making room for the high number of dependents seen in the statistics.

Where do we find in the socioeconomic statistics the visible beginnings of divergent growth patterns? It was not people's jobs or functions that were dramatically different in the two mercantile port cities. It was the traditionally assigned rewards for their work apparent in the wealth distribution. The early histories of the two cities clearly illustrate how these differences came to be.

PART II

CHAPTER 3

A MERRY PARTY AND SERIOUS BUSINESS

The Elite of Guayaquil

Because he was deputy mayor of the city, the young merchant Vicente Ramón Roca had to hear several criminal complaints every week. In 1823, under the new republic, Ana Yagual's uncle Mariano de la Cruz was brought before him, accused of making a violent attack on a white man. Roca and the consulting judge were desperately concerned about keeping order in their new political world. In this case, though, there was no actual proof that Mariano was guilty of murder—only that he had been "uppity." In the past, legal technicalities might not have saved an Indian, but now the judges themselves had just passed a series of laws to guarantee democratic rights to republican citizens. In this moment of fearful fluidity and general excitement, the two gentlemen decided not to condemn Mariano without proof; instead they issued a severe warning to him not to "exceed his authority" and released him under a bond for his good behavior.[1] In fact the gentlemen were not certain exactly whom they wanted to include as citizens in their new republican world. Far from being rigid, Vicente Ramón and his cohort were creative and thoughtful, intent on forging a brand new world. It was a tall order, however.

A recent visitor to the area had described a similar state of social flux and intense examination of the Guayaquileños' own society. Captain Basil Hall of the British Royal Navy was in the city for Christmas of 1821.[2]

Simón Bolívar was drawing near, and it was not clear whether the government of the tiny independent nation of Guayas would be willing to dissolve into the larger region the hero was liberating. Hall spent a happy day in the countryside with several charming young ladies from "good families" while they waited for the military men in the city to resolve the tensions, which they easily did. The captain hoped to continue his flirtations that evening at a social gathering. He found himself outmaneuvered, however, by the women themselves, who apparently had their own reasons for wishing to ignore him. "As they arranged themselves in two lines facing one another, in a narrow veranda, it became impossible to pass either between or behind them." He was reduced to listening to their conversation through a window that opened onto the balcony. At first he could not understand their rapid Spanish, but gradually he began to follow its outline: to his amazement, he found that they were hotly engaged in a political debate. It was not at all what he had expected ladies to be discussing. Captain Hall, after all, still had much to learn about how these people conducted their affairs and about the magnitude of the issues they were in the process of reassessing.

Basil Hall had been welcomed by the most elite families of Guayaquil. In his account of the days he spent with them, he described several aspects of their lives. In an architecture that emphasized the social hierarchy, they lived on the upper floors of some of the same buildings that housed tradespeople and servants on the lower levels. The buildings were of wood, plastered inside and out, and sometimes the inner rooms were painted pretty colors. They had balconies on the street side and on the inner courtyard. With the gauzy curtains or shutters left open, the cross breeze was delightful. Visitors always commented on the simple elegance of the rooms; they were not cluttered with much furniture, but what pieces they had were beautifully made. Every drawing room had a netted hammock: people could create their own breeze even on the stillest days. There were damask coverlets and china tea sets, with tiny spoons of silver or of shell for stirring coffee. All the best families also had a house in the countryside on a plantation. Those houses, accessible along a network of rivers and creeks, were also of wood, but usually gaily painted on the outside and with a tiled roof.[3]

The younger generations at least seemed to love their lives in the newly independent Guayaquil, welcoming the future and priding themselves on intelligent debate. A young man wrote to a near relation in Quito:

I feel the deepest desire . . . to see you and to talk to you . . . I hope I may some day have the joy of being with you in this beautiful province, which offers young people the brightest joys, especially now, when we are preparing so many diversions. On Monday the bull-fights begin, and every day throughout there is a dance in the evening . . . The city is beautifully decorated, and it is delightful as can be to see . . . the frequent meeting of free men of all nations; and the infinite public papers and pamphlets about all kinds of topics are bringing enlightenment to young people.[4]

These social gatherings "bringing enlightenment" were called *tertulias,* a word that has no exact English translation, but refers to an informal party in which conversation is the critically required element. Their *tertulias* were important, for they nurtured the independence movement and afterward shaped the new society. Historians have debated the reasons for the change in the thinking of the Guayaquil elite between 1810 (when they did not support an uprising against Spain that took place in Quito) and 1820 (when they declared the Guayas province an independent nation and began to participate with other rebels up and down the coast). Some have argued that the harsh reprisals of Spain's local representatives against the rash young enthusiasts in the city roused general sentiment against Spain. Others have argued that the elites simply saw what was undoubtedly coming: by 1820 Buenos Aires and much of the north coast of the continent had been liberated; the Mexican popular uprisings were gaining ground; and eager British merchant ships plowed the local seas.[5] Probably for all these reasons the change in Guayaquileño thinking rapidly took place at the *tertulias,* where a traditional form of entertainment was enlivened by heady talk of independence and the future.

By 1820 these gatherings invited general involvement among the elite. They were not only for excitable young extremists. Indeed, it was impossible for any gentleman to ignore the political debate; due to the women's participation, it had become part of the very fabric of a man's domestic life. The debate was intimately intertwined with his dinner and with any flirting that he chose to do. Vicente Ramón Roca, who at the age of twenty had nearly been exiled when an overly patriotic letter to a priest was intercepted by loyalists, went to the *tertulias* to court Juana Andrade. They participated actively with the patriots who staged the change of government in October of 1820, and one month later they were married. Once the fighting was underway, the traditional evening get-togethers often centered around groups of women in sewing bees, who had gathered to make shirts for the army or sheets for the military hospital. The merchant José Villamil gained stature in the city when his seven-year-old daughter made two shirts for soldiers with her very own hands and the story made the newspaper.

There was no question of the serious political discussions being held away from the *tertulias* where women gathered; in fact, the women were considered the hostesses and promoters of the political debates. Manuela Cañizares from Quito had become famous not long before when she held the 1809 party at which the 1810 antigovernment plot was hatched; when her participation was discovered, she fled to a convent and stayed there until she died in 1813. Since then, the Spanish in Gran Colombia had publicly executed at least 44 women and exiled at least 119; news of these events would have reached Guayaquil regularly. In like tradition, but escaping punishment, Ana Garaicoa, mother of the seven-year-old seamstress, held the dinner party designed to screen the final organization of the government takeover by the *independentistas* of Guayaquil in October 1820.[6]

We probably will never know exactly what was said in those airy drawing rooms looking out on the Río Guayas. But in the end the talk bred excitement in favor of the cause of independence and other social experiments. References in letters and memoirs have proven that the more liberal members of the social gatherings also read and discussed the works of Abbé Raynal, Jean-Jacques Rousseau, Baron de Montesquieu, Thomas Paine, Thomas Jefferson, and others. Several young Guayaquileños visited Spain at a time when these works were available there.[7] They clearly talked about the "infinite public papers and pamphlets" mentioned by one enthusiastic letter-writer. The outpourings of the press probably did seem infinite in the early 1820s, because it was the first time that Guayaquileños had ever had a local printer. Before the newly independent government purchased a press in 1820, people had gotten their reading material from Quito or Lima or off foreign boats. Suddenly there was something new to read every week in *El Patriota de Guayaquil* that was of immediate, local interest. José Valens had many visitors in his cafe, where he cleverly sold both lottery tickets and the latest issues of the papers.[8]

Of course, the world of newspaper readers was a relatively small one in the context of the city as a whole. Only about 150 issues of each paper were printed for a city of at least 20,000 inhabitants. Even assuming that each issue was read by more than one person, the proportion is small; but to elite families, it seemed that *everybody* was reading the new paper. Most subscribers were between thirty and forty-five years of age, old enough to be married and head of a household of people with whom they might share the paper. (Only two women subscribed for themselves—the unmarried sisters of the radical Ana Garaicoa.) At least half of the subscribers were merchants. Most members of the City Council added their names to the list. The little republic's governing committee was involved in the production of the paper. The first issue of *El Patriota* had waxed eloquent on the economic potential of Guayaquil and blamed Spain for the city's slowness to develop, accusing the mother country of having imposed "three centuries of ignorance, monopoly, shackles, and prohibitions."[9] The text of the paper and all succeeding issues consisted of articles by the editors, new laws, letters to the editor, and selections from other newspapers arriving in the port. The largest percentage always concerned the wars of independence in the Americas, and the message was clear: positive portrayals of the functioning independent areas of South America appeared side by side with pictures of chaos wherever the Spanish remained.

Yet even in these relatively controlled pages the elites did not present a seamlessly united front. They generally agreed upon the wisdom of self-government, but they disagreed as to what kind of new world they wanted to inhabit. The majority of the letters to the editor consisted of criticisms of other members of the elite: the subject of a letter was dishonest, was participating in contraband trade, was lobbying to join Peru for selfish reasons, etc. These mutual critics were quite direct: over half of the letter writers (53 percent) signed their names, and another 28 percent made themselves obvious by giving their initials. Only 19 percent submitted anonymous contributions. After only a few months of publication, the editors of the paper grew disgusted with the criticisms, which were even leveled against themselves, and announced that in future they would only publish letters of commercial or scientific interest. They reminded readers that any person who had anything to say in print was free to hire the press to put out a special pamphlet. Henceforth, public political debate continued in veritable pamphlet wars.[10]

Disagreements existed between the small rural planters and those large cacao planters who also controlled the import-export trade. Evidence appeared even in *El Patriota*. A group from the town of Samborondón wrote: "The people of the Province of Guayaquil, since the day of the transformation, have suffered under an unbearable yoke heavier than the one from before . . . Six families, without any other interest than the spirit of

commerce and their own aggrandizement, have thought to take our immense sacrifices and turn our Patria into their own inheritance."[11] Although all the major merchants, and many of the small ones, were also
landowners and cacao producers, thus blurring the one-sidedness of their
interests, the opposite was not true: there were many small planters who
were not also merchants. They harbored resentments against those who
had the power to buy and sell or to refuse to. During the period of Guayaquil's complete independence, between 1820 and 1822, merchants—or
those who defined themselves primarily as merchants—made up 36 percent of the governing body and landowners 39 percent. This is not as
balanced as it may seem. Out of all elite families, at least 40 percent were
major landholders, while fewer than 20 percent were import-export merchants. So the merchants' political influence far exceeded their numbers.
Similar percentages existed in the makeup of the municipal assembly later
in the 1820s and into the early 1830s. It is important, however, not to
envision any state of open warfare between merchant-landowners and
pure landowners: after all, the city assembly did remain mixed. And in the
case of the provincial assembly, to which representatives from all parts of
the province were sent, the rural elite themselves usually elected merchant
landowners. In 1831, for example, one of the signers of the angry Samborondón letter was part of a committee of four assigned to counting and
checking the vote, and four of the six men elected were merchants.[12]

Reacting against the perceived corruption of the Spanish government,
the council specifically allowed for disagreement and took pride in being
incorruptible. Both during the council's period of supreme authority and
under Gran Colombia, when it was concerned with purely city issues,
members took pride in their newly independent status: they made efforts
to behave in a professional manner rather than merely governing according to their own interests. They fined their colleagues for failure to show
up for meetings; they worked on Christmas Eve and even if necessary on
Christmas day; a member would withdraw if directly related to a person
under discussion.[13]

Despite being newly free of Spanish restrictions, the merchant elite did
not have the power to do what they would when they would. They were
only gradually able to shape financial policy to suit their needs, as is
evidenced in the story of their lingering low-intensity war against the
Customs Office. The various successive governments depended on the
Customshouse for their largest source of tax revenue. Local government
policymakers, many of them merchants themselves, believed they had

little choice but to raise duty payments because of the increasing demands of the Colombian federal government. But merchants who were not responsible for balancing the government's budget were not sympathetic. Importers of wine lodged a formal complaint against the Aduana office in 1825—among them the rich and powerful José Villamil and Vicente Ramón Roca and the British merchant William Robinet. Ship owner Antonio Durán also sued in 1828, for he was at a pitch of rage against the Aduana for an unexpected 8 percent increase that threatened to ruin him. But the government judge found against the plaintiffs in both cases. Many merchants simply did not pay what they owed for years at a time. An 1826 list of outstanding Aduana debts included the names of twenty-one men who owed between 158 and 9,497 pesos, almost all of them prominent and respected citizens. One of the largest debtors was a foreigner, a British merchant called Jonatas Winstanley. To everyone's amazement, he was suddenly arrested one day and forced to pay most of what he owed. The others waited no longer: within two weeks, all the small debts were cleared and many thousands of pesos had been paid on the larger ones. Unfortunately for the collections officers, the problems began anew immediately afterward: the government's records for the late 1820s reveal a continuous struggle against high-profile scofflaws.[14]

When the change in government came in 1830, as the state of Ecuador parted forever from Gran Colombia, merchants attempted to take advantage of the temporary legal confusion. They refused as a body to pay some duties, claiming that they had heard they had been suspended, and they unsuccessfully attempted to embark some lots of worked silver without paying any exit taxes, on grounds that it had not yet been named by the new government as a duty-paying article. Perhaps most enraging for these merchants was the fact that it was one of their own who blew the whistle: Juan Francisco de Icaza, fifth son of the prodigiously successful Martín de Icaza, whose ties to Mexican businessmen had nourished the cacao export trade for over a generation, took his role as an elected government officer very seriously.[15]

This, then, was the context for the merchant traders of newly independent Guayaquil. Theirs was a world of fearful and wonderful fluidity, of questioning old norms, widespread disagreement, and political dickering. Within that context of debate, they had to decide how to run their businesses. Their merchant culture evolved in many arenas—in the organization of their trade networks, the style of their day-to-day business practices, their investment strategies, their ideas on taxation and public investment, and their relationship with laborers. It is to the formulation of their merchant culture in these areas that we now turn.

Trade Networks

In 1835 there were 120 registered merchants in Guayaquil. Of these, 35 were large wholesale and retail merchants engaging in some form of international trade, and 85 were smaller, retail-only merchants. Relations between the two groups generally showed no strain: they took the form of patron-client ties. Pedro Galarza, for example, himself a small landholder and a retail merchant selling fine fabrics, leather, and paper, owed over 18,000 pesos to the more powerful wholesaler Miguel Ansoátegui and smaller amounts to two others. These debts arose when the men entrusted Galarza with goods they had imported and accepted his promises to pay them later. Foreign retail merchants—many of them Spaniards who had been expelled from Mexico—applied for citizenship by demonstrating that they had at least 2,000 pesos in capital and by obtaining the sponsorship of several prominent wholesale merchants.[16]

Some of the smaller merchants would themselves later move up into the ranks of the larger merchants: we know that for many of the retail-only merchants their status was only a temporary stage of life, for 61 percent of them were unmarried, far more than among men or merchants generally, indicating that they conceived of themselves as beginners. Other retail-only merchants, however, remained permanently in that category. When he died in 1823, the Chilean-born José de Echeverría had in his store some jackets, cotton cloth, fifty-three hats, one watch, a chair, five books, and two chests of china. Some of his customers owed him small amounts of money—six or seven or maybe twelve pesos—but he owed larger merchants almost a thousand pesos. Apparently there were more men in Echeverría's situation who believed themselves lucky to be in business at all than there were who harbored resentments against the larger merchants. At least they told an inquiring foreign visitor that there were more small merchants than heavy capitalists and that their small speculations allowed for a "considerable number of persons who enjoy a comfortable independence."[17]

Still, on at least two occasions, resentments surfaced. While Guayaquil was independent between 1820 and 1822, import merchants began for the first time to sell goods to the public straight off their boats, thus considerably underselling small retail competitors, who complained vociferously. The government sided with the larger merchants. Years later, in 1827, a group of retail merchants protested the city council's decision to do away with the stalls they rented, where in fact they made their greatest profits. They submitted two petitions, pulling out all the stops: "[Please consider] the prejudice which would result to us, and the indigence which many honorable people will be thrown into, and their families too . . ." "We trust that your integrity will never allow such a thing to come to pass, first of all because in no period (except under the Spanish) have the rights of the rich been favored over the rights of the poor . . ."[18] At first these petitions seem almost comic, given that they were signed by well-to-do businessmen, but they were writing to a council dominated by the even wealthier import-export merchants, to whom these smaller merchants inevitably compared themselves. It was specifically because of their position as men of property that the threatened "indigence" appeared so dishonorable.

The profitable external trade was limited to a select few who had the capital necessary to finance international shipping expeditions. These great merchants also developed a system based on personal connections. Before the independence wars, during the cacao boom that began in the 1790s, Martín de Icaza sent Francisco de Iraeta, a relative in Mexico, shipments of cacao grown on his own land and in return received shipments of cochineal and indigo (red and blue dyestuffs) that he could sell for cash at home. Iraeta for his part liked to order that monies due him be paid back "invested in cacao." The two men punctuated business news with mention of their children. Francisco even allowed himself to be fatherly, given his more advanced age. "You must have patience," he told Martín when the latter grew frustrated. Years later, in 1834, Martín's nephew was still writing to Francisco's grandson in the tone of a previous acquaintance, informing his relation that he was coming to Mexico and asking what goods he should bring to sell.[19] Yet this system depended on trust between people separated by weeks of travel, and sometimes it backfired. In 1799, for example, José Bustamente and José Ortega in Guayaquil contracted with Jacinto Vejarano, an acquaintance in Cádiz: he would send them 40,000 pesos' worth of manufactured clothing each year, while they would send him 10,000 cargas of cacao, to be sold at 4 pesos per carga. To make this work, Vejarano would use his influence at court to obtain for them the political governorship of the village of Palenque, so that the Guayaquileño businessmen might extract tax payments in cacao from the indigenous people there, at little or no cost to themselves. Vejarano did not obtain the *tenencia* of the village for them, and he persisted in selling clothing to other merchants in Guayaquil at low cost so that they regularly undersold the duo. At least this was how they explained to themselves their inability to sell all the clothing. They lost money for two years and then unilaterally annulled the contract. Vejarano sued them, and they countersued: the legal actions continued into the time of the republic and past Ortega's death.[20]

Intermarriage was usually what made the difference between a successful international arrangement and a disaster. The Iraeta-Icaza connection stemmed from the fact that Rosa María de Iraeta, Francisco's daughter, had married Isidro de Icaza, Martín's brother, and they lived together in Mexico, near the bride's family, according to merchant custom. Francisco and his other son-in-law, Gabriel, in writing to Martín, peppered their letters with references to "my son Don Isidro" or "my brother Don Isidro," constantly reminding Martín of their near relationship. Isidro and Rosa María were permanent hostages guarantying the good behavior of their families: if either side behaved dishonestly, their beloved family members would be made miserable for their remaining days. In this system, the women stayed where they were born, close to friends and family, and the men came to them. Thus in Guayaquil, as in other cities, there was among the elites a high frequency of marriage between foreign men and local women. Of the elite men involved in politics in the early 1820s where parentage is known, almost all had locally born mothers, while half had fathers from Spain. The practice continued after independence, although the foreign male marriage partners between 1820 and 1835 were generally no longer from Spain. They came from England, France, Sweden, Venezuela, New Orleans, and the sierra.[21] Many of them gained names for themselves in the independence wars and were generally liked and trusted.

Once in a while trust went awry. In 1827 María de la Cruz Andrade chose to marry Tomás Drinot, a ship captain and merchant from Saint-Malo, a seaside town in the north of France. Although "Cruzita's" family really knew little about him, they did not try to stop her. One day about a year later, when she was near term with her first child, her husband went out and came back in a miserable mood. He then shut himself up and shot himself. The judge was at first nonplused and suspected that someone else had killed him: he asked the servants if Tomás had ever mistreated Cruzita, if there might therefore have been someone seeking retribution, but they all insisted that this could not have been the case. Then it came out that Drinot was a bigamist. Ten years ago in Saint-Malo he had married a Frenchwoman named Catalina whom he had abandoned; she was still alive. Cruzita went into shock. She gave premature birth to a son. And then León Iturburu, another French merchant currently acting as consul, announced that it was his painful duty to bring suit on behalf of the other widow, Catalina. Half of Drinot's wealth—which was not inconsiderable—was returned to France.[22]

Between the ages of fifteen and twenty-five, Guayaquil's elite young women paid their money and placed their bets. They looked the young men over and chose the most likely ones.[23] Most who gambled won or at least did not lose so badly as María de la Cruz. Young men from home either were from "good families" or they were not; but in the case of foreign young men, it was largely up to the women to decide who would advance to become a successful merchant and who would not. If an outsider could not win the hand of one of the *señoritas* of good family, then he stood almost no chance of advancing to a position of acceptance, respect, and wealth. Some never did.

Compare the fates of Manuel Antonio Luzárraga and José Villamil. Due to their marriages, one became extraordinarily wealthy and one only moderately so. Manuel Antonio arrived from Spain just before the outbreak of the wars of independence and took up the cause with a ready will. He volunteered to serve first as captain of a warship and then as captain of the port (in charge of policing the river) and participated actively in several battles. Then he published a pamphlet account of the battles, mentioning his own role. As a war hero, he won the hand of María Francisca Rico, the daughter of the very wealthy Francisca Rocafuerte, who spent her time campaigning for women's education. He had some limited family money, but María Francisca brought him far more, and he went into business as a leading import-export merchant.

José Villamil, on the other hand, from a large land-owning family in New Orleans, had traveled widely in the Caribbean and participated in *independentista* activities in Venezuela before he decided to settle permanently in Guayaquil, probably because he had fallen in love with Ana Garaicoa. She, too, as noted, was a young enthusiast for "the Cause," known for her intellect and her laughter. Together, they made plans for the future of their country; they later named three of their children Simón, Bolívar, and Colombia. Unfortunately for José, Ana's dowry did not match her patriotism or her intelligence. He thus was unable to go into business as an import-export merchant on a large scale on his own. The couple put what money they did have toward the effort to impress the elite towns-people: they hosted frequent *tertulias*, and in 1821 their house was de-scribed as the grandest in the city. With his reputation as a great figure, Villamil was able to go into business as a co-signatory for other mer-chants. That is, for a percentage of the profits, he would vouch for another merchant's credit, arrange the details of shipments and storage and sched-ules, book passengers, and take charge of making repairs or ordering new equipment.[24]

Daily Practices

Generally the most successful merchants were hard-working, realistic, and careful. In the various emergencies of life, the locals knew where to find them—in their warehouse office or store. Not one sworn statement in any court case ever mentioned looking for one of the well-known mer-chants in a billiard hall or bar, though they looked for priests and teachers there. The lives of Vicente Ramón Roca, Manuel Antonio Luzárraga, and José Villamil, whom we have already met, all demonstrate the presence of extraordinary energy. They were always engaged in a multiplicity of projects, both mercantile and political, and consistently oversaw all cor-respondence. José Villamil reacted typically in the 1830s when he was awarded the governorship of the Galápagos Islands, where he intended to use convict labor to establish plantations as well as starting a whaling fleet to export the oil. He did not just send a representative: he went himself to the distant archipelago to make the necessary arrangements.

Most merchants seemed to put their faith in practical endeavor rather than leaving matters to God. Their letters to each other occasionally in-cluded brief prayers that the supreme being would guide their loaded ships safely through the high seas, but they always began and ended with necessary information and instructions, including advisories about what to do in case of disaster. The Icaza family wrote lengthy letters to their associates in Mexico replete with all the potentially necessary details and then made sure to send them in duplicate on separate vessels, in case one copy should be lost. When Antonio Sucre, the greatest Ecuadorian hero of the independence wars, was assassinated in June of 1830, the country went into shock and turned to its religious faith for comfort. The local government upheld special instructions from the national government that every person should wear mourning clothes for eight days and all the churches hold special services; even in this situation, however, not a word was said about stopping work.[25] Although businessmen here, as elsewhere on the continent, did try to please the divine by offering money to the church, they were rarely carried away in this regard. In their wills they left only small amounts beyond payments for their funeral masses; indeed, there is no record that Guayaquil's church ever amassed the quantities of investment capital that the church did in some places.

As long as they were working hard and guarding their wealth in practical ways, the merchant elite believed it made sense to operate according to the most sophisticated principles with which they were acquainted. Government account books, often kept by the same clerks who worked for the private companies, indicate a familiarity with double-entry bookkeeping and an awareness of the importance of perfect accuracy. They used paper money easily and effectively: from municipal workers and soldiers they bought at sharp discounts the IOUs the government often used to pay salaries and then used them at face value in paying their customs bills. Internationally, they relied on *libranzas* or bills of exchange.[26]

Institutional forms of credit were just beginning to be born. In general, loans were still personal affairs: merchants and merchants' widows lent money out at interest. They made private arrangements among themselves that only became matters of public record when the debtor died without paying or welched and the creditor went to court and produced some kind of a signed letter or note, often lacking the signature of a witness. Thus personal acquaintanceship and trust were of the utmost importance.[27] The institution that came closest to acting officially as a lending bank was the Seguridad Mutua or Mutual Security fire insurance company, founded in 1828 by Manuel Luzárraga. The company lent money—the collected dues of the insured members—for six-month terms at 6 percent interest, but first preference was always given to member subscribers, so it was not really a viable source of credit for most people. The founders were almost all prominent merchants who had much to lose in a fire themselves. Luzárraga himself served without salary as the director, but a treasurer and secretary were hired to do most of the work for 300 and 200 pesos per year, respectively. Luzárraga found he had to push the fledgling organization: in May of 1828 he wrote to the occupiers of government-owned buildings to remind them that, according to a new law, they were now required to buy insurance from the Seguridad Mutua. In June he announced in the papers that the new rules for fighting fires had been printed and were available for sale in a certain store.

The company was first tested seriously in December of the same year, when the Casa Consistorial, the main local government building, caught fire. The Seguridad performed its two assigned functions—helping to put out the blazes as efficiently as possible and later covering damages for insured tenants. It continued to operate well in other cases too. The voting members were called to meetings through notices in the newspaper. A person became a voting member by taking out insurance for at least a thousand pesos—and this could be distributed over several properties, as it sometimes was. At first these wealthy members seemed to believe that buying their shares was an act of generosity on their part, rather than an act of self-protection. Often they failed to make the payments due, especially if they were out of town. But Luzárraga was tenacious and the company did not die, though it struggled in the 1830s. He learned something, too, from the practice of lending out the company's funds for six-month terms. Years later, at mid-century, he would establish the city's first officially recognized private bank.[28]

Clearly, if they were to make such credit operations work, the merchants had to work together in a purely businesslike and rational way, divorced from their private passions and community fault lines as much as possible. Probably as part of a strategy to preserve their own interests, most merchants joined professional associations. In 1823 the Sociedad Económica de Amigos del País was founded by order of the Liberator, Simón Bolívar, with a chapter in Quito and another in Guayaquil. Vicente Ramón Roca was treasurer, and many others signed their names as members. As an imported organization, however, it did not thrive. Citizens and foreigners, big names and small, continued to use the courts to resolve their disputes.[29]

The merchants' cases were withdrawn from the public courts, however, when in September of 1829 most of the city's merchants met to form the Consulado de Comercio or Merchants' Guild. A full voting member had to have at least 12,000 pesos in capital, a second class member at least 6,000; a special member with a security of 500 pesos could be voted in by a majority of the full members. Plantation owners and ship captains who met the requirements were explicitly stated to be as welcome as merchants themselves, to avoid divisions within the elites. Their tribunal met Tuesday, Thursday, and Saturday at ten in the morning, with a rotating committee of judges. Within a year the members had hammered out a code of conduct that was to govern them in all their dealings with each other. They made use of it: in one month twenty cases might appear, and almost all of them were settled (*conciliados*). Even the most powerful merchants attended. They were bound by their own rules to accept the guild's decisions. When a merchant tried to overturn a ruling by going to the public Appeals Court, his peers reminded him and the governor of the illegality of his proceeding. On the other hand, occasionally the guild felt that a case was so complicated or so important that the committee would refuse to hear it and it would be sent into the ordinary courts of law.[30]

Perhaps the greatest challenge for the merchants lay not in convincing each other how they should behave, but in convincing their children. In this early republican moment, they and their wives were also still in the midst of determining how best to educate their children so they would be well equipped for the future. There were not many schools in the city. The best secondary institution was the Colegio San Ignacio Loyola, which had a rather rocky history. It had been closed in 1767 when the Jesuits were expelled and thus had not existed when the generation of *independentistas* were boys. They had been educated abroad. Only in 1816 did the Colegio San Ignacio reopen its doors, without Jesuit direction. It had almost no funding—the extensive Jesuit properties having been auctioned decades before—and the new treasurer was accused by many of mishandling what funds there were. In the early years of the republic he justified his activities by publishing a special pamphlet, explaining that the institution's income consisted of whatever cacao crops were left to it in people's wills and a share of the wealth of the suppressed monasteries. In 1827 the governor became disgusted and investigated the school's accounts: he issued strict orders about the budget and the handling of investments. Making the school a priority was part of the optimism of the new era. By 1829 the director had received a medal for his achievements in returning the school to its former glory. He expressed his "most glorious of sentiments and feelings of satisfaction" in a letter to the governor.[31]

In the 1830s the school ran efficiently and without major incidents. Its students were wealthy: expenses totaled about 100 pesos a year. The students rose at five, made their own beds, dressed themselves in their black suits and hats, and then began their schedule. They first studied Spanish, French, and English for six hours a day and then majored in either philosophy (including studies in the humanities, such as history and music) or *náutica* (including mathematics, geography, navigation, and ship controls). Those who planned to run a merchant business could select either course. All the students presented public examinations almost every week. Neither parents nor school authorities would brook any rebellion. If a

young man refused to comply with these expectations, he could be expelled for his "bad example" to others. And the rule was enforced.[32] In the
second half of the 1820s the Escuela Náutica was organized to train naval
officers. It provided an honorable but cheaper alternative to the *colegio* for
impoverished boys of good family. There was no cost to attend classes,
but the students repaid their *patria* by serving an apprenticeship on board
a warship before they graduated. The son of Miguel Casilari, a political
administrator and landholder, was killed while serving. One young Icaza
was on the list of students, but most of the names were of less-well-known
families.[33]

Until the 1830s there was no operating school for girls in Guayaquil.
As elsewhere in South America after independence, however, elite women
began to argue for the founding of one. How could they be useful republican citizens and raise successful sons if they were not educated? During
the 1820s the collection of funds was trusted to María Urbina, apparently
because she was the wife of the treasurer of the Colegio San Ignacio de
Loyola. María Urbina, however, consistently reported that there was not
enough money to start the school. Only when the wealthy Francisca
Rocafuerte founded the Junta Curadora de Niñas (Girls' Guardian Committee) and began to write regularly to the chief of police, who oversaw
all internal municipal affairs, did the situation change. Francisca's enthusiasm must have been contagious. She successfully collected public and
private funds and obtained some land that had been confiscated from the
Convento San Agustín. She was old and her signature shaky, but she dictated her letters to someone younger, probably her daughter María Francisca, who had married Luzárraga, the banker, and later became treasurer
of the school's Junta Curadora. The older Francisca wrote proudly of the
"greatest progress we are making in the education of our sex." By 1831
workmen were inserting two large windows in the girls' school building,
which was large enough to include living quarters for the directress and
studios for drawing and music. Every year the girls presented a public
examination, and the best students received special ink pens as their
prizes. When members of the Convento San Agustín sued to get their
land back, together with the buildings on it, in 1832, Francisca Rocafuerte
wrote straight to the governor, demanding that he help prevent them
from turning the tide of "progress"—and progress made after many years
of effort. He turned the issue over to the national government, and Quito
found in the school's favor. Apparently educating the mothers of future

merchants seemed more important than placating the church, at least in the current climate of Guayaquil.[34]

Investment Strategies

Perhaps most importantly of all, in deciding how to put their money to use, Guayaquil's merchants had to learn how best to deal with the British and other foreign traders now in their midst. Guayaquileños were not in the habit of trusting them. In fact, the Anglos had long had a reputation for piracy.[35] There were few resident British whom one could come to know well. In the colonial era foreigners were theoretically forbidden to enter as merchants and set up trade on their own: they could only work through a Spanish or Creole representative. During the independence wars some political leaders began to hope that foreigners from the North Atlantic would soon take on a different role—that of investor or trade partner. The young United States was far ahead in developing international trade connections. Henry Robinson, a U.S. ship captain, had been detained since June of 1820, when, during the last days of the royal government, he had been hauled in for suspected contraband activity. In January of 1821 the papers were transferred to the new attorney general (*procurador general*). In the summary he submitted to the judge he mentioned: "It is worth taking into consideration the extremely important role of foreign boats like *The Tea Plant*, which have been the only means of keeping alive the commerce of this area . . . "[36] The judge agreed, and Robinson had no more trouble.

That same year there was a widespread debate among the elites of Guayaquil as to whether the law should be changed and foreign merchants be allowed to conduct business on their own and import more freely. The talk made its way into the newspapers and into the diary of the visiting Captain Basil Hall.[37] "It was pleasing . . . to observe," he wrote, "more correct views gradually springing up, and in the quarter where they were least likely to appear—amongst the merchants themselves." The central issue here was whether or not foreigners should be required to become partners with Guayaquileños in order to invest in local businesses exporting cacao and importing manufactured goods, or whether they should be given free rein to set up their own firms and retain all net profits after customs payments themselves. The advantages of forcing them to work with locals were clear; others argued, however, that it would be better for everyone if the doors were opened. More British ships would come, and local merchants, who were also mostly planters, would be able to sell more cacao. Certainly the British would be better pleased with this arrangement and would prove friendlier, perhaps providing easier credit and refraining from participating in the smuggling operations that so badly hurt income from Customshouse payments.

The question of whether the increased goods coming off the British boats would hurt local artisans was only rarely addressed by the merchants who debated the issue: it was not a priority for them. It had already been made illegal to import cacao, coffee, purple and blue dyestuffs, sugar, molasses, rum, salt, or tobacco, as these were products of the country; indeed, the landholding merchants grew them on their own plantations. The issue of guarding small manufacturers against competitors was different, however. Merchants saw it as being more complicated and lobbied for varying tariffs from year to year, often depending on what was currently overstocked in the port. They did not solicit the opinions of artisan guilds.[38]

The laws were indeed gradually changed in accordance with the merchant-planter interests, and the British were the first to respond with enthusiasm. They had been waiting for years for this kind of legal trade in South America. "He must indeed be more than temperate, he must be a cold reasoner, who can glance at those regions and not grow warm," one member of Parliament had remarked in 1817.[39] Within a few years of the legalization, there were about twenty British merchants in Guayaquil, and by the end of the 1830s at least thirty-five. In 1826 the British merchants in the area took purposeful steps to increase demand for their goods in local markets. They sold goods to merchants heading for the interior at very low prices, hoping that the reduced retail prices would attract new customers. "It may be hoped that it will have the ultimate effect of creating a demand where none has hitherto existed," explained the consul. The merchants' actions did not have the desired effect: they found that the Guayaquileños had been right in not pushing the issue, as there simply were not as many people with the money to buy as they had hoped. They were, however, successful in other ways, having the capability of responding somewhat more effectively than locals wherever demand did exist. The Englishman Mr. Robinet was known for having the fastest sailing ships on the coast. He speeded goods to the locations with the greatest demand. Local merchants were not entirely frustrated by this in that those who had particularly good relations with the English were able to buy from them in order to profit from the retail sale themselves without having to invest in ships: Vicente Ramón Roca, for example, bought flour, furniture, copper, iron, European wines, and crystal.[40]

Yet there were constant tensions between local and foreign merchants. Local merchants sometimes expressed a belief that the foreigners were there to cheat them, and in fact they were sometimes right—as when a foreigner did not share profits as promised or returned home without paying a debt, after convincing another local to undersign for him. British and United States merchants also complained about being forced to pay the *empréstitos* or small forced loans to the government. At one point a U.S. citizen was actually temporarily confined for noncompliance.[41]

The case of Charles Swett, a North American, provides an excellent illustration of the Guayaquileños' respect for a foreign investor's capital as well as their resentment of any arrogance. Swett was a prominent citizen: when his house was advertised for sale it was a point in the house's favor to note that it had been his. But when he found some wine missing from his warehouse and accused master craftsman Juan Camacho of the theft, he aroused the ire of the whole town. Even the prominent Martín de Ycaza testified on behalf of Camacho. In 1829 the firm of Bartlett & Swett sold the army cloth in quantity; when the government later could not pay the bill, Swett gladly negotiated a discount on the firm's customs payments: only one month later, however, the same municipal officials who worked out the deal were pressured by locals into limiting the proportion of its customs bills that the firm could pay with its whopping IOU. In 1831 the provincial government borrowed money from him and ordered the treasury "to take proper measures so that Sr. Swett may be satisfied with religious scrupulosity in the time promised, as the honor of the government and the interest of justice both require it." Only a few months later Bartlett & Swett's ship, the *Maryann*, was occupied by soldiers looking for contraband. Swett complained to the British consul, who agreed to intercede, but then proffered the opinion that there had been nothing wrong with the search undertaken.[42]

There was a deeper issue, beyond the potential for the souring of individual business ties, that repeatedly surfaced with regard to the foreign presence. In times of political conflict, there loomed the possibility that outsiders might attempt to give material aid to whichever side promised them greater commercial advantage in the future. In August of 1832 Charles ("Carlos") Pflücker, a German who had been hired by the British merchant firm of Gibbs, Crawley & Co. to manage their office in Guayaquil, was suddenly expelled. The government claimed he and several prominent Englishmen had been involved in a plot to overthrow President Juan José Flores in favor of Rocafuerte, and they were all required to leave within four days. (Pflücker did not allow himself to be permanently defeated. He moved to Peru, where he became involved in mining in the 1840s and raged against obdurate peasants.)[43] Pflücker's assistant, Richard Wingate, said that the accusation was false and, furthermore, that five men were dependent on the Gibbs-Crawley store, which could not continue to function without a head. His plea did no good. Walter Cope as consul took over in directing the firm's affairs until a replacement could arrive and sent a critical report to his own government.[44] Most foreign residents apparently believed that Pflücker had been unjustly attacked and feared for their own safety. The commander of the USS *Falmouth* later visited and reported that during the disturbances

the citizens of the United States had suffered no molestation or interception in the pursuit of their business (except in the detention of an American ship for a few days) . . . However, the American citizens resident here were under very great apprehension in consequence of the question having been agitated, of banishing some of them from the country, for supposed political offenses of which they feel themselves entirely innocent . . . [45]

Ironically, Pflücker's assistant, Wingate, later demonstrated that the accusations against his chief were probably well founded, for he himself was caught on a ship in a meeting with the officers, attempting to convince them to change sides in the civil war. The consul expressed his gratitude that the young man was humanely expelled without any other punishment. He also said in a private aside to his own government that, had a British warship been present in the port, the first expulsions never would have occurred.[46] He assumed that might would make right. But there is no proof that this would have been the case. If anything, he tended to minimize the extent of local resistance to policy being dictated by the British.

Given that the merchant elite at this point were experiencing their relationship with foreign investors as a troubled one and that they were for the first time legally free to do as they chose, it should not come as a surprise that they took it upon themselves to diversify their investments in old and new ways.[47] They continued as landlords and cacao exporters, and some developed further the straw hat cottage industry on the coast. But they began to turn against their former practice of purchasing government contracts as a form of investment. Spanish-style monopolies were losing their traditional desirability. First, the question of fairness had been introduced in the early years of the republic. The newspapers had raged specifically against "three centuries of ignorance and monopoly . . ." Now when the council members sought to sign a new contract they had to advertise in the papers; or, if they made an arrangement privately, they then published news of it and asked that any objections be made promptly.[48] Second, the freer trade laws had increased the number of ships coming and going from every port and cove, so that customers were finding it easier to buy goods unofficially; thus those who had bid on the monopolies often found themselves losing money rather than profiting handsomely as in the days of old. Francisco Marqués de la Plata, an import-export merchant, had submitted the winning bid on the right to sell salt, for example. He complained bitterly that contraband salt was still brought almost to the doors of the retailers, so they were not buying from him. The primary *ramos rematados* (contracted branches) were the salt, tobacco, and liquor administrations; working these businesses came to be seen as a thankless task. The appeal of the monopoly was dying.[49]

There was, in contrast, heightened enthusiasm about the potential of a new area: manufacturing. Other than the shipyards, there was little large-scale industry in the area. Despite the abundance of timber, for example, and its regular export and its use in shipbuilding, there was no sawmill: a British visitor observed that merchants could induce workers to cut and saw the wood by hand at affordable prices. Thus investment in machinery would not have been justified. But in the new era thoughts turned in new directions. The Charity Hospital, under the guidance of the conscientious politician Juan Francisco Icaza, invested its funds in a factory (they did not say what kind), hoping that its profits would run the institution. José Villamil asked the City Council's permission to build a steam-engine–powered steelworks, but only if he could have monopoly rights, as he apparently did not believe there would be enough of a market to justify several such factories. Manuel Santos registered to build a cotton factory, in which he intended to use the most modern of equipment, and one of the Samaniego family registered for a playing card factory.[50] All of these ideas received enthusiastic responses from the local government—except for Villamil's proposal of a monopoly, the principle of which was now frowned upon—and the assurance that under the republic there were no legal barriers. And yet not one of the projects was ever mentioned again; I have found no evidence that any one of the three plants ever came into existence.

None of these merchants were known for being dilettantes or quitters. For what were probably rational reasons, given their usual behavior, they took the projects through the planning stages, even to the point of making them public, and then apparently decided to abandon them. Only Villa-mil's actions—in insisting on a monopoly—give us a clue as to their possible reasoning. Like him, they may have been concerned that the demand in Guayaquil could not support such ventures. Santos would have had to buy expensive machinery and then compete with cheap cotton imports arriving not only from England and the United States but also from the East. Samaniego could probably have sold his cards only to the limited numbers of elites, for the poor were proving unable to buy even tobacco.

At the time, apparently, no one commented on this quiet strangulation of incipient manufacturing ventures. There were other profitable ventures open to businessmen. Either they did not see the importance of their various decisions not to proceed in this direction in the context of their busy lives or they saw the matter as being of such grave importance that they could not bear to write about it.

Beliefs about Taxation

Under the Gran Colombian government, and then under the Ecuadorian, Guayaquil's provincial government worked closely with Bogotá and then Quito. There were four main sources of revenue, some part of which had to be submitted to the higher authorities: monies collected by the Customshouse, special sales taxes on items like tobacco or passports, the Indian tribute payments, and the government's one-third share of the tithes the church collected from farmers. The first sum was by far the largest (indeed it represented almost half of the national government's income in the year 1830). Tithe collections, on the other hand, in this area where the church was anything but dominant, were abysmally small. The local government retained varying percentages of these collections, depending on its own or the national government's emergency needs. Besides funding city and provincial maintenance expenses, the local government was responsible for meeting all public payroll, including the salaries for everyone from the Customshouse workers to the teachers in the Escuela Náutica to the military. Paying the soldiers alone absorbed from one-third of the budget (in a good month) to two-thirds (in a time of military emergency). Guayaquil's government was also responsible for paying back the public debt, and these outlays were second only to those for military expenses.[51]

The public debt was large because in times of crisis the government looked to individuals to supply loans rather than imposing a regular property tax. The burden did not appear to be especially onerous to the city's major merchants and the largest landowners. Indeed, the men involved in the highest city affairs expected to reap rewards in exchange for shoring up the poverty-stricken government. One of the wealthiest landowners living in the city offered to sell the new Charity Hospital 50,000 clay roof tiles at a good price; as he understood that neither the hospital nor the government had any money to spare, they could pay him by deducting payments from the duties he owed when he brought foodstuffs from his plantations into the port. The government was accustomed to turning to the wealthy—and most often to import-export merchants who themselves held government positions—when in need of quick emergency loans of thousands of pesos. They gave the lenders public accolades and up to 3 percent interest *monthly* or "the market rate" (*el de plaza*).[52]

These voluntary interest-paying loans, however, could not entirely underwrite the provincial government's budget, including the large amounts that were required to be paid to Bogotá and the military. Thus they turned irregularly to *empréstitos forzosos* or small, forced loans, which were progressively distributed among the city's relatively elite citizens by the City Council to come up with a large total sum. The quantities assigned ranged from one peso to a maximum—after August 1827—of two hundred pesos for the richest householders. As early as 1822 the independent government had used the pages of the *Patriota* to put pressure on readers to give or loan more money to the cause; by 1823, after incorporation into Colombia, there was no longer any choice. Most people paid their assigned share. The case of Santiago Vergara illustrated what might happen if they did not: in December 1823 he refused to pay the twenty-five pesos assigned to him, claiming that he had mounting debts. He was arrested and his property sequestered, although he was shortly released. Why he was selected to serve as a warning to others becomes clearer when we read in a separate legal case that in November he had been brought to court by his creditors and in desperation had spoken insultingly about some of the city's leading merchants—calling them thieves and rogues.[53] Most people paid up peacefully, however, or, if they did not, they wrote ahead of time to the intendent, explaining why they believed they had been assigned too high a share and how they currently stood financially.[54]

Voluntary loans were more likely than forced loans to be repaid, but the government made efforts to continue to repay all of them, even if years behind. The first intendent imposed by Bolívar announced in 1822 that all holders of the public debt should bring forward their papers for a general reckoning. No clear results came of this effort, but during 1826 and 1827 two leading merchants worked hard at developing a format to systematize the public debt and its repayment. Repayment continued behind schedule, however; in 1831, after the separation from Gran Colombia and the formation of the Merchants' Guild (Consulado de Comercio), one of the same men was part of a guild committee in charge of prioritizing the government's payment schedule. The guild then helped organize the new federal Amortization Bank. Over time, many of the import-export merchants who had put up the large voluntary loans earned their interest and received back their principle in the form of discounts off their customs bills. Some actually received cash payments when there was money in the public coffers. Expectations must have remained positive, for in 1835 Guayaquil's elite willingly met to discuss a project that essentially involved the issuing of local government bonds, and 140 were issued.[55] There remained problems, nonetheless, with the repayment of the internal debt, problems that only grew worse as time went on.

Though the budget problems showed no sign of abating, no creative tax restructuring was seriously proposed. Efforts were made to increase efficiency in collecting customs payments and Indian head taxes, but no regular property tax was promoted. As in colonial days, the only personal tax continued to fall on the indigenous, the poorest segment of society. Nor was there a discussion of delaying greater proportions of the interest payments to merchant financiers in favor of spending on what today would be called infrastructure. Money spent on roads, bridges, or agricultural experiments might have increased their lamented exports, but the tiny wealthy class did not want to shoulder the expenses of the entire population's needs. The British consul noted their refusal to invest in roads because the expense would be all theirs. At one point, the City Council considered getting around this by demanding that all citizens participate in building a bridge out of town by giving labor time if they could not give money: the scheme was unreasonable, however, and they apparently abandoned it.[56]

There were flashes of debate introduced by individuals and then si-

lenced. Street lighting was paid for from 1822 on through a slightly progressive tax on householders, but the official in charge had difficulty in
collecting it. In 1829, instead of sending out soldiers to improve collection through violence, Vicente Ramón Roca, as chief of police, issued a
new tax schedule that was more dramatically progressive than the last
one, to maximize people's ability to pay. (He did also threaten to arrest
people and, worse yet, publish their names in the paper to shame them, a
technique that might have worked with the recalcitrant wealthy.) On a
grander scale, Juan José Flores, the first president of Ecuador after the
collapse of Gran Colombia, proposed a progressive income tax in 1831;
but he received no legislative support, and none from the coast. The idea
was given up within a year.[57] The concept of spending for the "public
good" or "general welfare" (including their own) would have seemed ri-
diculous, for the elite called themselves *el pueblo*, the people.

Relationship with Labor

The merchant elites of Guayaquil, like people everywhere, were not always clear or uniform in their thinking about others. The issue of what to
do about the labor question surfaced with a vengeance during the years
of fighting against "tyranny" and the early republican fervor. Patriots
evinced some discomfort with slavery, for example, although they retained it for a whole generation after independence. While Guayaquil was
a sovereign state, the *importation* of slaves was outlawed, and a "law of the
free womb" promised that henceforth all children born to slave mothers
would be freed on reaching their majority.[58] The laws of Gran Colombia
were similar, and thus little changed in this respect when the province of
Guayas joined Colombia in 1822—except that a Colombian law of 1821
also decreed the establishment of a Manumission Fund from a minimal
tax on inheritances. After Guayaquil joined the nation a flurry of sales
occurred from pessimistic to optimistic slaveholders, for a sizable group
was convinced that Bogotá would shortly decree freedom for all.

Whites in general began to display a degree of discomfort with the
notion of slavery, given their current positions on liberty and tyranny.
The *procurador general*, whose job it was to represent the slaves in court,
delighted in playing on such squeamishness. He reminded the judges that
it had been the Spaniards who had introduced the practice of slavery,
speaking of the "unhappy class of people whose liberty had been cut short
so barbarously by the Spanish." His readers now did not want to think of

themselves or their laws as tyrannical, so in order to make an effective legal attack he spoke of the "capricious" qualities of slave owners. One owner wrote back and in a wounded tone said that the *procurador* did not know him well at all.[59] Whatever their discomfort, however, the slave owners were not by any means ready to sacrifice completely the institution of slavery. The practices of buying and selling continued. One slave trader even managed to import some slaves and sell them to locals after the passage of the new laws, on the grounds that he and his clients had acted in ignorance and good faith.[60] Although speculating in the slave market was now forbidden, and slaves had to be sold at the same price for which they had been bought by their current master, white friends and neighbors continued to sell to each other. They even continued to advertise in the papers.

In the same way, the coastal elites went back and forth in this period concerning the role of the indigenous people. In the late colonial era all male Indians aged eighteen to forty-nine (except the sick and the caciques) paid tribute in cash and were also subject to labor time requisitions; in the early republican period the tribute was abolished in accordance with democratic principles and then reinstated in accordance with government need. Only in 1835 were coastal Indians definitively freed of the tribute and rates then significantly lowered elsewhere. Many of the elite continued to be of mixed opinion: although Guayaquil's leading citizens were enthusiastic about the possibilities of free labor as opposed to peonage, and did not want their own hired laborers to have to pay the labor time tribute, they recognized that in demanding a *cash* head tax they guaranteed that at least some members of each Indian farmer's family would be willing to work for wages on plantations.[61] A priest from Santa Elena, Ana Yagual's home, articulated the concerns of many:

> The evil which is born with us and which comes from our sinful origin has taken greatest hold among the indigenous, for it is very well known that they are indolent in their efforts to leave behind the rustic life of their fathers. The slave has his master to make sure that he learns to save himself, but it is impossible to train the indigenous if he is not legally bound to certain requirements.[62]

While these men debated the proper course to take in future, they continued to rely substantially on coerced labor to get work done, even in the city. Groups of Indians were regularly drafted from surrounding villages

to work in the navy shipyard for a time. The shipyard then routinely sup-
plied Indian laborers to public projects "since they are very fit for this
kind of work." They might be called on to repair the hospital or build a
small boat. If there were absolutely no Indians available from the navy
yard, then on a rare occasion the government might insist that some of
the people living on the savanna, like Mariano de la Cruz, come and take
their place.[63] Cristóval de Armero, a prominent merchant, complained
about the drawbacks of such a system. He asserted to the governor that
rounding up Indians in this way was abusive as well as being a waste of
time. He suggested that instead fifty young indigenous men be selected
to come and live in the city for two full years, where they would be prop-
erly trained in the art of construction, thus eliminating the resentment of
the indigenous community and creating more useful workers.[64] Nothing
came of Armero's suggestion, though. Most of his colleagues assumed
that there were plenty of workers available for short periods who could be
forced to do an adequate job without being trained or paid.

Those who did not have access to indigenous labor time from the shipyard, including most private companies, could often turn to the prison or
presidio. Inmates had been sentenced for having committed a robbery or
because they had been rounded up as vagrants, "men without a known
profession." Some were recaptured army deserters who had been placed
in the *presidio* in order for the government to "economize in blood" or
spare needed hands a brutal punishment. Although there was some debate
about the wisdom of trusting such men with important work, most of
those eager to create labor gangs seemed to assume that they were simply
poor rather than dangerous. In exchange for the labor of a man from the
presidio, an employer had only to pay the government three reales a day
and he had at his command a man who was forced to work hard or accept being beaten. An entrepreneur who was planning to build a new
slaughterhouse was so eager that he promised four reales per day for any
man assigned to him. The only difficulty was that the workers frequently
escaped from their labor sites and rewards of up to eight pesos had to be
offered for their capture.[65]

A person who was unable to hire from the *presidio* but did not want to
hire free laborers might consider buying or hiring slaves. It was common
practice to hire other people's bondsmen. Said one owner of another: "He
is profiting from the considerable daily wage of a ranking shoemaker, for
such is his Zambo." He added that in four months the owner made
twenty-two pesos this way, not counting Sundays. Even the labor of an

unskilled young man was worth three and a half reales per day, slightly more than that of a *presidio* worker, and the domestic work of a woman was generally valued at three reales. Incipient industries, such as the larger bakeries, relied almost entirely on slave labor. The accounts of one *panadería* indicate that two partners had bought themselves the labor of twelve *negros y zambos* in order to operate.[66]

These were the same merchants who continued to debate appropriate new laws for a free country and even to discuss the possibility of freeing all labor. How they managed to negotiate contradictory thoughts and contradictory practices varied from person to person. To some extent, the *peones* or *esclavos* were of course invisible, not as laboring hands but as human beings. When a government official wrote out a passport, for example, the number of "peons" accompanying the recipient might be listed, but the "peons" themselves never received such a document.[67] On the other hand, probably to a greater extent, given the frequency of comment, the dark-skinned masses were extraordinarily visible, looming in the elites' consciousness as large, angry, and threatening specters. If they were evil, they had to be controlled and perhaps even punished for their natures by being forced to work. The fear of rebellion was a constant. The elites were ready to believe rumors of "subversive words against the white class" or even of plots to kill all whites, although no evidence was ever uncovered.[68] The newspapers cautioned against marauding runaway soldiers (and their women) turned pirates, and hosts cautioned a foreign traveler that her Indian guides would probably push her out of her boat to gain possession of her things. (This did not happen, although she did fall into the river on her own.)[69]

In the midst of the republican fervor, a relatively new framework gained in importance. The coerced masses *had* to be treated as they were, for they were lazy. Until they learned better habits, there would be no choice. If there were delinquent young people in the streets, it was because their parents had failed to do their duty and apprentice them to a trade. They should be turned over to a master for training. A newspaper editor commented that Indians should not complain about the supposedly exorbitant sums charged by priests for legal marriage ceremonies as long as they continued to waste their money buying *comidas y chichas*.[70] Clearly, the writer believed the Indians did not care if they lived in instability and sin and preferred to spend their money on food and drink.

Vagrancy and laziness were also concerns of the nation's highest governing officers. This is evidenced in an 1833 report of the minister of the interior, where vagrancy was listed as the nation's second greatest concern after public health. "Vagrancy: The government, convinced that this is the moth of nation states, the germ of vice and crime, has declared that the lower ranks of the army and navy shall be filled with [those who have been] vagrant, idle, and badly behaved." Guayaquil was singled out, because of a report submitted by its own governor, as having a particularly grave problem regarding vagrancy. The idle should be made to work "for rations and without salary." The government was sure of the efficacy of this plan, certain that it had worked elsewhere: "The nations that have progressed in civilization have, in this way, converted prejudicial types into virtuous citizens dedicated to useful occupations."[71]

The key was that in this new, enlightened era these people would be taught. Just as Guayaquil's delinquent young people would be rounded up for training, the central government also planned to reform the unemployed. The long-range plan summarized in the 1833 report was optimistic. The government was planning to build schools to teach "basic principles of morality, urbanity, and literacy." This budgetary allowance would be most useful to "agriculture, commerce, and crafts" in that the Indians might learn to emulate to some extent the republican *pueblo* and thus work harder and behave more responsibly. In reality, the new public schools almost never welcomed Indians as pupils, but instead opened their doors to the children of ambitious mestizos.[72] Still, the *idea* of teaching Indians to better themselves became a popular one. It surfaced in daily interactions. If Ana Yagual's uncle Mariano de la Cruz was not convicted of a crime, the authorities still assumed that he was a vagrant in need of appropriate threats to keep him on good behavior. Vicente Ramón Roca and his colleagues set him free to prove himself. As a good republican citizen, Roca could serve as an example to Mariano de la Cruz. Whether the state of being an oppositional example was in itself the subconscious goal or whether Roca deeply desired to see a world in which Cruz had achieved equality is another question.[73]

In some respects, Roca and his friends had demonstrated their enthusiasm, their will to analyze and experiment, their insistence on political justice. If they later found that poverty dogged their city, it would not be for lack of effort on their part. Yet some of their beliefs seemed too old to change easily and had wide repercussions. Certainly their culture influenced them in all their economic exertions, but not always in expected ways. To see clearly how their choices compared to those made by others, we need to look at these same matters in another part of the world.

CHAPTER 4

STRAWBERRY PARTIES

AND HABITS OF INDUSTRY

The Elite of Baltimore

Lydia Hollingsworth picked up a pen to write a note to her country cousin. "I hope you will pardon me for not writing you ere this, it was my intention to have done so . . ." She had been busy buying finery in the Baltimore shops that her cousin had especially requested and had only just worked out a suitable way of sending the goods. "William Cooch told me he would take charge of anything I had to send up, therefore I put them in a chair box which I will put under his care, and enclose the Key in this letter." Lydia had exerted herself. "On Tuesday Aunt D[ebby Cochran] and I shopped all the morning." And in general she was sure that her cousin would be pleased with the results. "The bombazet and bombazeen are handsome . . . I find it impossible to procure nice black beaver gloves as Miss Alexander tells me she was taken in. All the other articles are good. Cousin, Aunt and I thought the barcelona shawls would answer as they are large." She closed her letter with a detailed list of the twenty items purchased.[1]

Lydia and her cousin were hardly alone in their exacting concern with consumer goods and public appearances. One early spring day in 1827 the merchant Charles Moale sent off an angry letter to the mayor of Baltimore, who was a personal acquaintance: "Allow me . . . to call your attention to the [city] Lamp which is affixed on the House I occupy in Charles Street." Moale, it seemed, had suffered annoyances related to the streetlight for some time, but today's events had passed the limits of his patience. "The Watchman this afternoon in taking down that part which contains the Oil overturned the contents of it on my front Steps and there left it—The next person who came into the front door stepped into it and trod it all over my carpet from the front to the dining room door." Moale could not accept these events. "These things my Dear Sir are not to be bourne with, I can not tamely look on and see my Property destroyed in this wanton manner."[2] Moale's misery was not simply due to the pain of watching the destruction of that which was his. His expensive carpet led from the front door to the other first-floor rooms that visitors frequented: its good condition was essential for his image as a successful man, and that image was critical to the future of his business. He could not afford to leave the floor bare or use a plainer rug, despite the likelihood of its being trod on by dirty shoes.

The Baltimore that Frederick Bailey came to know so well was a culture of visible property arranged to impress all beholders. He learned young that he himself was a crucial part of the display. The master of his plantation had sent him to a city relation to serve as an errand boy and to impress upon the neighbors that the Auld family now held a slave. Most city slaves served a highly symbolic function in addition to performing their assigned tasks. Not only the fact of ownership but also its form served to show a master's status: "Every city slaveholder is anxious to have it known of him, that he feeds his slaves well."[3] Slaves like Frederick found themselves human props in a stage set of objects: their presence was as useful as bombazeen or Mr. Moale's carpet in reifying the power of a select group.

The rich wielded their property to reinforce their status and underscore the respect they deserved for the power they could exert if they chose. In their houses they sought to prove they understood elegance. When they painted their walls a shade of green, they called the color olive, sage, pea, or sea green; if yellow, then apricot, peach, fawn, or straw. They put "glasses" (or mirrors) over their mantles and always placed their candle snuffers on the tray designed to catch stray ashes. Their candlesticks were of brass and their furniture of mahogany. On the sideboard they left out their finest pieces of plate.[4] But to transform small displays into mighty ones the merchants and their friends needed to wield their property where more people could see it. The carpets leading from the front steps into the houses impressed visitors, but more public scenes were enacted when the wealthy left their homes. At church, for example, the ordinary parishioners—only a small percentage of whom could even vote in church affairs—watched the wealthy perform, for church leadership was the latter's avocation. In the Catholic cathedral the wives of the prominent parishioners dressed in some of the finest clothes available for purchase.[5] These families also went to the theater. Generally audiences were mixed, but the well-to-do reserved the highly visible boxes for themselves. These families put on dazzling functions for each other, which ordinary people could not attend as guests, but could not help but observe from the fringes. The wealthy went to well-lit balls: when the Marquis de Lafayette came to visit the city, they produced a garlanded spectacle that lived in people's memories for many years. Or they made noisy excursions to the countryside in the popular berry-picking expeditions called strawberry parties. In the summer they went back and forth to the shore at Cape May on frequent steamers or traveled in private carriages to interesting sites and spa towns within a few days' drive.[6]

Besides the presence of servants and slaves, clothing was a key element in all of these activities. Without impressive attire, the status of the actors might not be clear to all beholders both within and without their own group. Fourteen-year-old Eliza George, whose Quaker family generally discouraged vanity, wrote to her aunt about her desperate need for a new outfit: "My riding dress is getting so shabby that I am almost ashamed to wear it. I have been wanting a cloth one for some time and as cousin Mary and MN have cloth ones when I ride with them I am always odd." Generally it fell to women to supervise the procurement of clothing that would reinforce their husbands' and brothers' position in the world and hence their own. Occasionally outsiders condemned women for their role as clothing consumers. One Protestant Episcopal Female Tract assigned divine vengeance to a woman who loved finery too much and lived extravagantly.[7]

In fact, however, most elite women's accounts demonstrate that they considered it their duty to dress themselves and their families with as much appearance of richness as possible while economizing at every step. In letters and journals elite women kept careful track of all that they made themselves for family and friends and all that they budgeted for purchase. "Tell Sally, if you please," wrote Lydia Hollingsworth to her cousins, "I have looked for a shawl which I thought would please her. They had in many stores, white grounds with gay borders, but as she wished one not gay, I thought purple the most genteel. It was one dollar and seventy-five and I return her the 25 cents remainder."[8] Such women called their sewing "their work" and kept records of how many yards they had been able to buy with a given amount of money or how much needlework they had been able to accomplish within one day. They were masters of a complex language of fabric types, stitching patterns, and ever-changing styles and prices. Even a country storekeeper kept in stock literally dozens of fabric types and shades of color, both domestic and imported, and the cityfolk were faced with far greater selection than this in the shops near the wharves. The women kept themselves informed by reading the European periodicals advertising "coloured plates of the Fashions of Each month" sold in Baltimore bookshops. They were aware of their responsibility to maintain their families' status through their dress.

Some elite women demonstrated the extent of their families' wealth and power in a more concrete way than through displays of clothing: they interacted with each other and with those poorer than themselves through charity organizations. The city guide reveals an industry of women helping "less fortunate" women: they ran the Baltimore Female Orphan Asylum, the Benevolent Society for Educating and Supporting Female Children, the Female Penitents' Refuge Society, the Indigent Sick Society, and the Dorcas Society for clothing the poor. These well-dressed women advertised their activities in the newspapers and went regularly into the neighborhoods and houses of the poor with their munificence. They demonstrated their power to the needy when they petitioned the City Council to provide free firewood for "poor and worthy citizens" who were temporarily laid up during the cold months of winter.[9] In fact, in this case, they met both their goals: they did provide some relief and in doing so strengthened their families' position in the city.

Conspicuous consumption and conspicuous beneficence may have been especially important in strengthening the elite's authority in a place where their political power was far from absolute. In a world where the vote was not limited to a few property holders, but rather, since 1818, to white male taxpayers, a variety of men could end up holding offices and making important decisions.[10] Merchants in Baltimore found they had to share their political posts with upper-level tradesmen and others. Between 1820 and 1835 there were 166 elected City Council members. Of the 80 percent whom we can identify today, import-export merchants composed the largest subgroup (23 percent). They were surrounded by allies to whom they were often related and with whom they usually voted: local land-owners (11 percent), retail merchants (15 percent), and professionals, including lawyers, doctors, and administrators (15 percent). Thus the merchants could usually—but not always—count on dominating a total of 64 percent of the vote. However, they could not control the debate or even all of the decisions. The second largest subgroup was that of the master craftsmen (18 percent), and they too had their allies: small manufacturers (10 percent), publicists (5 percent), and the owners of small businesses, such as taverns and hack companies (3 percent).[11] Nor did merchants dominate the executive branch: during the late 1820s the city's popular and successful mayor was Jacob Small, a self-trained architect and builder. The merchants could have had no illusion that they were in complete control of political decisions within the city. The key to their power had to be their money. It is not surprising that they made its use a public act.

The life of the famous Robert Oliver demonstrates the political frustrations experienced by the merchant class. He was an Irish Protestant who had arrived in Baltimore at the end of the War for Independence. He married a wealthy young woman and embarked on an extraordinarily successful career that has already been well documented. The key to his success was the use he made of the European wars. Because his brother-in-law was known to the Spanish court, and his American ships were neutral, he obtained monopoly privileges in transporting specie from Mexican mines that was due to Napoleon Bonaparte between 1806 and 1808. The gross profit was a quarter of a million dollars. Although Oliver had officially retired in 1819, he did not in fact withdraw from mercantile affairs. He had a country estate, yet still spent a good deal of his time in the city. He was a founding member of the Chamber of Commerce and signed many merchant community petitions. Like other merchants who resisted the rising tide of manufacturing, he was in favor of internal improvements, which were not seen as incompatible with the import-export trade: at the end of the decade he was among the group of men who met to galvanize the founding of the Baltimore & Ohio Railroad and was a member of the first Board of Directors of that organization. As a Federalist, and as one who believed in protecting his own interests, Oliver had been and remained indirectly active in politics by offering financial support to candidates he deemed appropriate. Like others in the merchant community, he found himself unable to exert the level of control in politics that he thought he ought to have. It is likely that he complained of this phenomenon to his friends and acquaintances, for one wrote to him, "I know of the immense losses you have sustained by the sacrifices you have made for the party and by the treachery of those who paid your benevolence with the common coin of the world—base ingratitude." Oliver had always helped shape the polity and the economy; it was difficult for him to accept that his world was changing. It was perhaps more important than ever that he present himself to the public through his wealth as one of the "royal merchants of Baltimore, as the Medici of old were in Italy." [12]

Trade Networks

The Baltimore merchant Thomas Tyson did not have to stir from Baltimore to engineer profitable transactions around the world. From the moment the Spanish American independence wars began to render the southern climes more attractive to traders, Tyson's ships ventured outward in ever widening circles. After establishing a secure base in Havana and elsewhere in the Caribbean, he began sending them on to Rio and Buenos Aires. In later voyages, they rounded the cape. From Valparaíso the captain wrote that he had received glowing reports of the profits available in Guayaquil. Within a year Tyson was sending ships that far. In 1823 he sold almost one thousand dollars' worth of merchandise in Guayaquil alone, half of it in the form of crackers, the other half as Spanish cigars, and this was only a fraction of the total sales he made during that twelve-month period. His success in this far-off world was due to his making effective personal contacts, both with his trading partners and with his captains. [13]

In Guayaquil Tyson trusted the sales to Vicente Ramón Roca and later, once foreigners were allowed free reign, to the firm of Bartlett & Swett, in exchange for a 4 percent commission. This charge was Tyson's most serious expense. In turning the goods over to an agent he avoided the cost of storing or processing them in the unfamiliar foreign port. He was willing to do favors: a Caribbean trading firm in Florida later wrote to him specifically to thank him "for the strong support and friendly sentiments evinced by you towards us" and to assure him that "we shall ever feel greatly obliged" in case he should ever need a return favor in exchange for whatever it was he had done for them. [14] In the Guayaquileño case, Tyson also worked with a known ship captain who was an effective salesman: when he had trouble selling at a desired price in one port, the man was willing to move on to Lima or Montevideo. When he could not get cash, he happily filled the hold with the cacao and medicinal barks that could be turned to cash at home. The shipmaster was clearly willing to bestir himself for the ship owner. Indeed, Captain Breck, who sailed for him often, demonstrated in his correspondence that Tyson had not made him at all afraid to complain or report problems. Even after one disastrous voyage during which the cook was swept overboard and the boat accidentally became mixed up in a battle in the independence wars, Breck was mollified and convinced to sail again.

Thomas Tyson came from a wealthy family whose rise was a part of Baltimore history. Between the 1770s and 1790s several Quaker millers from the Philadelphia area who had been displaced by the disturbances of the Revolution moved south and established enterprises near Baltimore. The Tysons, Ellicotts, and Stumps were the most famous of these. Despite being early industrialists of a sort, due to their mills, they were essentially import-export merchants. They bought wheat from local farmers, processed it into flour themselves, and sold it on the international market; their return cargoes made them into international traders. Within a generation their milling establishments had become impressive sights. The late eighteenth century European wars gave these Baltimoreans a golden opportunity that they eagerly seized, as we have seen. In a rush, they crossed boundaries: flour merchants like the Tysons also imported fine coffees, and merchants with older names, traditionally importers of luxury goods, also exported flour. After the wars they could no longer compete with England, but they worked together to develop the inland trade they saw as a possible substitute. They hired master builders to plan possible canals and to prepare reports on the feasibility of "repairing" (or clearing) the rocky Susquehannah so that it would be safer to float goods down the river—and thus allow Baltimore's merchants to compete more successfully with Philadelphia's for the inland trade.

New water routes were the most popular, but other committees put money into turnpikes. The difficulty in this case was that the investors hoped to turn an immediate and tidy profit in the collection of tolls, while in fact the expense of maintaining roads was so high that they lost money for years. When a second set of stock shares was issued for the Baltimore and Harford Turnpike, the managers recorded that "no person applied to subscribe." But the landowners and major merchants understood the long-term benefits to themselves associated with lowering the cost of the transportation of goods: although they did not continue to invest as individuals, they did use their political positions to ensure local and state government aid for the new roads through taxation. They sent frequent petitions, many of them successful: "The President and Directors . . . are now and always have been very desirous of completing the turnpike to

Belle-Air, but cannot raise the necessary funds for that purpose. If, however, the legislature of the state would in their wisdom subscribe stock in the company to the amount of one half what it would require to complete the said Turnpike, the company will engage on their part to raise the remainder." [15]

The greatest project of all consisted of the railways. In 1827 a committee consisting of merchants whose families had been of three traditions—landholding, milling, and importing—met to lay their plans and became the Board of Directors for the Baltimore & Ohio Railroad. Though the prospects were exhilarating, the reality proved rougher going. As they changed from horse power to engine, or added another stretch with a new kind of rail, there were always unexpected problems that no one knew how to solve. The building of the B & O was a story of false starts and learning-by-doing, for the best planners, engineers, and workers in the city had no experience in building railways. [16]

In all of these endeavors connecting town to hinterland, the merchants' skills in manipulating personal contacts in other places and in exchanging information were as critical to their success as they had been in overseas trade. In this local arena they generally entrusted their wives and sisters with the task of forging and maintaining the personal relationships that they could later use. The women accomplished their task through visits back and forth and extensive letter writing. "Goods for ladies" advertised in newspapers consisted not of hats, but rather of sealing wax, pearl and ivory paper cutters, gold leaf and camel hair pencils. When they could not send a representative sister or niece to spend a fortnight or longer in another's house, they filled letters with the kind of details that brought their households to life in each other's minds: "He now speaks every short word," Lydia Hollingsworth wrote of a small future merchant, "and [he] connects some." [17] In this way actual and potential business ties became invisibly intertwined with strands of affection.

The social net began with blood ties. The Stumps, for example, were a family of merchant millers who had also expanded into the herring trade. The letters between the two brothers John and Samuel are illustrative of the way in which a number of such clans conducted their business. John, the elder, lived on a plantation in Cecil County at the head of the bay and supervised the collection of herring from local fishermen. He then sent these on to his brother Samuel in Baltimore, who served as merchant. When John could not find enough fishermen to work for him in a particular season, he asked Samuel to induce some from the city to sail up to see him. When there was a glut of fish on the market in the city, Samuel asked John to send only small barrels for retailers; on the other hand, when there was news of war from South America, he predicted fewer shipments of jerked beef to the Caribbean slave market and therefore expected they could sell more salt fish. John trusted his city brother to handle lawsuits in which the family was engaged; Samuel trusted John with large amounts of cash when he requested them. These arrangements and the trust which rendered them practicable stemmed from the faith both brothers placed in their tie of blood. In this case, bonds of affection did not seem to be strong. They did not refer to visits to each other or write with warmth. Although most relations did not open their letters this way, they began, "Dear Sir." They forwarded personal news rarely and laconically. Once when the older brother John was seriously ill, Samuel said, "Reuban has sent some lettuce and onions for you, which he says you are fond of."[18] A man who was probably a slave evinced more interest in John's welfare than his younger brother did. Yet the lack of warmth did not seem to lead to economic problems. The custom and culture of the family business held the brothers together effectively enough.

Intermarriage, however, was the most important social bond on which the merchant class depended: ties with immediate biological family were not sufficient for their purposes. Most of the leading families were united to planters by marriage.[19] Making these important arrangements was again left to wives. The task became time consuming for a woman once her daughters attained their late teens. She had to escort them to numerous events, oversee the purchase and production of more clothing, and train the girls to perform the roles expected of them. Sometimes a daughter did not follow willingly. Caroline Calvert consented to leave the plantation to stay with relations in Baltimore, but she refused to wear the revealing dresses brought over from Europe and insisted on something that came up to her neck. The girl's mother wrote often of her concern: "She is very reserved—too much so, I think. I never saw a girl so little the coquette."[20] The responsible older woman exerted direct pressure where necessary. Said an older sister to a younger: "What are you about, you lazy Girl—The present fashion is short courtships, and the Lady the difference on her side."[21] The marriage question had the potential to become exceedingly contentious if a daughter did not respond to pressure or even direct orders. In such cases, fathers became involved.[22] The townspeople claimed that when the renowned and wealthy Robert Oliver learned that his daughter was running off to meet a disapproved suitor he shot at her.[23] Oliver's loss of control in the political world seemed to be mirrored in his loss of control of the all-important marriage bond.

Daily Practices

The Hollingsworths, like many others of their kind, valued their enterprises exceedingly. Even in a moment of crisis their uncle Levi had put business first, although he continued to remind himself not to. Under the shadow of war with Britain, he wrote from Philadelphia, "It is not a time to trouble you with markets . . ." And then, unable to refrain: "Flour is dull 6-1/2 to 6-3/4$." Recollecting himself, he added a brief prayer: "God bless you all and take you under his Holy Keeping."[24]

Elite religious expressions indicate that they explicitly tied their success to their faith with approximately the same frequency as elites elsewhere in the nation did. There remained the more traditional types like Richard Dorsey—who paid for his pew promptly but said no more about church the rest of the year.[25] But at this moment, the nation was in the throes of the Second Great Awakening; indeed, the number of Protestant churches in Baltimore was growing almost exponentially. The elites were very much involved. One study has shown that during this time the percentage of the population that was church-going remained steady at about 50 percent, but that, while the proportion of laborers decreased from 30 to 20 percent, the proportion of wealthy attendees rose from 30 to 40 percent.[26] Reasons are harder to pinpoint. In New York the Awakening has been referred to as a "shopkeeper's millennium," as the rising upper bourgeoisie, rather than the traditionally wealthy, attempted to exert a moral influence and raise their stature. There is evidence that this pattern held true in Baltimore as well. We find religious fervor not among the older families, but among the newly well-to-do. A new soap factory ran a Sabbath School. A father who ought to have been satisfied that his daughter had married "up" in marrying into the Wilson family wrote her dire predictions as to her fate if she did not find it in her to be born again: "I use the freedom of a father in urging my Child to great watchfulness for we wrestle with subtle enemies, . . . the Christian life is a warfare, and remember the caution let them that stand take heed lest they fall . . ."[27] The father only ceased his warnings when the daughter died at age thirty-one.

Traditionally, much of the success of the merchants of the leading families has been ascribed not only to their piety but also to their hard work and excellent recordkeeping techniques.[28] If their piety was debatable or at least variable, the volume of their correspondence and activity demonstrates that they did indeed work efficiently. Their recordkeeping varied. In some cases, they insisted on modern double-entry bookkeeping; in other cases, they did not. By the late 1820s their businesses had created a demand for preprinted ledgers and business forms that increased efficiency. For the first time, the use of such papers became common rather than unusual. And the printers William and Joseph Neal, who sold merchant account books, felt that it would boost their business to promise to engrave bills or have "blank books ruled in any manner."[29]

The developing banks formed the nucleus of this world that was expanding through the use of paper. A large segment of society, including not only merchant investors but also some from the middling ranks, began to make deposits in these institutions so that they might receive up to a 5 percent return: meanwhile, the pool of deposits formed a growing surplus capital. The banks made more resources available for merchants to borrow than could be obtained through personal loans and were more permanently reliable than bills of exchange in transactions with foreigners. The story, however, seemed too good to be true: the banks were not universally trusted. The Franklin Bank, for example, still suffered from primitive recordkeeping and a poorly defined system of checks and balances among the staff. One Monday morning in May of 1820 the cashier of the bank went off in great distress to look for the president. He was referred to the barbershop on Calvert Street, and there he found his man. The story was briefly communicated in hushed tones: the elderly porter Enoch Churchman, who had charge of the keys to the vault, had just tendered his resignation and confessed to some minor misdemeanors during his term of office. The president ordered the cashier back to the bank and told him to wait for the board to convene. When the cashier got back, he learned that the porter had gone off in search of a drink of water, never to return. Later it became clear that Mr. Churchman had used his temporary solitude to secrete upon his person a significant additional quantity of cash.[30]

Nor was the Franklin Bank the only such institution to suffer fraud. Banks issued their own preprinted checks in lieu of cash, which could be redeemed for metal money later at their point of issue. If someone presented a check from another bank, he or she was first given a bank check and then after a certain number of days could exchange it for specie, at which point the paper was incised with a metal paper cutter. If the deposited check had been forged, the outlaw needed to try to exchange it before the forgery had been discovered and the bank cashier notified. In order to protect themselves, those engaging in such criminal activity would anonymously hire street boys to run to the bank for them to change a check. Sometimes they were caught, sometimes not.[31]

The process of learning to trust banks was a long one in Baltimore. Even turning to them as a source of funds for incipient projects was a relatively new idea. Most people were more comfortable with the idea of raising money through a lottery. Lotteries, after all, had been working well in the new nation. They funded the building of hospitals, cultural edifices, commercial buildings, and internal improvements. In Maryland they were carefully regulated by state law. Until the 1830s, when their numbers grew to such an extent that all possible demand for tickets had been saturated, no one ventured to criticize this technique for accumulating capital. Customers for the tickets came from all walks of life. They could buy whole tickets or parts of tickets. In newspaper advertisements finance houses vied to outdo each other in their claims that they sold the most winning tickets. In an expensive commercial directory aimed at merchants and their families several pages were dedicated to describing the best places for buying tickets; this volume also offered straight-faced assessments as to the relative likelihood of winning depending on where one purchased one's ticket.[32]

Jacob Cohen, the son of Jewish immigrants from Bavaria and Bristol, ran the most prominent lottery shop. He had set himself up in business by buying large blocks of lottery tickets at a discount and then selling them at full price to individual buyers. Between the War of 1812 (in which they fought) and 1831 Cohen and his brothers turned his lottery store front into a bank. In this they followed the general trend of their day, in which people turned from raising capital through lotteries to raising it through banking. There were times, however, when the two forms seemed to blend together in one shop. Cohen used several effective techniques in transforming his establishment. First, although the business was still run out of the Baltimore office, Cohen sent his brothers to five other port cities to open branches, as lotteries lasted long enough to make out-of-state ticket purchases not only possible but popular. The Cohens received a wide variety of bank notes in payment for tickets and were soon able to operate successfully in the exchange business. Indeed, if they received a bank note in payment for a lottery ticket, they would accept it at face value even if it came from out of state and thus ordinarily would be discounted. To raise their specie holdings, they also began to advertise that they would buy Spanish doubloons and other coins. By 1831 Jacob Cohen was ready to close his lottery operations and declare the opening of Cohen's Bank. At this point, he was also participating in the stock market trade, albeit hesitantly; he had only begun to accept share certificates as payment for tickets and then resell them to the public in the mid-1820s.

Cohen's success was noteworthy: by the mid-1820s his firm was competing against twelve other lottery sellers, at least six of whom advertised prominently in the papers just as he did. He, however, paid for larger advertisements than did his closest competitors. He also published his own small weekly, *Cohen's Gazette and Lottery Register*, which seemed to offer the public inside knowledge of the different lotteries and which contained fascinating stories about lucky winners who had purchased their tickets at Cohen's. It is possible that he had to counteract public suspicion of a Jewish firm. There is, however, no evidence of this in surviving papers of his contemporaries or in any of his competitors' advertisements.[33]

In these years of commercial transformation merchants felt vulnerable. In their letters and conversations with passing travelers they frequently bemoaned their risky environment and mourned the numbers who went bankrupt every year. In addition to feeling buffeted by their English competitors, they experienced tensions and rivalries amongst themselves. In 1820, when the postwar recession caused by the revival of Britain's trade was still very serious, a group of leading merchants met to reduce one source of stress by forming a union. In September they signed a constitution for their new "Chamber of Commerce." Robert Oliver signed at the top; he was followed by other such wealthy men as Levi Hollingsworth and Elisha Tyson (Thomas's uncle). In order to be sure that the organization would continue to defend their own interests, the merchants defined conditions for membership carefully: "No person can become a member of this institution, who is not a citizen of the U.S. and a trading merchant of the city of Baltimore." They defined "trading merchants" rather traditionally as owners of ships or import-export dealers, but also expanded the meaning slightly to include presidents of insurance companies. In using this language, they did not explicitly eliminate those trading merchants who chose to invest in manufactures—and indeed, several of them would do so—but they did exclude men who were primarily or exclusively manufacturers and whose interests they saw as being essentially opposed to those of import-export merchants. To maintain these standards in perpetuity, they wrote: "Every person desirous of becoming a member shall sign this Constitution before the 1st day of November next, or must thereafter be nominated by a member . . . He shall then be balloted for, and three negatives shall exclude any applicant."[34]

The power of the Chamber of Commerce existed as long as its members acknowledged it: the organization claimed for itself the role of settling disputes among members in order that they might avoid facing each other in open court, and the first rule was that no member could refuse the arbitration of the chamber and still remain a member. A four-man arbitration committee was replaced every month through elections. During the first two years of the chamber's existence the committee settled a flurry of cases. Gradually, however, the organization became less active. Some members may have become disillusioned when they realized that political and personal alignments sometimes impeded "objective" decisionmaking: when ship owner Jacob Daly brought a well-documented case against Thomas Tenant, he lost almost immediately. Although the fact was never mentioned, the members knew that Tenant was vice-president of the Chamber of Commerce at the time.[35]

Having arranged themselves in the ways that they wanted, it was important to the merchant families that they prevail upon their children, nieces, and nephews to make the vision their own and carry it forward. They saw the schools as being the primary locus of such persuasion. There the children not only acquired the basic skills that they would need, but also made friends among the people who would later supply marriage prospects and business associates; they came to care about the people with whom they would later sign petitions. A woman said of the institution she had attended: "These families [the dry-goods merchants, shipping merchants, and silversmiths] all sent their children to Dr. Bartow's school." The boys who attended the Bel-Air Academy remembered standing together for their public examination. The bonds were made fast not only though joint studies, but through their common amusements. The girls left their school to go "Maying" in the spring; the boys at Bel-Air were eventually forbidden to celebrate with guns and gunpowder after their examination in order to avoid "much possible and probable danger to their lives."[36]

For a young future merchant, there was one key element in his development that no school could provide: he had to learn outside of the classroom how merchants actually conducted their business. For this reason,

many fathers took their sons on "apprenticeship" voyages. The Hollingsworth boys used their allowance to buy sweetmeats in the West Indies;
they sold some of their cargo to their mother upon their return. Samuel
Spafford took Samuel, Jr., to Pernambuco in Brazil so he could watch his
parent conduct his affairs. The boy wrote to his mother once they had
arrived that he and his father were both well and hoped that she was. "My
respects to all my friends," he added earnestly.[37] A slightly older but
equally lonely J. P. Donaldson simply wrote straight to his friends and
asked that they greet his parents:

Callao Bay, February 26, 1829

. . . As it respects the markets flour is now selling at 10$ on board
and every prospect of it rising . . . The Brig Chilean of Baltimore is
here and they are purchasing flour for the purpose of going to Guayaquil where I expect they will get a very good price as the port
has been under a state of strict blocade . . . we shall sail for Paita in
1 or 2 days but god only knows when we shall sail for home. I am
now getting so sleepy that I can hardly see my pen therefore you
must excuse me if I misspell any words . . . I now having a few leisure
moments take up my pen to conclude my letter as the ship will sail
in a few hours. I have only time to wish that you will give my best
love to all the girls of my acquaintance—to your family—to my
friend Millington . . . I remain yours, etc. J. P. Donaldson
P. S. Be so good as to tell my mother and vater that I will write
them by the next opportunity . . .[38]

The boys were learning about the rigors of travel, the harshness of lone-
liness, the complexities of events in foreign nations, the need for personal
contacts, and methods of calculating profit in the buying and selling of
goods. These were not lessons they could learn in school, and all effective
merchants needed the knowledge. Even if they were not going to travel
extensively themselves, they would supervise the travel of their ship captains and correspond with representatives.

The case of future merchants' wives was quite different. They did not
need "little adventures," as the Hollingsworth women called the boys'
exploits. They needed to learn their parts as forgers and preservers of
social ties that would make their husbands' business lives possible. This
lesson could be taught in school, but in the case of resistant pupils families
had to bring some additional pressures to bear. They could not simply put

a recalcitrant girl on a ship and imply that she could either learn her part or try to swim home, as a family could do with an obstinate boy. They could, however, refuse to allow a girl to continue her education and remind her that she had no other options. Mary Alicia Mitchell, for example, who was of marriageable age, had interest only in her studies. At Mrs. McKim's School in Baltimore she took first place in etymology, composition, modern history, astronomy, ancient geography, writing, and arithmetic. She begged her uncle and guardian to be allowed to stay at school and received this reply: "I must conclude by a word of advice to you my dear Girl, that is, that you have now arrived to that age to know the value of time and the importance of an Education & as this is the last opportunity you will have, I am in hopes that you will make the best use of your time. You will quit at the expiration of your Quarter and return home. You will write me frequently and say if you want anything."[39]

Mary Alicia worked on reining herself in. Either at the behest of a teacher or on her own she wrote an essay on the natural place of woman. She began with this premise: "Man might be initiated into the varieties and mysteries of needlework, taught to have patience with the feebleness and waywardness of infancy, and to steal with noiseless step around the chamber of the sick; and woman might be instructed to contest for palm of science, to pour forth eloquence in Senates . . ." She concluded that such might indeed be accomplished, but "revoltings of the world would attend this violence to nature" and "the beauty of the social order would be defaced . . ."[40] Shortly after she left school, Mary Alicia married into the Stump family—dealers in flour and herring, as we know—and apparently entered into her new duties without complaint. She saved the seething commonplace book of her adolescence, but added no more to it. Before her marriage, in writing out a poem about "The Calm Sea" she had once asked herself,

> Is there such a calm for mortal breasts
>   when storms have once been there?
> When passion wild has swept along with heart corroding
>   care?

Mary Alicia's kin had established a way of life that worked well for them, and her teachers were their allies. Young people's deviations could destroy the family's accomplishments. Mary Alicia and her peers had to learn to find their calm within expected confines.

Investment Strategies

Baltimoreans knew that although their beloved lotteries pooled cash they did not produce money through credit. As they ceded merchant trading to the British and turned to infrastructural projects, the problem became more serious. Joint stock companies grew in importance, but they frightened people profoundly. The stock exchange—even in larger cities than Baltimore—at this time remained smaller than the banks in terms of numbers of dollars accessed.[41] The concern we have seen among bankers to prove to the public that they would be honest and invest depositors' funds wisely probably indicates that lack of trust was an important factor in limiting early interest in equity investments. It was hard for a man to turn his money over to the use of another individual's company. Even Richard Dorsey, a wealthy and knowledgeable landowner and part-time merchant, wrote fearfully to his banker in the late 1830s, authorizing him to invest in stocks on his behalf, "provided you think them safe."[42]

Most members of the elite were less afraid of city stock, also called municipal bonds. These were issued by the municipality for varying periods at 5 or 6 percent interest annually (depending on the length of term), which was slightly higher than the standard rate at most private banks. They were informally although not legally guaranteed by the local government through their access to the tax base. Investors knew that, in addition to earning interest, their money was funding the development of internal improvements that in turn were a benefit to themselves as well. These relatively safe investments became almost casual. Among themselves, investors treated city stock certificates as if they were money drawn on a bank and used them to pay debts to each other.[43]

Insurance companies invested money in the low tens of thousands of dollars in city stock. The city guide published by Fielding Lucas in 1832 listed eight such firms, most dating from the postrevolutionary war years, with two of more recent origin. In fact, there were several others, although lesser known. Certain members of the elites had designed them to protect themselves against fire and shipping disasters: the original founders of the Baltimore Fire Insurance Company, for example, included merchants Andrew Ellicott, Isaac Tyson, and Levi Hollingsworth. At first only major houses and businesses and large institutions bothered to insure themselves. The minutes of the meetings of the institutions indicate that even in those cases certain men had to remind others of the importance of insurance. But as time progressed the owners of small houses began to insure themselves with greater frequency as well. Advertisements reached out to them: "Establishments warmed by iron stoves, secured [to the floor or wall], rather than by wood fires, will be insured for one quarter percent less." John Chapman insured his house and apothecary stock, for example, and coal merchant Zachariah Woollen covered several small brick outbuildings. The companies were successful in their campaigns and assigned committees to investigate possible investments for their amassed funds. By the 1820s and 1830s they offered relatively large dividends that they happily announced on the front pages of the newspapers.[44]

At this point, the merchants used these various credit options largely in order to finance more of their traditional activities in agriculture and the shipping trade. Manufacturing formed an alternative area for investment. At first, however, most merchant families resisted backing such enterprises. Most believed that they would remain a minor element of a primarily agricultural nation's economy.[45] Only a few merchant-millers of grain had begun experimenting with textile mills as early as 1808, when the European wars ended; although their factories were considered fascinating, they were most often seen as tourist attractions rather than technological models for the future. "I must tell you of a projected jaunt of pleasure, Lydia and I have had. We have a beautiful ride of 10 miles, to Ellicott's Mills, where the Cotton Manufactory is established, it is a very fashionable and general resort, and on Wednesday last Lydia and I joined a party of ladies and gentlemen . . ."[46]

Twenty years later, exchanging information among themselves, elite families were still only beginning to be convinced of the efficacy and potential of these mills:

I am induced to trouble you with the present letter by a recollection of our conversation when I last had the pleasure of seeing you, respecting the best and most economical mode for a farmer to get his wool made into cloth for his people. I think you mentioned that it was your practice to send your wool to a manufactory near Baltimore where it was spun, wove, dyed felted and made into Cloth at a certain price per yard . . . Will you do me the kindness to inform me, what manufactory it is to which you have been accustomed to send your wool, the width and price of the cloth, and whether the stuff made is all wool or part cotton, and whether the owner of the establishment would make it either way at the option of the person sending the wool. I have so much difficulty here in procuring good weavers and in accomplishing the labour of spinning that I am inclined to adopt your plan of clothing my people . . .[47]

The farmer obviously did not want to relinquish control over the processes he and his wife were accustomed to supervising. But as the matter stood he was dependent on the labor of a number of his own household and of temporary hired hands; if they could not or would not work for him under his terms, he was unable to turn his wool into cloth. He began to pay attention to alternate suggestions.

However, although most wealthy landholders and merchants were slow to be convinced of the money-making potential of mills, master artisans in the city were quicker to be convinced of the virtue of turning their shops into "manufactories." They began to offer lower pay to more workers who were unskilled, without thinking of them all as future journeymen or masters. Through careful division of labor they would be able to produce more goods, which they would then sell to dealers in the city markets, for they believed (and shortly proved) that there were plenty of ready customers. They later insisted, for example, that an additional footbridge be constructed across Jones' Falls because they believed that only its absence prevented countless citizens of Fell's Point from spending more money in the center of town where their shops were. In 1823, of the twenty-six manufactories in Baltimore City, fourteen were of the type that had descended from artisans' shops—typefounders, weavers, soap makers, paper makers, and glass blowers. This number did not even include the tanneries and brickyards that had expanded from small shops. For the first time, a small paper guide was published in Baltimore that had never been needed before, giving charts of varying wages by the hour, week, and month, so that a boss could pay numerous employees with varying schedules more easily.[48]

Increasing artisan involvement in manufactories soon gave rise to a public conflict. An argument in favor of tariff protection for local manufactures had first been articulated immediately after the Revolution. Public debates on the issue had raged in newspapers, for many merchants who made their livings by selling goods from Europe did not like the idea.[49] In the late 1820s an aspect of the issue came home to Baltimore in a serious local crisis. A group of merchants protested against the mass-produced goods currently available in the weekly markets, claiming that they were mostly foreign and citing the anti-importation laws they had once abhorred. In January 1827 fifty-two successful import-export merchants submitted the following petition to their City Council:

The practice [of selling dry goods in the markets], from a small commencement only a few years ago has increased into an organized and extensive system, exceeding in the amount of sales of a variety of articles . . .

Your memorialists, are aware that there now exists an ordinance forbidding the sale of Imported goods in the markets, but this law, which but partially met the grievance, has never been enforced, on account it is presumed of the difficulty of distinguishing between foreign and domestic goods.

All of your memorialists are affected in a greater or less degree . . . but the operation is most ruinous on those of us who live in the vicinity of the markets and who have heretofore drawn their chief support from the custom of the country people and others frequenting the market . . .

[We] will conclude by imploring you to devise some means to protect us, as a numerous class of citizens, giving employ to a number of persons, and paying higher rents than any other portion of the community . . .[50]

This statement was buttressed by several neighborhood petitions from the businessmen located in the vicinity of each of the several markets, which mentioned not only dry goods, but also "shoes, boots, hats, tin and crocory [*sic*] ware." The one from Fell's Point was signed by seventy local notables, of whom thirty-nine are identifiable. They included twenty merchants selling imported cloth, clothing, shoes, soaps, and china; nine traditional master artisans (mostly shoemakers and tailors) who apparently did not sell any of their fine products in the market; and ten men in unrelated businesses, who should not have cared one way or the other, but who may have been pressured into signing.[51]

Almost immediately, the council received a contrasting petition, with sixty-seven signatures. But these signers were humbler men. Their signatures mostly lacked the scrolls and flourishes present on the other petitions, and only slightly less than half of them are identifiable today. They called themselves "the undersigned manufacturers, Citizens and dealers in the public markets . . . of Cedar ware, combs, shoes, tin ware and domestic dry goods." Their twofold argument was simple and brief. They could "conceive no harm can result to the public" from their sales, and they always paid their market license fees. Of those signers whom we can identify, an equal number were market dealers (storekeepers or peddlers, as they called themselves) and artisans with expanded shops. Among the artisans were represented soap and candle makers, carpenters, shoemakers, weavers, coopers, comb makers, and glove makers. The unidentifiable signers could have been more peddlers, laborers in the manufactory shops, or friends who were pressured into signing. There were also seven signers who operated taverns within the grounds of the markets, who apparently believed they would lose a significant share of their business if the markets reverted to selling foodstuffs only.[52] In another petition of shoe dealers only, the salesmen insisted that all the items they sold were American made and were not somehow slyly offloaded from foreign ships.[53] The following year, in the great craftsmen's parade, the weavers and dyers were to make the same point in displaying a giant figure of Britannia weeping for her lost trade.

The merchants apparently did not want the issue to be seen as one of merchants vs. artisans. Another petition was submitted claiming that "[the] merchandise is now sold to the great disadvantage and almost ruin of many manufacturers, merchants *and mechanics*" (emphasis added). Only twenty-five people signed this document, and in fact at least half of them were merchants, but the signatures of the few master artisans involved were placed very prominently on the first page.[54]

In its decision the council—whose mixed membership consisted of merchants and tradesmen—sided against the merchants. They said that the city needed the income from the market license fees. They also may have feared riots in the markets or massive complaints from the majority of the population, who, judging by the success of the new practice, liked both the convenience and the lower prices. The merchants printed a scathing response, urging the council to reconsider, and convinced the renowned Robert Oliver to sign with them, at the top of the column.[55] It did no good.

Some merchants adapted themselves to this new world by choosing to finance the expansion of artisan shops. Many craftsmen did not have the capital necessary to transform a shop, even if they believed they could make money by doing so. At this time, most Baltimore manufactories were under the personal direction of their owners, who worked on the shop floor just as master craftsmen had always done. "Thomas Fisher's dyeing establishment" and "John Chapman's Columbian Green Paint Factory" advertised on the basis of the special knowledge and skill of their masters. Foreign visitors said that these were not the operations of major industrialists. But times were changing. The way for a craftsman to finance a transformation of his shop was to go into partnership with a merchant or merchants who could provide the capital while he provided the expertise. Import-export merchants who feared they would meet their defeat in the market stalls were probably more and more eager to discuss this option. In 1820 Francis Hyde, a soap and candle maker, went into business with George Williams, a merchant. Hyde actually stayed on the shop floor and oversaw the work; Williams was not publicly attached to the new factory, but his name was prominent in the fire insurance records. In a more famous case in 1825, the McKims invested in the chemical-making shop owned by chemist Howard Sims. At first they kept him on, as he had expected, but Sims learned that the investors had the real power when they excluded him shortly afterward.[56]

Manufactories were also beginning to appear that were not attached to the name of a particular master craftsman, even at the start. The newspapers advertised a newly opened "Steam Engine and Jobbing Shop at No. 14 Fayette Street." They would take "orders for engines, pumps, soda water apparatus, hydraulic presses, printing presses, tobacco press screws and boxes, comb presses, lathes and circular saws."[57] Clearly, one tradesman was not expert in all of these areas, and the capital investment had been intensive. Thus, although the records of the business have not been preserved, we know that this was the project of the investors, whoever they were; the craftsmen who must have been present in the factory to direct the labor were there to work for the owners. The tradesmen had celebrated their victory over the import-export merchants in early 1827; one wonders how many of them then saw the writing on the wall—that they would shortly lose control. They had been right that there was a wide market for the goods they made; other, richer men were quick to learn the lesson. They channeled their investments accordingly.

Beliefs about Taxation

To the extent that they were involved in the formation of public policy, Baltimore's merchants attempted to understand their city's strengths and develop them to maximize their own potential for success. They supported the 1829 city budget that allotted the greatest share of public spending to support for the B & O Railroad. Next in order came the expenses of the city poor, watching and lighting, interest owing to city stock buyers, and finally the cleaning and clearing of the harbor. In other years the division was similar.⁵⁸ In all cases, the elites emphasized the involvement of as many people as possible. They protected both internal city business—through watching and lighting—and inland trade ties—through the support for turnpike and railroad building. They did not ignore external trade: they made the maintenance of the harbor a joint public expense, rather than leaving individual merchants to pay for clearing areas near their own wharves. They did not ignore their own most immediate interests in that they protected their investments in municipal stock.⁵⁹ But they placed keeping desperate poverty at bay even higher on the list. They behaved as if they knew that the other projects would have become more and more useless had an ever larger share of the population neared the point of being unable to function in city commerce.

Are we to conclude that they were figures of extraordinary generosity? Who provided the funding for these projects? The merchants and their friends, though they shouldered a share, did *not* provide all of it and had no intention of doing so, being no more inherently generous than any others. They shared the burden with the entire taxable population, whose total contributions were significant, as tax-paying citizens were distributed relatively evenly over the four categories they comprised, as we saw in Chapter 2. The most important tax was the direct property tax, although a separate "poor tax" was also levied to aid in supporting the Almshouse and in meeting other city poor expenses. The property tax at this time was $4.78 per $100.00 worth of property. The last assessment of values had been completed in 1813 and put the city total at four million dollars. By the late 1820s most merchants knew their total investments were worth far more than the value for which they were currently taxed. Taxes on the middling sorts, a larger share of whose wealth took the more immediately visible and measurable form of furniture and plate, retained a closer reflection of the current reality.

The City Council with its mixed membership—and led by Mayor Jacob Small, the builder—worked to ensure a more just distribution of responsibility. In 1827 the council accepted the report of the collector stating that it was necessary to legislate fines against delinquents to ensure timely payments. Baltimore's wealthiest men became angry at this. In January 1831 eighty-five of them submitted an emergency petition to the Maryland Assembly begging that the state government limit the city's "frightening power of taxation." Within two months the state legislators, who were their personal acquaintances and even relations, obliged the merchants; Jacob Small resigned as mayor. The City Council, however, shortly procured permission to conduct a thorough property reassessment. In 1834, after a careful study, the city's total taxable wealth increased tenfold.[60] The wealthiest merchants had won a battle but lost the war.

There were, of course, other city licenses and fees. If universally imposed, this kind of tax is regressive, weighing more heavily on the poor, but in their discussion of such taxes and in their practices most people indicated that they believed the wealthy should have to pay them while other people should not. The steep city dog tax of $2.00, for example, was zealously collected in some better-off wards by the superintendent of chimney sweeps, but the collector did not even make an effort in the Fell's Point area: in the late 1820s he made the ridiculous assertion that there were only fourteen dogs living in the first and second wards combined. Clearly he felt it would be useless or cruel or both to attempt to collect from more people in that neighborhood; his report was accepted without comment. Seven carriage owners signed a petition that the carriage tax was anachronistic in that it had been invented in an age when "few it is presumed kept carriages, and they being wealthy and using the streets for pleasure or convenience were able to pay it."[61]

Discussion of private spending on public projects was reminiscent of the forms of collecting and spending of taxes: most people believed that as many people as possible should be involved and that any investment toward the "public good" would reward the individual investors themselves rather directly. Improving the water supply was an example of a project that necessitated serious discussion of public and private spending. The Baltimore Water Company, a private venture operated for profit, ran pipes down from high-level streams, but it was known for being an ineffective organization. In 1830 the City Council began to pressure the company to sell its property to the city—either land and pipes or, better yet, pipes only (which would cost the city less). Meanwhile, the councilors also approached the owners of the ten closest mills on the Gwynn's Falls stream, offering to buy their land and especially their water rights, so that they could divert rivulets to the city populace. They told the elite men who were to lose the ownership of profitable ventures that they would gain by living in a city with an improved water supply and thus greater prosperity. But the merchants and mill owners wanted and expected a more direct return for their sacrifices. The water company stalled. The mill owners held a meeting, arranged among themselves a bottom-line price—higher than that which the city had suggested—and continued to maintain a relatively united front, although there was some disagreement at separate meetings.[62] Opinions ran high, as other people's interests were also at stake, and finally the City Council's Water Committee made a statement: "Being seriously impressed with the great importance of this subject with its immediate bearing upon the happiness and comfort of the inhabitants of this great City; and upon the increase and prosperity of the City itself; your Committee shrink from the responsibility of re-commending . . . any specific measures in relation to a supply of water until the sense of their constituents . . . shall be ascertained."[63] The City Council called a public meeting in each ward. The consensus was that most people supported continuing to investigate the taxpayers' purchase of the mills at a price that would satisfy the owners, in that the Baltimore Water Company was not performing effectively enough.[64] The public should make an investment for its own benefit.

Relationship with Labor

Employers in Baltimore depended on a range of labor forces. They still contracted individual indentured servants from Europe, but only rarely. Black slaves had been present in large numbers at the turn of the century, but by 1810 the figures had stabilized and were now decreasing every year. Most working men were still "apprentices," on the bottom rung of the craft system. Though they had been losing ground recently, it was not to coerced white or black labor, but to free labor, white and black.[65] New immigrants who had no ties to the guild system and freedmen of African descent were gaining ground in the population and certainly in the ranks of the "day laborers" who were available for hire by the hour. Indeed, the population swelled with such workers. Why employers gradually turned against the use of coerced labor can never be settled beyond a shadow of a doubt. It has been proven that slaves could be used profitably in the new industries and sometimes were. Yet in a world of slaves saving and suing for their freedom—as we shall see them actively doing in Chapter 8—it was hard to maintain discipline and prevent constant flight without pay-ing incentives or in other ways coming to terms with the enslaved. "For sale—A likely fine looking young mulatto man, who has about ten years to serve, is a good miller and cooper and will be sold to any good master *to whom he would be willing to go*" (emphasis added). Meanwhile, there were a range of new investment opportunities and more and more free men available to hire. Slave owners tried to placate their labor forces with long-term manumission dates and agreed-upon sale prices, but new employers turned away from the tensions embedded in the situation and hired free workers.[66]

As yet, the elites did not demonstrate great fear of the growing class of day laborers, many of whom were Europeans or their children. In the discussions of public investment, references to any fear of a multitude or a rabble potentially abusing the investment were rare. The rabble in general seemed very distant. During the War of 1812 one of the Hollings-worth women had summarized her household's view of the location and scale of such a threat: "I think the people in the southern States are in a wretched situation, those of Georgia who are now contending with the British. Blacks and Indians are worse off than any other class of citizens, and the [white citizens] appear to dread the latter foe the most."[67] Un-easiness over such a dark-skinned horde had reappeared most recently in editorials sympathizing with Simón Bolívar far to the south, for he was responsible for governing over "a set of wretches—natives and foreigners."[68]

Apparently, wealthy Baltimoreans considered themselves safe specifically because they were not surrounded by worse-off "Blacks and Indians" or "native wretches." Indeed, when they did experience fear, it was in direct proportion to their realization that the sizable dark-skinned minority that did live nearby might rebel. Newspaper readers were offered hideously detailed (and apparently satisfying) descriptions of the punishments meted out to black rebels in faraway places. During and after the Nat Turner scare in nearby Virginia in 1831, white fears rose dramatically. In September, before Turner himself had been caught, some letters about a planned uprising purportedly written by free blacks in the area were intercepted. Nerves remained taut. On October 17 the son of a factory owner wrote in his journal: "Spent this day attending to business . . . after which having heard that the blacks were about to raise a riot, I went with my father to that part of the City where they were; but they had dispersed."[69]

Slave crises aside, however, the idea that a property-destroying and undeserving horde of *poor* people also existed in Baltimore only made brief appearances in the discussions of the elite. Generally, such a horde was small, manageable, and perhaps even useful. Between 1822 and 1827 a number of wealthy men including one of the Tysons developed plans for a "House of Industry," designed to supplement and perhaps replace the Almshouse in dealing with the problem of the "shiftless" poor. The new organization would provide paid in-house work or outwork to the unemployed, subtracting from the clients' pay the cost of the food and firewood consumed. Children would be offered minimal schooling and then bound out as apprentices. The entire plan depended on two assumptions: first, that the laziness among inmates of which the Almshouse keepers often complained was in fact not prevalent, and, second, that the unemployed could be trained to be effective low-paid workers. However, despite the presence of these attitudes within the "charitable" merchant community, they were not strong enough to take root and grow branches: plans for the house died a gradual death.[70]

In 1829 a new law was made effective in Maryland that required that public education be available to all white residents, male and female. Student tuition was $1.50 per semester, including books, and by 1830 had dropped to $1.00, excluding books. There were even a few "certificate" students who paid nothing. A girls' and a boys' school opened in the western part of the city on Eutaw Street, and, at the same time, two tiny rooms on Bond Street were rented for the residents of Fell's Point. By 1830 these students had been moved to a decent room over the Engine House and another over the Watch House, both on Market Street. By 1831, although the Eutaw Street schools were prospering, the commissioners had to admit that the classrooms in Fell's Point were floundering, despite the move to better sites. Many people apparently felt too busy and too overwhelmed to send their children, or needed to have the children work, or could not afford the minimal fee. Teachers complained about the bad behavior of the students who did come, and parents complained about the excessive use of corporal punishment. Attendance continued to fall. The school commissioners considered closing the boys' school and allowing any who felt truly ambitious to walk to a school recently erected in Old Town, near Jones' Falls.[71]

In their report that year the commissioners, including the merchant Jacob Cohen, outlined their thinking about what the availability of education should be:

If we consider that under favorable circumstances, and strong and enlightened efforts, it is possible for society to bring three-fourths of the whole number of her children ... within the pale of education, leaving the others to that necessity which no human power can control, we have 5,000 children left [to educate] who [currently] receive no steady, nor uniform, nor enlightened instruction, in a word, who will arrive at years of discretion without being accomplished in a good English education, and for whom it is the bounden duty of society to provide.

In one sense, this philosophy was extraordinarily inclusive, speaking of the right of the vast majority to education and self-improvement, even if it meant that others in society would have to absorb part of the cost. And yet the writers also assumed that a certain minority was to be absolutely excluded. The context of the paragraph had made it clear that in speaking of "the whole number of society's children" the writers meant only white children. Furthermore, the commissioners posited as an unquestionable fact that there was no hope for one-quarter of the white school-age children, for whom nothing could be done. Most of these would be new immigrants. The commissioners were not confused by this idea: their society was to be inclusive of most and exclusive of a minority. It was as true that there would be schooling for most people as it was that there would be none for Frederick Bailey.

There was thus little sense that the poor were a "multitude" or a majority; they were not called so and it was assumed they ought not to be so. Rather, the poor were a painfully irritating distinct minority with whom "society" in general had been burdened. Then suddenly in the mid-1830s the issue loomed larger than it had before. In 1834 at least five different banks failed when they issued too many notes and could not meet withdrawal demands at a moment of crisis. Some working people lost their life savings; others simply felt themselves vulnerable to the machinations of the wealthy. In the early months of 1835 a wave of arson began, and some anonymous pamphlets drew attention to the issue in the late spring. Tempers simmered over the summer, until rioting erupted in the first week of August. On Thursday, Friday, Saturday, and Sunday bands of people formed sporadically, burned and smashed, and then dispersed. They targeted the homes of wealthy merchants and financiers. By Monday the rioters were tired and the militia far more active; the crisis ended. Several dozen people had been arrested.[72]

Lydia Hollingsworth recorded her rage when the men she believed to have destroyed her family's property were acquitted six months later. City authorities found it difficult to prove who had done what in a riot, and they wished to defuse any lingering rage in the city, but she did not see the situation as they did:

> But one opinion exists here, with regard to the ruin of our house, that it was wanton, unprovoked and unlooked for by all but the abettors. My Sister and I were ignorant of threats, and did not know until Sunday, it was necessary for us to leave home, which we did with the children and found refuge at Mr. Ridgely's . . . That night they profaned in the utter destruction of every article within our long cherished paternal home. Oh Cousin what a horrid State has been brought upon individuals; upon the morals of the young and old who united in the revelry, by the wickedness of these men, who were acquitted by a Court temporal. The testimony produced of their guilt and dishonesty was too well established not to impress those who attended the trial, although the Jury acquitted them. Our house in South Street was sacked, the very doors, shutters, mantles, stove carried off in open day during this mis-rule, and all the valuables theirs . . .[73]

The tenor of Lydia's rage and even confusion is explained when we think of the rarity of such an event in the world she knew. The words "wanton destruction" were used when a lamplighter accidentally spilled oil on a doorstep, causing it to be tracked across a merchant's carpet. Careless and disrespectful lamplighters were a more familiar enemy than masses of poverty-stricken and enraged people. Lydia Hollingsworth did not live in a world where the majority were drastically deprived or envisioned by the elites as being profoundly dangerous to their perfectly constructed lives. The extreme nightmare of an actual riot—always possible, but never expected—had for a few short days become real, but it was still not a coherently understood event. Only by placing the sudden violence in comparative context can we make sense of it; Lydia on her own did not have the ability to do that.

Comparison

When Vicente Ramón Roca and Lydia Hollingsworth made the decisions that governed their futures—and often the futures of others—they viewed the world from dramatically different positions. In 1820 Baltimore, although still a mercantile city, had already moved far beyond the just-freed

Guayaquil in terms of experience in international trade and in industry. A whole new generation had taken over from those who had been active adults at the time of the War for Independence. Indeed, the wealthy Baltimoreans had left concepts of revolution far behind them. If Vicente's world was one of buoyant optimism and experimentalism, Lydia's was one of brittle rigidity and reminders of hierarchy. While the Guayaquileños were intent on using their evening parties to plan rebellion against Spain and then formulate idealistic new laws, Baltimoreans attended strawberry parties for the simpler pleasure of inspecting each other's barcelona shawls. If in one place elite displays bordered on profligacy and waste, that place was Baltimore. There is less evidence that the elites in Guayaquil consumed a large proportion of their income on lavish living than there is in Baltimore. Without insisting on their having profoundly different characters, we can say that the two groups were at different points in their histories: one was feeling the flush of republican virtue and experiencing a strong sense of responsibility for the future, while the other had recently amassed significant capital even as their political authority was undermined, leaving a need to reinforce their power symbolically where they could. The attitudes displayed by the Guayaquileños might have positioned them well to attempt to make economic gains and overtake their peers to the north, or at least to prevent the gap from widening.

In many respects, the similarities between the two groups of people are more noticeable than the differences. In both places merchant networks depended on personal ties and especially on marriage. The South Americans, however, were apparently more successful in creating the ties that bind. Their merchant empires based on marriage were far-flung, covering many nations and outlasting generations. Maryland marriages were in general local affairs, more likely to solidify connections between a town merchant and his rural suppliers, for example, than to provide an exporter with a recipient he could trust in another nation. Guayaquileño merchants could also rely on these family connections for credit to an extent that apparently few Baltimoreans could. The informality and ease with which their system of loans worked is attested by the fact that so few examples exploded into acrimony.

There may be several reasons for the tightness of the family bond which existed in Guayaquil to a greater extent than in Baltimore. Elite families' sense of themselves as being tied together through Spain and their Spanish blood was still very recent, especially as many young husbands literally came from that country. Those families who had been encomienda recipients generations earlier kept close track of their genealogies, so their status remained expressly visible to each other. The ties, however, had to be affective as well as symbolic for the system to work well. Gender roles may partly explain the differences between the two cities in this regard. The maintenance of active family ties in many ways fell to the women; they had to be willing to play their part. In Guayaquil women were invested with a sense of their own importance to their families and of the importance of their families to the patriot cause and the future. In Baltimore, on the other hand, their purpose was becoming more clearly decorative as the era of the Revolution and republican motherhood passed away. The regular rebellion of a certain percentage of daughters would eventually coalesce into several nineteenth-century movements we now call feminist, but it had not happened yet. While the Garaicoa sisters subscribed to *El Patriota* and eagerly helped José Villamil from New Orleans establish himself, Caroline Calvert, Mary Alicia Mitchell, and numerous others writhed against the dictates of their guardians. One could argue that perhaps there were just as many examples of young girls in Guayaquil who were unwilling to carry the family torch and that we simply have not found them. If so, however, evidence of the fact seems to have been more systematically destroyed than in Baltimore, and that in itself speaks volumes.

The very efficiency that the Guayaquileño merchants displayed in creating family bonds strong enough to protect international trade agreements and guarantee the availability of credit may, ironically, have been part of their undoing. We may see a case of a machine working so well there is no need to fix it—even when it becomes outmoded. Thomas Tyson had no in-laws overseas, so he gave his ship captain greater latitude of action and a greater share of the profits. Likewise, if he needed credit, he could not be so sure as Martín de Icaza that he would meet with a warm reception from his cousins or in-laws in requesting a loan. The Baltimoreans developed other strategies: Tyson and his peers moved beyond a personalistic notion of credit toward impersonal investment banking schemes. Through their family networks Guayaquileño merchants accessed extensive capital for the projects in which they were interested: expanding their cacao holdings and outfitting ships and even armies. We have tended to assume that they did not invest elsewhere because they did not have institutionalized credit. We might ask ourselves the heretical question as to whether the reverse was not nearer the mark: perhaps they did not develop such systems because they did not need them.

That the difference between the cities' elites in this regard was more a function of their different situations than of a greater cultural tendency toward rationalistic organization in the north is evidenced in different ways. In Baltimore, as we have seen, there were still many who resisted the concept of lending banks and distrusted them, and in Guayaquil, although so recently freed from colonial status, there were already several who speculated in paper money and were interested in exploring banking. Merchants in both towns favored a rationalistic mode of settling disputes among themselves, but in this case it was the Guayaquileños who were better able to pull the project off: their Consulado prospered, but in Baltimore the Chamber of Commerce foundered while the members fought about who should benefit most by it.

The daily practices of the two groups of merchants were startlingly similar. They put in long hours, kept thorough records, and used modern bookkeeping methods. Both put greater faith in their own labors than in the hand of God, although in an era rife with disease and shipwreck they did not discount the latter. Both mixed suspicion of new risks with interest in them. Their investment strategies, however, show that Baltimoreans were if anything more cautious than the Guayaquileños. The former had grown cautious through the recent troubling times and believed the United States should not attempt direct competition with Britain now that the European wars were over: Britain was good at manufacturing, and the younger nation good at buying manufactured goods in exchange for grain. They saw no reason to argue with their own success and became enraged when other up-and-coming groups did not agree with them. Their petitions on the subject of manufactures demonstrate their feelings. Guayaquil's merchants, however, were experiencing a surge of nationalist pride and often in their dealings with foreigners insisted on their independence and self-reliance. They were interested in discussing protectionist ideas and adopted some. The people of Guayaquil were more deeply embedded in a literal sense than those of Baltimore in the traditional practices of profiting as landlords and contracted monopolists, but in their thinking they expressed some rejection of those modes and interest in newer kinds of ventures. The more enterprising considered which kinds of factories would be best to build. Ironically, the Baltimore merchants were rapidly convinced by the sizable profits of the manufacturing upstarts to follow suit, while the intrepid Guayaquileños could not find the demand for the enterprises of which they dreamed.

There are, on the other hand, some areas where the variations among the merchants of the two cities can better be described as forming a dichotomy rather than a continuum. In training their sons, for example, merchant fathers in Baltimore placed them aboard a commercial ship and expected them to work, to learn to be practical and to seek profit. Guayaquil's sons, as part of their period of study, were dressed in ornate uniforms and sent to risk their lives on warships. Such, at least, would be one interpretation of what we have seen. The facts, however, could be considered in another light: Baltimore merchants, despite the advancements of their era, continued to rely on a traditional notion of apprenticeship and so sent their youth out on ships with little trading chests so that they might observe their fathers; Guayaquil's merchants were more intent on founding two new schools that offered the latest scientific perspectives, as well as training the boys to cope with the continuing wars.

Some of the greatest differences between the merchants of Guayaquil and those of Baltimore are found in their attitudes toward taxation and infrastructure, which are related to their beliefs about labor. Baltimore's elites obtained labor largely through contracts with free workers of more limited means than themselves, while Guayaquil's traditionally preferred to rely on coerced labor wherever they could or on a combination of coercion and less-than-subsistence wages. The divergence is particularly interesting, as employers in both places were in many ways facing a similar situation: slavery was becoming less popular in the hinterland, due to a recent change in export crop. A steady stream of freedmen and of slaves saving for their freedom filled the city. In Baltimore employers gradually yielded their conception of "worker" to the demands of free men; in Guayaquil they sought other forms of coercion in rounding up Indians or turning to the *presidio*. In a related vein, Baltimoreans believed that internal improvements and public investments were key to a healthy economy. The merchants taxed themselves and shared the burden with others, in order to make these investments. They also bought city stock and encouraged others to do so. In Guayaquil merchants avoided such expenditures, seeing quite accurately that the burden of a progressive tax would fall almost entirely on themselves. They defined *el pueblo* as a very narrow stratum and considered the masses to be beyond the pale of people who counted. They were surrounded by a majority of extremely poor and physically different people whom they had been accustomed to considering as almost another species, and they made their decisions and formulated policy accordingly.

One historian has made the case that the antiaristocratic tradition in economic policy formation in the United States dated from the days of the founding fathers, who were schooled in the idea that relative equality in wealth distribution was an antidote to political tyranny.[74] By the 1820s the merchant elites were certainly motivated to school themselves in this tradition. They had no choice, since the popular pressure in the early republican era had given the vote not only to property-owning white males, but simply to tax-paying ones, working men had been using their power. Landowning merchants had to serve on the assembly alongside master craftsmen and even work under a mayor who was an architect and contractor. The tax laws were made more progressive despite merchant resistance.

Guayaquileño elites, on the other hand, though they argued among themselves, did not share their power with other groups, certainly not with craftsmen. It was not that they were unfamiliar with Enlightenment thinking or particularly resistant to it. On the contrary, it was in Guayaquil, we remember, rather than Baltimore, that abolition and emancipation were discussed freely at this time. The habit of assumed privilege, however, does not dissipate on its own, and despite their thrilling theoretical discussions they continued to take unpaid labor for granted. The balance of power in the two places contrasted in interesting ways: the Baltimore elite normally did not fear "the horde" as much as did their counterparts in Guayaquil, probably because the world in which the Baltimoreans lived was structured in a relatively more equitable way. Yet it was structured thus because the reaction of the mob would be more immediate and more violent if the elite overstepped themselves, as most of the poor did not conceive of themselves as being deeply and inherently different from the rich: so it had been in the seventeenth century and so it was still when the banks failed in 1834.

Interestingly, the points at which the economic cultures of the two merchant groups are most starkly opposed all concern attitudes toward workers. Where work itself was concerned—whether we speak of style of trading interactions or work ethic or rationalistic pursuit of profit—the two groups behaved remarkably similarly. They had, however, imbibed very different attitudes about their position in relation to others within their communities. Thus they parted company in their thinking about who should pay taxes, how the money should be spent, and what the rewards for laborers should be.

PART III

CHAPTER 5

THE QUEST OF THE

"PERSONAS DECENTES"

The Middling Ranks of Guayaquil

A soldier named Pedro was looking for some evening entertainment. He walked out toward the outskirts of town on the edge of the open grass-lands. The petty officer sat down outside a certain house where someone was playing a guitar and people had gathered to dance or simply to listen. Ana Yagual, who lived there, was serving rum. She and her mother had found no other work than this, but they were earning a living. Later in the evening, though, Ana had to accost Pedro and demand the money he owed her—whether for rum or other services rendered was not clear. Pedro merely laughed at her and commented on the delicious amuse-ments provided by the place, despite the annoying qualities of the *indios*. He assumed that Ana Yagual and her house were at his disposal.[1] When, in a different incident, a small shopkeeper was asked why he treated a city police guard in a similarly insulting manner, the man responded that he observed a separate code of conduct in his dealings with dark-skinned people and only respected "personas decentes."[2]

Neither the storeowner nor the soldier Pedro felt the need to demon-strate in any explicit way their own qualifications as "personas decentes." Membership in this small group was generally a birthright, not an ac-quired characteristic. Those who considered themselves "personas decen-tes" had almost always been born into a minimal amount of property and prestige; their kin had probably spent several generations effectively shedding any familial associations with slaves or peons. Many members of the lower orders, however, did *attempt* to amass enough property to establish some claim to "decency" in the immediate future: they spent years saving to buy jewelry, the only investment of permanent value that they felt they could make in their situation. "My black washerwoman once came to me to borrow a doubloon, with which to redeem from pawn a massive gold chain and medal, which I had often seen her wear." At a baptismal party, free blacks gathered to present gifts to a new baby and loaded the table with silver and jewelry.[3] It was apparently rare or impossible, however, for any family to be able to buy their way within one generation into the ranks of the "personas decentes": I cannot offer one concrete example where such a phenomenon definitely occurred. Accumulation of a small property and the prestige that came with having money to spend were not enough, for the second qualification—the shedding of personal associations with the lowest ranks—was equally important. The latter was a function of the ability to make repeated distinctions between one's own family and the majority, distinctions that could not be made while one still had sisters or cousins or in-laws who were slaves or peons or people easily confused with such. Outsiders could not necessarily count on their obscure backgrounds to guarantee them a place among the *decente*. On the contrary, they might be particularly subject to suspicion. A lonely schoolteacher from Quito said he felt he was in a foreign country.[4]

Only a closer look at the lives of the middling ranks can illuminate the feelings of vulnerability that explain the hostility visible in their behavior in the early republic. Because of their small numbers, many of the middle-ranked people in Guayaquil knew each other and shared their community life to a certain extent. They were divided among themselves, though, and cannot be immediately examined as a unit. We must consider the artisans, professionals, and entrepreneurs, asking how each group envisioned their own choices: how they thought they could succeed and how they strategized. Only then can we return to the question of their interactions with and expectations of the majority.

The Artisans

The shops of most shoemakers were clustered together on certain streets. So were those of most carpenters, tinsmiths, painters, and every other group of artisans. Each trade was in some ways a world unto itself, to the extent that the members of each guild knew each other and participated in governing themselves. Every year, each guild selected a new *maestro mayor*, who was officially invested by the City Council. These rotating chiefs represented the painters, silversmiths, blacksmiths, tinsmiths, tailors, shoemakers, bloodletters, musicians, and household carpenters (as opposed to the black ship carpenters and caulkers, who did not send a representative for investiture but seem to have had their own form of union). Members of a *gremio* or guild consisted of masters of the trade only. These were limited in number. In the case of the shoemakers in the late 1820s, there were 35 masters to about 300 journeymen and an unknown number of apprentices or assistants.[5] Masters maintained personal authority over their workers: they labored alongside their employees throughout the six-day work weeks, rather than moving around and supervising several projects at a time.[6] In some cases masters obtained their own employment, and in others the *maestro mayor* assigned a master to a job that the guild as a whole had been offered. All masters were deemed worthy of respect and responsibility: in court they were frequently trusted with the evaluation of the property of elite figures during disputes over estates. They were themselves the heads of large households that often included slaves.

It was not assumed that all or even most workers would eventually rise to become masters of their craft. *Indios* or *zambos* were usually permanent assistants. According to Spanish law in the Americas, they had been specifically excluded from joining guilds, though, of course, not from working in the shops.[7] Each new generation of master craftsmen was to come from a certain class of people. These ideas were rarely stated explicitly in the early republic, but they did not disappear. In one interesting case, the family of a young man confused these separate sets of expectations for different groups of people. The boy had worked for his uncle for years without receiving any pay other than his food and was disappointed when his uncle died and he found he had been left nothing. He sued. His uncle's wife and her lawyer argued that they had fed and clothed him as masters do for their assistants and in exchange they had full right to his *jornales* or days of labor. But the judges responded that, although ordinarily such an analysis was apt, in this case uncle and nephew were "men of the same class" and the boy must be treated better and be paid, as he himself was a potential master.[8]

The guilds, then, were useful to the master craftsmen in making the rules by which they wished to live, but they were not necessarily useful to the majority of the practitioners of a craft. The workers could not use them, for example, to demand better pay for themselves, while the constituent masters did use them to set their own daily pay rates. In fact, the apparatus of the guilds sometimes became a tool for coercion. A governor or a general could write to a *maestro mayor* and demand that he put a certain number of hands on a certain job immediately, whether or not they were otherwise engaged.[9]

Still, the fact remained that even without being able to become masters or advocate for themselves through the guilds, for most ordinary artisans life was more than bearable. Those who practiced a trade at all were the fortunate few. They made a living wage and could nearly always find employment. Indeed, the differential between their pay and that of a master was not huge. Throughout the period from 1822 to 1835 a master earned approximately two pesos a day, sometimes slightly more or slightly less, depending on the trade. His immediate underlings earned about one and a half pesos, and the ordinary journeymen about one peso. Only the lowest-level assistants (who were really day laborers) earned the more negligible four reales (half a peso). A high-level assistant under twenty-five years old could earn nine pesos a week, enough to support himself and his mother and her household "decently."[10] These rates even applied to some men too dark to be included in the official *gremios:* although apparently almost all cabinetmakers and household carpenters were white (almost certainly including mestizos who passed as whites), and they had their own carpenters' guild, woodworking blacks, mulattoes, and *zambos* did not necessarily face an impossible future. Craftsmen aboard ships (carpenters, caulkers, and riggers) were predominantly black, including many of the masters, and they were paid the same wages as other artisans. This tradition extended back into the colonial period and did not disappear with the coming of independence.[11]

Examining the life of a printer, Manuel Ignacio Murillo, helps to illuminate both the possibilities and limits in the life of an artisan. Murillo was a nineteen-year-old with some smelting experience when Vicente Ramón Roca's brother Francisco imported a printing press in 1820 and set it up in a storefront in the town hall. He smelted the letters and demonstrated aptitude in setting up the new equipment and so became a valued employee. At first the *Imprenta de Guayaquil* was under the direction of one Vicente Duque, but by 1827 Murillo was the *encargado* (the person in charge), who made reports directly to the City Council. The printing office was a busy place where an efficient person might make a difference: the workers printed not only the newspaper *El Patriota de Guayaquil*, but also other papers and large numbers of pamphlets and private orders.

They handled subscriptions and advertisements and may even have done some of the writing. When a character was damaged, they needed to make it over themselves, as there were no more experienced letter-smelters in the city. Until it was fixed, they used their ingenuity: the British pound symbol turned upside down, for example, could serve as a *J* in a pinch.[12] In June of 1828 Murillo advertised that his contracted period as the *encargado* was up; the city was requesting bids for taking over the press and its tools. Apparently, no one responded. In July the City Council decided that their budget could no longer allow for paying the newspaper's required salaries and stock: they would actually give the equipment to anyone who wanted it, provided the person would do all municipal printing free. Murillo responded that he would accept this bargain *if* the city would pay him a mere twenty-five pesos a month for their jobs, and the council agreed. As it turned out, Murillo accepted a bid from the city rather than the other way around. Murillo continued to gain confidence as the years passed, writing to the governor himself on official business and organizing the presentation of a comedy play, probably for profit. In the early 1830s the City Council decided that they did indeed need to maintain a press of their own rather than expecting a private printer to do everything they needed for twenty-five pesos a month: they signed contracts with a series of men and ran into numerous difficulties until finally they decided to give that business, too, to the experienced Murillo.[13]

Despite his successes, Murillo never became a rich man. In 1832, when he had accepted the city's contract, he was in the lowest or poorest category of people required to contribute a share of the "forced loans." He was thirty-one years old, as yet unmarried, and lived with his twenty-five-year-old sister María. They owned no slaves. On their block, which was far from the center of town, lived other artisans—mostly shoemakers and tinsmiths—who were not wealthy. Murillo himself was partially of African descent: a military captain who was one-quarter black was his direct ancestor, probably his grandfather. Although he did exceptionally well for himself, due to obvious talent and some good luck, there still existed clear boundaries he could not cross. He almost never mingled with the elite citizens except in his workshop. His success did make one key difference, however: probably because of it, his son was able to find backers to found a newspaper fifty years later that became Guayaquil's major daily. His grandson, in turn, was able to marry the rebellious daughter of a leading family directly descended from an encomendero. After his death, Manuel Ignacio Murillo was allotted an honorable paragraph in every genealogical dictionary of Guayaquileño society and for the first time was called "Don Manuel." In print, Dolores Arzube Febres Cordero was never acknowledged to have married the grandson of a commoner.[14]

The Professionals

Men and women who sold their services or their knowledge, rather than practicing a craft, were quite limited in their options. The legal profession was reserved for sons of the highest families, and the clergy did not welcome many children of the middling sorts. In the Andean highlands poor men frequently entered the ranks of the church, but in this commercial and secular city there were fewer regular churchgoers and thus fewer churches and relatively few opportunities for clerics. Not having a high status to lose, the *padres* were not jealous guardians of their own or their orders' reputations. In fact, they became notorious for wild living, and most of the public attention they received was negative: they were criticized for demanding unnecessary pay raises, for refusing to go and hear the confessions of the dying, and for womanizing. One *fray* so far forgot himself as to have an affair with a dancing girl. Her other lover became so enraged that he hired an assassin to do away with the priest. He apparently thought this would be more effective than making a public accusation, as his announcement would have surprised few people.[15]

Equally unfortunately for the ambitious, there were also few opportunities for architects or engineers. Although invisible in the census, they did exist as the partners of contractors or carpenters: those businesses wishing to design and then build the chapel for the new cemetery Pantheon were invited to request the necessary dimensions and instructions from the chief of police before submitting plans and bids. But for work requiring novel technical expertise, foreigners were often hired. "A foreign engineer, who has selflessly served our government many times, undertook to direct the work [of the new tribunal building]." These examples show that local builders certainly did develop practical experience and were able to construct needed projects; on the other hand, local builders apparently had not sought more advanced instruction in the most modern techniques. The relatively low demand for new kinds of buildings, bridges, or mills would have rendered the decision to seek higher education in this area a rather foolish one.[16]

The best opportunities existed on boats or in the military. Guayaquil's pilots were known for their skill in navigating the riverine network and were organized in their own formal union, with their own chief. Along with worthy heads of state, *los pilotos* were singled out in one government report as being necessary for the progress and development of any nation with port cities. British visitors acknowledged: "They know their business perfectly." Recognition in this case went hand-in-hand with pay: they received eighty pesos a month. Petty army officers could also do well for themselves. Their resumes indicate that they had to serve for many years and in many actions in order to be promoted, but they could advance; the inventories of their worldly goods at the end of their frequently truncated careers show that they were able to buy far more than most people in their city. They lived in rented rooms, rather than in houses of their own, but, in varying proportions, they owned several sets of clothing, pieces of silverwork, crystal, maps, and books.[17]

A far larger group, however, was the army of clerks and bureaucrats who worked for businesses and public offices and who were not deemed so indispensable as the pilots and military officers. They tended to occupy a set of rented rooms in one of the tiered buildings, being unable to afford the cost of a full house. In the public agencies, their salaries ranged from 300 to 500 pesos a year, while those of the directors were at least 1,000 pesos, although the clerks did literally all the documented work that has survived.[18] Though he could never become the director of an agency, a clerk could rise through the ranks to attain a better job. Domingo Sánchez, for example, worked for the tobacco administration in 1825 and had to spend at least part of his time away in the isolated town of Daule, but by 1827 he had been rewarded with a position in the Treasury Department. Rewards like these were attained partially through length of service, but they were also a question of merit. Sometimes a wealthy patron insisted on a candidate's merit, but the patronage system was not all-encompassing: often a candidate defended his own cause. "I, Francisco Ruiz Díaz, officer of the Post Office of this Department, . . . for the space of four years have served in this position with the delicacy of a good employee, giving to my superiors and to the public irrefutable proofs of my honesty and excellent comportment."[19]

The labor of these public servants was not highly valued by their superiors. Perhaps this was because there was always another white mestizo able to read who could take their place. Thus if a clerk quit, there would be no visible emergency. If an army officer quit, on the other hand, his company might go marauding; if a pilot quit, a merchant's ship might run aground. Their salaries were low enough so that there was no room for

them to involve themselves in the financial investments that their superiors made, and they were not supposed to operate any kind of business
on the side anyway. They frequently complained that they and their families could not live without the immediate receipt of their pay. The City
Council sometimes attempted to enforce reductions, but then the directors of city agencies, who did not usually advocate for the employees,
would finally speak. They insisted that they could not find a capable person who would work for a smaller amount of money or that it was ridicu-
lous for the state to cut workers' pay to save money so that—theoretically—the government might meet other state salary obligations (the
military's). Extra duties were added as a matter of course: once it was even
suggested that municipal office workers be required to patrol the streets
in shifts at night to strengthen the police force. An officer of the port felt
so overworked that he dared to use sarcasm in answering a reprimand
from the *intendente* about having fallen asleep on duty: "The priority work
of disembarking the last troops to arrive at this port in the corvette *Pichincha* and the schooner *María* kept me on the docks from two in the
morning till six, and needing some rest so that I could continue the paperwork, with the permission of the Comandante Mariano Necochea, I
retired to rest a little; thus I provide you with my reason for not being
awake at the time you sent me your much appreciated note."[20]

Clerks' salaries in merchant firms were known to be higher than they
were in government offices, but the work may have been more demanding
and possibly equally devalued. Certainly the workers had to be well qualified: one man advertised in the paper that he could speak and write Spanish, French, English, Italian, Portuguese, German, Greek, and a bit of
Quechua! The merchants' guild once claimed they were temporarily unable to pay their employees, but the same members later became enraged
when the scribe at their Saturday morning meetings said he had other
responsibilities that day at another job he held. The man quit, and the
merchants announced that in future they wanted someone who would be
willing to work only for them.[21]

Some professionals were what we would today call "self-employed."
These included musicians, doctors, and tutors. The possibility that almost
anyone with a bit of talent might work in one of these areas began to
disappear in the early republican period, as professional structures—and
therefore strictures—multiplied. Leaders in these fields, like the artisan
maestros mayores, were concerned with proving that they were *not* just anyone; they were anxious to tighten policies of exclusion. In 1828, for the

first time, the *maestro mayor* of the musicians asked the City Council to pass an ordinance denying musicians the right to play for private parties without a license issued by him. Four other musicians protested this idea vehemently. The results of the debate are unclear, but the fact remains that this type of regulation was now under serious discussion.[22]

A similar issue appeared in the medical field in the same years. Traditionally, there were several kinds of practitioners, but their work often overlapped. Barbers sometimes let blood, but they were not officially *flebotomistas* (bloodletters and pharmacists) registered in their own guild. A surgeon or *cirujano* had more medical knowledge or at least experience than the latter and might serve as the only medical man on board a warship. Still, not being a "doctor," a surgeon remained officially of lower value: he earned not more than forty pesos a month in the military hospital, less on shipboard, while a man who had been to a medical school in some part of the world claimed seventy pesos a month in the same military hospital. In reality, any of these could earn almost equivalent amounts in private practice if accepted as "doctors." On the surface, these groups seemed to coexist rather peacefully. Then in 1827, without publicizing his reasons, the public prosecutor announced that *flebotomistas* who had not been officially examined would no longer be allowed to open their own shops. One year later the chief of police called a meeting of all doctors, surgeons, and pharmacists and announced that all of their establishments must henceforth advertise who had authorized them to practice under their respective titles and that an official committee would be visiting their shops to regulate the prices of medicines. In 1830 the law went so far as to specify that none but licensed doctors could practice and, more concretely, that only doctors could prescribe medicine and that barbers were not to be caught bleeding patients. According to a British commentator, these different types of medical practitioners were all "persons of color"—by which he meant not *negros* or *indígenas*, but rather various mixtures that only excluded pure-blooded Spanish. None of them were accepted in elite social circles as equals. But the leading professors of medicine, the trained doctors, did visit the elite in their houses. They gave and received favors. Dr. Manuel José Brava was called *mulato;* although he could not have married a merchant's daughter, he was widely respected and his presence much in demand. Men like Dr. Brava, who had something to gain by separating themselves from the more plebeian medical practitioners, were probably the ones who urged the changes in policy instituted by the authorities.[23]

The teaching profession offered opportunities to other professionals. Traditionally, teachers practiced their trade by hanging out a sign or placing an advertisement until they had sufficiently developed their clientele. They offered music, French, math, or "liberal arts" to likely young people or adults. These people also worked part-time for private schools like San Ignacio de Loyola and the Escuela Náutica. The best paid of these received only about twenty pesos a month. The directors of the latter two institutions, who were gentlemen by birth, were the only educators in the city to be paid significant salaries, earning over 1,000 pesos a year. Once the employees of the Colegio San Ignacio actually protested, not so much against the large discrepancy, but against what they felt to be an injustice that occurred during the Peruvian occupation: during that time the school had been shut down and teachers went unpaid, except for the director, who continued to draw his own substantial salary. The governor sided with the director, and the teachers were forced to withdraw their complaint.[24]

In the late 1820s teachers also did battle to protect their professional turf. At that time, according to the mandate of the Quito government, the city founded the required set of public schools. Teachers who ran their own miniature primary schools for neighborhood children were concerned about the appearance of the new normal schools: an exam would determine who might become a teacher, rather than social acceptance in the small world they had previously controlled through the extension or withholding of mutual recommendations and referrals. They badmouthed the "Lancasterian" system upon which the schools were based. According to the plan a teacher taught a few monitors who then turned around and taught subsections of a large class. Elite city officials, enraged that their project schools were being condemned by local teachers, debated the possibility of requiring that *all* teachers who advertised lessons of any kind be able to pass a publicly administered examination. Possibly because of this struggle, the city at first had difficulty in finding teachers willing to work in the normal schools, despite the relatively high advertised salaries. When they finally had a list of men and women who had signed up and passed their exams and were willing to work in the city or in the surrounding provinces, an article praising the teachers' patriotism appeared in one of the newspapers.[25]

The traditional teachers' concerns proved not without foundation. The new bureaucratic procedures made it possible for people to enter the field who would not previously have been able to convince their neighbors that they were respectable and knowledgeable enough to teach. A man whose handwriting was barely legible and who had obviously been given little formal training begged that he be allowed to present himself for the examination in order to prove himself and become a public school teacher.[26] By the mid-1830s there were so many teachers available that the government could pay the man working in the poorest parish less than the legally required thirty to thirty-five pesos per month. Although he complained about his treatment, his position was precarious. There were many men and women able to teach themselves to read and eager to enter the ranks of the "personas decentes" if allowed any channel.

The Entrepreneurs

It is impossible to count the number of Guayaquileños with little or no capital who nonetheless hatched schemes for making money. Small ship captains sometimes entered into a form of partnership with the owner. Handling all the booking, loading, unloading, and duty payments, they apparently kept some share of the profits, although it is unclear how much.[27] Many people who started out with even less went into business as peddlers. They would borrow money from a local merchant with whom they had a personal connection of some kind. It was never a large amount: 80 or 120 pesos or the right to use a small rowboat. They would carry city goods to rural areas and try to sell them at a profit. Sometimes the plan worked very well: at least one man was able to make enough to maintain one wife in Guayaquil and another in Daule. But often goods were damaged or failed to sell, and the men wound up in court for failure to pay the debt to the sponsoring merchant. For women it was harder to work as wandering peddlers themselves, but they still managed to participate in the business. Felipa Andrade lived in Guayaquil but operated a small business in Caracól by sending men out to buy goods and transport them to the little town by the sea. Of course, this was risky: she was badly burned when she gave one Manuel Bersoso 180 pesos and he never came back.[28]

The pooling of resources through marriage could also launch a business. Women with sizable dowries could maintain a small herd of cattle on the savanna and build a butter- and cheese-making business, though they could never afford to become sellers of hides, like the large landowners. María Francisca Alvarado married her husband when they were both young and poor and recently orphaned. He was a carpenter and built them a house, but never rose to a very good position. She, meanwhile, slowly built a small herd of cattle out on the savanna. Twenty years after their marriage, her husband was living with another woman. María Francisca wanted a divorce and half of their "fortune." María de la Cruz Castro had brought her husband a huge dowry for one of her class (500 pesos) and with it they had built a small dairy that produced about 500 pesos a year. She remained firmly in control of the family finances until her death, when she distributed the property among her husband and seven children.[29]

A few entrepreneurs found that profits were to be made in entertainment activities. Domingo Gonzales, who also later bid on the military hospital pharmacy contract, drove a hard bargain with the municipality in settling on a contract for running the cock-fighting pit. He was offered sole rights for five years if he would turn over 800 pesos a year to the government, but he was not satisfied. He said that the start-up cost of building a modern amphitheater would be extravagantly high and that he wanted sole rights for ten years. He got ten years, but at a cost of 1,200 pesos per annum. Apparently finding the activity less profitable than he had thought, he later extricated himself from the deal.[30] Those with fewer resources available opted for smaller projects: they sponsored one-day horse races and acrobatic shows, opened another billiard hall, built pleasant shacks for bathers by the riverside.[31]

Illegal entertainment schemes could be profitable, but they were dangerous. A woman named Beatriz López who operated a bar decided to take a risk by allowing illegal gambling in her establishment. She was fined once and had her name published in the papers to shame her. She continued to allow the profitable but reprehensible activity and was caught again when her gamesters cheated the wrong person (an angry priest). In court Beatriz attempted to draw on public support for people who had to pay *empréstitos* although they were too poor and on images of women as unable to fend for themselves: "The debts that plague me are huge, for I have to pay 50 pesos a month for the rooms I use and 32 pesos within four months for the taxes levied against me . . . The solution I chose was motivated by the fact that I am a pitiable woman who cannot bargain for herself." The judge was unmoved and forced her to sell the tavern.[32] Like many others, Beatriz López had tried to make the most of her circumstances. She took a risk, and in this case she lost.

Given the limited nature of the print culture, Beatriz and other entrepreneurs relied on word-of-mouth and on demonstrations of the attractiveness of their establishments to advertise their businesses. They had to assess risks and potential profits and make their decisions. Although it was illegal for bars to remain open after hours, for example, and they sometimes were fined for doing so, many owners chose to leave their doors wide open far into the night, letting the light and music and laughter stream out into the street. Although it was illegal to sell pornographic engravings from Europe, Telemaco Guillén distributed enough of them to bring large numbers of customers to his store in the Ciudad Vieja. When caught, he managed to convince the authorities that he had no idea he was doing wrong, since they were living in an age of independence and freedom.[33] A few business owners attempted to use newspapers to advertise in a more "legitimate" manner, but these were generally *avisos* or announcements that someone had a particularly large or fine supply of an item, rather than attempts to generate special interest in an establishment.

Craftsmen, as we have seen, still administered their shops personally, directing the handiwork themselves: generally not even the most successful experimented with expansion into a manufactory with divided labor. Yet when a larger demand for a certain good appeared, there were entrepreneurs who responded. Ignacio Roldán and Miguel Palacio expanded their bakeshop into an industrial bakery during the wars, hiring only one baker to help supervise and then buying the time of untrained slaves to do specific tasks as directed. What made them more adventurous than Petra Paredes, for example, who never moved her business beyond its one oven? Apparently the answer was that they had plenty of customers who could afford to pay, as they had received contracts to provide bread to the military hospital, the army, and several warships.[34]

The Middling Ranks in Public:
Civic Involvement and the Economy

It is easier to see how the middling sorts defined their work and strategized in their careers than it is to learn how they envisioned their broader relationships to the polity and economy. They were usually absent from official public spectacles. On July 13, 1822, for instance, over three hundred "heads of family" met in Guayaquil to ratify Simón Bolívar's decision regarding the political fate of their city. All three hundred signed an elaborately worded document. Most of them were fine men in fine clothes, not middling sorts. Only a handful were master craftsmen and lower-echelon priests or other professionals.[35] From today's vantage point, it is difficult to determine exactly how many of the middle-ranking citizens of Guayaquil felt themselves to be intimately involved with politics and public decisions or how many thought of such matters at all. First of all, they were not generally expected to vote. When Ecuador's first constitution was later promulgated in 1830, many of them were officially excluded: suffrage was limited to literate heads of household over twenty-two having at least 300 pesos in property or a firmly defined profession. (Servants and day laborers were specifically excluded, so that there could be no upset if any of them should happen to come up with 300 pesos.)

Almost none of the middling sorts subscribed to the city's newspapers. There were a few exceptions, such as Gaspar Casanova, the municipal notary public, and Fernando Sáenz, the master of carpenters. But some of them probably bought individual copies of the papers, which were always available for sale in certain bookstores at about two reales each. Certainly some of the printed debates were directly related to their own lives, and the authors of the articles called for their enthusiasm or caution: a circulating pamphlet insisted that average citizens were about to benefit mightily from the destruction of former monopolies over commerce, and an anonymous writer from the provinces warned that six unnamed families were attempting even as he spoke to use independence for their own aggrandizement.[36]

We can guess what responses to such articles probably were, based on observations of people's actions when they faced other demands for civic involvement: they generally tried to elude participation in public life, viewing it as more of a burden than a privilege. In fact they saw it as something of a disaster to be named by the municipality to the post of *teniente corregidor* of a parish. As such, a man was responsible for composing tax lists, making collections, and generally maintaining discipline. To avoid the responsibility, those named often claimed illness, a need to work full-time to support a family, or inability to read and write. Only the last excuse was officially acceptable, so usually the men were eventually forced to serve. Being an important employee of an *hacienda* was another legitimate excuse, as the large landholders did not want to lose their best accountants and foremen. When elite city officials attempted to organize a local brigade of guards, they complained again of a lack of popular enthusiasm, themselves evincing a lack of respect for the middling sorts. "[We must relate to the Government] the story of the storekeepers and other vagabonds who have missed roll call every Sunday and Thursday, and who have collected their matriculation papers [only] to make sure that they will not be drafted, and in this way have avoided any kind of public service." [37]

City elites also found that although they tried to present being included on certain tax lists as an honor or mark of civic involvement, it was not always perceived in this way. Regular taxes were imposed only on the Indians, but in times of need "forced loans" were frequently demanded of the upper-level citizens. The rates assigned to each household were somewhat progressive. But at one point a city official admitted frankly in a letter to the *intendente* that in order to raise the quantity collected many citizens had been listed in a higher category than they should have been. Another tax which was mildly progressive was the street lighting tax, but it, too, in reality fell most heavily on the middling ranks. The "principal houses" and major commercial addresses paid twelve reales each, and the small houses and *chinganas* only eight—but eight was a much larger share of their income than twelve was for the rich. Flat taxes imposed only on the businesses of the middling sorts sparked overt resistance: when the city government tried to collect four pesos from each small grocery store in 1828, the owners made it necessary for the collector to call in armed Customshouse guards. [38]

Leading villagers in neighboring Indian communities on the savanna and further afield responded with even greater rage. Unlike whites or white mestizos, they could not accept these taxes as at least a flattering mark of their identity, proof that they were more than *indios*. Those Indians who owned more than one thousand pesos' worth of property were defined as "citizens" under the new republic; they had all the rights and responsibilities of other middle-ranked citizens. They were no longer allowed to speak for the *indios* as they were no longer their legal peers, and they owed forced-loan tax payments. Not surprisingly, rather than being gratified, they protested vehemently. One man wrote that he had been unjustly *accused* of being a citizen. [39]

Although in general the middling sorts would not have said they felt accused of citizenship, they clearly were excluded from the process of deciding how tax monies were to be spent. Given that they rarely saw the results benefiting themselves, and often bore the financial burden, they never made demands of their own for urban improvements which they felt would only end up costing them more than they were worth. Their situation in the early republic was not uniformly bleak, however. The founding of a public school system in 1826 formed a partial exception to the patterns of exclusion that middle-ranked people experienced. The elites, as we have seen, were interested to some extent in experimenting with definitions of citizenship. It remained to be seen what the middle-ranking people believed they got out of it.

After receiving word of the new national law passed in Bogotá requiring the building of the schools, Guayaquil's municipality began to take concrete steps—finding sites for classrooms, searching for teachers and a director, hiring a porter for the office. There were 120 students enrolled almost immediately, but we do not know who they were. It is difficult to determine exactly whom the city officials intended that the schools should serve. The surviving correspondence implies that, although the most elite families never planned to send their sons, the school planners also never had in mind the poorest folk. The sons of upper-level artisans and doctors and small businessmen were apparently the targeted population. The City Council, for example, insisted that the teachers did not have the right to expel students who misbehaved—a stance they most likely would not have taken regarding day laborers' and peddlers' children. They later insisted that all *padres de familia* meet to discuss the new schools' progress and predicaments, definitely indicating that they did not have in mind a collection of *zambos* and Indians.[40] By 1829 there were two functioning public schools, one with fifty-five students and the other with seventy, but they continued to struggle financially for lack of funding.

There were also a limited number of scholarship students—no more than eight at any one time—in the elite Colegio San Ignacio Loyola: these boys had a choice of paying back the school in money once they started working or serving six years in the *marina* instead. Even they, though, came from the upper echelons of the middling sorts or from wealthy families currently in financial straits: one well-known doctor, for example, had graduated from the school as a scholarship student. Theoretically, the only requirements were that a boy be the legitimate son of free parents with good manners and a previous knowledge of reading and writing. Yet these seemingly loose rules could ensure that there was no room for a peddler's son and many other children of similar background.[41]

The children learned young—whether their parents were artisans, professionals, or entrepreneurs—that they could never expect the rights, privileges, or pay of the elite citizens. Murillo and his cohort worked hard: there can be no question of that in looking at the remaining records of their efforts. A number, as we have seen, maximized possible profits within their own niche, but they could not challenge the parameters of the niche. When they were fully counted as citizens or members of the *pueblo* in any way, it was usually so that the elite members of the government might make exactions upon them, rather than elicit their opinions. Probably for that reason, there is no record of their suggesting any public projects, such as new streets, bridges, or schools. To the extent that they were offered education, it was largely to enable boys to do as their fathers had done. They could have a better life than the majority, but they could not ask for more than their own parents had possessed. Even the extraordinarily successful Murillo, who rose from a young errand boy to be the city's leading printer, never owned significant property or attained the title *don* in his lifetime. His family would wait for the grandson's generation for begrudging acceptance by the elites and then received it as a single exception.

In this context the pervasive pattern seen in trade after trade of devoting their early republican energies to processes of delimitation and exclusion of those beneath them appears understandable, some might even say commendable. The middling ranks were fighting to define themselves in the best way they could. Despite hard work, theirs was a precarious position, never entirely secure, never very well rewarded. They had no opportunity to move beyond the limits imposed both legally and informally. So they expended their energy where they might see some results—in distinguishing themselves from the masses. The soldier Pedro certainly did his best in this regard, choosing to insist that he was above the class of *indios*, rather than saying something to the effect that he had the military behind him. He found it more effective to demonstrate who he was not, rather than who he was.

CHAPTER 6

THE QUEST OF THE

CONTRIBUTING CITIZENS

The Middling Ranks of Baltimore

Frederick Bailey found life difficult in the shipyards where his master hired him out to work. He had not expected to confront any tensions. "Until a very little while before I went there, white and black ship carpenters worked side by side." But suddenly the white carpenters began to define solidarity among themselves as being equivalent to the exclusion of certain others. "All at once, the white carpenters knocked off, and swore they would no longer work on the same stage with free negroes." Things progressed by the day; the hostilities shortly extended to all "the niggers," including the slaves. "My fellow apprentices very soon began to feel it to be degrading to work with me," Douglass later remembered. It was not long before they physically attacked and nearly killed him.[1] Not long before these events, a group of white carters had similarly attempted to have free black men banned from their profession. They first submitted a complaint in 1827 and were ignored—apparently even by most of their fellow draymen—but then pushed harder the following year and succeeded in having the issue brought up in the State Assembly. The lawmakers were unwilling to give a group of carters such power over their competition, however, and they had to remain content to work side by side with free blacks.[2]

These events were particularly striking in their context. Generally, Baltimoreans' assertions of their political and economic rights went hand in hand with the assertion that the speakers were themselves a part of the polity and the economy, rather than the assertion that certain others were not. This was traditionally as true of the carters as of everyone else. In 1827, for instance, the same year in which a few of their disgruntled brethren began to complain about the black competition, most of the draymen, black and white, were busy working together to try to resolve their "informer" problem. Every summer, as everyone knew, the fleas of Baltimore had a field day. The horses suffered especially, strapped to their carts and quite unable to relieve the itching. The drivers of empty carts often left them standing on one side of a city street in Fell's Point, while they went down to the wharves to rustle up a job. Then the irritated beasts would begin to jerk backward, pushing their carts until they crashed into other masterless horses and wagons behind. A man short of money was nearly always on the lookout: as soon as he saw one of these tangled messes he would run for a bailiff and report that a certain driver had failed to maintain the required distance of twenty-five feet from the nearest standing cart. Informers were careful to ascertain that the bailiff recorded their names, so that they could receive half the fine collected.

In 1827 sixty-three draymen submitted a petition to the City Council complaining of these "hourly vexatious suits." They began by insisting on their rights: "We the subscribers, owners and drivers of carts within the City of Baltimore beg leave respectfully to represent that we and each of us contribute to the funds of the City by paying taxes on our real and personal property or by paying for licenses to use our carts on the streets of the City."[3] The men went on to make a practical suggestion, that they be allowed to park their carts "with the tails to the curbstone" so that the curb would act as a brake when the horses attempted to shove the carts backward. Their plan was approved, but the council's problems with the demanding carters did not disappear. Arguments continued over their right to park in certain genteel streets and over the rights of rural and urban wagoners to park near the market the evening before market day. Ordinances were passed and repealed, with the mayor sometimes being drawn into the fray. At one point he vetoed a movement to place chains across the avenues of the markets to keep horses and carts out until a given hour. His vision of the moment when the hour arrived, the chains were removed, and the assertive carters were free to make their dash for a position was a veritable nightmare: "All the officers of the City could not prevent the state of confusion that would inevitably ensue, and which may be more easily imagined than described."[4]

The draymen were not the only Baltimoreans to argue that as contributing citizens they had the right to command attention. Even a man who could barely write was convinced of the importance of his participation to society as a whole: "This petion [sic] to the honour of City Council on account of my fire buckets that was lost in the public servis as they are recorded in the register by Mr. Hargrove and i wish that your honours please to grant me some satisfaction for them as your honours think proper. Your friend, Anthony Fleishull."[5] Anthony, we may note, did not hesitate to refer to the councilmen as his "friends" even as he also called them "your honours." In another case a number of residents of Old Town next to Fell's Point had a meeting to produce a document demanding flagstones that would allow them to cross even the muddiest streets. They felt strongly that the fact that they lived in the poorer section of town "east of the Falls" (and bordering Fell's Point) should not mean that their neighborhood ought to be left out of the municipal budget:

These houses are all . . . tenanted by a meritorious class of citizens who of course contribute to the public fund and expect their own and the public convenience promoted, in common with other sections of the city. And, it is believed to be the common custom to furnish at least one set of flagstones at each intersection. Baltimore Street, west of Jones' Falls, it is believed has long since received at every intersection, the attention now solicited for these intersections; and if they do happen to be East of the Falls, the undersigned cannot see any reason for passing them by unnoticed . . . [6]

The people who expressed themselves in this way had at least two recent experiences of public debate about the rights and responsibilities of contributors to society: the processes of street widenings and street paving were occurring all around them and making a great impact on small property owners. Not everybody owned a small plot of ground or a house, but almost everybody had at least one near neighbor who did, and the processes were too noticeable to everybody, including renters, to escape attention. When people petitioned the city because of the loss of a home due to eminent domain, they did not always win what they were demanding—whether it was a tax break or a larger reimbursement—but they sometimes did; it was clear to everyone that as taxpayers—or at least license buyers—they had the right to make their request.[7]

It was not a monolithic segment of the populace who believed that they were owed something by their society in exchange for what they contributed. In fact, these were people of widely varying types. They ranged from the sweating draymen urging on their horses to the well-dressed and precise accountant William Murray, who had joined his neighbors in demanding flagstones for the Old Town section so that, as the signers put it, they would not get their shoes muddy on the way to church. Despite their differences, these groups did share not only their sense of entitlement but also a lack of desperation. None of them starved; the poorest would not perform just any task, even for money. The elite merchant Sam Spafford wrote to his country relation: "I have been through the Market talking with the Butchers about your Cattle—they say the weather is too hot at present to leave home, when the weather gets a little cooler I think I will get some of them to go up [to Cecil County]."[8] Meanwhile, William Murray added up his family's expenditures with great concern. They kept one servant, no horses, and a modest house. Yet they overspent their income. "Without retrenchment we shall soon be in a bad way," he moaned in his diary. However, his experience of a crisis did not indicate that the wolf was at the door, but rather that he had gotten carried away in the purchase of such things as new clothing, an extra stove, and some baby-sized furniture.[9]

These people lived near each other in relatively mixed neighborhoods. They avoided the poorest narrow alleys and could not afford the lovely streets where there were only one, two, or three houses to a block. But between these extremes there were many blocks of mostly rented two-story brick row houses "in good repair" and with numerous windows. Frederick Bailey's master, the foreman of a shipyard, lived on Aliceanna Street in Fell's Point surrounded by wealthy families and laborers. Seamstress Maria Clemm (Edgar Allan Poe's aunt) rented the upper floor of a corner house in Old Town while a drayman rented the floor below her, and on their block lived two laborers whose families shared one house, two widows of sea captains, the merchant son of a master wheelwright, a customs official, a successful brickmaker, and a small bookstore keeper.[10] Before we try to decide how much these people had in common or did not, it will help to look more closely at each group. Then we can return to the same questions asked in the last chapter: how did they believe they could succeed and how did they strategize? How did they relate to others?

The Artisans

The work of artisans was spoken of with respect by people around them. When a master artisan wanted to obtain a contract, he often emphasized the skill of his journeymen. "I have constantly in my employ the best mechanicks . . ." "I . . . have in my employ the best of workmen—my materials are new, and I will agree to do all work at short notice . . ." "In addition to [my] former good workmen in the bell-hanging line, [I] have employed an extra superior hand, just from London, who has worked for the nobility."[11] An artisanal tradition of pride in one's work was old even in a relatively young city such as Baltimore, where most men did something similar to the work their fathers or fathers' friends had done. The proportions of the types of artisans remained almost unchanged from the years immediately after the Revolution. At the end of the War of 1812 those in the clothing industries still made up 28 percent of tradesmen; those in the construction trades had gone from 25 to 21 percent; those in shipbuilding were still about 12 percent.[12]

Informal guilds had been and still were active in celebrating their members' accomplishments. They participated, for example, in the grand and memorable 1828 parade in honor of the laying of the first stone of the new railroad, advertising with dramatic symbols the sources of their pride. In that parade, 100 or more marchers generally represented each trade: bakers, tailors, blacksmiths, tinsmiths, millwrights, weavers, dyers, carpenters, stonecutters, masons, bricklayers, painters, cabinetmakers, chairmakers, tanners, shoemakers, hatters, machine-makers, coopers, saddlers, coachmakers, wheelwrights, coppersmiths, printers, bookbinders, jewelers, silversmiths, glass cutters, ship carpenters, pump-makers, ropemakers, riggers, and, finally, sea captains. They came with giant floats, on which they had prepared huge displays, which were all very dramatic and demonstrative of pride. The blacksmiths had a clanging, red-hot working shop atop their stage. The weavers and dyers had their effigy of Britannia, weeping for her lost trade in textile exports. The carpenters had piously built a temple of wood. The stonecutters offered four pure white horses carting a load of white marble. The saddlers impressed the audience with two Arabian-clad grooms leading beautiful horses. The coachmakers displayed a modern, elegant barouche. The ship captains, coming last, had placed a real ship called *The Union* on wheels; for this day only, the captains had become the crew, in the age-old pattern of reversal on festival days.[13] In a twist that was becoming more typical, only black craftsmen were excluded. Even some white women marched.

Master tradesmen were largely the ones who orchestrated and participated in these memorable displays, benefiting from the power they already had and at the same time increasing the esteem in which they were held. It was no accident that James Mosher, a bricklayer, and Robert Carey Long, a carpenter, who grew to be successful builders, also both took leading roles in trade organizations: the former was president of the Apprentices' Library, and the latter secretary of the Carpenters' Society. People who achieved such respected positions carefully cultivated their power in several ways outside of their professional activities as well. They established themselves as patrons in informal relationships with others. Nowhere is this more evident than in the records of "Mister Barney." Bernard Labroquère was a well-known white cooper who had fled Saint-Domingue in the wake of the successful slave revolution there. He was about twenty when he arrived and at first worked as a journeyman for other coopers at $1.50 per day. After about twelve years he went into business for himself and, at the same time, began to put poorer men in his debt: for William Rose, who could not sign his name, he rented a shoe-making shop, probably in exchange for part of the profits. He sold some tools to John Ashland and later bailed him out of debtor's prison. He offered to pay for the schooling of the son of his two indentured servants.[14]

Master craftsmen also asserted themselves through legal channels. When a group of bread hawkers and small bakers—including one woman—petitioned to be allowed to sell loaves lighter than the legally required minimum on grounds that their poorest customers could only afford small ones, the established bakers—all male and better-known—flew into action. They wrote to the City Council: "The fact is, Gentlemen, your petitioners want the trade *totally unrestricted:* should this ever be the case, then the Public may look out!!—There are a few bakers who are not prepared to go all lengths!! . . . The signers [of the petition] may be *Pharasees* [*sic*] or *Publicans;* but as to that we care not, convinced as we are, that they are not the friends of the Poor!!"[15] The bakeries continued to be regulated.

Apprentices as a matter of course became journeymen, and a large percentage—at least a large minority—later chose to set themselves up in business as master craftsmen, who had the potential to gain profits and notoriety.[16] The life of William Minifrie provides an interesting illustration of the extent to which the ambitions of a young carpenter were likely to be achieved. He was born in England and by 1828, at age twenty-two, had completed his apprenticeship to a carpenter. His diary was full of "going to America." As part of his preparations, he wed his sweetheart Mary in January ("Went to Parson Lanes to get the License, was told to look grave, Laughed all the time"); in March they sailed for Baltimore, where his uncle lived, arriving on April 7.[17] They walked about town and rented a room with money he had brought with him, probably due to the generosity of his family. One week after docking Minifrie spent $2.25 on some pine wood and "begun to work" on furniture for himself and Mary, which might possibly also have served as a public sample of his craftsmanship. He also began to attend different churches, clearly with a view to choosing the congregation that most pleased him—and would, possibly, serve as the best social network. By May 5 he still had not found employment with a master carpenter, but his uncle began to hire him irregularly to do odd jobs.

Another month went by. On June 3 he had a fight with his wife, and on June 4 he suddenly became much more active in looking for regular work. "Went to several places to try to get work . . . none to be had, some thoughts of going to Philadelphia." This time he was persistent, though, and within less than a week he was working for a Mr. Denny, sometimes in his shop and sometimes aboard a boat. After this, Minifrie worked hard by his own standards—mentioning his labors in his diary on almost all days except Sundays—but he also recorded a serious amount of drinking in "porter cellars" with his friends. And on two Sundays that summer he and Mary spent money on excursions—a day trip on a steamer and a trip to a revival meeting outside the city, which he found highly entertaining. By the end of August they felt they could afford to rent an ordinary small house in Fleet Street for $6 a month. In September his uncle paid him for the work he had done for him when he first came to Baltimore, and that same day Minifrie recorded purchasing the first clothing he had bought since his arrival (a pair of pants). During the autumn he also bought a small stove, some pieces of furniture, and some books at an auction.[18] The books may have included some of the guides for builders interested in adding to their knowledge through study. There were several such guides available, such as *The Practical Builder's Assistant* and *The Timber Merchant's Guide*.[19]

Minifrie's diary reveals him to have been a man of zest and good humor, and he was probably a talented craftsman as well, for he seemed to impress numerous customers. He did not record making any connections through churchgoing, but he did use religious holidays to good effect: on Christmas day he went duck hunting with a group of friends. On February 9, 1829, after only eight months of working, he recorded that he "quit Denny's employ." He then worked directly for various clients, and on April 13 he felt ready to rent a shop and house on Baltimore Street in Old Town for $10 a month. Less than ten years later he announced himself an "Architect and Builder" and became very successful. In Minifrie's case, his youthful enthusiasm had not proven mistaken. He had moved up according to the classic design. Nor was he alone in this. Indeed others, such as Robert Carey Long, became far better known and died wealthier. Minifrie had advantages not shared by the most destitute: these included an established connection in Baltimore, a family nest egg large enough to pay his passage over and leave him something with which to get started, and the skin color and social graces necessary to win the confidence of paying clients. His advantages, however, were hardly unique; it is easy to find similar success stories.

Artisans who had more difficulty in obtaining clients than did Minifrie had various options to expand their base. They might, for example, do cheaper work available to more people. Carriage maker John Finley in the spring of 1830 suddenly began to submit a splashy, noticeable advertisement with a large picture to the *Baltimore Gazette*, in which he mentioned, to those who might not have been in the habit of thinking that they could afford a carriage, that he was quite willing to sell coaches secondhand. He was also in the business of repairing coaches for their owners; there came a point when the wealthy might decide to sell their old coaches to the craftsman. Craftsmen could develop client bases outside of the city in addition to their customers in town. Brassfounder Ebenezer Hubball offered: "Workmen sent to any part of the country within the distance of two days travelling." The craftsmen brought their own tools to the site and were expected to pay for the food they consumed. Yet it was considered desirable work. Even in his most successful years, cooper Bernard Labroquère was willing to take one journeyman and travel to Virginia.[20]

Other artisans attempted to obtain work from the municipality to supplement their income from individual clients. When the Washington Monument was built, for example, even though most of the pieces were imported, several local artisans provided services: William Woodall (pumpmaker), John Jubb (scaffolding carpenter), Mordecai Kennedy (blacksmith), Willard Rhodes (glazier), George and Michael Warner (brickmakers), James Hinds (bricklayer), John Hitzelberger (carpenter), and Mrs. Rebecca Clackner (stonecutter).[21] The city's business, however, proved disappointing to many. The workers were paid with "paper money": they first went to present a bill to the City Commissioners' office, which issued a "voucher" that had to be signed by all three commissioners. The recipients then took this piece of paper to the City Register, where they received a check to be drawn on a local bank. When the city was short of money, however, petty tradespeople did not always receive permission to turn in their vouchers for checks. Helen Wolff, widow of Samuel Wolff, pumpmaker, wrote to the city begging to be paid at least part of the $71.62 the city had owed her late husband. Others wrote on their own behalf that they felt poorly used by the "gentlemen."[22] They were almost always eventually paid, but delay caused hardship. Perhaps because artisans who were once bitten were twice shy, or perhaps because city officials chose to spread the wealth, most people who presented bills to the municipality did so only once or twice.

A small handful of men received contracts for the majority of all city work done: Frederick Crey, Matthew Benzinger, William Barker, and Alexander McDonald. They were clearly men who had started with some capital and considered themselves businessmen or "contractors" more than craftsmen. Yet the first two had some experience as actual pavers and builders, probably from their youth, and apparently had not received a gentleman's education, as they were poor spellers. Barker called himself a shipbuilder and charged $2.00 a day for his time, a master artisan's wage. Crey and Benzinger, who worked separately during the 1820s (the former as a paver and the latter as a wharf and bridge repairman), had combined forces to form one firm by 1830. They had two more investing partners, whose names did not appear on any records of the actual work done, but who apparently helped by offering their credit for the bonding that the city insisted upon for large jobs.[23] The minutes of the meetings of the city commissioners and the signed contracts reveal that Crey & Benzinger received almost every job they wanted, even when other contractors put in similar bids. It could be that the commissioners simply trusted the familiar or that they had been bribed. But the one explanation for which there is some real evidence is that the city officials were content to work with companies large and strong enough to withstand delayed payments without complaint. They were constantly in debt to Crey & Benzinger. Indeed, after the spring of 1830, when Alexander McDonald went ahead and began work on a certain job without any advance payment or even any assurance that he would be paid, he, too, began to receive larger contracts.[24]

For some artisans, the key to material success did not lie in any of the common techniques of cultivating work in rural areas, or reselling used goods, or obtaining municipal contracts. Instead, some of them considered the possibility of expanding their shops to manufactories and producing more. We have seen how their activities in this area, both alone and in partnership with certain merchants, led to a major political argument in the city and that those interested in manufactories eventually won the day. They could not have known then that the event marked the beginning of the end for artisans as a significant social force.

The Professionals

Law, medicine, and the church generally drew from the upper ranks in Baltimore, but despite this there were numerous other opportunities for those who had some education or special experience. Men who navigated the rivers and the seas formed a large contingent in Baltimore. The pilots were much better paid than ordinary seamen. Immediately after the Revolution, a law was passed in Maryland requiring that they be tested and registered in order to practice. It was also required that a pilot own a small boat; but as many of them could not afford this alone, they formed partnerships among themselves. So many black men used this career as an avenue for advancement that after the War of 1812 a law was passed that every pilot must have at least one white apprentice. (This fact raises the as-yet unanswered question as to whether there were white boys training under black men, as would seem necessarily to have been the case.) On board ships, they were treated with respect and often received food as good as the captain's. Nor did they have to travel for lengthy periods, as ships always put them ashore on their way out to sea at Cape Henry. Ordinary fishermen could do extraordinarily well in certain seasons if they owned their own boats. A young white man who did not have a boat but did have an education could sign on as a ship's officer. Petty officers could hope to work their way up to the rank of captain, and a captain was free to join the ship owners in engaging in merchant trading, to whatever degree he could afford.[25]

Jacob Hugg had just such a career. He was the youngest of six children and was raised by his mother alone, for his father, a small grocery store operator, died when he was a small child. When he was a young man he went to sea for the wages. In 1821 he was hired as shipmaster for the first time. His letters home included thoughtful observations of the people in the South American cities he visited. Probably because he was so attuned to his environment, he was able to gather information quickly when he arrived in each port, and his employers apparently learned to trust him to make marketing decisions. He wrote to his brother from Río: "[I] hear the market is overstocked with flour and that is our principle [sic] cargo—we shall sail tomorrow for the River Plate." When he was not writing letters, he used at least some of his leisure time to practice his handwriting on the pages of the ship logs. He copied out endlessly such sayings as "Frugality with industry is Duty of man" or "Riches have wings." Occasionally, he also attempted sample math problems or astronomical calculations. After only a few years at being a shipmaster, he began to invest in affordable amounts of cargo himself, so that he might keep the profits.[26] Hugg considered that he was especially successful, but not unique. He did not attribute his success either to luck or to remarkable virtue, but rather to the necessity that had inspired him. In the late 1820s he wrote the following note on a blank page of his ship log:

There is one thing that softens and sweetens all my toils. It is that I am enabled under the auspices of a Kind Providence to assist and Rendor [sic] the latter days of a dear mother comfortable . . . Had I been born to fortune I really think I should have been good for nothing—my nature required a spur to action and my mind would scarcely have wandered beyond the limits of my native City. In being as it were forced to visit foreign climes I experience all the pleasures and adventures of travel without the expence and at the same time reap all the advantage of commerce.

Other citizens who had a decent education became teachers. Those who were lucky or who had wealthy connections became the sought-after tutors of elite children. Miss Chatterdon was the organist at the Catholic cathedral and thus music teacher to wealthy young ladies. Monsieur Gilles, a Frenchman singled out by Lafayette during his visit, also gave music lessons. Those who did not have the social connections required to develop a clientele as tutors could sometimes open schools for "infants," which accepted weaned children up to age seven or eight. In their advertisements these schools offered clergymen as references. Their most serious problem seemed to be the strength of the ties existing between the students and their mothers: at one school the teachers insisted that visiting would now be forbidden until after a child had been four weeks in attendance.[27]

Beginning in 1829, there were a few positions available in the newly developed public school system. The work was hard. The schools were run according to the popular Lancasterian system that had already spread as far as South America, in which one docent was expected to teach scores of young people through the use of monitors. Not surprisingly, the teachers made frequent complaints about discipline. Still, for the males at least, the pay was good in comparison to many other jobs. The men, who taught the boys, received $800 a year, and the women, who taught the girls, $400. After the first year the school commissioners suggested placing all male students under the age of eight in women's classrooms, to save the city money, and their plan was readily adopted.[28]

Black students were excluded from these schools, as were black teachers. Undaunted, black teachers created, ran, and taught classes in a system of their own design. The churches played a leading role. Both the Sharp Street Methodist Church and the Bethel African Methodist Episcopal established schools that lasted for many years and employed several teachers each, while other Protestant churches operated schools intermittently. In 1828 Sister Mary Elizabeth Lange from Haiti founded a Catholic order, the Oblate Sisters of Providence, and a year later the nuns started the Saint Francis Academy for Girls. They accepted day students and boarding students who came from a distance. At first most of the girls were from families who had come from war-torn Saint-Domingue, but soon the school became known to all groups. Many graduates went on to become teachers themselves, starting lay schools which were not affiliated with churches. Such teachers made their living off the tuition payments, but, unlike white teachers, they generally did not advertise in the newspapers; apparently they relied on word-of-mouth communications to advertise for them. Those who did advertise had to be cautious and cultivated an image of pathetic students in need. Jacob Greener ran a school for "indigent coloured children." He requested the patronage of wealthy white benefactors, explaining that a white treasurer would husband all donations.[29]

The black intelligentsia remained the lifeblood of the black professional community: the role of teacher was one of the very few channels open to the educated. Public debate about political issues relevant to black

Baltimoreans spilled out of the classroom and into streets and houses. William Watkins, who ran the most prominent lay school, led a campaign against the back-to-Africa colonization schemes that were largely sponsored by whites. Memoirs reveal that people also discussed the potential political role of free black nations such as Liberia and Haiti. They read popular schoolbooks like *The Columbian Orator* and newspapers like the *Freeman's Banner*. Nor, at this time, did they hide the fact that they did so: a white bookstore owner in Fell's Point did not hesitate to sell a copy of the former to a black child. As early as 1826 politicized free blacks petitioned the legislature concerning a law that required unemployed free blacks to leave the state: "We reside among you and yet are strangers; natives, and yet not citizens." [30]

There were of course fields other than teaching open to educated whites. The men had the opportunity of becoming clerks and administrators. Employers and employees advertised for each other. "Situation wanted in a shipping or commission house . . . by a youth in his sixteenth year of respectable family and good education." "A youth of 15 or 16 . . . of correct moral habits, and who writes a good hand . . . is wanted in the office of a Gentleman of the Bar." By the early 1830s there were also four notaries public in the city. One of them worked at the Customshouse, drawing up inventories of incoming goods. For fifty cents each he received the required sworn statements from individual travelers that the goods they brought with them were for their own use and not for resale. The city also employed clerks and accountants. When they did good work, the City Council sang their praises. The committee charged with inspecting the work of the clerk of the city commissioners (in charge of paving streets and dredging the harbor) said that "if it was their province, they would have no hesitation in saying that the compensation allowed their clerk is by no means adequate to the amount and character of the duty performed by Him." [31]

There was in fact a rather extensive municipal bureaucracy. The salary range for full-time employees was remarkably narrow, ranging from the $600 to $750 per annum paid to the city commissioners, Almshouse superintendent, and other officers to the $2,000 paid the mayor. Such workers as market clerks received only about $200 a year, but they themselves operated market stalls with a large discount in the rent and did their work as clerks (which consisted mostly of cleaning and billing other stall holders) in combination with their daily labors as salesmen. [32] Tax collector Francis Dallam did not receive a salary at all, but this was because he was instructed to keep a percentage of what he collected. It was up to him to decide how much of what he gleaned he wished to invest in an improved collection apparatus complete with more clerks; he often complained miserably that because of all the necessary expenses involved in his task, it was very difficult for him to make a profit at all.[33] City bailiffs (who guarded the markets and were considered a cut above the city's night watchmen) received only the pittance of sixty-two cents per day, but this was because they kept one-half of all fines paid. Most days they recorded, "Nothing done," without any apparent embarrassment, but on other days they stood on a corner and fined everyone who came by "driving at a trot." They often were accused of adding to their income through socially unacceptable activities, such as keeping stolen goods that they confiscated or, in the case of one man, asking to buy liquor on the Sabbath and then informing on and fining the person who sold it to him.[34]

The legally required inspection of foodstuffs—barrels of pork, beef, butter, lard, salted fish, flour, liquor, and also hay for animals—constituted a little industry. Vendors could not sell goods that had not been branded after inspection, and producers had to pay to have their goods inspected. The inspectors retained a percentage of the income thus collected and were empowered to fine producers whose goods did not measure up in quantity or quality. Irate producers frequently appealed to the mayor, in one case even creating a disturbance on a Saturday afternoon by insisting on immediate action even though the mayor's office was closed. Sometimes decisions were reversed, but usually they were not, and the inspectors remained in power either way. Probably because of these facts, most petitioners were careful to word their complaints in the most inoffensive way possible. "Not that the present Inspectors were inattentive but because the work was too great . . ." began a group of dealers in whiskey.[35]

Most people agreed that public employees should be well qualified and well recompensed. In February of 1830 the Board of Visitors and Governors of the Baltimore County Jail announced in the newspapers the opening of a search for a new warden and welcomed applications. By the end of the year they had selected David Hudson, who had been director of the Maryland Hospital. The board commented to the City Council on their vision of the necessary qualifications for a warden: "He should be honest, sober, intelligent, vigilant, firm and humane: a person who will devote all his time and all his energies to his appropriate duties. Now it cannot be expected, that a man having these qualifications will long remain in the office unless he have a liberal compensation, and decent accommodations for his family." They carried their point: Hudson received a good salary and a new house.[36] Such a man and his work were publicly valued.

The Entrepreneurs

Other people set out to make money without training as artisans or as professionals. Most commonly, they went into business as salespeople, ranging from itinerant peddlers to shopkeepers. Each year, at least 500 people purchased $5 "ordinary licenses" allowing them to sell their wares. Of these, one out of ten were women. Blacks, again, were legally excluded. Many of these licensed salespeople remained poor and could barely make the payments necessary to keep themselves in business the next year, but others had a little capital and operated established businesses. Vendors who worked in the markets illustrate this wide range. They all paid market rental fees, which varied from the $2 per month required to work a movable stall or cart to the $20 demanded of the butchers. Women tended to be more active in the areas requiring lower capital outlay: in 1830 in Fell's Point they occupied one out of four movable stalls, but there was only one woman (a widow) among the twenty butchers.[37]

Men could establish themselves as wood corders who received the goods that the rural woodchoppers brought to the base of Jones' Falls. Corders who paid the highest price per load had the most customers: sometimes the boats were lined up in the water in front of certain dealers. The dealers could increase profits by turning out more cords than the amount of wood they had actually warranted, through the use of certain deceptive stacking methods that enraged the townsfolk. Others took the corded wood to woodyards in the backstreets of the poorest sections of the city and then corded it over again in slightly smaller bundles that no one took the trouble to inspect.[38]

The majority of the entrepreneurial projects involved public entertainment. Inns and taverns attracted customers based on their ability to provide amusement: bagatelle tables, billiards, bowling, and lotteries. A woman—even a "respectable" woman in a "decent" house—could set herself up as a fortuneteller and develop a wide-ranging clientele. Mr. and Mrs. Timmerman operated "pavillion baths" just outside the city in the summer, the former keeping them clean and the latter attending to the lady visitors. Mrs. Macdaniel offered for a few nights only the entertainment provided by a "Papyrotechnick Gallery," consisting of a "Handsomely lighted display of taste and novelty."[39] The theaters were the most capital-intensive entertainment ventures; only some of them were owned by men of middle rank. The Holliday Street Theatre was financed by a group of stockholders and offered relatively erudite plays—at least in comparison to those of the new Theatre and Circus, operated by and for humbler people. There tickets were cheaper, only twenty-five cents in the pit or up in the "gallery for colored persons." In the winter the audiences at this establishment complained to the owner that they were cold, but they came anyway.[40]

In a relatively literate society, reading and reading aloud were also popular forms of entertainment that could prove profitable to the enterprising. Newspapers vied for readership. The *Baltimore Minerva and Saturday Post* insisted in 1830 that it had more subscribers than any other paper in the city; in that way the editors hoped to attract even more. And the number of subscribers was not necessarily as great as the number of readers. An annual subscription rate to a newspaper was about $8.00, more than the cost of a month's rent for a small house, so people clearly read secondhand materials. For publishers and booksellers, the goal had to be to interest as many people as possible in a certain publication or book, even through secondhand circulation, so that an increasing number of issues would actually be purchased. The large percentage of newspaper space devoted to book and magazine advertisements is astounding to the modern observer, until it becomes clear that most of the material was of purely entertainment value. Scanners of the newspapers learned where they could buy (for fifty cents) *The Library of Useful Knowledge*, containing information about the hyena, camel, llama, giraffe, and reindeer. They also found advertisements for celebrated trial reports, such as "The Murder of Mr. White in Massachusetts," or ladies' magazines consisting of "coloured plates of the Fashions of each month." The materials available were often topical: Fanny Wright, for example, delivered some of her famous radical lectures in Baltimore in December 1828; within a year her speeches were available in book form.[41]

Almost all entrepreneurs relied on such advertising techniques, but they had to proceed cautiously, for they faced some cultural resistance to these practices. Mr. Barnum, for example, placed a notice in each room of his hotel that his establishment sold linen, razors, hair dye, tobacco, etc., but his decision to do this was unusual and noteworthy, provoking negative comment from at least one guest. Rubens Peale was forced to take a pleading tone when he asked the City Council for permission to put up a sign on the sidewalk advertising his museum. Newspaper advertising appeared to be eminently acceptable, on the other hand, probably because the papers were marked as the locus of commercial information, and here businesses experimented with different techniques right on the front page. They began to introduce larger graphics than they had ever used before or threatened for weeks that a visiting anaconda was in its final days and about to be moved south or that a magazine was on the verge of selling out even when it was not. The most extensive advertising space was given over to testimonials for various medicines. These often included gruesome details that may have been as fascinating to the healthy as they were to the sick. "Sixteen large ulcers were on my leg, one on the calf, one on my knee, one above on the outside of my thigh, and thirteen small ones. On the 8th of April, 1827, I began on the Colombian Syrup, and in two months and a half my leg was healed up soundly." [42] How much of the desired effect these advertisements had we cannot know, but they at least brought their submitters some business and they had an audience, for they continued to appear. There were either enough people who could afford to buy papers or enough papers that were passed from hand to hand to make the ads profitable, and, perhaps more importantly, there were enough literate people who had money to spend who could choose whether or not to respond to them.

The Middling Ranks in Public:
Civic Involvement and the Economy

The citizens of Baltimore liked parades. When they marched, they marched in groups. At the procession marking the deaths of Thomas Jefferson and John Adams in 1826, the various clergy, soldiers, and politicians appeared in their respective bodies, followed by "the youths of the several schools," then by the more general "citizens, eight abreast." A note was attached to the program instructing that "those . . . who prefer joining the procession in classes or societies, will report themselves to the Chief Marshall of the day, who will have places assigned to them . . . " The parade in honor of the new railroad also displayed people's pride in their clubs and societies, even ending with various "juvenile clubs": the pride in belonging started young. Indeed, the city teemed with organized groups—the Newtonian Society, the Economic Society, the Agricultural

Society, to name but a few. Hundreds of white men were members of volunteer military brigades. They put time and attention into their drills and their uniforms. "Some of the companies are composed of respectable tradesmen, who have expensive dresses, with ostrich feathers on their caps, which gives them much the appearance of the ancient Spanish dress."[43]

Others joined the volunteer fire companies, whose members were subject to both intense feelings of camaraderie and passionate disagreement. After one violent argument, a particular group of men swore that "they would never take hold of the ropes of this Company again." They burned their badges and applied for membership elsewhere. Frequently men who were members of a certain club also participated in political events together. The minutes of a volunteer fire company read, "After a half hour's pleasant discussion the company adjourned, some to Monument Square to hear the candidates for electors of Jackson and Adams, and some to hear their wives and children prattle."[44]

The exclusion of certain ethnic groups from these activities fueled the formation of other clubs and societies. The first Hebrew Congregation, for example, was founded in 1830, immediately after the passage of "the Jew Bill" made it legal to do so. The first president was John Dyer, a butcher, and the first treasurer was Levi Benjamin, a former peddler who had opened a secondhand store. (Wealthier Jews like the Cohens belonged to a synagogue in Philadelphia.) The congregation rented a room over a grocery store at the corner of Bond and Fleet Streets, in Fell's Point, but by 1837 they were able to obtain a three-story brick building of their own in a better neighborhood. Dues were a relatively steep $5 per year, payable in biweekly installments, and collection was strictly enforced. For practical or for social reasons, many Jews also reached out to form bonds with other groups in the city: of German descent themselves, they remained active in the German community by advertising in the German-language newspaper and inviting the Christian readers to their charity functions.[45]

Black citizens formed their own philanthropic and mutual aid societies. Between 1820 and 1835 about forty of them came and went, and some were permanent. They were usually church-based or trade-based. There were, for example, societies for porters and coachmen, barbers, brickmakers, and caulkers. During the period two to three thousand black Baltimoreans became members of at least one of these groups. At least half of these people were women. The Union Female Society was actually for women only: each member paid 12 cents a month and then could receive sick benefits of $1.00 per week for six weeks. The clubs also covered the costs of a member's funeral. "Some of these [societies] have uniforms, and few objects strike the eye of the stranger more forcibly than the processions of them that are occasionally to be seen in attendance upon the funeral of a member."[46]

For the white Christian majority, the schools were another locus of public involvement and investment in the future. The experience of the son of a shoemaker was typical of many: his mother had a dairy business and sent him from a young age to Miss Mary Baker's school for small children. Then he went to one of the new public grammar schools and was placed "with other small boys in the female department." At the age of seven, he graduated to the all-boys class. These schools had been founded for the "poor," who were not defined as the children of the most desperate members of society, but of needy tradespeople and small business keepers. The theory was a relatively inclusive one and required public participation through taxation if not through attendance. The schools attracted hundreds of students from the targeted group. Attendance rose so dramatically within the first few years among students of the middling sorts that a large new building had to be constructed in Old Town. Current thinking on education insisted that assigning children work to be done independently while the teacher worked with another grade allowed young minds to wander; it was better, said the school commissioners, for the students to spend their time listening or reciting to teachers' assistants, if they were to improve themselves. The books they chose were in keeping with these ideas: the practice sentences of *Warner's Primer* and the contents of the *Public School Song Book* printed "by order of the commissioners" were equally designed to be morally uplifting and to leave no room for questions. And yet the schools were not meant to dampen all ambition: they were explicitly designed to turn out workers with enough knowledge to be able to move beyond day labor and enter a trade, according to the originators' own statements. "We have the means of bringing these wandering sheep, many of them, indeed, astray, into the folds of education."[47]

Private schools, of course, had existed since long before the founding of the public schools. Most of them were for the well-to-do, but some of them had operated according to the belief that there was a demand among working people for "self-improvement": in the early part of the century there was indeed a national movement spawning tradespeople's schools—

the same movement that had given rise to the demand for the public schools. In Baltimore Mr. Bennett's Male and Female Academy had provided a separate "Night School" since the mid-1820s, and by the mid-1830s advertisements for such adult schools were numerous. They offered "systems of writing," bookkeeping for clerks, even French and German. The Straw School on Water Street taught girls the business from "the preparing of the straw to finishing the bonnet."[48]

To some extent, the middling sorts of Baltimore were literally investors in their own future. That is, they could buy shares in joint ventures if they chose. The concept that working people might make limited investments, according to their abilities, was a common one. When, for example, the Second Dispensary, the medical facility open to the public of Fell's Point, could not raise enough funds from local dignitaries to continue functioning, its directors made the suggestion that the minimum share of $5— which allowed a sponsor a vote in hospital affairs—be divided up among several less-wealthy families who might wish to participate as a unit.[49] There also existed a tradition of such families' making investments for profit. During the War of 1812 almost one hundred men who could not be considered elite made one-time investments in the outfitting of privateering vessels. Seamen, sailmakers, chandlers, and others were swept up into the patriotic fervor. These should not be confused with the more than one hundred established merchants who made large and repeated wartime investments, profiting enormously. More than two-thirds of these small risk-takers lost their money, but a few were lucky. Sailmaker Jacob Grafflin was apparently one of the latter. In the early years of the century he ran an ordinary sailmaking business, but in 1813 he borrowed several hundred dollars from an insurance company for an unstated reason. By 1820 he was drawing huge sums of money from the Farmer's and Merchant's Bank and stocking a ship bound for St. Thomas with apples and vinegar belonging to him.[50]

The belief in widespread investment in the commonwealth affected the development of banks as well. "The Mechanics' Bank" had been founded in 1806, with the twin ideas of ordinary citizens becoming commercial investors and loans becoming more accessible to artisans. A battle occurred among the originators as to whether mechanics themselves or a group of merchants would actually control the bank's finances. A conservative partnership between certain relatively elite tradesmen and their merchant allies won the day, but the bank's policies were permanently influenced by the demands of the radicals. The shares sold easily, many to tradesmen, as they were offered in smaller and therefore cheaper units. Profits were more than respectable. By 1833 the bank held $384,000 worth of assets, approximately equal to the average among other commercial banks in the city if the two largest and most elite were excluded. Perhaps equally importantly, the belief began to grow that even the poor could participate in investment indirectly, by depositing their weekly savings in an institution. Baltimore's first "Savings Bank" was established for people of limited means in 1818. There a customer could deposit any amount no matter how small during the business hours of any day. This contrasted with most banking institutions, where large minimum deposits were required and could be made only at certain times on certain days. Several other similar institutions appeared in the following years. The black women's Union Female Society entrusted their resources to such a bank. Reports of the activities of both kinds of banks appeared in the newspapers and were consistently before the public eye. The constant news, however, while dispelling some of the sense of mystery, did not entirely allay public fears that these investment opportunities might possibly be in reality only a way for elite citizens to rob common ones. Most people, in fact, had not yet been won over to the new concept. The riots after the bank failures of 1834 and 1835 cannot fail to remind us of the latent hostility. Many of the participants in the violent confrontations were said to be ruined tradespeople: how large a proportion of the rioters they actually formed we cannot know, but the significant fact is that the whole city could easily believe such a rumor. The concept of popular investment was growing, but was not at all universal.[51]

In the late 1820s between one-quarter and one-third of people who died holding stock of some kind were small investors who held equity in the Mechanics' Bank or some other bank or who owned city stock. The initial purchasers of the 5 percent twelve-year notes issued by the city in 1832 included eleven merchants or major landowners or their widows, but also five master craftsmen, a milliner, and a grocer; those takers whom we cannot identify are also likely to have been tradespeople. The combined equity of such investors was a small portion of the total capital invested in Baltimore, but it was not a meaningless portion, and it was destined to grow. About half of these small holders were widowed women, who partially or entirely met their living expenses with the interest or dividends earned.[52] Elizabeth Luke, for example, whose husband had been a grocer before he died, owned some municipal stock. She was far from being an elite figure and could not write her name. When her signature was needed on a document, she went to the table and made a large "X." Yet her money helped the city meet the expenses of internal improvements and even helped subsidize the new railroad. Like the draymen who demanded the right to park their wagons where they liked, she knew she was a part of the polity and the economy. She was included.

Did Elizabeth ever see Frederick Bailey? Did she ever wonder about those who were not included?

Comparison

Despite profound differences between their expectations of themselves and their futures, middle-ranked people in Baltimore and Guayaquil were in some ways startlingly similar. We glimpse people in both places working hard and hatching creative money-making schemes; we see them in both places laughing and dawdling when they might have been working. It is a mistake to imagine the artisans in the young United States hard at work in their leather aprons while their counterparts in the southern hemisphere idly chat with friends. William Minifrie's wife had many an argument with him before he could be convinced to work more regularly, while Manuel Ignacio Murillo's sister and then wife watched him work creatively and persistently year after year to better his position. These are only two men, but the descriptions of Baltimore's raucous theaters indicate that Minifrie was not alone, while the anxious and carefully notarized business records left by Guayaquil's middling sorts demonstrate that Murillo was not unique.

In neither city did the middle-ranked people demonstrate a particularly profound religious influence. Evidence of their religious expressions does not appear in the preceding chapters because it would have had to be negative evidence. In the aftermath of the second Great Awakening, religious pamphlets from organizations such as the Young Men's Bible Society were certainly available in Baltimore; but other people did not refer to these documents in the ordinary course of events, and no printer continued to work with the society for more than a couple of years. Nor did overall church attendance among the middling sorts go up at this time.[53] If people were working harder out of a Protestant sense of responsibility for self, they left no proof of it. On the other hand, if in Guayaquil the middle-ranked people were spending time or energy in traditional Catholic religious practices, they likewise left little proof of it. If Manuel Ignacio Murillo prayed to a saint before he ran a printing job, we will never know it. Certainly there is no evidence that he or anyone else avoided responsibility on grounds that the saints wished it so. Neither in their wills nor in their business records did ordinary people indicate that they devoted many resources to the church. In their wills they were more likely to pride themselves on their accomplishments rather than crediting the divine. One *cofradía* member went so far as to plead with his brethren that they come to mass more often, consider spending a little more to attend to the upkeep of the figures of the *santos* in their church, and even work together to prevent theft from the church.[54]

Perhaps because of their equally irreligious attitudes, people in both cities were willing to be lax in their morals where profits were concerned. In Baltimore we need not look beyond the subjective inspectors, the court informers, the cheating wood corders, the wildly popular fortunetellers, and the successful theater owners to see this willingness to be flexible. In Guayaquil, too, bar owners allowed cheating and left their doors open if they thought it would be profitable, while other men invested capital in cock-fighting.

Attitudes about labor (and leisure) remained in fact remarkably similar, though the attitudes about groups of people and the relationships between them were profoundly different. Despite the people's relatively equal willingness to work hard and take risks, the difference in attitudes about people had a direct impact on the proportions who were able to conceive of themselves as "middling sorts" or "gente decente" and also on the resources they were able to accumulate. Cultural forms of inclusion and exclusion are visible in an analysis of widely varying groups of middle-level citizens.

In Baltimore Elizabeth Luke's sense of being counted as a contributing citizen was common. People made small investments, demanded work, joined clubs, and signed petitions with alacrity. They insisted that they were like the majority. In the recent period one crucial exception had emerged: it was only in relation to free blacks who were in competition for work that whites defined themselves as middle-ranking citizens based on the claim that they were different from others and should be in a privileged position over them. Such thinking could flare out violently, as Frederick Bailey learned. His shock and his rage were all the greater because the phenomenon in his experience had until then been rare. This picture is a peculiar one, and not at all universal. If in Baltimore one usually proved one's worth by demonstrating that one was like the majority, a ratepayer to be included in all reckonings, then in Guayaquil one proved one's worth by demonstrating that one was *not* like the majority, not like the common hordes. Ana Yagual's client Pedro and many others like him used this tactic.

The lives of artisans, for example, were strikingly different in this regard in Baltimore and Guayaquil. In Baltimore the value of artisanal labor was mentioned frequently; it was well paid and was a source of public pride on the part of the artisans themselves. Master craftsmen certainly benefited from the good pay and the ceremonial displays more than did their apprentices. But advancement was at least theoretically merit-based, and the statistical and anecdotal evidence suggests that it was usually real for the majority, in that most white men did advance rather than remaining permanent apprentices or low-level journeymen. In Guayaquil, on the other hand, the situation was far different. The value of a worker's labor was never emphasized. Master craftsmen were the only members of the *gremios*, rather than merely the leading members, and most assistants never rose within the ranks, or apparently even expected to. Their pay remained low. There were similar differences between the lives of professionals in the two places. In Baltimore professionals were still trying to encourage others to join their ranks through education. In Guayaquil musicians, doctors, and teachers who organized in the first flush of independence expended their efforts in attempting to draw a circle around their profession that no one would be allowed to cross, in order to render themselves more secure.

The explanation for these contrasting attitudes seems to lie in the different degrees to which middling sorts felt valued by each other and by their social superiors. In Baltimore an artisan's work was respected, and a hard-working one had a good chance of becoming a well-known and well-to-do figure like William Minifrie, or Bernard Labroquère, or Mayor Jacob Small. In Guayaquil even the most successful craftsmen like Manuel Ignacio Murillo had to temper their expectations, and there were few who accomplished as much as he did. A sea captain of a Baltimore ship had a much greater chance than a Guayaquileño peer of being welcomed by the ship owner as a fellow investor. In Baltimore clerks were promoted to administrators; they were offered public accolades, and the best ones were retained by offering them the inducements of higher salaries and other benefits. In Guayaquil clerks were not valued, and the titular heads of their offices, although they might do little or none of the recorded work, received three and four times their salaries. Successful Baltimore entrepreneurs, including innkeepers and circus managers, were praised to travelers writing their narratives, but in Guayaquil similar businesspeople had to fend off the accusations of the authorities that they were not conducting themselves in a seemly way. It is no accident that ordinary white Baltimoreans did turn with hostility on another group—the minority of free blacks—when they felt their own value threatened for the first time, for the free blacks were working hard, competing with whites for the specialized jobs, prestige, and self-respect that accompanied them, while industrialization raised the specter of becoming an unskilled day laborer.

These contrasting patterns of exclusion versus inclusion in turn left their mark on the decisions of middle-ranked people as to whether or not they should invest in any way in expanding their shops or businesses. In Baltimore there were many master craftsmen who turned workshops into small manufactories, even braving the anger of the import-export merchants. They knew that they were producing goods for a public that was, by and large, not destitute either of money or of a vision of themselves as people with rights: the artisans who chose to expand their shops made more soap, candles, paper, and clothes with that public in mind. Entertainers also produced more plays for them; the educated opened more schools; and storekeepers lobbied for more bridges to connect their streets. In Guayaquil the situation was different. The hesitancy to expand probably stemmed from lack of demand, for when demand did exist expansion occurred. For example, there were not enough well-to-do families to keep alive a large bakery selling pastries and pies—which travel narratives tell us people certainly liked—but two merchants and a baker opened their large shop when the army demanded a regular supply of loaves. Likewise, an investor was willing to risk extensive funds in a cockfighting theater, certain that he could make the place attractive to people, but only if he received a monopoly contract, as he feared there was only a limited level of discretionary income. The decisions of the middling sorts as to whether to change or expand their businesses or conduct them much as always had to be connected to their assessment of the likelihood of any such changes proving profitable. We can see from their everyday behavior that they knew their own situations best and operated rationally within their own frameworks.

Probably because of the belief in Baltimore that most people were ratepayers, demands for street improvements and new schools were frequent: no single small group feared that they would have to foot the entire bill, and the results were of obvious benefit to many people. The success of such projects may in turn have helped to fuel people's faith in the profitability of buying shares in other joint ventures. In Guayaquil, on the other hand, the middling sorts were almost as few as the elites; when they were forced to pay for projects through *empréstitos*, they felt the effects most painfully. Recall the wealthy Indian who went to the extreme of saying he had been *accused* of citizenship. Such people almost never attracted attention to themselves by making demands. Certainly they were not invited to participate in making decisions as to how the public monies should be spent, and they rarely benefited from public projects. Even the new public schools ended by being of more use to upper-level artisans and to the relatively high-born who were temporarily in need than they were to most of the middling sorts. Despite similar attitudes toward work, contrasting attitudes about people were bound to lead to different kinds of commitments to economic development.

PART IV

CHAPTER 7

WORKING ON DEAD MAN'S ROCK

The Poor of Guayaquil

People up and down the street insisted they did not have three pesos to give. They did not even offer one peso to the tax collector, for they said they could not. On every street it had been the same. Vicente Ramón Roca was in a quandary: he had consented to be the chief of police this year, and it was his responsibility to direct the collection of the sum. He wrote distraught letters to the governor about the weight of "carrying on my shoulders an immense hatred." In early 1827 the Colombian government in Bogotá, concerned about a possible Peruvian invasion, had issued an unusual edict, demanding of Guayaquileños "a head tax of three pesos on all free men, without exception of class, condition, or state." Later, to clarify that they did indeed mean everybody, President Bolívar added that "all day laborers should pay, per head."[1] People had responded particularly negatively: they jeered or referred to "the tribute" instead of the tax, obliquely referring to the fact that they were *not* Indians and therefore should not be assigned a head tax as Indians traditionally were. The women were the worst, according to Don Vicente. They displayed a degree of anger that was scandalizing.

Don Vicente decided to resort to armed force. He went to each of the military barracks in the city and commanded them to extract the money from the people by arresting anyone who refused to pay. But public opinion was so strong that the officers knew ahead of time that they could not swim against the tide. Three of them did do their best over several weeks, but in the city's wealthiest neighborhoods; three others politely sent out soldiers for two hours and then announced the job had been done as well as it could be. One officer simply looked at Don Vicente and said, "I am not your hook"—meaning your arresting officer—"and you must give it up."[2] Don Vicente reported the officer, of course, but he still had very little money to turn over to the national government. He wrote defensive letters to his superior and attempted to explain the level of resistance he was encountering.

In retrospect, the popular anger is not profoundly surprising. To understand it, we must understand who these people were who sarcastically referred to the "tribute." When the elites were taxed over and over again in various impromptu situations, they complained vociferously, but they did not rush to distinguish themselves from tribute-paying indigenous peoples. The comparison does not seem to have occurred to them. These jeering *jornaleros*, on the other hand, were freed slaves who had only just ceased to turn over a weekly payment to their masters or indigenous people who had only recently escaped their identity as tribute-payers and learned to blend into the city. Or they were the children and grandchildren of one or both of these. These people lived in Guayaquil purposely so that they might live as they chose and not have to turn over whatever surplus they had to a figure of authority. These were generally not people who wanted to participate in open rebellion: there was in fact a strong tradition of social banditry in the region which they had rejected for themselves.[3] If they had wanted a life of open warfare, they could have had it, but they did not. They had either chosen to come to the city or, if born there, had elected to remain despite the risk the men ran of being drafted into the military. Perhaps they knew people who had gone to the mountain strongholds, but they themselves had chosen another way. They resisted the city "tribute" tax in every way possible short of armed rebellion. They wanted only to be left alone to work and spend their money as they chose. For many of them even attaining that goal represented a tremendous victory. They and their families had been peons or slaves and had only recently walked onto the stage of city life.

Enter the Indian

When the indigenous immigrant Mariano de la Cruz was hauled before the court, he did not give his judges much information. "I am a weaver of straw hats, and a peon day laborer who will put my hand to anything."[4] He was from Santa Elena on the coast and was now living in the house of his sister María Magdalena on the edge of the city. He thought he was at least thirty-five years old; he was Catholic. Mariano de la Cruz never explained why he had left the balmy littoral and made his way to the city, and his questioners displayed no curiosity on that front, apparently not finding his arrival particularly surprising or unusual. In these years the region was experiencing an influx of indigenous peoples coming down from the mountains, and some of these newcomers along with some of the province's own natives were traveling on to the city. Indigenous tribute payments on the coast were lower than they were in the Andes and were gradually being abolished.[5] Given the problems that highland Indians were experiencing with their own tribute payments and the decline of their textile production, it is small wonder that many came down from the mountains. What is more interesting is that so many moved to the city, rather than staying in more familiar rural areas. A closer look at the region reveals some of the reasons.

Mariano's people of Santa Elena were descended from the Huancavilca seafarers, but in these days everyone spoke Spanish and had Spanish surnames. Their chieftainships had been disbanded years before, in the 1780s and 1790s, following the rebellion in Peru of Tupac Amaru II, who claimed to be the last Inkan prince. Deputy mayors chosen by the literate indigenous now controlled native political affairs in the area, but there were still some shamans who retained traditional healing practices and were regarded as authority figures by most people.[6] There was a variety of economic activity in the area: fishing, weaving straw hats, honey bee farming, mining salt, diving for the caracolillo shells used in making purple dye, raising cattle. Further inland, where the dry land gave way to fertile green, people also cut timber and produced coffee, cotton, tobacco, fruit, and cacao. Traditionally, there had been large plantations side by side with Indian communities that owned some land of their own. Now, as cacao became more profitable, some of the plantations expanded, swallowing up large tracts of the Indians' land. The owners pressured the formerly independent peasants to work for wages and to do more unpaid "tribute time" on the plantations. This pattern had been most pronounced in Machala, but the new dynamic was visible in other places as well. The village authorities in Yaguachi tried to explain local tensions to officials in Guayaquil:

The individuals who have contributed the rice [requested by the government] absolutely refuse to thrash it, claiming that it is not their role, not being harvesters themselves but rather buyers of the services of harvesters; and those who do have that role, as they are poor men and maintain their families by day labor, resist with force the work that has been demanded of them [without pay].[7]

The expansion of *hacienda* holdings usually occurred through the courts. As early as 1822 a local gentleman had written in distress to the newspaper that the "miserable peasants" were being defrauded of their lands by a court system uninterested in protecting them. First Bogotá and then the regional government continued to pass laws encouraging the "adjudication of empty lands." Indian groups were to be given every opportunity to demonstrate how much of their traditional holdings they actually put to productive use, and the rest of the land—even if the use rotated—was to be sold to more efficient agriculturalists, who were generally people who had more money. In areas where this had not already occurred some indigenous groups fought to prevent it. In El Morro, near Ana Yagual's birthplace, they submitted a petition to the governor claiming their lands were *not* empty.[8]

Some of the rural indigenous also began to writhe under what they viewed as a centuries-old tradition of disrespect. When the republican government was born in Quito, it began to receive daily complaints of abuses by local *alcaldes* (mayors), as some of the Indians saw the change in government as an opportunity to complain about grievances they associated with the old regime.[9] Though most of these came from Andean villages, a goodly share originated in the coastal lowlands near Guayaquil. Generally the indigenous petitions concerned tax collection and collectors. Occasionally women complained about cases of assault.[10] In addition to experiencing old wrongs with more resentment, Indian communities also faced new kinds of abuses: they suffered when marching troops passed through. The soldiers came hungry and in great numbers. Most communities, however, could feed them and then recuperate. Disaster did not strike unless the military commandeered their mules and horses, their "only patrimony" and the means by which they earned their living. To avoid this, the communities, both Indian and Hispanic, always tried to please by providing as much food and cash as possible and by thanking the government when they ordered that the beasts of burden be left alone. Sometimes, however, the armed soldiers simply took the animals even without official approval. In the worst cases the soldiers were unable to feed the livestock they appropriated, and the roads through which they passed were spotted with the rotting carcasses of mules.[11]

That which the indigenous most resented, however, was the *contribución* (tribute) not only of several pesos a year, but also of days and even weeks of labor time, as demanded by the local government. Unenforced and then revoked edicts banning tribute on the coast probably helped resentments grow. At the demand of the regional government, Hispanic *alcaldes* sent the requested number of native men to Guayaquil to labor on public works projects. In the correspondence they were bandied about like bags of salt. In one case the local mayor actually stated that he would agree to send one hundred men, but he wished to remind the government that his town was in dire need of salt: he hinted that it would be only fair to arrange a trade. Soldiers might be sent "to collect the canoe and the peons," and the mayors would answer, "I remit to you the men who are to serve in the Arsenal."[12] Most of the men sent to the city were put to work building and maintaining the arsenal of the navy station. The military staff lists generally included between fifty and eighty indigenous men, sometimes paid only in rations ("con sólo ración") or sometimes given a token salary of between two and four pesos a month. (Twenty pesos was considered to be enough for subsistence for a town person.) The forced recruits complained, however, that often they were not paid the cash they had been promised, and occasionally they were not even given their daily food rations. The government tried to resolve this problem by issuing a paper exempting each worker from the head tax for that year if they were not able to pay him his salary. On the other hand, when the workers *were* paid and were working on a ship in the port while the head tax was being collected in their home village, the chief of police made certain that the navy sent someone aboard to collect the tax from them.[13]

After Ecuador separated from Colombia in 1830, and there was more talk about ending native tribute on the coast, either the indigenous men began to protest more often against the required labor time or the local officials began to notice their resentments. For whichever reason, the latter began to complain frequently to each other about the high rate of desertion: "They simply return to their houses." In one case officials were concerned that the men were somehow finding out ahead of time about the sending of labor draft notices and then making themselves scarce. Finally the commandant of the Navy Station wrote a complaint to the governor: "Even though the number [of requested men] is quite moderate in comparison to the number of people in these towns [of Santa Elena, el Morro, etc.] it has been noted that the Alcaldes have been gradually diminishing the number sent . . ." The new government in Quito did in fact change the law, making it illegal to force Indians to work without pay, but there were no provisions for enforcement, and this law could be circumvented by assigning a nominal salary. Years later, a scandalized gentleman sympathizer was still writing letters to the editor about the presence of Indians being forced to labor on the *malecón*.[14]

It is not surprising that many of Guayaquil's rural indigenous attempted to discard their identity. Some went through the court system in an effort to prove that they were really mestizo and thus should not have to pay the head tax or serve time. They worded their cases almost exactly as they had in colonial days: those who won their point were those who could prove that their mothers had been mestizas or *zambas* and their fathers unknown.[15] Far more simply left the place of their birth, where they were known to everyone, and attempted to pass themselves off as mestizos somewhere else. The large, anonymous city of Guayaquil was the most likely spot for them to choose. Because they were trying to disappear, it is difficult to track them now. Sometimes those who were already there, living on the outskirts of the city, helped newcomers: literate *indígenas* even helped groups of tributary laborers sent from the countryside adjust their paperwork before presenting themselves to the authorities so it would look as though fewer had been sent. Some would then be able to melt away into the city. Only a few, like Mariano de la Cruz, were nabbed by the city authorities, and then only because they had committed some other crime: the Indians of the coastal region, after all, had been speaking Spanish and wearing Hispanic clothing for several generations, and the children of the migrants from the highlands probably grew up similarly.

In most cases, the evidence for the presence of these migrants in the city must be indirect. We know there was a rising tide of strangers in the city. That a number of these newcomers were "passing" Indians is evidenced in a series of incidents demonstrating that confusion about people's identities was almost unlimited. According to a law of 1828, the indigenous did not have to pay any duties on the foodstuffs they brought into the city to sell because they paid personal tribute and did labor time. Government officials became incensed when they found that many arriving white mestizos were convincing the police that they were in fact indigenous people who did not have to pay duties on the goods they brought, even though they had been previously taken to be Hispanic mestizos who did not have to pay tribute. A community of *naturales* grew on the savanna hugging the edge of the city. Most officials assumed that they were really indigenous or partly indigenous.[16] When they arrested and questioned one, such as Mariano de la Cruz, they found their assumptions to be grounded. He offered them no easy access to information about himself and convinced them that he had not committed the crime of which he stood accused. He clung to his privacy and his independence: these were probably all he had to call his own.

Enter the Freedman

In 1825 Alejandro Campusano recalled the day he had left his master's house forever: "The sweet voice of the Patria came to my ears, and I, wanting to be one of her soldiers, both to help shake the yoke of the General Oppression and to free myself from the slavery in which I was held, ran quickly to present myself to the liberating troops . . . "[17] Now, only a few years later, this black man living free in the city had to go to court to defend the rights he had won in fighting for his country. With his eloquence and his record, he carried the day. Meanwhile, María Manuela Arteta, a slave apparently born in the urban home of the wealthy José Garostiza, managed to gain her liberty and that of her children in quite another way. Vicente Mata, who operated a store on the first floor of one of the Garostiza houses, had fallen in love with her long ago, and she had agreed to enter into a relationship with him. She became close friends with Vicente's sister, who bought María Manuela and gave her to her brother on the explicit condition that she be freed when Vicente died *or* when she chose to marry someone else. Vicente never mentioned this last possibility in his writings, and the idea probably did not please him. María Manuela apparently never tried his patience by asking to marry someone else; she and her children received their freedom when he died.[18]

After the elite of Guayaquil declared the independence of the region in 1820, and throughout the ensuing years, the slaves in the area began to fight ardently for their own freedom. They used every method at their disposal in record numbers: they joined the army and filed lawsuits and worked and stole and saved money and argued and ran away. They clearly talked aloud about their hopes and plans, for even the slave owners were aware of them, sometimes mentioning almost pityingly "the desire for Liberty that every slave has."[19] The fervor of Enlightenment ideology combined with changes in the economy helped the slaves find white sympathizers. Cacao plantations needed many workers in frequent bursts, but they did not need them consistently throughout the year, and masters disliked feeding slaves in idle times. Thus over the past two generations the number of slaves in the province had been cut roughly in half through manumission, self-purchase, and a failure on the part of masters to reinvest in human chattel. Many rural villages and small towns now consisted of a few Hispanic officials and petty merchants surrounded by a population of free blacks and mulattoes who worked as paid day laborers. Despite the wealth implied by nearby cacao trees and orangeries, these people had little or no land themselves and their villages took on a "miserable" appearance, especially in periods when there was no harvest.[20] Some of them made their way to Guayaquil.

An unknown number of slaves did not wait to receive freedom legally but chose to run away to the city. The fugitives were extraordinarily creative in their attempts to elude the searches that were made after the police received letters from their irate masters. One man—who came from almost as far as Quito—told authorities he belonged to the brother of the man from whom he had actually run away, so that his accent and origins would not arouse suspicion and it would be assumed he could not be the man sought by the angry master. The deception worked for eight years. Free women of color were occasionally fined for sheltering runaways, although anyone who committed such a crime had earlier been publicly threatened with dire punishment. It was indeed a risky way of life. Owners had long memories. Once an *hacendado* announced that he had spotted in the city the peon with whom one of his slaves had fled twelve years earlier.[21] In 1834 the newspaper *El Colombiano* began to publish the names of "apprehended slaves," and there were usually two or three each month.

The largest number of former slaves living in the city had not left their rural bondage either legally or illegally. Rather, they had won their freedom since being sent to Guayaquil by their masters while still enslaved to swell the number of domestic servants and artisans who turned over their pay to their owners. These more than the rural slaves were exposed to the ideas behind the new laws made after independence.[22] They were surrounded by a rhetoric of independence and liberty, by changing laws, by free people of color—black and indigenous. Many of them had the experience of being paid for their work. And yet it was clear that their urban owners had no intention of freeing them all voluntarily. If they wanted their liberty, they would have to fight for it. And they wanted it.

In theory each region was home to its own *junta de manumisión* that met at least once a year to choose the slaves who would be freed through the funds of the Bank of Manumission. In Guayaquil the bank was to receive money from two sources—an inheritance tax and weekly deposits made by the slaves themselves. It seems that at first, however, the inheritance tax was not collected. In 1822 six slaves petitioned the government that the bank actually be established to help them purchase themselves. In 1823 slaves came in large numbers to leave money with the employee working out of an office on the Plaza de San Francisco. The bank suffered from serious problems in its administration, regularly misplacing the money. There were many stories like Petra Iler's: "I had to do well in putting in the funds in the Bank of Manumission, according to the custom, and with the security given to the slaves by disposition of His Excellency the Liberator. I have almost contributed half my worth, and after I've gotten nothing for it, now they tell me the bank is out of money." [23]

As Petra went to court and fought hard for her rights, the administration finally found the funds necessary to buy her liberty. In January 1826 the national government became concerned about the general lack of compliance with the manumission laws at the local level. The Bogotá government sent a severe letter to the governor about "abuses" in this area, and a year later Simón Bolívar refounded the Bank of Amortization for Slaves in Guayaquil's Casa de Gobierno, through which slaves could buy themselves by paying at least one peso a week. The *junta de manumisión*, consisting of a judge, a vicar, a treasurer, and two private citizens chosen by the governor, had the responsibility of meeting at the end of each year to choose which slaves were to be freed. Those who had contributed the most in weekly payments or who had fought for the Patria were the most eligible. But nobody could be freed if the junta did not meet, and it could not meet, one member fretted, if the other members did not bother to show up.[24] Despite delays and obstacles, Guayaquil's slaves continued to try to profit according to the law. In their court cases many demonstrated the eloquence of Alejandro Campusano. Some even refused to call themselves slaves. "I who was a slave . . . ," "I, a resident of this city and son of the Chocó region . . . ," "I, *vecina* of this city . . ."

Most of the men who presented claims had fought for the army of independence, which they proved with witnesses and documentation. Some former owners presented no problems. "Now that I see how well-founded is his request to be free, and that he has committed no crime for which he should lose his right, I say to the judge that I have no difficulties with this . . ." He was, after all, to be paid by the bank. It was not exactly necessary to obtain the permission of one's former master in order to gain freedom, but a strongly opposed owner could be damaging to one's case. The widow of General Juan Paz de Castillo, for example, said that a boy who had followed her husband into battle could not possibly have fought, "much less wield the weapons of the army . . . for he was so little as to be incapable of even serving as a drummer." The ex-slaves did everything they could to stand up to such an owner. One Pedro Franco responded, "I don't think such claims are legal, because I am free, and I am ready to take up arms again, . . . as a loyal Colombian soldier." He added that his former master was not very patriotic, mentioning certain details that provoked an investigation of the man's conduct during the war. His former master was left to stew in his own shame and rage, and Pedro Franco kept his freedom.[25]

Women had to look for other legal ways to win their freedom. They worked for wages, with and without their owner's permission, saving every penny in the bank and hoping that their regularity and their earnestness would induce the committee to come up with the balance at the end of the year. The price that an owner was willing to accept became an important element in the relations between master and slave. When, for example, one owner wanted his slave to feed and raise the baby of a friend who had no milk, instead of offering her money he lowered the price he was asking for her freedom, and she was quite satisfied. In 1822 and 1823—and perhaps in other years if we could find the records—most of the cases settled out of court were between masters and women slaves and concerned the setting of a just sale price or the renegotiating of a plan already made. Usually, the owner and the slave both signed a *papel de venta*, and according to its terms the slave could leave the master's house to work and beg for money from friends, paying the owner a certain quantity each week. The question became more complicated if, as often happened, an owner later reneged and refused to sell.[26]

A few slaves were fortunate and were freed in their masters' wills, so they did not have to spend their life savings just to get started. Occasionally they were willed a bit of property in addition. When the mistress of José Sánchez died, she said he had been a good and faithful servant; as payment for many years of service she gave him thirty pesos in cash and a coral rosary.[27] She particularly specified that her more valuable pearl and gold rosaries should go to family members. After a lifetime of working for another's benefit, José Sanchez walked out into the streets as a free man with only one month's salary and a coral rosary. And he was one of the lucky ones.

Working in the City

Once they were living free in the city, a new life for former tribute-payers or slaves depended on their ability to get work. It was often difficult to find. Those who had work to offer seemed to prefer to employ coerced laborers, the kind they knew best. Incipient industries like the larger bakeries and tanneries depended on slave labor. Employers with a large job who could not hire enough slaves petitioned the government for access to the labor of the *presidio* inmates or tributary Indians temporarily in the city. Even a traditional shoemaker who wanted more help was likely to hire a slave from a rich man rather than take on a free man.[28] Still, there were not enough coerced laborers to go around; potential employers complained about the perennial shortage of labor, meaning coerced labor, as they were surrounded by unemployed free hands. Willy-nilly, they had to hire some of the free laborers.

The vast majority of all *jornaleros* were either servants or food and water sellers, all of whom were spoken of with contempt. Free domestics did the same work that slaves did: they carried water and messages, cooked and cleaned, laundered and ironed. In the larger houses these tasks were divided, but in a house with one servant a lone woman might be expected to do everything. The women were sometimes also pressured to serve as concubines. Service extended beyond private homes, for there were servants working in all bars, schools, and offices. Most could expect to receive a daily meal in addition to their pay, but when, for example, the private high school was having budget problems, records show that food for the domestics was one of the first expenses to be reduced. The food purveyors were the most visible workers. Every day they brought to the city fish, produce, pigs, and chickens. They started selling even before they got to the city if they could: in his diary a Baltimore traveler described them climbing onto his ship from their canoes, offering their luscious goods. When they arrived at the river port, all nonindigenous were required to pay some minimal import taxes, but the municipal authorities frequently complained that many avoided this by unloading in secret above or below the city. Despite their being needed—or perhaps indeed because of it—these workers were not considered to be worthy of making a profit off their trade. In 1831 Luis Tobar, in the name of himself and the other market hucksters of foodstuffs, submitted a petition to the City Council which by implication would have solved the problem of illegal importations: they begged that the duties paid on goods from the river be lowered. When the council turned them down, they added insult to injury: "It is well known what these market hagglers are, and what are the frauds that they continuously commit." [29]

The water carriers urged their laden donkeys through the streets with sticks. The beasts traditionally were dressed in red leggings to protect them from the mosquitoes. During some seasons the tides carried the sea salt far upriver, and *balseros* had to make trips toward the mountains to find fresh water before they began to distribute it. These workers had less freedom than did the food-sellers. Their activities and the prices they charged were strictly monitored by the municipal police, and they were fined for deviations reported by the populace. The well-publicized prices depended on the distance the water was carried and remained the same for many years. These laborers were acknowledged to have a hard lot: even the strict Vicente Ramón Roca referred to them as "miserable day laborers." The elites knew that if they quit others would replace them, but they had to take care not to make the work so unattractive and unprofitable that even the starving would reject it. Once when a four-peso tax was imposed on each loaded raft arriving from the mountains, the *balseros* collectively petitioned the governor to be released from it. He eventually agreed, on the condition that the water carriers be required to provide any government office with as much water as desired, on demand.[30]

What most day laborers aspired to, however, was not domestic service or the selling of food and water. They spoke instead of "learning a trade." Some were able to do this. The artisans' guilds depended on a certain number of poor people of color to be responsible for doing low-level tasks within each trade. But there were two serious problems: first, the competition was stiff for the places available, and, second, even if one could obtain a position, there was no guaranty that people of that low level would be regularly paid or would ever advance. In solving the problem of securing a place it helped to have an influential friend. María Manuela, the slave of José Garostiza who secured her freedom through her relationships with her white-mestizo lover and his sister, convinced her master to help her apprentice her so-called free *zambo* son to a shoemaker. Unfortunately, the young adolescent boy wasted his chance: he was thrown out when he continued to laugh at the master shoemaker despite reprimands. Years later the penniless young man probably regretted his behavior, for he complained that there were not many other opportunities open to him.[31]

The difficulties of obtaining good treatment and proper payment were constant. Big jobs were distributed by the *maestro mayor* to the city's master craftsmen, and payment was received through him as well. In 1835 Fernando de la Cruz received for his guild of shoemakers a promissory note for 1,200 pesos as payment for outfitting some military troops with boots, belts, cartridge holders, and leather packs. Because the government's credit was shaky, Fernando was only able to sell it to a speculator for 159 pesos, which he used to pay the higher-ranking shoemakers, but none of the fifty-eight men who had been called on to work a few days each. Several men and one woman (who worked with her husband and represented him), apparently middle-aged people, presented a protest in the court. They were each to receive only a minimal amount of money even if they won, but to them it seemed to be a matter of utmost importance, for they had nothing to spare.[32] A similar case concerned the carpenters. The lowest-level assistants received four reales a day, one real higher than the rate charged for unskilled *presidio* labor, yet they were last on the list to be paid. When the master of the guild received payment for a canoe day laborers had made, he used it to pay other debts. They went to court and petitioned: "We are poor, and our existence, and that of our families, is by the sweat of our brow . . . "[33] After two years they were still waiting. Three of them were able to sign their names to their petition—not elegantly, but legibly. And yet it seemed to have done them little good to have studied a trade and learned to sign their names, for their claim was still regarded as unimportant by the authorities.

Some men who could not enter a trade tried to obtain a "post," a low-level municipal job that presumably would at least be permanent, if not terribly lucrative. Such jobs were obtained through a patronage system: one had to make oneself known to the authority charged with recommending men to the governor. Womenfolk working as domestic servants in elite houses may have been useful in this regard. In this period of war, however, with the municipality constantly short of money, the money earned by a man at a post was rarely enough to feed a family. There were two garbage collectors who led less trustworthy men from the *presidio* in hauling refuse away in carts. The two men were to earn fifteen pesos a month, while the two mules who dragged the carts were to have six pesos spent on them. After several years of experience the municipality found that these men had to be strictly forbidden to be boisterous or make a party of their job.[34] After the separation from Gran Colombia, a company of night watchmen was created; each man was armed with a pike. They were paid twelve pesos a month, a sum that the municipality frankly admitted was not enough to live on, suggesting that they supplement their income by working for private citizens.[35] Between twelve and twenty-four men worked as guards for the Customshouse at different times, and several others were employed by the government's Tobacco Warehouse. Some of these knew how to read and write a little and were expected to be responsible, as it was their job to keep the goods safe from robbers; they were paid the minimum salary of twenty to twenty-five pesos a month (the equivalent of eight reales a day, the pay of a skillful low-level craftsman). When the financially strapped government ordered that salaries were to be temporarily cut across the board, the director of the Tobacco Administration wrote in defense of his agency's guards. He pointed out that they simply could not eat with only eleven pesos a month and that they would be forced to look for other work and neglect guarding the precious tobacco. They were exempted from the order.[36]

Esteban Recato, the city gravedigger from 1825 on, was probably the crankiest municipal worker or at least the staunchest in defense of what he viewed as his rights. When he could no longer keep the savanna's cattle from wandering through the cemetery, he complained to the council and insisted that they build a fence, which they agreed to do. The city's financial records show that in 1832 he was regularly paid between ten and twenty-two pesos a month, depending on the number of burials. Soon he insisted that this was not enough. The arrangement had always been that he would be paid one peso for each soldier brought to him and one and a half pesos for each body from the hospital. (Private citizens paid him on the side.) This had been satisfactory during the years of war, he explained, but now there were very few soldiers available for burial. Esteban wanted a raise. There is no record of his receiving one, however.[37]

People who did not have another occupation did odd jobs: they took what work they could get, day by day. Women often took in laundry or became wet-nurses. Men loitered around the shipyards or buildings under construction, hoping to be hired for lifting or unloading or hauling or holding. Common sense would suggest that an entrepreneur may have tried to organize some of them into labor gangs, so that merchants and tradesmen would not have to do their own negotiating directly; indeed, there is at least one surviving bill for such a service. Smaller odd jobs were available to those in the right place at the right time. Account books refer to paying peons to look for a lost canoe, scrub an empty house, deliver newspapers and pamphlets, shout news aloud, etc. If a person could read and write even poorly, she or he could, upon demand, serve as a "scribe" for completely illiterate acquaintances. Other such temporary work was closely linked to entertainment. Woodsmen guided gentlemen in hunting deer on the savanna, and boatmen escorted elite young people in Sunday pleasure parties to the countryside. Others reared fighting cocks or bulls and then staged battles, before which gentlemen could place their bets. Until the practice was outlawed, unspecified "ferocious animals" were harbored, probably so that their owners could charge admission for a view. Holidays and presidential visits were indeed occasions for celebrating, for there was plenty of work building triumphal arches and balustrades, making costumes, and, at Carnaval, cleaning out, decorating, and selling the eggshells filled with water.[38]

Many Guayaquileños subsisted on what they made working permanently as entertainers. Foreign ship captains complained that their sailors always came back from the city thoroughly inebriated. It was true that the *chinganas* were numerous and highly entertaining: a man could drink, enjoy the music and the dancing, play cards, hire a prostitute. Many of the city's women worked there; at least eight such establishments were even owned and operated by women. Sometimes a *chingana* grew informally and disappeared quickly: a group of young black women rented a room and offended the neighbors with their late-night dances and bawdy behavior. Women who were or called themselves "mestizas" living on the savanna near the city were also involved in the business, as we know from the story of Ana Yagual. Indeed, if a woman believed she had no choice but to work in this trade, she was better off in the city, where she was generally allowed to practice with the authorities' taking less notice. In the small towns in the countryside a prostitute ran the risk of having her children removed from her home and placed in foster care. The *chinganeras* were willing to take risks to increase their profits. They often allowed gambling with cards, even though it was illegal, and took precautions to make sure they were caught as rarely as possible. Acting on a tip, police chief Vicente Ramón Roca once burst into a billiard hall. Inside, all was tranquil. He found "no disorder at all."[39] The grapevine had worked, with at least a minute to spare.

Many people—probably far more than we will ever know—were reduced to supporting themselves through crime, generally theft. Meat sold in the warren of narrow streets in the Ciudad Vieja rather than in the market had often been stolen. Someone could take a cow from a nearby *hacienda*'s herd, tie it in the savanna near the Old City, slaughter it by candlelight when most people were asleep, then bring it to sell in the early morning. When such cases were uncovered, they revealed a complex network of thieves and receivers, including people of all colors, both sexes, slave and free.[40] Some thieves were professionals who knew how to make master keys and could clean out a watch repairshop, a Customshouse warehouse, even a church altar.[41] Most theft cases, however, concerned items stolen from living quarters by someone known to the complainant, often living nearby.[42] There were always those who were ready to profit from moments of crisis: during a fire in a school some items were saved, but others were stolen; and while the police force was occupied by the coming Peruvian invasion, the criminal world worked "with the most scandalous impunity."[43]

The contraband trade provided an illegal living for other people. The business usually involved, at top levels, at least one Guayaquileño merchant and one foreign ship captain, but plenty of others were involved. Small boats flitted in and out of the port at night, sometimes drawing near enough to the large boats to pass packages to them. Greater quantities of illegal goods were loaded and unloaded on deserted beaches at night, at a distance from the city. Occasionally workers were paid to repackage foreign rum (a forbidden item) inside whale oil casks that effectively covered any telltale smell. Sometimes the underpaid municipal guards were bribed to become involved, working with the men they were supposed to hunt down, some of whom may even have been their friends or neighbors. Families living in the Ciudad Vieja were paid to store goods, and in one case they secretly processed the smuggled tobacco right on the premises.[44]

Because of such activities, many people had seen the inside of the jail. As damp and dirty as it was, it did not seem to have a reputation as a terrifying place apart from the rest of the world. For the poor, it was a porous institution, almost a part of their community, a place where they waited for short periods either to be released or to be sent to labor in the *presidio*. For at least a few years one of the upstairs rooms was used as a school for children of artisans and tradespeople, who trooped in every morning. All prisoners were supposed to pay for their own food. For most this was impossible, so the guards either gave it to them anyway or, apparently, allowed food to be brought to them by friends from the outside. Escapes were reported constantly, and the police noted that it was almost impossible to recapture a man "of that class." For over a month in 1831 a gaping hole in the prison's chapel wall went unrepaired, and in 1832 guards and prisoners gained a reputation for partying together late into the night.[45]

A sentence to serve time in jail became more serious after 1832, when an experimental labor colony was founded in the Galápagos Islands, and the government began to order the deportation of minor offenders. When it became known that the first group was to go, the agitation in the prison bordered on riot for weeks, and there were even more escapes than usual. Even after this change, however, there is some evidence that the residents of Guayaquil continued to view their incarcerations as temporary, troublesome stopovers that did not by any means cut them off from the ties they had formed or change the fact that they had few alternatives. Domingo Delgado, an indigenous man from the Cuenca area who called himself a *peón jornalero*, came to live in Guayaquil in 1826; shortly afterward he was arrested for stealing two trunks of clothes from a man who had hired him to guide a boat. He was caught because he himself wore one of the bright nankeen jackets. Delgado was jailed. He escaped then was arrested again for another theft. This time he was sent to the *presidio*, but he escaped again. Later he was arrested and sent to the Galápagos, where they put him to work on a ship. By 1838 he was back in Guayaquil.[46]

For a few strong and brave souls, there was one form of high-paying work available to ordinary men of Guayaquil within the formal economy: one might travel for a living. Men charged with carrying the mail were respected *señores* of middle rank, but they almost always hired assistants. Trustworthy workers were also needed to cart goods between towns—to distribute the salt from Santa Elena's mines, for example, or to bring Cuenca's cloth down from the mountains. There was less work available during the rainy season, but even then some goods and mail continued to pass. This was not easy work. The crags rising to the Andes were beautiful but deathly. Even in the dry season, when the roads were in good condition, mules sometimes fell off the narrow mountain tracks. There were rumors that in the rainy season, when the roads were rivers of mud, mail carriers sometimes climbed trees and "scrambled from bough to bough."[47]

In a port city the sea might have offered other men employment if they were willing to leave their homes and families. And indeed, local pilots who knew the tricks of the river and the unlighted coast could demand from foreign clients as much as 150 pesos for a safe round trip, from the open sea to port and back again. Sailors were not paid so well, earning only nine to twelve pesos a month. Still, they had no expenses while they were at sea and could come back from a voyage of one or several months with an impressive lump sum. There should have been a sizable number of Guayaquileño sailors—but there were almost none. Juan José Flores explained this to posterity in a letter detailing how he planned to staff a ship that had just suffered mass desertion. As usual, he said, indigenous men or vagrants from the street could be impressed as ordinary seamen. To obtain enough "first-class sailors," who had some skill and experience, he could bribe some of the British and North American men now serving on other boats. Indeed, ship records indicate that there were usually dozens of the latter in port at any one time and that they filled most of the positions for first-class sailors.[48] So there was, after all, no need to train or to pay significant salaries to Guayaquil's own ordinary citizens.

Buying in the City

After work one day a slave stopped by his favorite store to look for his friend, a free man. He found him and repaid a standing debt of one real.[49] It was a small sum, but for the slave and his acquaintances money was hard to come by, and they remembered the exact amount a long time later even though a distracting, exciting brawl occurred that day. They did not have a large number of purchases and debts to recall.

The difficulty of finding mention of popular spending may be a function of the sources, but it seems to me that this reflects the fact that common folk rarely did spend, except on market food. They had almost no discretionary income and had almost no choices to make. Their inflexible budgets are evidenced in numerous ways. One government official remarked that in his city people of both sexes chewed tobacco from the age of six until death, and the administration should have had cause to congratulate itself on imposing a government monopoly over the product so as to secure all profits. Yet somehow people were not paying the new higher prices. Either they had stopped chewing or they were risking prison in receiving smuggled tobacco sold at the old price. Hunters may possibly have brought some of the area's abundant waterfowl to the back doors of the rich to sell to their cooks, but they did not bring such meat to market. Fish was easier to catch in quantity and therefore less expensive, and people apparently bought only the meat that was the cheapest. In a town full of people with few formal entertainment options, the one theater owner complained he could barely stay afloat because attendance remained so low. Yet people attended free public spectacles with enthusiasm. Those who drank ordered the very cheap rum made by neighbors of the *chinga-neras* in illegal stills.[50]

It had to be apparent to the poor that governing figures were aware that the majority of the population did not have even a few pesos to spare. A gentleman requested by the City Council to make a list of contributors to a forced loan demanded by the government said that he left out "the poorest class of society" because it would be "impossible" to ask them to pay. The national government did not like his refusal to include more people on the register, but the Ministry of the Interior later admitted in its own report that it was almost impossible to collect taxes from such people due to the *miseria general* and that a four-peso tax could shut down the smallest businesses.[51] If the elites were divided in their willingness to blame the poor for their inability to buy anything or to pay taxes, perhaps it was because they knew that the people's having nothing stemmed from the fact that they were offered so little. It was in fact their role to have nothing. Once during a raging fire a few individuals saved the building of the merchants' guild from going up in flames. The merchants were extremely grateful and decided to award the men a "large prize." They gave them two pesos each.[52]

Reaching for a Better Life—Or Deciding Not to Try

The new republican enthusiasm for education left the poor unmoved. If most people accepted their situation as it was, it may have been because they saw no alternatives. Education might have provided some hope in other circumstances, but here it did not. What good would learning to write do a boy from Ciudad Vieja? People would still know where he was from and offer him low-paid positions. Probably for this reason, combined with the expense, very few had sent their children to private charity schools that had existed under the colony.[53] The young republic founded two public primary schools, but these, as we have seen, were intended for the middling ranks and did not make the destitute feel welcome. The municipal government talked about starting another in one of the poorer neighborhoods, so that those children could easily walk there, but it would be many years before that project materialized. In 1831 a rare event became the exception that proved the rule: José María Bolaños, one of the teachers of the *escuela normal* that opened in 1826, asked the City Council for permission to offer a special handwriting course that would allow adults of the common class to improve themselves. He received permission and probably offered the class. There seems to be no record that Bolaños ever offered the course again, however. His students may well have learned what they probably already suspected: the children of a *zambo* shoemaker were still the children of a *zambo* shoemaker even if they could write.[54]

Some of the populace may actually have harbored suspicions—not entirely groundless—that education might do them more harm than good. In the first fifteen years of the republic indigenous peoples saw taxes levied against them and some of their community lands sold on the grounds that the money was needed to pay for schools for their children.[55] Furthermore, when a man was chosen by the City Council to be a neighborhood *alcalde*, whose job it was to enforce discipline, help collect taxes, and generally make himself unpopular, the *only* acceptable excuse he could make was that he "did not know how to read or write."[56]

Joining the army might have offered some possibility for social advancement. Yet except for the former slaves—who fought to keep their freedom—and the men drafted in times of emergency, most of the military force consisted of foreigners, generally men of African descent from Colombia and Venezuela. The local men's hesitancy to enlist could only have been due in part to the horrors and atrocities of the battles, for engagements were actually few and far between, and if the possibility of social advancement were real it might have been an inducement. Their reluctance may have been related to the poor quality of the food offered, the rate at which diseases were passed among soldiers, the hardship of travel, the lack of living quarters, and the low pay. Soldiers earned one real daily, minus any days spent recuperating from wounds or illness. Their salaries were famous for being months in arrears, and they knew full well that their officers always received theirs. Most importantly, perhaps, it was probably clear to them that the promotion of common soldiers was actually quite rare. Joining the army did not bring much added wealth, and it did not even bring greatly increased status. The reputation of soldiers preceded them: they enjoyed the *fuero militar* and, subject only to a military court of law, were known for loitering, gambling, and generally setting a bad example. At the end of the 1830s a debate in the newspapers of the city's elite demonstrated that common soldiers were held in extremely low regard by the wealthy.[57]

For a poor man or woman, the only really effective way to improve the situation was to form ties with others, preferably with those others who had more material resources. Usually the most useful kind of social tie was a close personal relationship. In one case Manuel Ojeda, a property-less man from the mountains, probably an Indian, worked for Vitoria Bernal, a woman who owned a store: he would go out for days at a time in a canoe, bringing back goods for her to sell. They were involved in a romantic relationship; when it ended, Manuel went into a rage and sued Vitoria. He wanted a share of the money made while he had thought they were partners. It was much more typical for a woman to depend on a man. A woman might move in with a printer or a lieutenant or a baker. She would serve as both his mistress and his maid, but her standard of living and that of her children were the same as his, as long as the relationship lasted. One woman named Andrea Miró was as intrepid as Manuel Ojeda, and she met with more sympathy in court. She sued Justo Aguilar for 300 pesos in back-pay for years of domestic work. He claimed that she had shamelessly seduced him, but the judge ordered that he pay her 30 pesos a month until the debt was paid and that, if he would not, his furniture should be sold.[58]

Andrea Miró was lucky as well as strong-willed. Most women, however, raised their children alone or lived with other day laborers who could not offer them financial resources. They lived close to the edge all of the time, and their anger boiled over when a man like Vicente Ramón Roca came to collect "tribute" from them in the form of a head tax they could not possibly pay without suffering. They and their men wanted to be left alone to work and make their own lives. They themselves or their parents or grandparents had been peons and slaves, with their labor and time and the pesos they could gather together extracted from them year by year. Even now these cityfolk, after years and lifetimes of living free in the streets of Guayaquil, still had almost nothing to show for it. Their labor was degraded and devalued at every turn, so that many if not most of them relied at least partially on an informal economy based on dangerous, illegal activities. They would have liked to buy shoes and many other things, but they could not. They might have sent their sons to school or to the army if they had believed it would do any good, but they did not believe it. All they could do was refuse to give Roca the three pesos he wanted.

Every day the gray waters of the River Guayas floated tranquilly by. Near the mouth of the river emptying into the sea, a person could see El Enamortajado (The Corpse or Dead Man's Rock). It had had this name since colonial days, because it looked like the corpse of a friar, lying on his back. But in these years a new tale was born to explain the little island's name.[59] In the early years of the republican government, so went the story, some gentlemen decided to build a lighthouse on Dead Man's Rock. They left four workers there with tools and supplies of food, but without a boat, so that they could not steal anything. The gentlemen had meant to pick them up again once they finished the lighthouse, but in the intervening months they forgot all about them. The men finished their work and then they starved. They died there on the rock.

This is not to say, however, that people necessarily accepted their role with tranquillity, with nothing more than a joke and a story. We saw Ana Yagual following after her absconding client with loud complaints. Her uncle Mariano de la Cruz rushed to her defense. The visiting military man merely laughed at them, but later that night the once-merry officer was found dead. When Vicente Ramón Roca and the other authorities tried to determine who had killed him, they met with a stony wall of silence. No one was ever convicted of the crime.

CHAPTER 8

"TO BECOME THE UNFORTUNATE

TENANTS OF YOUR ALMS HOUSE"

The Poor of Baltimore

Margaret Tagert was twelve years old when the imposing door of the Almshouse closed behind her and she found herself inside its walls. On New Year's Day, 1826, Margaret was the most recent arrival in the house; she was quite alone. "She has," wrote the stern director, "a father and mother whose character is bad."[1] Many such children repeatedly found wandering in the streets because their parents were not at home were taken to the Almshouse by the city's bailiffs.[2] This was a memorable trip for them. The house was "situated on a big hill, three miles distant from the center of town, and surrounded by tufted trees and green fields."[3] It was located at the intersection of Franklin and Pulaski Streets, at the far northwest corner of the city. In order to get there, the city's cart and its occupants had to leave behind the narrow byways that children like Margaret knew well and pass by "pleasant houses where life looked delicious."

On that first day of 1826 there were 354 people in the house, if Margaret had cared to count them. That year the daily average was 322, but it was cold: there were always more people in January and February.[4] Seventy-nine of the residents had at least one family member in the house, but they did not live together in family units, as they were assigned dormitories. The huge Almshouse contained rooms for every kind of person: white men and white women, black men and black women, orphan children, children brought by their parents, the sick, and women about to give birth or nursing their infants. There was an infirmary, school room, chapel, dairy, storage house, and various kitchens, dining halls, and work-rooms, besides the garden and farmland outside.

Margaret was placed with the other white girls. There was sickly Sarah Ann Turner, for example, whose three brothers were in the room for white boys; they had all come in with their Irish-born mother, Jane, after their father had abandoned them last summer. Their mother knew how to spin and card wool; when she found employment she was discharged, but she left her children in the house. Five-year-old Mary Ann Mosher had been accompanied by a little sister named Louisa, but the baby had died before Christmas. Anne Higab was the same age as Margaret. She had come from Ireland with her parents when she was eight, but they had both died since. She had been bound out twice as an indentured servant and was back in the house now with memories like nightmares. Her first master had left Baltimore, and the second had returned her as unfit. Someone in one of these houses had propelled her into sexual activity at a young age, and she suffered now from venereal disease.

Often girls like these were assigned to care for the youngest children, black and white. Margaret Catherell was a white baby found the previous August in a Fell's Point hog sty by Mr. Catherell Cooper. Henry Young was already a toddler: he had come a year ago with his German-born mother, who was then at least seven months pregnant. After the lying-in she left with the infant she had to breast feed, but little Henry stayed behind in the house. Baby Sally Salmon had been named in the Alms-house, possibly because she was a bright rust-gold color. She had been left on the doorstep of Lucy Johnson, a "decent coloured woman" living near the Lutheran Burial Ground, and Lucy, unable to care for her, had brought her to the house. The experience of a child living alone in the Almshouse may not have been as alienating as it would appear: the or-phaned and abandoned young people did not die in appreciably higher numbers than those whose parents were with them.[5] People who had no family ties with the children must have looked out for them—must have offered affection and seen that their food was not snatched from them and that they had blankets.

All of the children, from the infants to those Margaret's age, black or white, faced the same array of alternative futures. One-quarter of them would eventually go home with their mothers. Another quarter would die or run away. Half would be bound out as apprentices. When they were old enough (usually at least seven), and, apparently, if they were behaving passably well, their names were listed at a Meeting of the Trustees of the Poor. They were then matched with people who had requested a workhouse child as a servant or apprentice, and the city paid the cost of the indenture where it was necessary. In Margaret's case all of this happened unusually quickly: she was bound within a month of the day she entered the house. The trustees signed the same type of legal document that they signed for all the young white paupers:

> [We] . . . do hereby put and bind the said Margaret Tagert unto Charles Slack as a faithful apprentice from this day until the 30th December 1831 when the said Margaret Tagert will be eighteen years of age or until she become married. During all which term the said apprentice shall not be absent without leave; but shall perform lawful hard work, behave orderly and obey all reasonable commands. And the said Charles Slack doth hereby bind himself to teach or cause to be taught the said Margaret Tagert the art and mystery of housework and plain sewing, also reading, writing and arithmetic as far as the rule of Three and provide her good and sufficient diet, washing, lodging and apparel . . .[6]

The trustees further reserved the right to stop by and check on Margaret without giving advance notice. Then the girl was sent to live with Charles Slack and his wife on their farm near the city.

In an institution not governed by many rules or guarded by many staff Margaret Tagert would have been able to wander the halls before she left. There were several memorable characters staying there. In the black women's dormitories lived Effa Hutching and Mary Merican, both ninety-one years old and both born in Africa. Twenty-two-year-old Hetty Turner said she had "lost the men of her family." She was one of the only black women who, when asked her religion, did not either name the sect or avoid the question. She announced that she had none. In the white women's rooms lived, among others, Nancy Everett, who had come in almost three years ago to give birth to a baby she named Sarah Ann. The child was not strong; possibly it was her tenuous hold on life that caused Nancy to stay within the relative safety of the Almshouse. When Sarah Ann died shortly after Margaret Tagert's stay in the house, Nancy did not remain many days after. The men's rooms were equally full. Philip Johnson, a forty-three-year-old black man who had somehow lost his wife, had entered with his two small children when he lost the use of his legs. There in the house the doctor had told him he had to have them both cut off to save his life. He consented to have his two children bound almost immediately: his son went to Ann Arundel County and his daughter to someone in Fell's Point. John Burke, a white man who had worked as a baker for forty years, had been in the house before during drinking sprees, and now he had the fever that was currently prevalent in the city.[7]

People who visited the Almshouse noticed that it was a scene of great activity, not sloth.[8] During the day the school-age children such as Margaret Tagert went to the classroom, and on the Sabbath some people took advantage of the church services offered. As many people as possible were engaged in productive labor—indeed, the *per capita* annual cost of supporting the poor decreased dramatically during the 1820s as a result of the people's labor—but most "hands" were unable to work. Usually close to 100 of the residents were children, and significantly more than 100 were maimed or very ill. Of the remaining "able-bodied" people, many were needed to care for the first two groups—watching over, cooking, cleaning, and laundering. Those who were able to exercise crafts, however, must have put their hands to work with a will. In the six months before and the six months after Margaret Tagert's stay the farm and garden produced over $3,000 worth of goods, the carpenters about $2,000, and the women's spinning, weaving, and sewing over $1,000. Only a few could work at a trade at any one time, as the Almshouse inventory included five carpenters' workbenches, eight shoemakers' seats, three sewing lapboards, and ten spinning wheels. Since the goods produced exceeded those of some comparable private businesses, the totals suggest that the residents may have competed with pride to see who could bring in the most money. The farmworkers labored under a hired expert superintendent, who may have driven them unmercifully, but this would not explain the productivity of the other shops, where the workers superintended themselves. By 1835 the residents were actually paid by the piece and in turn charged for their board in order to encourage hard work, but in Margaret Tagert's day this was not yet the case.

Yet these hard-working people seemed at least temporarily unable to support themselves outside the Almshouse. Although Margaret's stay was brief, most people remained far longer. The average length of stay among the people present in the house on New Year's 1826 was just under three years, longer among the children (who were mostly waiting to be bound out), slightly shorter among the young and middle-aged adults, and longest among the very old (who generally expected to live out their remaining years in the house). The numbers of men and women were exactly even. Slightly more than half the adult men were unskilled laborers. The rest had been trained in a trade, but most of these were apparently low-ranking workers within their trades: barbers, carpenters, mariners, shoemakers, and weavers (there were five or six of each in the house). Other trades had only one or two representatives. Thirty-seven of the women (or 30 percent) said they could perform some combination of knitting, sewing, spinning, or carding. The others must have been "accustomed to housework," as a few claimed, and an unknown number would have supported themselves or supplemented their income through prostitution.[9]

The director usually recorded adults' reasons for entering the house on the day of their admittance. Twenty percent were unable to function due to drink. Another twenty percent were ill. The latter were divided into three very nearly equal groups: those suffering the fever in the city, those with a venereal disease, and those who had a permanent and often progressively worsening disease, such as blindness or consumption. Fifteen percent were experiencing a temporary (or occasionally permanent) loss of the use of a limb, usually due to an accident. Ten percent suffered from some form of mental impairment, and another ten percent simply from old age. Six percent had rheumatism, and another six percent were transients, newcomers in town. Five percent were women who were pregnant or caring for more children than they could handle. Three percent were women whose male providers had died or run away or beaten them or thrown them out. The records kept by the doctor in the Almshouse indicate that in fact many people were underreporting their health problems upon entry. Many, for example, were suffering from acute diarrhea, but only a handful mentioned this.[10]

Almost all the officials who had experience working in the Almshouse, however, were convinced that alcohol played a larger role than the numbers suggested. They saw heavy drinking and said that far more than the twenty percent who were clearly driven to the Almshouse by drink were indirectly led thither by "intemperance." The residents' personal crises, illnesses, and accidents, they claimed, were often a result of overindulgence of their taste for liquor. No one discussed the opposite possibility—that their drinking might sometimes have been a result and not a cause of their painful personal crises, illnesses, and accidents. The doctors' and employees' views were common in their social world. There was a strong sentiment that the rising poor tax burden could be controlled if the sale of alcohol were limited: a petition was even presented to the City Council demanding that a waiting period be required before a license to sell alcohol be issued to any citizen while a background check was done to ascertain the man's moral character.

John Morton, the director, turned away paupers who had previously come to the house to spend a few days drinking and then had run away wearing clothes issued to them by the establishment without paying for them or asking to change back into their own old clothes. He might, he admitted, even have gone so far as to tell such vagrants that they might perish in the street for all he cared. Elected officials who did not actually work in the Almshouse did not always share Morton's attitude. John Robb was enraged about this issue: as manager of the poor in Fell's Point, it was his job to send the indigent to the Almshouse, and he did not want them sent back. He wrote to the mayor: "It has been necessary to send from the Point a number of poor miserable objects who must be provided for or die in the street, which I am informed in some instances has given offence to Mr. Morton . . . Under those circumstances, I would beg leave to resign this office . . ." [11]

Despite the Almshouse staff's obvious frustration with alcohol and the damage it caused, their own statistics do not bear out the supposition that constant drunkenness was what brought people to the house. Of the 273 adults in the house with Margaret, 97 were known to have stayed several times. These would be the most likely to prove to have a drinking problem, but in fact more than two-thirds of them were considered "sober." The distinctions between those who never entered the house, those who came once in an emergency, and those who came repeatedly arose due to differing levels of available resources. Resources would have included even minimal family savings or property that might serve as a cushion in emergencies, a network of social relations and ties with others who had assets to spare, and education or a completed apprenticeship, preferably under a locally known master. This seems apparent because the residents as a whole—and the group of frequent visitors most especially—were disproportionately non-natives, who had had less time to develop any of these kinds of resources. Only one-seventh of the residents were whites who had been raised in Baltimore, and many of these were children: Frederick Douglass later remembered this type of child as having been willing to do anything—even teach a slave to read—in exchange for some bread. There were more visitors to the Almshouse who had been born in Ireland than had been born in Baltimore, though this did *not* match the city's statistics at the time. (Margaret Tagert was among them.) Finally, the records of the doctors working at the health clinic in Fell's Point tell us that all the people there suffered from the same kind of crises relating to accident, illness, and alcohol that the people in the Almshouse experienced.[12] But not all of them ended up in the poorhouse—only those who had no safety net.

At first glance, the numbers of black men and women seem to point to an exception to the rule, given that they certainly had been prevented from amassing resources and yet their proportion of the Almshouse population was slightly lower than their proportion of the city's population (just under one-fifth as opposed to just over).[13] This might partly be explained by the fact that it was riskier for a black than for a white to proclaim indigence, as a black Baltimorean could always be accused of being a runaway slave. But there was more: a higher proportion of black men than white men in the Almshouse had a trade, indicating that a profession provided more limited insurance for a black man than it did for a white. This can most easily be explained when we consider that the black community had been prevented from building the same resources as whites in addition to their trade skills.

The Almshouse drew its residents from those streets and alleys where people lived close to the edge of survival all the time. A pregnancy, illness, or abandonment drove people to its walls. Sometimes desperation was so great it exceeded the ability of the house to offer a solution: "a black girl child" or a "female white infant" might be found drowned in a privy.[14] From whence did this stark reality come? We must step back to see how such people first came to the streets of Baltimore.

Enter the Freedman

Frederick Bailey lived in an urban world in which slaves worked without flagging toward freedom and in which whites were beginning to feel threatened by the phenomenon. As in other places in the United States, there had been a moment of shared enthusiasm for democracy after the War for Independence, and until 1811 some black citizens had even been able to vote in Baltimore.[15] As elsewhere, the enthusiasm on the part of most whites had waned. Now free blacks had to request permission even to have a party—and successful requests included the testimonials of several white friends.[16] Various "back-to-Africa" colonization schemes became favorite charities. Laboring whites were afraid of the free blacks' capacity to compete in the working world. Plantation-owning whites were concerned that the presence of free blacks would make those who were still enslaved discontented. "That [my slaves] were content with their condition, I do not doubt, and would have remained so but for the evil which resulted from their intercourse with free persons of Colour, whose efforts, I have every reason to believe, are unceasing in poisoning the minds of Slaves, wherever they can meet with them." [17]

The concern of the whites, however, did not stop the blacks from coming to Baltimore in search of a new life. The free black population continued to grow. The people poured in from three sources. In a countryside changing from tobacco to grain, as we have seen, many came with legal manumission papers. They also came as runaways. And they came as slaves who saved their money carefully to buy themselves in the same way as their peers did in Guayaquil.[18] For each group, for different reasons, it was nearly impossible to get a leg up out of poverty. Success required a flawless performance: there was no room for crisis or illness or error.

The fugitives, though the smallest of the three groups, received the most attention. They came to the city partly in search of anonymity and partly in search of acquaintances whom they thought would help them. "50 Dollars Reward! Ran away on Wednesday last . . . a dark mulatto boy named Nick, or Nick Brooks . . . Nick has been seen loitering about the city since he left my service . . . he has a grandmother and two aunts living in the city." "Ran away on Sunday night . . . a coloured boy named John Dowing . . . It is likely he may have gone to his father's, near the Falls Turnpike Road . . ." The owners threatened sympathetic whites who might give them jobs: "Ran away . . . [six weeks ago] a dark mulatto woman named Milky . . . Having been satisfactorily informed she is employed in a family in this city, the person (whoever he may be) is hereby requested to deliver her up or abide the consequences." [19]

For a runaway slave to get a new life started in the city was an extraordinarily difficult task. Potential employers probably hesitated to hire anyone they suspected might be a fugitive, and there were people in every neighborhood only too happy to supplement their income by recapturing a slave and collecting the reward. The former slaves, who did not know the city and its personalities well, were especially vulnerable to tricks and subterfuges of eager bounty hunters. "He had made the Black man believe he was Mr. Tyson [Thomas Tyson's uncle Elisha, a well-known abolitionist] and that he was going to send him to his country estate. . . . He was [really] going to take him to the watch house." [20] Beginning in 1830, advertisements were placed in the newspapers describing the blacks currently committed to jail as probable runaways. If no one claimed them after several months, they were discharged, as the city could not afford to continue to pay for their maintenance in the prison.[21] Some of those arrested told the officials to whom they belonged; others insisted that they were not slaves. "He says he is free born." "She says she is free." Any white person who could satisfy a judge with some sort of documentation could take them away; however, the fact that many of those arrested remained unclaimed while the ads ran for months would seem to indicate that claiming a slave who was not really former property was actually not a common practice among whites. Probably neighbors who knew a slave had never belonged to a certain person would have protested the sudden increase in wealth when the person came home from the jail with this "reclaimed" property.

Former slaves who had been legally manumitted and had their papers in order were relatively safe from being grabbed and having their lives and earnings interrupted and possibly their freedom taken. Even they were at risk, however. When a Baltimorean was manumitted, he or she was supposed to register at the City Court.[22] If a person had been freed years ago but had not registered at the time, it was never too late to do so. It was necessary to bring at least one white witness to the court appearance to have the certificate of freedom recorded. Most of those manumitted were no longer young when they received their freedom and, for the first time, could begin to keep what they had earned. They had already given their best years of labor to another. Often they had more years ahead of them in which they would need to spend every surplus penny in trying to free those whom they loved. A free washerwoman named Anna who was in love with Frederick Bailey spent years collecting money to help him and later became his wife.

Many of those who were in a position to act did not wait for the manumission that most likely would never come on its own or, if it did, would come late. But buying oneself and one's family was a process of years, which eliminated all hope of gathering surplus resources during one's youth. Even those who labored apparently tirelessly and learned to negotiate the city's financial world as well as any upper-level tradesperson had to turn over almost every penny gained to another. At the age of fifty-four, a former shoemaker's apprentice-turned-preacher and his family were still in the midst of their hardships. His story speaks for itself and deserves to be heard for what it teaches about the economic straits in which freedmen were placed and the strategies they used:

[My wife and I] were both slaves . . . We have lived happily together, as husband and wife, for the last twenty-eight years. We have had nine children—seven born in slavery, and two since my wife's freedom. Five out of the seven in slavery I have bought—two are still in bondage . . .

The cause of my failure to raise all the money [in a speaking tour], I believe, was that I was unaccustomed to addressing large congregations of strangers, and often . . . I would feel such embarrassment that I could scarcely say anything . . .

[Later] my wife's mistress agreed to sell to me my wife and our two youngest children . . . My salary [as a minister] was only three hundred dollars a year, but with hard exertion and close economy, together with my wife's taking in washing and going out at day's work, we were enabled by the first of the year to pay the two hundred dollars our dear friend had loaned us, in raising the six hundred dollars before spoken of. But the bond for three hundred dollars was now due, and how must this be met: I studied out a plan; which was to get some gentleman who might want a little servant girl, to take my child, and advance me three hundred dollars for the purpose of paying my note, which was now due in Virginia. In this plan I succeeded, and had my own life insured for the seven years for five hundred dollars, and made it over to this gentleman, as security, until I ultimately paid him the whole amount, though I was several years in paying it.[23]

Noah Davis clearly had the financial ingenuity to create and finance a manufactory or any other business. He was, however, forced to spend his talents and his resources in another way.

Enter the Immigrant

The British officer Edward Coke was revolted by the "steerage passengers," the pathetic-looking "emigrants" with whom he occasionally had to rub shoulders during his voyage to America in the summer of 1832. In the port of Baltimore a doctor gave a cursory check to all incoming ships, looking for any evidence of contagious diseases. He, too, was offended by what he found in some of the newcomers. "The condition of many is deplorable indeed! both as to their pecuniary resources, as well as to their infirmities, mental and corporeal, moral and physical."[24]

The doctor reported that 1,843 foreigners had arrived in 1828, 2,074 in 1829, and 4,084 in 1830. And the numbers were to continue to rise. Between 1820 and 1850 Maryland would receive 130,000 immigrants. Many of them chose to stay in Baltimore, where their numbers grew so that they soon dwarfed the free black population and caused it to decline in its relative proportion. In the 1820s Baltimore's Naturalization Docket recorded the declarations of arrivals from Ireland, England, Scotland, France, Prussia, Sardinia, Saxony, Switzerland, and Sweden. The majority of new arrivals were from Ireland. They had nearly all come to grow wheat or to work on the wheat farms of others. They came also as artisans who planned to work in Baltimore or in a nearby town and as laborers who hoped to find jobs working on canals and roads and bridges. A few still came as precontracted indentured servants. Because of their employment connection to someone well-to-do, such temporary bondsmen may ironically have sometimes had a higher chance of living as well as they had hoped. Mr. and Mrs. Parks, for example, were the indentured servants of a successful cooper in Baltimore, and it was their employer who paid the school bill for little Thomas Parks.[25]

Despite the "deplorable condition" of some who came off the boats, others in fact arrived with some "pecuniary resources" and with personal ties they could put to use. Farmhand Joseph Pickering wished he had brought all the letters of introduction people had offered him when his savings began to run low before he found work. We met carpentry apprentice William Minifrie, who was able to write home for money until he found regular employment.[26] What of those, though, who did not arrive with resources of their own? Despite his condescension aboard the ship, Edward Coke made special note of the fact that after he began his tour when on the other side of the Atlantic he never again felt surrounded by hordes of such bedraggled folk. Once they reached the shore, most of them apparently did find the work they had hoped to find. Then they received a laborer's pay of seventy-five cents to one dollar per day. They could spend what they earned, as they did not need to begin by buying their own freedom. Yet the fact remained that a minority lived in misery and ended up in the poorhouse. Some, like Margaret Tagert's parents, even felt unable to tend to their daughters and their sons. In choosing to come to Baltimore, they had all indicated they had hope for their future there. Some lost their hope; some did not. In searching for understanding it is important to look specifically at the ways in which they were all trying to subsist, although with differing degrees of success. The fate that awaited the immigrants makes sense only in the context of the working lives of everybody else, including both the free blacks and the whites who had lived in the city for many years.

Working in the City

Only young males were overtly set aside as a class apart, a group doomed to evil habits and to poverty. In their daily lives most people did not tend to complain that either blacks or immigrants were causing most of the city's problems, but rather that "boys" were. Older citizens complained of "Boys and other evil disposed persons" who waited in the dark for boats to unload their goods so that they could grab something and run. The mayor ordered city bailiffs to "arrest all boys and others . . . who are in the habit of annoying [Meetings for Worship] by false alarms of the cry of fire." All boys, not only the destitute, were assumed to be miscreants who might be tempted to commit crimes. Pawnbrokers were under strict orders not to receive goods from *any* "minor, apprentice, servant, or slave." In other words, even employed young men were not held in high regard. In lists of unskilled laborers waiting to be paid, only "boys" were listed without their names and received pay drastically lower than everyone else's. In the latter case they were, perhaps, not only young, but also black. Young apprentices were assumed to be incompetent, the bane of their masters' lives: citizens complained that "coopers' boys and apprentices" were making a mess of their job of inspecting barrels of mackerel, as they opened them carelessly and spilled the pickling solution. They were even accused of being physically abusive to their teachers in the public schools.[27]

It was, then, not too much to hope that once past this "evil disposed" phase of life, any male citizen could aspire to becoming a respected member of society, for all Baltimoreans grew older every year. Generally, the traditional artisanal apprenticeship system still functioned here: most workers had reason to hope to rise to master status. For several generations, the proportions of mechanics and day laborers had not changed much. Some trades in the process of early industrialization, such as the shoemakers and some construction contractors, had indeed begun to take on more apprentices than could ever possibly be trained as journeymen, but thus far this had not become a clearly recognizable problem.[28]

It remained a reality, however, that in fact *not* all Baltimoreans had an equal chance at graduating from miserable boy to successful citizen. In the great parade of 1828 that marked the laying of the first railroad, every artisan group in the city supposedly participated. Almost everyone felt involved in the city's future on that day—almost everyone, but not everyone. Trades dominated by blacks were not represented, nor certain other menial jobs even if mostly done by whites. No chimneysweeps or bootblacks or wood sawyers or servants or day laborers marched—no one who provided a menial service rather than a handcrafted product. Most people really were invited to participate in the hopes and dreams of this relatively inclusive society, but there still remained a smaller class of people who were subtly set aside as permanent drudges.

Such a day laborer might try to form a connection with a well-off family, so that they would always call on him when they had work beyond that which their permanent servants could do. Mordecai Chalk, for example, worked frequently for the wealthy Spafford family for "1/4-day" or "1 day." He did such seasonal and short-term tasks as sowing their garden turnips and killing their hogs. Others entered into relationships with contractors, who were often looking for gangs of men and who tended to hire those they had hired before. The contractors included firms who had offered the lowest bids to clean or pave streets, dredge the harbor, unload goods from ships, dig canals, etc. Often they needed large groups of laborers. The force employed to dredge the Basin, or Inner Harbor, included fifty-eight men and thirteen horses, plus several higher-level "superintendents."

Most of these men received seventy-five cents per day. A few who did less physically demanding jobs, such as tending to the horses or guarding the tools at night, received fifty cents. A few others, who probably had longer experience or assisted the superintendents, received eighty-seven and a half cents. The latter amount was also the going rate for everyone who worked for street paver John Hetzler and several other employers. In a world where one could rent a tiny house for $4.25 or $5.00 per month in an alley of Fell's Point, this was a livable wage. In employers' records labor costs regularly exceeded outlay for materials, and they assumed that it must be so if they were to get good work out of the laborers. The problem was that the work was not regular, and not everyone had ties to those who gave it out. Foreign observers tell us that both black and white men hustled employment on the wharves, but we do not know how many of each were hired, as employers noted only a man's name, job, and wage, not his color.[29]

Many people felt that obtaining work from the city would be a positive step forward, probably because they believed this would ensure a more reliable future income. Most of the tasks the municipality assigned to day laborers were temporary, however. The mayor once hired men to try to catch the marauding hogs that roamed the city, so that they could be sold to the Almshouse for bacon. Because the muddy beasts were either hard to find or hard to grip, the men did not have much luck and were dismissed after a week. When large quantities of manure piled up in the streets, workers gathered it and deposited it in special lots where it was later sold to farmers. Other city jobs were permanent. There were seventeen prison guards, for example, and one city hall messenger and caretaker earning $75.00 per year. It must have been assumed that he would find other part-time work as well. The best position available was that of a nocturnal policeman or "night watchman." In the eastern district of Fell's Point, there were eleven "privates" in the force, earning $25.00 per month each. Until 1827 they had been paid a minimal amount per shift worked, with no pay when "taken sick"; but they had protested that they, like other citizens, deserved a regular income, and they had gotten it. The men who applied for these jobs could usually sign their own names, even if they could not write their own letters, but some could only put their "X" mark at the bottom of the page. They were day laborers who were only sporadically employed. One had some limited experience as a rigger, but he had never become officially apprenticed to a master.[30]

To secure such work, it was helpful to have worked previously for one of the high-level tradespeople known to the city officials. But it was the appeal for pity that was most effective. Henry Lutger, for example, went to William Hubbard, a successful pumpmaker who knew him, and asked him to write a letter on his behalf so that he might get work painting the city springs. "I do it with great pleasure," wrote Hubbard ". . . and as he has been sick this winter, being very much reduced in circumstances, you would be realizing a charity by giving him employ . . ." Another laborer wrote directly to the mayor himself: "Dear Sir: I am entirely out of work and have a poor helpless family and being deprived of work for at least two months past they are actually in want of the necessarys of life. I made application to Mr. Crey for day work . . . but he does not appear to be willing to give me [any]." They sometimes claimed good characters: one pointed out that he was also a good patriot and had been a soldier in the late war. But they felt that the argument that would carry the day was that they were in need and had many mouths to feed. No one, they argued, deserved to live in such poverty as they did. "You cannot give it to one who needs it more than myself." "Your petitioner respectfully represents that he is at this time unable to support a small family that is entirely depending on him for support." "Your petitioner has a large family to support and has never learned any trade and depends on labouring for the support of his family . . ."[31]

Other kinds of day laborers included fishermen and seamen, chimney-sweeps, and wood sawyers. Some of these earned as much as artisans, but most did not, and their status was lower, judging by the number of derogatory comments made about them. Chimneysweeps, for example, often boys, charged eight cents per chimney where the flue was one story, twelve cents where it was two, and fifteen cents where it was three, but most worked for companies who collected the money and gave them only part. Depending on how fast they worked, they could earn varying amounts in a day. During the season when chimneys were in constant use and many became clogged, they could spend days at a time flying from emergency to emergency, and these cases were probably more time-consuming.[32] Seamen's labor was even more dependent on the seasons. When the waters were frozen, there was little work, but in the spring their time was in demand. Common sailors earned less than $10.00 a month, although they were given their food and often a shirt as well. Theoretically, they had the possibility of arriving home with a lump sum, but in reality it was often spent in other ports or sometimes advanced to them for their families before they left. Their lifespans were short, and they did not always die at home.[33]

Some laborers found work in the new manufactories. Here the work was divided into small tasks; workers who were hired knew that the owner had no intention of treating them all as apprentices. They were usually paid the day laborer rate of seventy-five cents. Conditions at these sites of intense productivity left much to be desired: one traveler reported that the owner of a local steel manufactory said himself that his employees were "poor wretches." Traditionally, such work had gone to less-than-free laborers. Earlier in the century new factory owners had often taken young people from the Almshouse who were the wards of the city. Records of indentures for the 1820s, however, indicate that this was no longer current practice. Some plants, such as McKim's Maryland Chemical Works, had moved from being a slave operation to relying on a small number of slaves in conjunction with free workers.[34] At that time a number of the manufactories relied on "female hands." In the early 1800s master tailors had begun giving out slop work to women to take home and sew in their houses because they would work for less money, and the trend in textiles had continued until women were even the preferred workers for the new power looms. "It is an operation better adapted to females," wrote one supervisor.[35] Despite women's supposed docility, the son of the manager of a soap and candle factory encountered resistance when he demanded more than their labor. He was a devout evangelical who insisted that the workers pay attention to his teachings in addition to doing their work: they mostly ignored him. Young Moses was forced to be content with any response at all, however small. "Spent the greater portion of this day attending to business; spent part of the time in conversing [again] with the Females in the Factory on the subject of Temperance, and by the blessing of Providence I got one of them to consent to sine [sic] her name to the constitution of the Temperance Society . . ."[36]

There were only a few manufactories in each ward, however. They could not account for a significant number of workers. Certainly most women who needed employment did not depend on them. Far more worked as domestic servants. They cooked, cleaned, hauled and heated water, tended fires, cared for children, laundered, and ironed. Their wages varied and often depended on whether or not they had any children of their own to mind, who would make them less efficient workers. Many women, especially black women, did not work for one family, but rather hired themselves out as laundresses to many neighborhood residents. When a poor woman lost a baby and had milk available, she could advertise herself as a wetnurse in the newspapers and maximize her chances of finding a customer.

Another large group of women worked as hucksters. Men could be wandering salesmen as well, but the profession was dominated by women. One observer said the markets in other North American cities were more "orderly," but she liked Baltimore's busy centers: "Nothing pleased me more than the markets . . . Here an old woman sitting with a table spread with nice bread and butter, veal cutlet, sausages and coffee; there another, with a table bending under the weight of candy, sweet cakes, oranges and apples . . ."[37] In reality, most food sellers in this city were *not* poor: as we saw in Chapter 6, they brought in large wagonloads of goods and sold them from fixed market stalls. But there was still room for smaller businesspeople. People living on the edge could take out a huckster license but not rent a market stall to go with it; instead, they carted about small amounts of goods themselves. Sometimes two people put their money together to buy one such license, operating a miniature "partnership," as they themselves called the arrangement when they had someone write out a "contract" with each other on a slip of paper. Other people tried to sell goods in the market without spending the money to take out a license at all. When they were caught, they were fined. One man left when he was issued a fine, but shortly afterward his wife appeared in the market to take his place. Unfortunately for them, the bailiff noticed and fined her too. Some sellers—mostly women, black and white—were even more itinerant than the market vendors without stalls: they traveled "through the several streets," selling small amounts of oil or chunks of bacon or peaches and pastries, seven days a week, and they were "not without customers." Marketeers who paid for stalls protested their success.[38]

In some ways the market was its own social world. It came complete with its own style of crime and its own law enforcement official—the market day bailiff. It was this bailiff's job to prevent people not only from selling without a license, but also from committing such offenses as sleeping in the marketplace or fighting or "rioting." As he could not be everywhere at once, he depended on "informers" to report wrongdoing to him. The informer was allowed to keep one-half of any fine when it was collected—which it often was not, as some of the miscreants were "good for nothing," meaning they had no money with which to pay. Some people undoubtedly acted as informers in hopes of turning a profit; they may even have come to market with this in mind. The decision to inform depended on a person's power relative to the offender. Blacks never informed against whites. Women never informed against men. Women did occasionally, however, inform against each other. Harriet Collins, for example, was fined $1.00 for throwing stones. She immediately informed against two other women who had done the same thing and thereby got her money back.[39]

In 1827 a movement gained momentum among more-established marketeers and some City Council members to curb the activities of the itinerant peddlers and hucksters. Some were to be removed, and others to pay higher fees. A man was accused of being a "public nuisance" who often sold lemonade at Centre Market after market hours, when people were on their way home, hot and tired. He responded vehemently, noting that he personally kept the whole fountain area clean, at no cost to the city, and that lemonade was not "an expensive or injurious article, but a refreshing draft accommodating to persons passing . . ." He attached the signatures of over twenty-five respectable citizens.[40] A group of eighteen widows, each of whom carefully enumerated the number of children she was supporting, put those with the most dependents at the top of the page and protested the "too prevalent bias" against them. They entreated:

> ... that your Memorialists may be enabled further to prosecute their humble but lawful traffick, as the only means of their support and maintenance in Life, and which, should your honorable body still continue to tax and burden with heavy restrictions, your Memorialists will be compelled to abandon, and many of them by consequence in all probability, will be thrown upon the charity of your City and forced to become the unfortunate Tenants of your Alms House.[41]

There was actually a double threat enclosed in the message of the widows: although they were now among the contributing citizens, they might have to turn to the poorhouse and become a public expense, or, one could not help noticing, they might turn from their "humble but lawful traffick" to "traffick" that was *unlawful* or at least shady. Blacks and whites both bought charms from fortunetellers (powders wrapped in dirty bits of paper), and circus advertisements nearly always mentioned a woman who would put on an exotic performance, such as wild feats of horsemanship. Prostitutes looked for work every day on the wharves of Fell's Point. Market women illegally used their ordinary sales licenses to sell seafood and grog in tiny hole-in-the-wall "oyster shops" filled with enthusiastic patrons. When Catherine Oliver was cited for keeping her bar open on a Sunday, she insisted she had done nothing wrong, as she did not have a license for a tavern but an ordinary license that could be used on any day. Her judge admitted she had a point and wondered how the city could prevail on "this class of persons" to buy the right license. Meanwhile, they went on with their businesses, attracting customers with games of "ten pins" (which were to be bowled down) and "pitching pennies" (gambling on heads or tails). By 1831 the former game had become so profitable to barkeepers that the city began charging $25.00 per year as a license fee.[42] Sometimes these miniature tavern keepers took their businesses on the road and went to those who could not come to them. A harbor official complained that

> evil . . . has repeatedly arisen from the practice of Boats from the City, in charge of Petty Vendors of Spiritous Liquors, [coming] in order to sell or furnish the liquor to the seamen; the persons in the boats, laying on their oars a few rods ahead of the Vessels at the

Quarantine ground, and paying out line, to which is attached a Bottle or Bottles of liquor, partially filled, which in that state are buoyant and float leeward, carried by Wind and tide, towards the bows of the Vessels and are thus easily hauled aboard by the seamen with Boat Hooks, and unperceived by the Officers.[43]

Some people went beyond shady activities for which they might be fined or held in ill-repute and committed acts for which they could actually be jailed. About 1 percent of the city's population was tried for a criminal offense in a year.[44] How many of these were foreign-born we do not know. We do know, however, that only 20 percent were black, in a city where blacks made up about 23 percent of the population. While only 20 percent of whites were convicted, 50 percent of the people of color were. The overwhelming majority of those tried of both races were accused of stealing. (Larger numbers were brought to the jail for being drunk and disorderly, but these were fined and released and not entered in the "Criminal Callender [sic].") A few attempted spectacular thefts, such as robbery of the federal mail coach, but most robbed in a more prosaic way, taking advantage of a situation that was familiar. Workers complained that if they left large tools at a construction site overnight they disappeared. A black couple from the countryside who had come to market to make purchases were pulled aside by a friendly and knowledgeable urban black man, who promised to show them where they could buy used clothes. He did—and they said he picked their pocket too.[45]

Life in the city's jail was changing during this period. There were four compartments—one for male debtors, one for male criminals, one for all the women, and another for the ill. Within each section the prisoners could circulate during the day. Until 1830 they had no work to do and were left to talk. Also until that year they were issued raw meat and bread each morning and then cooked it themselves on stoves present in each compartment. But in keeping with broader changes in the nation's penal system, a new system was soon put in place. Prison staff took charge of cooking and distributed the stew twice daily. Criminals were further subdivided between the "hardened" and the new, and some of them were put to work. It became the onerous duty of the warden to enforce the collection of a fee from each prisoner to pay for his or her keep.[46]

People convicted of serious felonies had a different fate meted out to them: they were executed or went to the penitentiary, across the street from the jail, where they stayed for one to seven years. Here, according to the new "panoptican" plan, 17 guards watched over 300 prisoners separated by race and sex. On 5 floors, a total of 320 cells faced the inner hall. Each day groups were taken to workshops. The men made sails, rugs, combs, shoes, brushes, and furniture. The women carded wool, wove, sewed, laundered, and made "fine hats." By the mid-1820s the penitentiary store was in operation, advertising that it sold good-quality products at "reduced prices." Customers must not have been lacking, for returns were high. One visitor was scandalized that the inmates did not seem at all ashamed of themselves, but showed him the work they did quite proudly.[47]

There was, however, a far worse, almost unimaginable punishment that had been reserved for some. Black Baltimoreans may have known that a full two-thirds of the residents of the penitentiary were black, but this was not the worst threat they faced. In 1825 and 1826, according to a new law that was passed and then revoked, a free black could be sold into slavery for a period of two to ten years for committing a crime against property. A few white men would buy many convicts at a time: at least one was a known slave trader who advertised himself publicly as such in the papers. One man named John Brown was sold to serve a two-year term in June 1826. In April of the next year the bailiff brought him into court again. He had been sold, as ordered, and had run away from his new owner. Now he was caught again. This time he got ten years.[48]

There were some repeat offenders within the criminal system, but there does not seem to have been any sense that the prison or the penitentiary was a porous part of the community or that a stay there should be taken lightly. The massive brick structures were on the edge of the town. The surrounding wall boasted a great iron gate, "the opening of which takes no little time." There were even iron bars ranged across the tops of the chimneys. Escape was not tolerated. In 1826, in a huge trial involving over twenty subpoenas, a man was convicted of having tried to set fire to the jail and was sold into slavery for a term of ten years. When, several years later, some prisoners did effect their escape, the city poured money into efforts to recapture them, and they were caught.[49] Everything about these buildings indicated that the planners, builders, and inmates considered Baltimore's prisons a place apart—and, indeed, they were. The vast majority of the populace would never see their insides and never expected to. Most people never came near to supporting themselves through any kind of crime. Even most of the poor did not have to give serious consideration to this option. Statistically, a stay in the Almshouse at a moment of crisis was a real possibility. The choices of the poor were not attractive, but they were not indicative of desperation. Their work was paid, not coerced; even day laborers were paid seventy-five to eighty-seven and a half cents a day, close to the $1.00 earned by lower-level artisans. Men and women who provided a service—whether offering taxi rides or cleaning chimneys or selling lemonade—complained about their problems, but they did not complain of a lack of paying customers.

Buying in the City

In a locked closet in the Almshouse the director stored the most precious possessions of the residents. When residents died or ran away, their things became the property of the house; after several years the pile included some changes of clothing, a silver buckle and thimble, a watch, and several pairs of earrings.[50] It was a sparse collection: these people did not own expensive items. Yet even they had owned things beyond necessities, things which they had not hesitated to bring with them to the institution. We have seen poor Baltimoreans at the racetrack, in the theaters, aboard boats, and buying stoves. Their purchases can essentially be explained by the fact that wages were structured to provide more than subsistence for most people. When there was work available, even a man without a trade could earn seventy-five cents per day, more than enough to rent a house at $5.00 per month and buy food for at least two people. There is a catch in this reasoning, though: often such an individual did not have work or could not work. If buying were really so easy for everybody, there would not have been several hundred people in the Almshouse on any given day. So how could so many poor people buy? The answer is that there remained the expectation that any able-bodied person *could* later get a decent wage.

So it was that people regularly bought on credit. The jail was filled with people—easily eighty in a month—whose creditors had them detained for a couple of days, until they paid or satisfied a judge that they would, or had their case dismissed if the plaintiff did not follow through with his part of the procedure. Almost half of these were low-status working people who owed very small amounts of money under $6.00. And these were only the ones selected by creditors to be prosecuted in order to frighten the others. There were probably many more who also owed, but who owed less or else were making more successful efforts to pay a little at a time. In this case the proportions of blacks and whites detained exactly matched their proportions in the city at large. Women were only barely represented: they probably did more buying than men, at least of food-stuffs, but during the 1820s it became legally almost impossible to arrest them for debt.[51]

The relatively easy accessibility of small amounts of credit probably explains how such poor people as, for example, the widowed market huck-sters managed to stock themselves with some peaches or oil to get their little businesses going. Otherwise, it would have been impossible to col-lect the goods to sell, since most of them were not vending products they had grown themselves. Buying without ready money was easier if a person had an employer or relation who was known in the neighborhood. Suc-cessful men who did not want to be considered liable for purchases made by dependents who were no longer in their favor placed notices in the papers. Mr. Bool, who owned a bookstore and auction house, announced:

A WARNING. A Colored Lad by the name of Samuel Jones, about 20 years of age who formerly lived with me, has in some instances assumed the privilege of obtaining goods in my name. It is well that the public should be on their guard, and act accordingly, as he is discharged altogether from my service.

Another ad read: "All persons are warned not to credit my wife Milly Adams on my account, as I am determined to pay no debts of her con-tracting after this date. James Adams, Colored Man."[52] What happened when people lost the ability to buy on credit we do not know. It is very possible that Milly Adams and Samuel Jones managed to find other ways to continue to buy at least some of what they wanted. Or it is possible that they were part of a small group who really had no other human resources and, when these ties were broken, had to go to the Almshouse to avoid starvation.

Reaching for a Better Life—Or Deciding Not to Try

The fact that people were working, as well as buying what they needed to eat and some of what they wanted, still tells us little about their thoughts of the future or their degree of frustration. Theoretically, Baltimore's schools provided a way out of the worst alleys of Fell's Point, but in reality they seem to have failed. By the end of the period wealthy City Council members had published their conclusion that nothing could be done for one-quarter of society's white children—and, implicitly, all of the black children. Although they left no written comments, the poorest of the poor had voted with their feet when a private school was founded specifically for them. In 1821 Isaac McKim funded the opening of a new school that was to be free to poor youths. The trustees advertised it and found that many of the students who applied were currently attending other private schools where their parents had to pay a small fee. The indigent families whose children had never before attended classes did not line up. The trustees wanted to reach out to the latter, so they rejected all of the former and hunted up the kind of pupils they wanted. They emphasized order and self-control with their new, previously uneducated students. The school never had much success. By 1826 only very small children still attended.[53] Either the parents or the children—or both—were overwhelmed by their situation. They did not see value in the children's studying; there were clearly other things they felt they needed to be doing. School did not seem to offer them a way out of their situation.

Practical training, however, was another matter. In a city filled with artisans who had come up through an apprenticeship system, there was always the hope that someone in one's own family would do the same, attaining at least the level of journeyman, if not master. Fathers and mothers came to court by the dozen in most months to apprentice their children to artisans: many of them could not sign their own names and could barely come up with their required financial contribution, but they still insisted that their children learn not only the trade, but also reading, writing, and arithmetic by going to school part-time.[54] Apprentices were poor—and often they were known for being bad boys—but they would not always be apprentices.

Even among the very poor, then, there was apparently reason for hope. Yet was there really? Those young people most in need of an apprenticeship were the least likely to be prepared in terms of basic education, and their parents the least likely to have the required fee, which, though not high, could be prohibitive for a person with no excess money. Many women seem to have worked out a strategy, however. They would go to the Almshouse with their children, stay for a few weeks, and then leave when they found new employment. The key was that they left their children in the house, to be bound to masters at state expense sometime in the next few months or years. Perhaps these women never thought about what they were doing and only wanted to abandon their children in a safe place when they were desperate. Margaret Tagert's parents do not seem to have examined their actions. The high numbers who did this, though, and the fact that the Trustees of the Poor never commented on the practice as being evil or a mark of laziness both indicate that many parents knew exactly what they were doing.

Records of the Almshouse indentures show that the plan worked to some extent. In this period we do not find children from the house being bound to tailors or shoemakers, who were essentially running small factories, but rather to individual artisans, who only took one or two children over the course of several years. Those who took children from the workhouse signed legal contracts promising more education and benefits than some parents were able to obtain for their children in private indenture contracts. Of course, despite the statements of the Trustees of the Poor that they reserved the right to visit at any time, we do not know that they actually did so: there may have been no one to hold the masters to the promises they made concerning the children's welfare and right to "improvement." But the facts that the trustees were so consistently scrupulous in their legal arrangements, that their stated goal was to help the poor "improve" themselves, and that they even made sure that white girls were promised as much education in reading and math as were boys—although public opinion would not have necessitated this demand—all indicate that at least some of the indentured children did receive what was promised them. Certainly they received more training than they would have in the streets of Fell's Point.

There were, however, fewer reasons to be optimistic if you were black. The apprenticeship system that once trained the enslaved now closed its doors to free blacks. There *were* some positions available. "Wanted: a Negro Boy from 14 to 17 to attend in a Printing Office." But boys like this one were usually considered general messengers and servants and not taught a specific skill. Even if a young black boy did learn a skill, his indenture contract usually did not include the same promise of additional education offered to most white children of both sexes, though only slaves were legally barred from reading. Some few trades, like caulking, still included blacks: in the 1820s there were at least nineteen free black caulkers listed in the city directory. By the mid-1830s, however, white workers demonstrated resentment of this work of free blacks, despite the fact that they labored in separate fields. Frederick Bailey, as we know, became involved when the white apprentices in the shipyards suddenly turned violently on their black co-workers. Perhaps most ominous of all, the rising numbers of white immigrants were beginning to take over some of the nonartisanal work that free blacks had previously been expected to perform. There were now Irish hack drivers, in addition to the black ones. Some job advertisements were beginning to indicate a preference. "Wanted, a drayman—strict honesty and sobriety . . . a white man would be preferred." "Chambermaid wanted—A white woman who understands chamberwork and plain sewing." The percent of free blacks who were unskilled laborers steadily increased, as did the frequency of attacks upon them in papers for being poverty-stricken.[55]

What kind of future could the poor of Fell's Point believe in? The reality was double-edged. Margaret Tagert's parents probably would have laughed at the idea that hope or justice existed, and Frederick Bailey knew for certain that neither existed for him here. Yet Margaret herself may possibly have left the backstreets of Fell's Point behind forever through her stay in the Almshouse; and Frederick believed that a better future was attainable. He was in love with the free black woman named Anna who had been saving money for him. Together now they laid specific plans. It would not be long before he would make good his escape on a train to the north. He would wait for days alone in a room in a boardinghouse in New York until Anna could come to him. When she found him there, they would flee further north, to some place where they might attain their impossible dream, where they might work in peace and keep their money for themselves, using it to raise their family as they chose. It did not seem like too much to expect.

Comparison

Both Baltimore and Guayaquil were home to people starting over. In Baltimore the economic "boom times" brought freedmen and immigrants; in Guayaquil the political and economic changes associated with independence brought freedmen and indigenous people in from the countryside. What is consistently remarkable about people at this kind of crossroads in their lives is their extreme willingness to work. In both cities they worked hard, for long hours, at a great variety of jobs. They showed ingenuity in finding and even creating tasks that paid. From the evidence on the ground, it is impossible to build a case that the poor in either city resisted hard work in any way. Not that there is necessarily anything noble about people who are starting over: they also demonstrated a willingness to cheat, steal, and lie—to do whatever it took to stay afloat.

What does evidently distinguish the poor of the two cities is their relationship with their employers and with the elite classes generally. In Baltimore free employees were rapidly becoming the workforce of choice for employers; in Guayaquil they were not. In Baltimore the rate paid to day laborers was a living wage. In Guayaquil they were paid a rate so low that their employers frankly admitted they could not live on the sum. In Baltimore apprentices were expected to pass through the stage of obnoxious youth and become journeymen. In Guayaquil most tradesmen's assistants remained as they were. In such conditions, petty crime became rampant in the South American city and even somewhat accepted: the jail was familiar to many of the townspeople as inmates or visitors, including schoolchildren, and escapes were so frequent as to be almost unnoticed. The percent of people reduced to making a living illegally was smaller in Baltimore. The prisons there were a draconian presence, an entirely separate space reserved for criminals, not a part of the wider community.

In Baltimore even those most excluded from sharing in profits were generally thought to have the right to sustenance. Even they, to a limited degree and with the exception of the slaves, were seen as part of the polity and the economy taken as a whole. Thus the Almshouse existed. It almost never occurred to the Baltimore elites that they should do without any kind of poor relief system. In Guayaquil, on the other hand, it rarely occurred to the elites that they should create one. They saw an alien population whom they believed had lived this way for centuries, who were a resource for the *pueblo*, rather than being the *pueblo* themselves. The Almshouse in Baltimore physically and symbolically walled off the most desperate people, rendering them an isolated minority who probably lived with some form of shame. In Guayaquil such poverty was an average condition, visible in almost every street, not hidden, not shameful, and not to be changed. The fact remained, however, that the Almshouse, although humiliating in its form, functioned to prevent starvation and in some cases to resuscitate people and return them to their daily lives when they were better able to handle them. It also allowed for apprenticeship of even the poorest white children and some of the black ones.

It is, however, at "white children" that the line was usually drawn in Baltimore. Baltimore's very sense of inclusiveness depended on the exclusion of someone. Black Baltimoreans could not count on the same wages or on access to regular work. They were specifically denied apprenticeships in most trades and held accountable for a high percentage of crime. As a harassed minority, they shared many of the same problems known to the majority in Guayaquil.

We can see the differences between the two cities encoded in the ways laborers chose to address employers concerning their right to work. In Guayaquil they insisted on their own honor, on being hard-working patriots. They emphatically denied that they were slaves or tribute-paying Indians. In Baltimore they demanded pity if they were in distress, pointed out their right to a job on grounds that their families were hungry. There are two ways we might interpret this. Perhaps they needed to cast themselves in the role of supplicant by making some dramatic gesture because the wealthier addressees would otherwise be unlikely to see themselves as benefactors and act accordingly. Or the poor deeply believed in their own right to avoid hunger. In either case—and we can assume that both interpretations may be partly true—the statements bespeak a relatively egalitarian world. The women hucksters could threaten that if they were not allowed to make a living selling goods as they chose they would throw themselves on the municipality and force the general public to maintain them. The same statement would have elicited a mixture of confusion and laughter in Guayaquil.

In Guayaquil the systematic exclusion of the majority from profit-sharing severely reduced the demand for any goods beyond foodstuffs. There was no lack of what we might call creative consumerism. There are more descriptions of frills and furbelows on the working people of Baltimore than of Guayaquil, but we know from the preceding chapter that the people of Guayaquil also longed for new clothes. For economic reasons they simply could not buy them as often. A Baltimorean who did not have money still had the possibility of buying on credit. It was assumed that an able-bodied person would earn enough to pay later. This option, however, was rarely open to Guayaquileños. There footsoldiers and shoemakers complained bitterly when paid in IOUs, because they themselves were expected to buy goods in cash. Given this context, it is not surprising that there were enough people in the city of Baltimore interested in buying a small carpet, for example, to make the new carpet manufactory a worthy investment; while in Guayaquil, despite the existing love of bright colors and traditional textiles, no one considered such a venture.

The differences between the two worlds are more subtle than stereotypical. In the end, the critical judgments rendered by the poor of our two ports were very different. In Guayaquil, in the murder of Ana Yagual's soldier client, we saw the kind of violent retribution that was only too common; in Baltimore, in the final action of Frederick Bailey before he became Frederick Douglass, we saw an instance of a frequent decision on the part of a slave to attempt to attain a better life. Yet we have seen no evidence that the people of Guayaquil were inherently more violent or less willing to start over and work harder. They were only less hopeful. The majority in Baltimore did not have to swallow their pain instead of food. That fact would not have eased the weight of what Margaret Tagert or Frederick Bailey carried with them. Perhaps the weight was even greater when a similar burden was not shared by almost everyone. In the worst alleys of Fell's Point, the residents might well have asked what difference it made to them if the majority did not live as they did. Yet it remains true that a system relying on the exclusion of a few and a system relying on the exclusion of the majority will yield very different futures for the societies as a whole.

CONCLUSION

When he was an old man, Bernal Díaz de Castillo, who had once accompanied the famous Hernán Cortés, looked back on the days after the conquest of the New World. "Learning from Montezuma's account books the names of the villages which sent him tributes of gold, and where the mines and chocolate and cotton cloths were to be found, we decided to go to these places; and our resolve was strengthened when . . . we realized that there were no gold or mines or cotton in the town immediately surrounding the city of Mexico, only a lot of corn . . ."[1] The followers of Cortés and their descendants spread throughout the southern continent, building their towns over older towns and regarding an area as settled only when they had established dominance over the tribute-paying indigenous peoples. The pattern of treating native peoples as a resource extended long past the initial period and place of conquest. Indeed, three centuries later, Ecuador's Treasury Reports of the 1830s were startlingly similar to Montezuma's account books as they were understood by Bernal Díaz. The government ministry listed four sources of wealth: agricultural products (mostly cacao and chocolate), mines (referring to a little gold), industry (meaning highland cloth production), and the *indígenas*, the Indians.[2]

In a different new colony in the Americas Cotton Mather had once bemoaned alternate developments. Far from spurning "a lot of corn," he feared his New England parishioners had become so dedicated to its cultivation that they were not taking the time to worship as they should. He did acknowledge: "It is true the condition of many amongst you . . . is such as necessarily puts you on to have much imployment about the things of this life, and to labour with care and paines taking in the workes of husbandry."[3] In saying this, Mather implicitly acknowledged that where there was no gold or chocolate available for the taking, and no lines of indigenous people waiting to pay their tribute in goods or in labor time, the colonists themselves had to work long hours in the fields and avidly count their bushels, despite the disapproval of their pastor. Years later when independence came to the colonies, including Maryland, the citizens there were still forced to do much of their own work or make bargains with others much like themselves in order to induce them to do it. They had only a minority of enslaved Africans to count as a form of living wealth.

The words of men like Bernal Díaz and Cotton Mather have long been used to exemplify the cultural differences between the colonizers of North and South America and to emphasize the exceptionalism of the former. Most often they have been used to contrast the supposed sloth and greed of the Spaniards with the energy and practicality of the Puritans, underlining a purported difference in work ethic. But if the lens is shifted one might observe that the Spanish acted with remarkable efficiency in maximizing their profits and that, according to their own pastor, the Puritans labored not with alacrity but out of necessity. In order to question our most common assumptions about economic culture without discarding it as a concept, we have stopped to look closely at the two small worlds inhabited by Ana Yagual and Frederick Bailey in the early years of independence. In these two places, removed in time and space from the original interactions described by European colonists, how can we characterize the economic cultures that were taking root in the new nations of the Americas? The choices made by Ana and Frederick and those who lived in their cities inform us about the economic cultures within which they led their lives. The differences are worth noting.

On Difference

The Weberian dichotomy concerning attitudes toward work and the pursuit of profit that culturalist analyses in this century have most often relied upon, implicitly or explicitly, does not seem to be applicable in our cities.

This study has found little evidence to support the conclusion that the people of Guayaquil were somehow culturally inept in handling their business; nor were the people of Baltimore necessarily adept. The laborers of Guayaquil worked hard; the middling ranks competed; the elites made fortunes proudly and planned a brave new world. They did so, too, in Baltimore. The lives of Guayaquileños were not free of superstition or corruption or error; but neither were the lives of the Baltimoreans. Neither group spoke often of religion or provided us with enough evidence to connect it to motivation. Sometimes, in fact, we find the reverse of what our preconceptions might lead us to expect. The workers of Guayaquil asked for jobs based on their patriotism and talent, while the Baltimoreans pleaded for work on the grounds that it would be an act of charity to give it to them; the merchants of Guayaquil eagerly proposed new manufacturing schemes, while those of Baltimore fought against the prospect of building factories. The reader, indeed, can find such examples in any chapter.

Yet the two worlds can hardly be said to have been "culturally interchangeable." There are clear differences to be found in the attitudes toward laborers and in the envisioning of relationships between groups in the population. The two port towns reveal strikingly different patterns of inclusion and exclusion in profit-sharing of all kinds. We have seen contrasts, for example, in the elite preference for coerced vs. free labor, in salaries employers were willing to pay, in access to education on the part of the poor, in the expectation that apprentices would rise to master status, in the assumption that a sizable number of people normally would or would not rely on the informal or criminal sector. Such relational issues would once have been considered structural factors over which humans have no control. There has been more than enough work in the past twenty years, however, to demonstrate that such issues are profoundly cultural or at least are a function of a shifting nexus between the material and imagined worlds.

We have direct evidence concerning human decisions made about public investments in infrastructure. The elites in Baltimore believed in the importance of a broad tax base and waxed eloquent about the profits that internal improvements would bring to investors given the existing domestic market; they spoke of the need to educate more citizens so that they might become productive members of society. In Guayaquil the elites specifically envisioned a limited *pueblo* living amidst an infinite and dangerous horde. When they considered building a road, they rejected the idea on the grounds that it would cost too few people too much money. They built public schools, but never intended that they should be for the majority. And without a viable infrastructure, of course, Guayaquil's problems became circular: the poor and middling sorts had no outside help in their attempts to attain a profitable lifestyle and so were less likely than ever to reach a point when they might participate significantly in making public investments. We have indirect evidence that these limitations in turn deterred otherwise eager entrepreneurs from creating new goods and services: although the businessmen of Guayaquil did not leave explicit statements to that effect, they demonstrated both an awareness that there were few people whose work rewarded them well enough that they might spend in creative new ways and an unwillingness to consider changing such a reality.

The concept of "economic culture" may be as useful to us in our thinking as the concept of "culture" has generally proven to be. It can only be so, however, if we resist static and reductionist ideas of other people's economic world views and instead consider defining the term to include dynamic relations between people. From this perspective, race is of necessity a key factor—not in that certain races will have certain attitudes toward work and business, but rather in that the racial composition of a social universe has been seen to shape people's envisioning of themselves and each other. We now take such a concept for granted in our analyses of politics and artistic expression; the evidence of this book suggests that it is equally relevant in terms of economic self-understanding.

On Exceptionalism

We have seen that the cultural dynamics visible in the 1820s in both cities had deep roots. The patterns of exclusion in Guayaquil were continuously renewed in the rules handed down by authorities and in the interactions that unfolded between people. There was a moment of contingency after independence, when the Guayaquileño elites were for the first time free to make their own laws and policies. Yet although they behaved radically in some ways, they continued to make decisions that economically marginalized the majority of the population. To some extent, their decisions stemmed from what had by then become deeply embedded cultural attitudes. For many readers, the thought cannot help but occur that perhaps Weber was right in essence, though for the wrong reasons. That is, perhaps the differences between North and South are cultural after all, though the distinction would not be one of work ethic, but rather one of attitudes toward working people.

Here there is a cautionary note to be made. "Persistence is not necessarily essence," writes one historian.[4] To me, the evidence is clear that the causes were not a function of *necessarily* inherited culture (i.e., Mediterranean versus northern European or Afro-Indian versus white) but rather of flexible relationships between different social groups of people present in any given mix. The initially powerful sectors in both New Worlds defined themselves against the people who surrounded them. Assertions of racial difference worked against only a minority in Baltimore, but against the majority in Guayaquil. In Baltimore the rule-makers governed working people, the majority of whom, but for a slight change of historical fortune, might have exchanged places with themselves and whom they therefore had to take into account as at least nominal political peers. In Guayaquil they governed people distinctly different from themselves, historically and physically, whom they viewed as conquered, lesser, and inherently foreign beings, as had their forebears for many generations, and who on their part were more likely to view themselves as alien from the elites rather than as their competitors. And behind this cultural barrier there loomed the harsh material reality that the majority had been reduced to poverty through many generations of extractive practices: no small wealthy class is ever eager to take on the problems of an overwhelming majority.

Lydia Hollingsworth and her friends had the same instincts concerning popular hordes as did Vicente Ramón Roca and his peers. Had Lydia envisioned the majority of those surrounding her as brutes of an alien species, she would have asked for the same rules as did Vicente Ramón. She proved this in her reaction to the mob that once formed in her world. Frederick Bailey recognized the principle of exclusion. He was as intimately acquainted with it as was Ana Yagual. He knew how brutally efficiently it functioned in the world in which he lived. Those who were more powerful wielded the weapon against him and the minority of other people like him. It was not used against the majority, but only because it could not be. The rule-makers could not use racial difference as effectively against a majority who were not racially different from themselves.

One might argue that it was not even a question of what the local elites could consciously "get away with." One could argue that the local elites in each place literally *could not* understand themselves except in relation to those from whom they could distinguish themselves: we know who we are in that we know who we are not. We thus will have different understandings of ourselves and our world based on those who are available to contrast ourselves against and will make our decisions—including economic decisions—accordingly. In that case, readers who use this work as a source of evidence for North American cultural superiority must do so at their own peril. They will have to demonstrate on their own the superiority of the culture that attempted to eliminate the native peoples rather than incorporate them, then filled parts of the land with African slaves, and finally systematically excluded the descendants of both groups.

The postindependence period was a moment rife with possibility. If some of the people in Guayaquil made decisions that were not beneficial in the long run, they were still rational beings who were taking action in ways that made sense within their own immediate context. Others in their situation would almost undoubtedly have done the same. When it becomes clear to enough people that, despite the intentions of their forebears, the decisions made are not working then to benefit the whole, posterity will not be bound to continue on the same path. If in Baltimore people made decisions that were more effective in the long run, then their decisions need to be continuously reiterated, not taking the effects for granted.

On Economic Significance

This has been a study of culture, not economics. I have asked what was in people's minds as they made their decisions and took action in their lives. An economist would jump to another question and ask why those decisions did or did not work to increase their nation's wealth over the course of time. In the introduction I pointed out that our economic assumptions generally color what we look for when we consider culture. I now turn the question around: is it possible that what we learn about culture can affect what we look for when we study economics?

Before asking whether or not this cultural study has anything useful to say about the economic question of why the Baltimoreans' decisions worked better in the long run than the Guayaquileños' decisions, I must face the fact that there is a division in the field which will probably always exist. The unanswerable question is which is the "motor" of an economy: production (supply) or consumption (demand)? Theoretically, we acknowledge that the relationship between the two is the engine, but in fact most of us privilege one over the other in our thinking. We each make a choice: in an economic analysis, can an inequitable distribution of wealth be used to explain stagnation, or must this factor always be that which is to be explained? Robert Brenner writes: "Economic backwardness . . . cannot be regarded as the result of dependence upon trade in primary products . . . Indeed, it would be more correct to state that dependence on grain exports was a result of backwardness."[5] Some agree; others do not. Economic historians will be building their opposing cases as long as there are economic historians.

This study supports one side of the argument in its findings. It provides little evidence of culture having a direct impact on production, either in terms of laborers' willingness to work hard or in terms of investors' ability to rationalize and take risks. It does, however, demonstrate numerous points where culture had an impact on demand. We do *not* see a more "creative consumerism" in one place than in another. Rather, we see relations between people in the South American arena continuously envisioned in such a way that very few were allowed discretionary income or even imagined themselves as people who should have such income. With local consumer demand stifled, there was little impetus to industrialize or otherwise diversify. For the same reasons, infrastructure, including transportation and schools, remained nearly nonexistent, rendering it more difficult to change the situation in the future.

Readers who privilege production over demand will of course remain unmoved by these arguments. The cultural differences between the two cities do not prove the case that demand matters; they merely support it. However, I hold out the possibility that if the usual assumptions in studies of production are altered, then the culturalist differences seen here are relevant. Years ago Arghiri Emmanuel pointed out that although economists make various assumptions about the mobility (competitiveness) of labor and capital, the one pairing which is rarest—and in his view also most accurate—is that of mobility of capital together with immobility of labor "due to the socio-historical element"—a pairing which leads to the permanent devaluing of goods in certain parts of the world.[6] In plain words, in parts of the world it is possible to harvest or process resources cheaply due to the low cost of labor, which is held down artificially by those in power. Investors and customers from around the world fly to the site of the latest "cash cow" and are equally free to leave for better options, thus eventually equalizing profits, as capital must "compete." Hence in the interest of this competition the price of the good falls as low as it can in the context of the low wages. Whence these artificially low wages? The "socio-historical element" in today's language would be called the human element, or culture. Humans are taking actions, making decisions, that affect the way other humans are treated and paid; those others then respond somewhere along the continuum between complete acceptance and outright rebellion. Both sides make such decisions in the context of the cultural relationships that exist between them—relative education and expectations of life, habits of privilege and deference, traditional methods of choosing who shall govern and who have arms, etc.

It is without smugness and with genuine fear that I insist that the *longue durée* will prove those scholars who emphasize the economic importance of such cultural relationships to have been correct. It is in those nations that allowed the most extreme concentration of wealth where economies have failed to thrive and suffering is greatest now, not only on the part of the poor, but also on the part of the rich, who must live in fear, surrounded by stagnation.[7] We will all pay for our decisions to whatever extent we go that route. Like the people of early republican Guayaquil and Baltimore, we continuously face choices as to how to shape our worlds in the context of traditions handed down to us. The definition of "self-interest" may not be what we have thought it was. It may be that the society that finds in its imagination and cultural repertoire a willingness to include more people in resource sharing, even at the expense of the privileges of the wealthy, will achieve far more in the long run.

Frederick Douglass became a world-famous politician. Ana Yagual disappeared in obscurity. Yet neither is dead in that they live in our minds, in the dynamic ways in which we continuously interpret their lives.

NOTES

Abbreviations Used

ABC	Archivo del Banco Central, Quito
AFL	Archivo de la Función Legislativa, Quito
AHG	Archivo Histórico del Guayas, Guayaquil (EP/J Escribaro Público: Juicios)
ANH/A	Archivo Nacional de Historia, Núcleo del Azuay, Cuenca
ANH/Q	Archivo Nacional de Historia, Quito
ASM	Archivo de la Secretaría Municipal, Guayaquil
BCA	Baltimore City Archives
BMG	Archivo Histórico de la Biblioteca Municipal, Guayaquil
EPL	Enoch Pratt Free Library, Baltimore
MHS	Maryland Historical Society, Baltimore
MSA	Maryland State Archives, Annapolis
PFL	Princeton University, Firestone Library Special Collections
PRO	Public Record Office, London (FO Foreign Office)

Prologue

1. AHG,EP/J , document 536 (1823), "Criminales contra Mariano de la Cruz."

2. William Bennet Stevenson, *A Historical and Descriptive Narrative of Twenty Years' Residence in South America*, p. 204. Similar descriptions appear in various traveler accounts: Joaquín de Avendaño, *Recuerdos de mis viajes: Primer viaje a*

América—Ecuador; Friederich Hassaurek, *Four Years among Spanish Americans;* James Orton, *The Andes and the Amazon; or, Across the Continent of South America;* Enrique Onffroy de Thoron, *Amérique Equatoriale: Son histoire pittoresque et politique.* Even a traveler who otherwise refused to find beauty in South America was impressed: Ida Pfeiffer, *A Lady's Second Journey round the World.* Wherever I have drawn from accounts dating from the 1850s or 1860s, I have been careful to include only those descriptions that I was certain would have been relevant to the 1820s and 1830s.

3. Onffroy de Thoron, *Amérique Equatoriale,* p. 326.

4. Frederick Douglass, *Autobiographies,* pp. 209–211. Note that "Bailey" was Douglass's name before he freed himself and chose his own name. Among literary critics, there is currently a debate on invention and self-fashioning in Douglass's narrative, but this discussion affects interpretations of the man and his vision of himself and does not change the chronology of his experiences in Baltimore. See Eric Sundquist, ed., *Frederick Douglass: New Literary and Historical Essays.*

5. Joseph Pickering, *Inquiries of an Emigrant: Being the Narrative of an English Farmer from the Year 1824 to 1830,* p. 17. Other travelers who noted Baltimore's striking appearance when approached by water included August Levasseur, *Lafayette in America in 1824 and 1825;* Edward Coke, *A Subaltern's Furlough: Descriptive Scenes in Various Parts of the United States, Upper and Lower Canada . . . during the Summer and Autumn of 1832;* and Tyrone Power, *Impressions of America during the Years 1833, 1834 and 1835.*

6. Frances Wright, *Views of Society and Manners in America,* p. 249. Frances Kemble Butler, *Journal, in Two Vols.,* p. 73.

7. Douglass, *Autobiographies,* p. 214.

Introduction

1. Peter Temin, "Is It Kosher to Talk about Culture?" *Journal of Economic History* 57, no. 2 (1997).

2. The idea that human beings understand themselves only in relation to each other is often called "Lacanian," after the French psychoanalyst Jacques Lacan, who effectively brought the concept into public discourse. Lacan built on the work of other great thinkers—like analyst Sigmund Freud and linguistics scholar Ferdinand de Saussure—and he in turn influenced a key generation of structuralists and poststructuralists. Among those who attended his lectures were Roland Barthes, Julia Kristeva, Michel Foucault, and Jacques Derrida. They developed their thinking in unique directions, but common to all as a "jumping-off place" was the notion of the de-centered self. For a current theoretical discussion of these issues, I recommend Nicholas Dirks, Geoff Eley, and Sherry Ortner, eds., *Culture/Power/History: A Reader in Contemporary Social Theory.* For the application

of these ideas to the question of economic culture, albeit largely within European tradition, see Thomas Haskell and Richard F. Teichgraever III, eds., *The Culture of the Market: Historical Essays.*

3. Max Weber, *The Protestant Ethic and the Spirit of Capitalism,* pp. 39–40.

4. For highlights in the debate, see Gabriel Kolko, "Max Weber on America: Theory and Evidence," *History and Theory* 1, no. 3 (1961); S. N. Eisenstadt, "The Protestant Ethic Thesis in Analytical and Comparative Framework," in his *The Protestant Ethic and Modernization;* and Gordon Marshall, *In Search of the Spirit of Capitalism: An Essay on Max Weber's Protestant Ethic Thesis.* The idea of Spanish— or Catholic—irrationality and even incompetence, especially as opposed to post-Reformation northern Europe, was in fact, of course, more older than Weber. Jeremy Adelman in *Colonial Legacies: The Problem of Persistence in Latin American History* has provided a superb portrayal of the notion's birth in the sixteenth century and its various reincarnations in the ensuing centuries.

5. Thomas Cochran, *The Puerto Rican Businessman: A Study in Cultural Change.* William Glade, *The Latin American Economies: A Study of Their Institutional Evolution.*

6. Tomás Fillól, *Social Factors in Economic Development: The Argentine Case,* p. 12. Although more complicated, the views of such widely respected scholars as Frank Tannenbaum and Richard Morse were compatible with these ideas. Even Octavio Paz, whose brilliant and subtle thinking continues to influence us in important ways, relied to some extent on a belief in inherent national character.

7. Lawrence Harrison, *Underdevelopment Is a State of Mind,* pp. xvi and 164. Harrison's book is valuable for its summary of the many twentieth-century scholars whose views have been similar to his, beginning with Weber. His comment on Costa Ricans and Nicaraguans seems particularly ironic today, given that the half-million displaced Nicaraguans who are currently living in Costa Rica in order to obtain work have developed a reputation for being so energetic and hardworking that nationals say they are embarrassed when they compare themselves.

8. Marc Egnal, *Divergent Paths: How Culture and Institutions Have Shaped North American Growth,* preface and p. 101. This kind of analysis is very popular in recent lay works on the subject. See, for example, Kevin P. Phillips, *The Cousins' Wars: Religion, Politics and the Triumph of Anglo-America.*

9. David S. Landes, *The Wealth and Poverty of Nations: Why Some Are So Rich and Some So Poor,* p. 177.

10. Ibid., pp. 29–34 and 238–241.

11. Ernesto Laclau, "Feudalism and Capitalism in Latin America," *New Left Review* 67 (May–June 1971): 35. Laclau later added a "Postscript" analysis in response to Wallerstein. See "Feudalism and Capitalism in Latin America," in *Politics and Ideology in Marxist Cultural Theory.* This kind of debate among Marxists about the relative importance of internal and external relations was not unique to

the New World arena. The famous Maurice Dobb–Paul Sweezey debate of the 1950s concerned this issue in the European context, and the discussion was revivified when Robert Brenner published "Agrarian Class Structure and Economic Development in Pre-industrial Europe" in *Past and Present* 70 (February 1976), stimulating a number of responses. Some of these were collected in T. H. Aston and C. H. E. Philpin, eds., *The Brenner Debate: Agrarian Class Structure and Economic Development in Pre-industrial Europe.* Brenner noted that certain demographic patterns and/or the rise of trade between eastern and western Europe have been used by some to explain the abandonment of serfdom in the West, while the very same phenomena accompanied serfdom's reification in the East. Thus Brenner insisted that it is not the international trade itself that ultimately makes the differences, but rather the preexisting local relations between lord and serf or master and laborer. "Most crudely stated, it is the structure of class relations, of class power, which will determine the manner and degree to which particular demographic and commercial changes will affect long-term trends in economic growth—and not vice versa" (*Brenner Debate*, p. 11).

12. Steve J. Stern, "Feudalism, Capitalism, and the World-System in the Perspective of Latin America and the Caribbean," *American Historical Review* 93 (1988). The article is followed by a reply from Wallerstein. Stern articulated a rubric under which many scholars were working, some in their monographs and some in their theory. It is noteworthy, for example, that in this period Albert Hirschman insisted that the concept of "linkages" which he had articulated years earlier was connected to culturally induced forms of social organization. He had said in *The Strategy of Economic Development* that an export product could enrich or impoverish a nation depending on whether its extraction and shipment was "linked" backward and forward to other elements of the economy—such as the processing of other raw materials needed for its own processing, etc. Other scholars sometimes treated the idea simplistically and decided that the resources available in any area were either "left-wing goods" (such as copper) that lent themselves to equitable distribution or "right-wing goods" (such as sugar) that favored extreme capital accumulation. In the 1980s (*Rival Views of Market Society and Other Recent Essays*), Hirschman insisted that there is "no necessary one-to-one relationship" between certain commodities and certain forms of economic organization. Culturally determined relationships among people play a part. "Even in the famous case of the sugarcane-slavery complex, . . . [it is true] the prevailing technology of sugarcane lent itself to the introduction of an enslaved labor force, but the way of life the conquerors of the New World in the tropics wanted to establish for themselves made them look for the kind of economic activity that would best fulfill their wishes, and from a number of possible land uses they chose the cultivation of cane by imported slaves as the most fulfilling" (p. 74). The most cogent argument against the kind of product determining a nation's wealth has been made by Arghiri Emmanuel, *Unequal Exchange: A Study of the Imperialism of Trade.* He demonstrates, in economic terms, how political relations both within

and between countries (tending to allow for unequal or noncompetitive wages and the mobility or competitiveness of capital, respectively) determine the value of products.

13. These ideas appeared implicitly in some work in the 1970s, but were not well developed at that time. See, for example, James Lang, *Conquest and Commerce: Spain and England in the Americas.* Lang's work primarily consists of a relatively traditional contrast of imperial policies, although the question of social relationships is embedded in it.

14. Charles Bergquist, "The Paradox of American Development," in *Labor and the Course of American Democracy: U.S. History in Latin American Perspective,* pp. 32–33.

15. Stanley L. Engerman and Kenneth L. Sokoloff, "Factor Endowments, Institutions, and Differential Paths of Growth among New World Economies: A View from Economic Historians of the United States," in *How Latin America Fell Behind,* ed. S. Haber, pp. 260–262.

16. There is an immense literature about indigenous resistance to conquest in Latin America; the point here is not to be in any way dismissive of the strength of the efforts made. The fact remains, however, that the *overall* pattern of response in Nuclear America (where the Aztec, Maya, and Inka lived) was profoundly different from the pattern among nonsedentary hunter-gatherers, such as the Algonkians in the Northeastern Woodlands where the northern Europeans settled. Adelman in *Colonial Legacies* reminds us of the pressing need to problematize persistence, and not simply fall into the trap of replacing the traditional Weberian-style rubric for explaining all of Latin American history with a new but equally flattening model. Yet the notion of learning to emphasize the cultural interactions of the people present in a colonial social universe seems particularly promising for a variety of reasons. The cultural total in this case is more than the sum of its parts, not simply an inherited set of qualities. The idea also allows for contingency and for change, as history in this view becomes subject to variable human decisions on the part of multiple peoples.

17. Stanley Stein and Barbara Stein, *The Colonial Heritage of Latin America: Essays on Economic Dependence in Perspective,* p. 128.

18. Engerman and Sokoloff, "Factor Endowments," p. 291.

19. Ivan Molina, *Costa Rica 1800–1850: El legado colonial y la génesis del capitalismo.*

20. Karen Ordahl Kupperman, *Providence Island, 1630–1641: The Other Puritan Colony.* One might also consider English behavior in the Caribbean or in India before concluding that they were inherently opposed to the seignorial way of life.

21. Gordon Wood, "Ideology and the Origins of Liberal America," *William and Mary Quarterly* 44, no. 3 (1987): 639.

22. Stephen Innes, *Creating the Commonwealth: The Economic Culture of Puritan New England.*

23. The most useful analytical piece regarding comparative history remains Theda Skocpol and Margaret Somers, "The Uses of Comparative History in Macrosocial Inquiry," *Comparative Studies in Society and History* (1980). This type of study is different from what Skocpol and Somers have labeled "parallel demonstrations" or "macrocausal analyses." In the former, several similar cases are used to illustrate and uphold a theory. In the latter, two apparently different worlds that have yielded similar results (revolutions, for example, or industrialization) are examined for the key similarities that may thus offer an explanation (the method of agreement); or, alternatively, two previously similar worlds that have diverged dramatically are examined for the key differences that may provide the explanation (the method of difference).

24. Baltimore's section of the 1820 census can be assumed to be relatively accurate. Gathering evidence as to Guayaquil's population has been more problematic. An official church census of the period gives a total of just under 17,000, but we know from several sources that this was a drastic undercount. For reasons connected with tax and draft evasion, as many people as possible avoided being listed. Furthermore, numerous travelers and local elites commented on the growing numbers of people settling at the outskirts of town on the "savanna," and the church census ended with the well-defined city blocks. One newspaper article referred to the possibility of taking a separate census of the savanna. The municipality may have done this, for in 1831, when the church census was taken, the City Council reported a population of 24,000. See *El Colombiano,* January 3, 1829; and the municipal Actas de Cabildo, May 14, 1831. For a general discussion of the problems of undercounting, see Michael Hamerly, *Historia social y económica de la antigua provincia de Guayaquil, 1763–1842.*

25. Edward K. Muller and Paul A. Groves, "The Emergence of Industrial Districts in Mid–Nineteenth Century Baltimore," *Geographical Review* 69, no. 2 (1979).

26. In their introduction to *Colonial Chesapeake Society,* Lois Carr, Philip Morgan, and Jean Russo make the case that the Chesapeake and Maryland, rather than being seen as "deviant" in comparison to the Puritan North, ought to be envisioned as "the norm" within U.S. historiography.

CHAPTER 1. In the Streets of the Cities

1. R. A. Humphreys, ed., *British Consular Reports on the Trade and Politics of Latin America, 1824–1826,* pp. 227–228.

2. Adrian Terry, *Travels in the Equatorial Regions of South America in 1832,* p. 74 (quotation). Pfeiffer, *A Lady's Second Journey,* p. 337.

3. The best of the hats, later misnamed "Panama hats" because they were shipped via the isthmus, were marketed in the United States at good prices. Stevenson, *Historical and Descriptive Narrative*, p. 234; and Terry, *Travels*, p. 87. A good summary of the industry is found in Linda Alexander Rodriguez, *The Search for Public Policy: Regional Politics and Government Finances in Ecuador, 1830–1940*, pp. 20–21. For an analysis of its importance, see Juan Maiguaischca, "El desplazamiento regional y la burguesía en el Ecuador, 1760–1860," in *Segundo encuentro de historia y realidad económica y social del Ecuador*, vol. 1.

4. Goods on all classes of boats were recorded in *El Patriota*. See, for example, June 9, July 21, November 21, 1821. For government reports, see ANH/Q, Fondo Gobierno, Caja 70, I-VIII-1822. ANH/A, Fondo Administración, Carpeta 44.249, 1823; Fondo Hacienda, Libro 188, 1828.

5. Edward Stanley, Earl of Derby, *Six Weeks in South America*, p. 70. Terry, *Travels*, p. 81. Stevenson, *Historical and Descriptive Narrative*, pp. 249–254.

6. Stevenson, *Historical and Descriptive Narrative*, p. 254 (quotation). PRO, FO 145.1, March 16, 1827. *La Balanza* (January 4, 1840) reported approximately 200 arrivals for the calendar year 1839, and similar numbers appear in other papers. Thus the average by 1839 was more than one arrival every two days, but there would have been fewer in 1835, when the wars were still recent. A discussion of the Indians' boating techniques can be found in Julio Estrada Ycaza, *El puerto de Guayaquil*, vol. 2, Chapter 1.

7. Lawrence Clayton, *Caulkers and Carpenters in a New World: The Shipyards of Colonial Guayaquil*. Joaquín Acosta to General Pedro Alcantara Harrán, Guayaquil, September 19, 1838, cited in Estrada Ycaza, *El puerto*, p. 166.

8. BMG, vol. 91, May 7, 1830.

9. BMG, vol. 102, January 11, 1830. See also Estrada Ycaza, *El puerto*, pp. 107–114.

10. Stores described their addresses this way in newspaper advertisements, and houses at auction were described as being near the homes of certain individuals. The census takers organized their lists around major houses; when a yellow fever epidemic broke out in 1842, the sanitation plan divided districts according to lines beginning with well-known residences.

11. Hamerly, *Historia social*, pp. 16–17. Estrada Ycaza, *El puerto*, p. 85 (quotation).

12. BMG, vol. 133, December 21, 1831. Stevenson, *Historical and Descriptive Narrative*, p. 201. Hassaurek, *Four Years among Spanish Americans*, p. 5.

13. Stevenson, *Historical and Descriptive Narrative*, pp. 216–218. Terry, *Travels*, pp. 83–84.

14. Hamerly, *Historia social*, pp. 143, 206. Mark Van Aken, *King of the Night:*

Juan José Flores and Ecuador, 1824–1864, pp. 60–64. For the cost of rooms, see AHG, EP/J, document 1004 (1828). The prices of foodstuffs appear in several government documents: see, for example, BMG, vol. 67, March 20, 1827. There were eight reales in a peso.

15. Stevenson, *Historical and Descriptive Narrative*, p. 209. When Stevenson published his book, Guayaquil was part of a republic, not a colony, but he still used the language he knew best.

16. Avendaño, *Recuerdos de mis viajes*, p. 194.

17. Camilla Townsend, "Story without Words: Women and the Creation of a Mestizo People in Guayaquil, 1820–1835," *Latin American Perspectives* 24, no. 4 (1997).

18. Hamerly, *Historia social*, pp. 99–100.

19. Pedro José Huerta, "Las cofradías guayaquileñas," *Cuadernos de Historia y Arqueología* 3, no. 9 (1953). The *cofradías* were still occasionally involved in the city's court cases because of their property holdings and their involvement in money lending: see, for example, AHG EP/J document 2077 (1828).

20. Stevenson, *Historical and Descriptive Narrative*, pp. 209–210. Terry, *Travels*, pp. 70–71. The travelers describe a flamenco-style dance. Police reports published in the newspapers between 1822 and 1831 indicate that patrons of bars were frequently fined for gambling and barkeepers for keeping their establishments open "beyond the hour." *El Colombiano del Guayas*, June 21, 1828. BMG, vol. 109, June 28, 1831. Actas de Cabildo, September 22, 1831.

21. These same events were described repeatedly by travelers and every year in the newspapers.

22. Terry gives the best contemporary description of this holiday in *Travels*, p. 80. *El Chispero*, January 26, 1826 (quotation). BMG, vol. 73, February 24, 1827; and vol. 133, March 3, 1832.

23. *El Patriota de Guayaquil*, November 16, 1822. I cannot calculate complete statistics on murders because records are missing, but there are records of many other brutal cases.

24. *El Patriota de Guayaquil*, May 23, 1827. *El Colombiano del Guayas*, November 12, 1829. BMG, vol. 92, June 4, 1830; vol. 109, January 11, 1831; and vol. 111, January 13, 1830 (quotation). Public plans for dealing with fire began to change at this time and became much more effective within a generation.

25. Ronn Pineo, "Misery and Death in the Pearl of the Pacific: Health Care in Guayaquil, Ecuador, 1870–1925," *Hispanic American Historical Review* 70, no. 4 (1990): 612–618. Hamerly, *Historia social*, p. 182. *El Patriota de Guayaquil*, November 30, 1822. *El Chispero*, December 15, 1825. Actas de Cabildo, July 31 and September 21, 1827. BMG, vol. 75, n.d. 1828; and vol. 135, May 22, 1832.

26. B M G, vol. 61, December 15, 1826. *El Colombiano del Guayas*, December 31, 1829.A S M, Particulares, April 23, 1832.

27. B M G, vol. 61, January 6, 1826; and vol. 84, September 21, 1829. See also A S M, Documentos Varios, February 26, 1828. Actas de Cabildo, January 22, 1827, December 24, 1827, and January 4, 1828. A S M, Particulares, May 7, 1830.

28. *La Opinión*, November 13, 1839: "¡Entonces el barrio más despreciable de Liverpool o de Baltimore vale más que cualquiera República de las que se han levantado sobre el suelo de la América antes Española!"

29. Douglass, *Autobiographies*.

30. Pickering (*Inquiries*), an immigrant from England, did not change his mind about the town even though he did not find employment as he had hoped. Anne Royall, a woman from the western territories, was "overwhelmed" but then decided she found the place inspiring. See *Sketches of History, Life, and Manners, in the United States*. Christopher Phillips has written about blacks' belief in the potential of Baltimore in *Freedom's Port: The African American Community of Baltimore, 1790–1860*.

31. B C A, RG 41, Reports and Returns, documents 1416 and 1422, Record of Incoming Ships, 1825–1830, February 1831. *Baltimore Republican*, August 2, 1827. *Baltimore Gazette and Daily Advertiser*, February 13, 1830 (quotation). See, more generally, shipping announcements in the latter and in the *American and Commercial Daily Advertiser*, 1830–1834.

32. *Baltimore Republican*, September 6, 1827. *Baltimore Gazette and Daily Advertiser*, June 1, 1830. *American and Commercial Daily Advertiser*, January 1–7, 1834.

33. B C A, RG 16, City Council Correspondence, document 469, January 2, 1830 (quotations). See also City Council documents 453 and 533, (1830); documents 407, 425, 429, 442, 485, 522, 548, 604, 659 (1827). Raphael Semmes, *Baltimore as Seen by Visitors, 1783–1860*. See also Barbara Jeanne Fields, *Slavery and Freedom on the Middle Ground: Maryland during the Nineteenth Century*, pp. 40–45.

34. B C A, RG 3, City Commissioners Correspondence, document 122, December 3, 1830; documents 88–90, September 1830.

35. Pickering, *Inquiries*, p. 27 (quotation). Charles Steffen, *The Mechanics of Baltimore: Workers and Politics in the Age of Revolution, 1763–1812*, p. 22. *American and Commercial Daily Advertiser*, January 3, 1834.

36. Steffen, *Mechanics*, pp. 27–37. Semmes, *Baltimore*, p. 35.

37. Douglass, *Autobiographies*, p. 343. See Phillips, *Freedom's Port*, pp. 104–107, on whites moving out of the alleys and the overriding poverty of the blacks left living in the alleys.

38. Fields, *Slavery and Freedom*, pp. 2–3. Steffen, *Mechanics*, p. 6. On the lan-

guage used to portray black poverty as proof of criminality and worthlessness, see T. Stephen Whitman, *The Price of Freedom: Slavery and Manumission in Baltimore and Early National Maryland,* Chapter 6.

39. Pickering, *Inquiries,* p. 31. See also Catherine Courtland, "Reminiscences of an Old Lady Eighty-one Years of Age," unpublished manuscript, ca. 1890, housed in the Maryland Historical Society, for a description of the overflowing of Jones' Falls.

40. *American and Commercial Daily Advertiser,* January 1, 1830. Similar ads appear in almost every issue of every paper.

41. *City Directory* for 1831. Newspapers advertisements in the *Baltimore Gazette and Daily Advertiser* and *American and Commercial Daily Advertiser.* Basil Hall also mentioned the popularity of the rubber overshoes imported from South America in *Travels in North America in the Years 1827 and 1828,* vol. 1, p. 380.

42. Pickering, *Inquiries,* pp. 18, 32–37. Wright, *Views of Society,* p. 249. Kemble Butler, *Journal,* p. 75. See sample advertisements in the *Baltimore Gazette and Daily Advertiser* on February 13, 1830, and May 1, 1830.

43. Terry Bilhartz, *Urban Religion and the Second Great Awakening: Church and Society in Early National Baltimore.* John M. Duncan, *Travels through Part of the United States and Canada in 1818 and 1819,* p. 239 (quotation).

44. Duncan, *Travels,* p. 223. James Stuart, *Three Years in North America,* vol. 2, p. 12. Anne Royall, *The Black Book,* p. 303 (quotation).

45. Ramón de la Sagra, *Cinq mois aux Etats-Unis de l'Amérique du Nord,* June 17, 1835. Royall, *Black Book,* p. 192. There is extensive documentation on issues of public health. See, for example, BCA, RG 16, City Council Correspondence, document 567 (1827) and documents 529 and 562 (1830); RG 19, Health Department Reports, document 332 (1820). MHS, Rare Book Room, "Baltimore Eastern Dispensary Minutes of the Board" (1820), December 31, 1830.

46. Pickering, *Inquiries,* p. 25.

47. *Baltimore Gazette and Daily Advertiser,* December 1, 1830. Most of the travel narratives previously cited describe Barnum's Hotel, as it offered lodging to nearly everyone who came through Baltimore. Stagecoach newspaper advertisements indicate where the company offices were.

48. Douglass, *Autobiographies,* p. 341. Fields, *Slavery and Freedom,* p. 45. Frederick Fitzgerald de Roos, *Personal Narrative of Travels in the United States and Canada in 1826,* p. 33 (quotation).

49. Henry Tudor, *Narrative of a Tour in North America in a Series of Letters Written in the Years 1831–1832* (quotation). See also Ele Bowen, *Rambles in the Path of the Steam-Horse,* pp. 35, 57. MHS, MS 1993, William Minifrie's journal, July 4, 1831. *Baltimore Gazette and Daily Advertiser,* July through October 1830.

50. Hall, *Travels in North America*, p. 399 (quotation). Pickering, *Inquiries,* pp. 35, 39 (quotation). *Baltimore Gazette and Daily Advertiser,* March 15, 1830.

51. *Baltimore Gazette and Daily Advertiser,* March 15, 1830.

52. *Baltimore Gazette and Daily Advertiser,* April 2, 1830 (quotations). Literally all newspaper issues in these years contain advertisements for such shows. Power, *Impressions,* p. 140. Several visiting observers, including Edward Coke and Fanny Kemble Butler, comment that the audiences included many people of the "lower" orders.

53. *Baltimore Gazette and Daily Advertiser,* December 24, 1830.

54. Pickering, *Inquiries,* p. 26. Duncan, *Travels,* p. 229. De la Sagra, *Cinq mois,* June 18, 1835. Levasseur, *Lafayette in America,* p. 240. *Baltimore Gazette and Daily Advertiser,* October 1, 1830.

55. *Baltimore Gazette and Daily Advertiser,* April 2, 1830.

56. Douglass, *Autobiographies,* pp. 336–337.

CHAPTER 2. Conquest and Colony

1. See, for example, Fields, *Slavery and Freedom;* and Michael Conniff, "Guayaquil through Independence: Urban Development in a Colonial System," *Americas* 33, no. 3 (1977).

2. A comparable medieval European example would be the arc from Paris to Rome, in which French gradually becomes Catalan, which becomes Spanish, which becomes Italian, while neighboring villages can consistently understand each other. Personal communication from Una Canger.

3. John V. Murra, "Historic Tribes of Ecuador," in *Handbook of South American Indians,* ed. J. H. Steward, vol. 2, pp. 799–805. Linda Newson, *Life and Death in Early Colonial Ecuador,* pp. 62–74. Doris León Borja, "Prehistoria de la costa ecuatoriana," *Anuario de Estudios Americanos* 21 (1964), 35–39. Segundo Moreno Yánez, "Formaciones políticas tribales y señoríos étnicos," in *Nueva historia del Ecuador,* ed. Enrique Ayala, vol. 2, pp. 104–119.

4. Newson, *Life and Death,* pp. 74–77. James J. Parsons and Roy Shlemon, "Mapping and Dating the Prehistoric Raised Fields of the Guayas Basin, Ecuador," in *Pre-Hispanic Agricultural Fields in the Andean Region,* ed. W. M. Denevan, K. Mathewson, and G. Knapp, pp. 207–209.

5. The debate on the nature of the Inca state is old and complex. For an over-view, as well as a discussion of the ways in which the central government used gender ideology to create a family network, see Irene Silverblatt, *Moon, Sun and Witches: Gender Ideologies and Class in Inca and Spanish Peru.* For the highlands of Ecuador, see Frank Salomon, *Native Lords of Quito in the Age of the Incas.* For Inca attempts to conquer the coast, see Borja, "Prehistoria."

6. Robert C. Murphy, "The Earliest Spanish Advances Southward from Panama along the West Coast of South America," *Hispanic American Historical Review* 21 (1941).

7. The best account of these events remains John Hemming, *The Conquest of the Incas.*

8. Newson, *Life and Death*, pp. 247–250. Julio Estrada Ycaza, *Guía histórica de Guayaquil: Notas de un viaje de cuatro siglos*, pp. 3–15, commenting on his own *La fundación de Guayaquil.*

9. For an introduction to the nature of Spanish institutions in the New World, see the classic work by Charles Gibson, *Spain in America*. For a detailed study of Spanish interactions with the indigenous in the wake of the fall of Atahualpa, see Steve J. Stern, *Peru's Indian Peoples and the Challenge of Spanish Conquest: Huamanga to 1640*. For the fate of Inca noble families, see Udo Oberem, "Notas y documentos sobre los miembros de la familia del Inca Atahualpa en el siglo XVI," in *Contribución a la etnohistoria ecuatoriana*, ed. U. Oberem and S. Moreno.

10. Newson, *Life and Death*, p. 251–252. Murra, "Historic Tribes," p. 814.

11. Javier Ortiz [de la Tabla Ducasse], "El obraje colonial ecuatoriano: Aproximación a su estudio," *Revista de Indias* 149–150 (1977): 510.

12. Newson, *Life and Death*, pp. 13, 256–259.

13. Ibid., pp. 254, 259. For ways in which indigenous communities were able to use European commerce to gain their own ends, see Stern, *Peru's Indian Peoples*, as well as Brooke Larson and Olivia Harris, eds., *Ethnicity, Markets and Migration in the Andes: At the Crossroads of History and Anthropology.*

14. Estrada, *Notas de un viaje*, p. 26. Newson, *Life and Death*, pp. 250–51, 255.

15. William Simmonds cited in Warren Billings, ed., *The Old Dominion in the Seventeenth Century: A Documentary History of Virginia, 1606–1689*, p. 27.

16. A good introduction is Helen Rountree, *Pocahontas's People: The Powhatan Indians of Virginia through Four Centuries*. A useful discussion of Algonkian forms of government is Francis Jennings, *Invasion of America: Indians, Colonialism and the Cant of Conquest.*

17. John Smith cited in Edmund Morgan, *American Slavery, American Freedom: The Ordeal of Colonial Virginia*, p. 77. Morgan demonstrates that there was a long English tradition of placing hopes on natives to be found in colonies: he sees evidence of it in Sir Thomas More's *Utopia* (*American Slavery*, pp. 23–24).

18. J. Frederick Fausz, "Merging and Emerging Worlds: Anglo-Indian Interest Groups and the Development of the Seventeenth-Century Chesapeake," in *Colonial Chesapeake Society*, ed. Lois Green Carr, Philip D. Morgan, and Jean B. Russo, pp. 52–53.

19. William Cronon has studied this phenomenon elsewhere in *Changes in the*

Land: Indians, Colonists and the Ecology of New England. On tensions between the Algonkians and Baltimore-area colonists, see Louise Akerson, *American Indians in the Baltimore Area*, pp. 11–13.

20. Fausz, "Merging and Emerging," pp. 65–72. James Horn, *Adapting to a New World: English Society in the Seventeenth-Century Chesapeake*, pp. 28, 54.

21. Alan Kulikoff, *Tobacco and Slaves: The Development of Southern Cultures in the Chesapeake, 1680–1800*, pp. 3–7, 30–31.

22. Horn, *Adapting to a New World*, pp. 147–148.

23. Ibid., pp. 1–2. Russell Menard, "British Migration to the Chesapeake Colonies in the Seventeenth Century," in *Colonial Chesapeake Society*, ed. L. Carr, P. Morgan, and J. Russo, p. 121.

24. David Galenson, *White Servitude in Colonial America: An Economic Analysis*, pp. 102–113. See also Menard, "British Migration," pp. 107, 114, 126. Horn disagrees with their perspective; see *Adapting to a New World*, p. 76.

25. Menard, "British Migration," pp. 101, 119. Kulikoff, *Tobacco and Slaves*, p. 35.

26. Horn, *Adapting to a New World*, pp. 138–139, 151–154, 293–328.

27. Henry Miller, "An Archaeological Perspective on the Evolution of Diet in the Colonial Chesapeake," in *Colonial Chesapeake Society*, ed. L. Carr, P. Morgan, and J. Russo.

28. Jack Larkin, *The Reshaping of Everyday Life, 1790–1840.*

29. J. Thomas Scharf, *The Chronicles of Baltimore*, p. 9.

30. Morgan, *American Slavery.*

31. Paul Clemens, *The Atlantic Economy and Colonial Maryland's Eastern Shore: From Tobacco to Grain.*

32. Scharf, *Chronicles*, p. 20.

33. Kenneth J. Andrien's comprehensive study *The Kingdom of Quito, 1690–1830: The State and Regional Development* covers the entire region, including the articulation of the Guayas province in the wider economy. Valuable earlier studies of the city on its own were María Luisa Laviana Cuetos, *Guayaquil en el siglo XVIII: Recursos naturales y desarrollo económico;* and Hamerly, *Historia social.* Karen Powers in *Andean Journeys: Migration, Ethnogenesis, and the State in Colonial Quito* demonstrates that migration was an old and effective strategy for indigenous survival.

34. Doris León Borja and Adam Szászdi, "El comercio del cacao de Guayaquil," *Revista de Historia de América* 57 (1964). Carlos Contreras, *El sector exportador de una economía colonial: La costa del Ecuador, 1760–1830.*

35. Andrien, *Kingdom of Quito*, pp. 119–121.

36. BMG, vol. 72, May 4, 1827. PRO, Foreign Office, 144.2, November 28,

1828, and December 9, 1832 (quotation). Van Aken, *King of the Night*, p. 55; and Rodriguez, *Search for Public Policy*, p. 76.

37. Actas de Cabildo, March 3 and 12, 1831. AHG, EP/J, document 2082 (1835).

38. ABC, Walter Cope's British Consular Reports for 1834–1835, p. 29.

39. Henry Wood in *British Consular Reports* and the paper *El Patriota de Guayaquil* repeatedly confirm each other. It is possible that these numbers are slightly distorted, as one Englishman suggested that some British or American shipowners may have put their vessels to sea with Peruvian flags in order to profit from the lower tariffs the Pacific neighbors offered each other. Still, the predominance of Peruvian ship names and staff for the Peruvian entries indicates that such a phenomenon could only explain a minority of arrivals.

40. Goods on all classes of boats were recorded in *El Patriota*. On the trade as a whole, see Contreras, *El sector exportador*, pp. 79–80; and Willington Paredes, "Economía y sociedad en la costa: Siglo XIX," in *Nueva historia del Ecuador*, ed. E. Ayala.

41. Humphreys, ed., *British Consular Reports*, pp. 230–240.

42. ABC, Walter Cope's British Consular Report, Ship Returns, December 1834. Consul Gosselman's report to the Swedish government, in Magnus Mörner, ed., *Informes sobre los estados sudamericanos en los años de 1837 y 1838*.

43. Andrien, *Kingdom of Quito*, pp. 99–100. Hamerly, *Historia social*, pp. 91–92. Nick D. Mills, "Economía y sociedad en el período de la independencia (1780–1845): Retrato de un país atomizado," in *Nueva historia del Ecuador*, ed. E. Ayala, pp. 155–156. Stevenson, *Historical and Descriptive Narrative*, pp. 227–231. BMG, vol. 100, May 21, 1830.

44. James W. Livingood, *The Philadelphia-Baltimore Trade Rivalry, 1780–1860*.

45. This has been documented by Fields in *Slavery and Freedom*; Phillips in *Freedom's Port*; and Whitman in *Price of Freedom*.

46. The best study of this era is Gary Larson Browne, *Baltimore in the Nation, 1789–1861*.

47. MHS, MS 1849, Hollingsworth Letters, Deborah Cochran to Ruth Tobin, September 15, 1814.

48. BCA, RG 32, City Register, 1826 lawsuit against the U.S. Treasury. MHS, Defense of Baltimore Collection, MS 2304. For the depth of the crisis experienced nationally, see Charles Sellers, *The Market Revolution: Jacksonian America, 1815–1846*.

49. Browne, *Baltimore*, pp. 222–224. Fields, *Slavery and Freedom*, p. 17.

50. *Baltimore Gazette and Daily Advertiser*, January 14, 1830 (quotation). Charles Steffen, *From Gentlemen to Townsmen: The Gentry of Baltimore County*,

1660–1776, pp. 110–112. See also Jacob Price, *Capital and Credit in British Overseas Trade: The View from the Chesapeake: 1700–1776*.

51. MHS, Rare Book Room "A Brief Statement of Facts, Shewing the Importance of a Bridge over the River Susquehannah . . ." (1816).

52. On population counts, see note 24 of the Introduction. On becoming an industrial city, see Muller and Groves, "The Emergence of Industrial Districts."

53. Steffen, *Mechanics*, p. 13.

54. Jacob Price pioneered the method of using occupational profiles to study the varying roles of port cities in "Economic Function and the Growth of American Port Towns in the Eighteenth Century," *Perspectives in American History* 8 (1974).

55. To analyze the people of the Matriz, I relied on the *padrones* or census compiled by church officials in 1831–1832, after the declaration of the new republic, the purpose of which was to provide a tax register for *empréstitos*. It provides the name of every individual and the occupation and income category of the head of household. It is stored in the Biblioteca Municipal de Guayaquil. To analyze the people of Fell's Point, I established correlations among three documents: the 1830 census (giving the number of people in each house and their age and race), the 1827 city directory (giving the occupations of most householders), and a surviving 1827 tax assessor's notebook recording house-by-house summaries for the ward, which is stored in the Baltimore City Archives, RG 4.

CHAPTER 3. A Merry Party and Serious Business

1. AHG, EP/J, document 536 (1823). They castigated him "por haberse salido de su autoridad."

2. Basil Hall, *Extracts from a Journal Written on the Coasts of Chili, Peru and Mexico*, pp. 124–129.

3. Almost all travel narratives contain descriptions of these houses. Stevenson, *Historical and Descriptive Narrative*, pp. 207–208. Onffroy de Thoron, *Amérique Equatoriale*, pp. 328–329. Pfeiffer, *A Lady's Second Journey*, pp. 336–337. Avendaño, *Recuerdos de mis viajes*, p. 194. Stanley, *Six Weeks*, p. 63. For an example of the household goods carefully saved by an elite man, see the limited estate inventory of former colonial governor Juan Manuel Mendiburu, AHG, EP/J, document 908 (1827).

4. José María de Arteta to Pedro José de Arteta, August 14, 1824. Private letter submitted as evidence in a civil suit, preserved in ANH/Q, Fondo Gobierno, Box 71, 3-VI-1824.

5. Julio Estrada Ycaza, *La lucha de Guayaquil por el estado de Quito*. Enrique Ayala Mora, *El Bolivarianismo en el Ecuador*.

6. *El Patriota de Guayaquil,* June 2, 1821. Evelyn Cherpak, "The Participation of Women in the Independence Movement in Gran Colombia, 1780–1830," in *Latin American Women: Historical Perspectives* ed. Asunción Lavrin, pp. 220–224. Jenny Estrada, *Mujeres de Guayaquil,* p. 39.

7. Mariano Fazio Fernández, *Ideología de la emancipación guayaquileña.* For more general works on the intellectual history of the era, see, for example, Peggy Liss, *Atlantic Empires: The Network of Trade and Revolution, 1713–1826,* especially pp. 127–147; and Mario Rodríguez, *La revolución americana de 1776 y el mundo hispánico,* especially pp. 30–43.

8. Olivia Codaccioni, *"El Patriota de Guayaquil, 1821–1822:* Instrument et miroir de l'imaginaire politique guayaquilène." The practice of selling newspapers in bookstores also developed, according to advertisements in the papers.

9. Codaccioni, *"El Patriota,"* pp. 48–53. *El Patriota,* May 26 and June 2, 1821: "Tres siglos de ignorancia, monopolio, trabas y prohibiciones . . ."

10. Codaccioni, *"El Patriota,"* pp. 65–66. *El Patriota,* December 22, 1821. There are nine pamphlets from the exchange on the question of joining Gran Colombia vs. Peru preserved in the BMG, Biblioteca Rolando, Folletos Nacionales, Second Series, vol. 53.

11. *El Patriota,* July 20, 1822.

12. Contreras, *El sector exportador,* pp. 67–69. David Cubitt, "La composición social de una elite hispanoamericana a la independencia: Guayaquil en 1820," *Revista de Historia de América* 94 (1982): 15. BMG, vol. 122, election results, 1831.

13. Actas de Cabildo, May 27, August 18, and December 25, 1827; January 20, 22, and 27 and December 25, 1831.

14. BMG, vol. 69, February 15 and July 28, 1827, as well as year-end Aduana Report for 1826 and summary statement prepared in June 1827; BMG, vol. 72, year-end report for 1827; vol. 81, October 3, 1828; vol. 82, December 23, 1828; vol. 85, year-end report for 1828. AHG, EP/J, documents 502 (1826), 887 (1825), 2076 (1828).

15. BMG, vol. 92, November 8, 1830; vol. 100, October 12, 1830. Throughout the period, those merchants who were not themselves the elected officials responsible for balancing the budget made conscious efforts to change the customs laws. Joaquím Ponce, the customs administrator in the new republic, himself a relatively low-level retail merchant, eventually came to blows with the dashing and powerful import-export merchant José Villamil: he was forced to resign. Francisco Bernal, another international trader, was put forward to take his place. One cannot believe that a man wealthy in his own right took the office for the trappings: the inventory of the office furniture and equipment showed a rather barren place, and an inspection of the house made available to the head customs officer revealed a building in need of serious repairs. His purpose in wanting to become more familiar

with the functioning of the Aduana became clearer in 1828, when he and three other extremely wealthy import-export merchants submitted a privatization proposal to the government: they offered to take over completely in the management of the customs office and promised to turn over a fixed amount every year to the public coffers. They were turned down. Bernal did not give up his hopes of having an impact, however. Not long afterward, the newly formed Merchants' Guild was given the opportunity to work on developing a new rate schedule, and Bernal was actively involved in that project. BMG, vol. 67, November 13, 1827; vol. 69, June 30 and November 16, 1827; vol. 80, June 21, 1828; vol. 111, August 18, 1831. ABC, Fondo Jijón y Caamaño, 55:85 (1829). BMG, vol. 91, February 18, 1830; vol. 92, November 27, 1830.

16. ASM, Representaciones, Merchant Matriculations (1836). This volume is currently missing some pages, but fortunately the collection was published while it was still whole in the *Revista del Archivo Histórico del Guayas* 6 (December 1974): 113–124. AHG, EP/J, document 687 (1827).

17. AHG, EP/J, documents 687 (1827) and 791 (1823). ANH/Q, Fondo Gobierno, Box 77, June 16, 1831. Stevenson, *Historical and Descriptive Narrative*, p. 226 (quotation).

18. *Adición al Patriota*, September 21, 1821. BMG, vol. 67, *cajoneros'* petitions, n.d. 1827: " . . . los perjuicios que nos resultan, y la indijencia en que van a sumirse tantas personas honradas, tantas familias . . ." "Confiados nosotros en la integridad de Uds. creemos no pueda jamás llegue este caso, lo primero porque en ningún tiempo (salvo el Español) ha sido . . . más preferido el derecho del rico que del pobre . . ."

19. PFL, Iturbe e Iraeta Collection, July 22 and December 4, 1795; March 2, April 26, and July 8, 1796; May 2 and October 8, 1797; July 19, 1834.

20. ANH/Q, Fondo Gobierno, Box 72, February 15, 1825.

21. Susan Socolow reports similar findings in *The Merchants of Buenos Aires: Family and Commerce*, pp. 37–41, 174–175. She gives the startling statistic that while only one-half of merchants had sons in the business, fully two-thirds had merchant sons-in-law. For Guayaquil, see Cubitt, "La composición social," p. 13. Camilo Destruge's *Album biográfico ecuatoriano* reveals birthplaces and marriage dates for merchants. Frederico Freundt's successful marriage to Josefa de Arce Coello is mentioned in Gosselman's Report to the Swedish Government, in Mörner, *Informes*.

22. AHG, EP/J, document 2069 (1828). For other cases of this phenomenon, see Cook and Cook, *Good Faith and Truthful Ignorance: A Case of Transatlantic Bigamy*; and Richard Boyer, *Lives of the Bigamists*.

23. Marriages among Latin American elites have often been discussed as if they occurred between fathers and sons-in-law, with the daughters pulled out only

for the ceremony and then put back in a closeted apartment. There is little evidence for such an interpretation, however. Recorded stories about elite girls and young women in Guayaquil suggest that they were strong-willed characters accustomed to getting their own way and doing as they chose. Mercedes Decimavilla married John Illingworth, an English naval officer, when she was fifteen, in 1824. Because he was a friend of Bolívar and she so very young, it is easy to suppose that she was presented to him by her family and had little to say about it. But then we learn that at sixteen she decided to accompany him to sea despite protests; when she was twenty, during the Peruvian invasion, she attempted to cross the province, was nearly captured by the enemy, and was forced to hide as a commoner (Jenny Estrada, *Mujeres de Guayaquil*, pp. 51–54). There is also more systematic evidence to indicate that in many ways elite women were independent agents and thus often may well have made their own decisions about whom to marry and why. They did their own household planning as regarded purchasing. When a single woman or widow—or a married woman whose husband was out of town—wanted to sell her house, she advertised and only rarely named a male relative to act on her behalf. On the unusual occasions when their husbands did not leave them as guardians of their minor children, women could (and did) sue for custody after their husbands' demise. They lent money to businessmen and sued to recover bad debts or inheritances. When their husbands tried to spend their dowries—a man having legal right only to the interest or income, but not to the principal without his wife's signature—they went to court and won.

24. *El Patriota de Guayaquil*, June 30 and December 22, 1821, and June 22, August 24, and November 2, 1822. See also AHG, EP/J, document 673 (1823).

25. PFL, Iturbe e Iraeta Collection. The letter collection consists almost entirely of outgoing letters from Francisco de Iraeta, but in his letters to Martín de Icaza he summarized what he had recently learned from the latter's correspondence, giving us some idea of its depth. BMG, vol. 101, June 25, 1830.

26. These four-way agreements functioned as follows: a Guayaquileño merchant might owe a Baltimore merchant a thousand dollars. If he did not have cash or did not wish to send it, but the Baltimore merchant insisted on receiving specie instead of goods, he would write to some second Baltimore merchant, who himself owed a fellow Guayaquil merchant at least one thousand dollars. The first Guayaquileño would instruct the debtor Baltimorean to settle his debt by paying the creditor Baltimorean, and then he himself would settle with his friend in Guayaquil.

27. AHG, EP/J, document 787 (1823). Informal arrangements appear in nearly all lawsuits between merchants. For a discussion of the banks that were to appear a decade later, see Julio Estrada Ycaza, *Los bancos del siglo XIX*.

28. BMG, vol. 73, December 24, 1827; vol. 75, May 24, 1828. *El Colombiano*, June 21 and December 27, 1828, December 10, 1829, and January 21, 1830. AHG,

EP/J, document 3482 (1830). BMG, vol. 93, January 30 and April 23, 1830; vol. 135, list of members, n.d. 1832.

29. Actas de Cabildo, January 25, 1828. BMG, vol. 75, April 5, 1828. ASM, Documentos Varios, February 22, 1826. AHG, EP/J, document 1494 (1822); document 779 (1823); document 583, merchants' *conciliaciones* (1827).

30. *El Colombiano*, September 3, 1829. AHG, document 664, Merchants' Code (1830). BMG, vol. 110, April 6 and 21, 1831. ANH/Q, MS Hacienda 200, vol. 286, January 1832.

31. Nicholas Cushner, *Farm and Factory: The Jesuits and the Development of Agrarian Capitalism in Colonial Quito, 1600–1767*, pp. 161, 176. *Adición al Patriota*, undated, found with 1822 issues. BMG, vol. 84, December 11, 1829 (quotation).

32. *El Patriota*, April 13, 1826. *El Colombiano*, August 2, 1828. Actas de Cabildo, January 29, 1827, and December 9, 1831. BMG, vol. 109, April 13, 1831. ANH/Q, Fondo Gobierno, Box 79, Constitution for the Colegio de Guayaquil (1836).

33. *El Colombiano*, September 13, 1828, and September 3, 1829. BMG, vol. 79, August 17 and 31, 1828; vol. 120, July 15, 1831. ABC, Fondo Jijón y Caamaño, 53: 111 (November 1827).

34. Evelyn Cherpak in "Participation of Women" argues that the one advance women made during the early republican era was in education. Actas de Cabildo, January 22, 1828. ASM, Particulares, May 20 (quotation), August 12, and August 16, 1830. BMG, vol. 114, June 27, 1831; vol. 118, June 4, 1831; vol. 130, July 17, 1832. Pedro Robles y Chambers mentions the role of María Francisca Rico Rocafuerte in "Los Luzárraga," *Cuadernos de Historia y Arqueología* 44 (1982): 77.

35. PFL, Iturbe e Iraeta Collection, October 31, 1799.

36. AHG, EP/J, document 979 (1820–22). "Es de tenerse en consideración el importantísimo servicio de un Buque Estrangero como la Tea-Plant, por cuyo único medio ha podido de alguna manera respirar el comercio de esta carrera . . ."

37. *El Patriota de Guayaquil*, December 1, 1821. Hall, *Extracts from a Journal*, p. 115.

38. David Cubbitt, "El nacionalismo económico en la post-independencia del Ecuador: El Código de Comercio de Guayaquil de 1821–1825," *Revista Ecuatoriana de Historia Económica* 1, no. 2 (1987). For the Peruvian elite's postindependence resistance to "instant liberalism," see Paul Gootenberg, "Beleaguered Liberals: The Failed First Generation of Free Traders in Peru," in *Guiding the Invisible Hand*, ed. J. Love and N. Jacobsen. There also existed the separate issue as to whether or not the government should allow foreigners to exploit the coast's natural resources. They could, after all, finance such development projects much more

immediately than could the local business owners, and they were willing to pay generously for the permits. Thus certain British merchants had special privileges granted them by the Gran Colombian government. Francis Hall (a naval hero of the independence wars) and a few other partners received the right to sell the lumber from large tracts of land near Esmeraldas; in exchange they were to leave the land planted with cacao and tobacco after cutting the trees. The Pearl Fishery Company obtained permission to employ local boats and captains in their deep-water searches: they met with only limited success, however, for some of their British equipment could not be used near the projecting rocks where most of the pearls were found. Then, too, other British ships tended to follow them around, hoping to discover the best locations without buying a permit. PRO FO 145.1, December 11 and 14, 1825, and May 29, 1826.

39. A member of Parliament cited in Humphreys, *British Consular Reports*, p. ix.

40. PRO FO 145.1, September 22, 1826, and February 24, 1827. See also January 14, 1825, April 6, 1826, and October 14, 1826, same vol. AHG, EP/J, document 887 (1825).

41. AHG, EP/J, documents 777 (1823) and 901 (1827). See also Julio Estrada, "El comercio de armas en la guerra de independencia: La Compañía Muñoz-Henderson en 1820–1821," *Revista del Archivo Histórico del Guayas* 16 (1979): 29–59. BMG, vol. 82, n.d. 1828; vol. 113, November 2, 1831. PRO FO 145.1, March 4, 1827.

42. AHG, EP/J, document 6165 (1826). BMG, vol. 84, August 12, 1829; vol. 85, September 9, 1829; vol. 102, January 11, 1830; vol. 110, July 5, 1831: "... tome las providencias más eficaces para que el Sr. Swett sea relijiosamente satisfecho en el tiempo pactado, pues así lo ecsijen [*sic*] el honor del Gobierno y los intereses de la justicia ... "; vol. 110, September 30, 1831. PRO 144.2, May 20, 1832.

43. Florencia Mallon describes his later antics in *The Defense of Community in Peru's Central Highlands: Peasant Struggle and Capitalist Transition, 1860–1940*, pp. 55–56.

44. BMG, vol. 129, August 11, 1832. PRO FO 144.2, September 8, October 15, and October 30, 1832. PRO FO 145.2, September 10, 1832.

45. BMG, vol. 129, October 9, 1832.

46. PRO FO 144.2, March 2, 1833, and January 29 and April 6, 1834.

47. The only area of potential investment that the elites seemed to reject out-right was mining. French and English visitors faulted them for this, insisting that there was gold, silver, and mercury in the area. In 1829 the government in Bogotá did order that a local study be conducted on this issue, but there is no record that any report was ever submitted in response. Although the locals were accused of being shortsighted, it may well be that, rather than simply being resistant to a new

idea, they were relying on well-founded knowledge that there were no significant deposits: by the twentieth century this had been demonstrated to be the case. PRO FO 144.2, August 6, 1830. Onffroy de Thoron, *Amérique Equatoriale*, p. 337. BMG, vol. 89, December 22, 1829.

48. *El Colombiano*, December 31, 1829.

49. BMG, vol. 91, February 10, 1830. The term "government monopoly" was used to describe three entirely different types of arrangements: that in which the council paid a private citizen to handle a certain government function, that in which the council accepted payments from a private citizen so that he might be the sole holder of a potentially lucrative position, and that in which no money changed hands as a certain government function was temporarily privatized. The first kind of arrangement was simple enough. The government took bids, for example, from people offering to provide daily rations or clothing for the soldiers in town. Usually merchants who had already been successful in other arenas won these contracts: Joaquín Febres Cordero was awarded a rations contract when he said he could wait to be paid at the council's convenience, while his competitors insisted on being paid every month. The second format was the more important and more complicated one. In the case of the major *ramos rematados* of salt, tobacco, and liquor, the *asentistas* (contractors) were required to pay into government coffers a pre-agreed sum of money every month for a number of years. In exchange, they were to be the province's only legal dealers in those goods. In the third type of contract no money changed hands. In June 1828, for example, the council advertised in the papers that they were seeking to contract out the city's public lighting: the man who would take it over would suffer all losses or gain all rewards. They accepted Antonio Boloña's proposal, in which he promised to serve for five years. He would charge citizens by the number of doors they had, and there would be different rates for stores and residences. When he died a few months later, leaving his accounts in disastrous condition, the City Council fairly groaned.

50. Stevenson, *Historical and Descriptive Narrative*, p. 221. Actas de Cabildo, June 16, October 29, and November 9, 1831. BMG, vol. 112, July 26, 1832. ASM, Documentos Varios, April 20, 1826.

51. Figures for 1822 were published in *El Patriota* throughout the year. Figures for 1825 through 1829 are found in BMG, vols. 41, 72, 85, and 90, respectively. The early 1830s have been analyzed by Rodriguez in *The Search for Public Policy*. See also Gerardo Fuentealba, "La sociedad indígena en las primeras décadas de la República: Continuidades coloniales y cambios republicanos," in *Nueva historia del Ecuador*, ed. E. Ayala.

52. Actas de Cabildo, July 14, 1831. ABC, Fondo Jijón y Caamaño, 52:130, October 18, 1826. BMG, vol. 62, December 14, 1826; vol. 82, June 2, 1828; vol. 108, July 12, 1831; vol. 129, n.d. 1832. Manuel de Luzárraga was also heavily involved in these activities.

53. Actas de Cabildo, August 24, 1827. *El Patriota*, March 23 and May 4, 1822. AHG, EP/J, documents 615 and 617 (1823).

54. BMG, vol. 67, pleas submitted by Tomás Espantoso and José Antonio Roca, n.d. 1827. Actas de Cabildo, August 10, 1827. Generally the only delinquents were those who had been asked to contribute to the collection effort both in the city and at their country homes. Rosa Herrera, who in June had to turn over two horses for the use of the army (in a drive to collect a total of forty), was still delinquent in Guayaquil in September. Another gentleman who had paid his quota in Daule complained when he was charged another seventy-five pesos because he owned some rental property in the city. (In fact, he owned an industrial tannery.) The man who had been angry at not receiving his rent from the Tobacco Administration was conspicuously absent—out at his estate—when collection time came around a few months afterward. But later that year the intendent issued explicit orders that no one could dodge payment in this way: if any of the city's citizens were not to be found in Guayaquil, then they must contribute in the area where they were living. See Actas de Cabildo, August 28, 1827; and BMG, vol. 72, September 18, 1827; vol. 75, June 19, 1827; vol. 83, September 4, 1828; vol. 86, December 1, 1828.

55. *El Patriota de Guayaquil*, August 10, 1822. BMG, vol. 63, February 27, 1826; vol. 67, n.d. 1827; vol. 109, June 9 and July 7, 1831. *El Colombiano*, August 27, 1829. ANH/Q, Fondo Gobierno, Box 77, 18-VIII-1835.

56. PRO FO 145.1, October 14, 1826. Actas de Cabildo, February 29, 1828.

57. *El Colombiano*, December 31, 1829. See Van Aken, *King of the Night*, pp. 70–71.

58. The decree was published in *El Patriota de Guayaquil*, May 4, 1822. For a study of emancipation in this era, see Camilla Townsend, "En busca de la libertad: Los esfuerzos de los esclavos guayaquileños por garantizar su independencia después de la independencia," *Procesos: Revista Ecuatoriana de Historia* 4, no. 1 (1993).

59. AHG, EP/J, documents 698 (1822), 1546 (1822) (Quotation: "Los infelices de dicha clase cuya libertad fue arrebatada tan bárbaramente por los Españoles"), and 6237 (1826), among others. Concerning the changing concept of slavery, see Camilla Townsend, " 'Half My Body Free, the Other Half Enslaved': The Politics of the Slaves of Guayaquil at the End of the Colonial Era," *Colonial Latin American Review* 7, no. 1 (1998); and María Eugenia Chaves, *María Chiquinquirá Díaz, una esclava del siglo XVIII: Acerca de las identidades de amo y esclavo en el puerto colonial de Guayaquil*.

60. AHG, EP/J, document 985 (1821).

61. Mark Van Aken, "The Lingering Death of Indian Tribute in Ecuador," *Hispanic American Historical Review* 61, no. 3 (1981). Heraclio Bonilla, ed., *Los Andes en la encrucijada: Indios, comunidades y estado en el siglo XIX*.

62. BMG, vol. 130, July 17, 1832.

63. BMG, vol. 69, August 21, 1827; vol. 102, March 5, 1830; vol. 118, March 5 and May 30, 1831; vol. 128, August 7, 1832: "... siendo muy aparentes para esta clase de trabajo ..."

64. BMG, vol. 118, April 25, 1831.

65. *El Patriota de Guayaquil,* April 27, 1822. BMG, vol. 26, September 5, 1829; vol. 67, February 9, 1827; vol. 73, October 17, 1827; vol. 75, April 1 and May 21, 1828; vol. 77, February 15, 1828; vol. 93, January 18, 1831; vol. 122, September 27, 1831. ABC, Fondo Jijón y Caamaño, 54:74 (1828). ASM, Representaciones, April 13, 1836.

66. AHG, EP/J, documents 696 (1823) (quotation), 776 (1825), 3478 (1825), 6247 (1826), and 4321 (1836). Christine Hunefeldt has found that such bakeries literally functioned as repositories for recalcitrant slaves in Lima in the same period. See *Paying the Price of Freedom: Family and Labor among Lima's Slaves, 1800– 1854.*

67. BMG, vol. 91, Passports Issued, May 1830.

68. BMG, vol. 104, November 1831: "... palabras subversivas contra la clase de blancos ..." For other examples of rumored plots, see AHG, EP/J, documents 6219 (1827) and 1420 (1823).

69. Pfeiffer, *A Lady's Second Journey,* p. 396. *El Ecuatoriano del Guayas,* March 26, 1835.

70. Actas de Cabildo, undated pamphlet inserted 1827. *9 de Octubre,* July 6, 1833.

71. AFL, Report of the Minister of the Interior for 1833: "Vagancia: Convencido el gobierno de que ella es la polilla de los estados, y un jermen de vicios y de crimines, ha dispuesto el gobierno que las bajas de ejército y la marina se reemplasen con los vagos, ociosos y mal entretenidos"; "Las naciones que han adelantado en civilisación han convertido por este medio a los hombres perjudicales en ciudadanos virtuosos y consagrados a ocupaciones utiles."

72. See Chapter 5 for a discussion of these schools.

73. Carlos Aguirre has shown that similar ideas concerning the "vicious classes" and their need for improvement came to dominate in Lima by the second half of the nineteenth century in "Mapping Lima's Morals: The Construction of the 'Criminal Classes' in Late Nineteenth Century Peru." Gabriel Gutiérrez, the author of many of the ideas, was born and raised in Ecuador.

CHAPTER 4. Strawberry Parties and Habits of Industry

1. MHS, MS 1849, Hollingsworth Letters, Lydia Hollingsworth to Ruth Tobin, April 23, 1817.

2. BCA, RG 9, Mayor's Correspondence, document 1005, March 9, 1827.

3. Douglass, *Autobiographies*, p. 38.

4. John Haviland, *Practical Builder's Assistant*, pp. 31–33. MSA, Baltimore County Register of Wills, Estate Inventories, 1827–1830.

5. Bilhartz, *Urban Religion*, pp. 28–37. Stuart, *Three Years*, p. 250.

6. *Baltimore Gazette and Daily Advertiser*, March 1, 1830. For a sample of the many ads, see August of the same year. The cost of a trip was $5.25 one way, the rental of a worker's house for one month or about one week's wages. De Roos, *Personal Narrative*, pp. 39–40. Levasseur, *Lafayette in America*, p. 164. Charles Latrobe, *The Rambler in North America*, pp. 31–32. MHS, MS 833, Wilson Papers, "Journal of Priscilla Stansbury on a trip to Bedford Springs in 1824."

7. MHS, MS 194, Pleasants Papers, Box 12, "7th month 29th, 1829." MHS Protestant Episcopal Female Tract Society of Baltimore Rare Book Room, "The Christian's Idols, or the Story of a Poor Widow," January 1823.

8. MHS, MS 1849, Hollingsworth Letters, Lydia Hollingsworth to Ruth Tobin, May 9, 1811. See Amy Osaki, "A 'Truly Feminine Employment': Sewing and the Early Nineteenth Century Woman," *Winterthur Portfolio* 23, no. 4 (1988); Suzanne Lebsock, *The Free Women of Petersburg: Status and Culture in a Southern Town*, pp. 152–154. *Baltimore Gazette and Daily Advertiser*, April 2, 1830, advertises a collection of back issues of fashion magazines.

9. BCA, RG 16, City Council Correspondence, document 504 (1827) and 447 (1830) (quotation). Fielding Lucas and John Latrobe, *Picture of Baltimore*. The membership lists for these groups are not extant, except in rare cases where groups individually signed letters to the City Council. If it were possible to do a careful study of the composition of the societies, we would probably find a complex female world deeply divided along class and professional lines. For an example of such a study, see Nancy Hewitt, *Women's Activism and Social Change: Rochester, New York, 1822–1872*.

10. Browne has discussed the reduction in property qualifications for voting in local elections that occurred before 1810 in *Baltimore*, pp. 105–106, 218–220.

11. The Baltimore City Archives maintains complete alphabetical and chronological listings of all past City Council members, which I have analyzed in order to obtain these statistics. The composition of the council does not appear to have changed dramatically from the beginning to the end of this period.

12. Stuart Weems Bruchey, *Robert Oliver: Merchant of Baltimore, 1783–1819*. MHS, MS 626.1, Oliver Papers, Frederick Shaeffer to Robert Oliver, September 19, 1821 (quotation). *The Diary of Philip Hone, 1828–1851*, ed. B. Tuckman, vol. 1, p. 132 (quotation).

13. MHS, MS 2371, Jesse Tyson and Sons (1800–1826). This collection is extensive and provides excellently detailed information about a merchant family's

activities. Much has been written about Elisha Tyson, but very little about any other member of the clan. Jesse, a shipping merchant, was Elisha's younger brother, and Thomas, his son, had taken over the running of the business by the 1820s.

14. M H S, MS 2371, Jesse Tyson & Sons, May 22, 1825.

15. M H S, "Report of the Baltimore and Harford Turnpike Road Company to the Legislature of Maryland" (1830). These issues are thoroughly discussed in Livingood, *The Philadelphia-Baltimore Trade Rivalry.*

16. The most complete work on this topic remains Edward Hungerford, *The Story of the Baltimore & Ohio Railroad, 1827–1927.* For a brief overview, see Alfred James, "Sidelights on the Founding of the B & O Railroad," *Maryland Historical Magazine* 48, no. 4 (1953).

17. *Baltimore Gazette and Daily Advertiser,* August 16, 1830. M H S, MS 1849, Hollingsworth Letters, December 22, 1812, and April 21, 1818.

18. M H S, MS 1706, Stump Family Papers, Letters, April 16, 1828.

19. Fields, *Slavery and Freedom,* p. 22; and Leroy Graham, *Baltimore: The Nineteenth-Century Black Capital,* p. 38.

20. Rosalie Calvert to her sister Isabelle van Havre, January 11, 1819, in Margaret Callcott, ed., *Mistress of Riversdale: The Plantation Letters of Rosalie Stier Calvert, 1795–1821.*

21. M H S, MS 1849, Hollingsworth Letters, Deborah Cochran to her sister Ruth, January 30, 1814.

22. Robert Oliver was not the only such father. A Virginia father, for example, sent an anxious letter urging marriage to an unmarried daughter staying in the home of a married daughter in Baltimore. M H S, MS 833, Wilson Papers, Thomas Cruse to Eliza, September 3, 1822.

23. M H S, Courtland, "Reminiscences of an Old Lady Eighty-one Years of Age," p. 9. It is uncertain whether this event, which Courtland claims to remember, actually took place. For years a story loomed large in Baltimore's urban folklore that Oliver had actually killed his own daughter, but his descendants are quick to point out that there is no record of the death of a daughter of marriageable age. See M H S, Vertical File, Robert Oliver. One daughter did die as a child, however, and another made an unhappy marriage that ended in a divorce after her father's death. If Oliver had shot at the latter (and missed) under the circumstances described, that story could have merged with the story of his tragic loss of his other daughter to create the legend of the murder. Whether the story is true or not does not matter in some ways, in that the entire city believed it could have been true.

24. M H S, MS 1849, Hollingsworth Letters, n.d. July 1814.

25. M H S, MS 1653, Richard Dorsey Correspondence, bills for 1830.

26. Bilhartz, *Urban Religion*, pp. 26–27.

27. MHS, MS 833, Wilson Family Papers, Thomas Cruse to Mary Wilson, January 1, 1822. See Paul E. Johnson, *A Shopkeeper's Millennium: Society and Revivals in Rochester, New York, 1815–1837.*

28. Stuart Bruchey, "Success and Failure Factors: American Merchants in Foreign Trade in the Eighteenth and Early Nineteenth Centuries," *Business History Review* 32, no. 3 (1958).

29. *Baltimore Gazette and Daily Advertiser,* January 1, 1830.

30. MHS, MS 2631, Franklin Bank Minute Book, August and September 1820.

31. *Baltimore Gazette and Daily Advertiser,* August 16, 1830.

32. MHS, Rare Book Room, Lottery Laws (1820–1830). Joshua Shaw, *U.S. Directory for the Use of Travellers and Merchants.* John Ezell, "The Church Took a Chance," *Maryland Historical Magazine* 43, no. 4 (1948).

33. The progress of the Cohens is visible in the advertisements appearing throughout the 1820s and 1830s in the *Baltimore Gazette and Daily Advertiser* and the *American and Commercial Daily Advertiser.* A careful study of Cohen has been done by W. Ray Luce, "The Cohen Brothers of Baltimore: From Lotteries to Banking," *Maryland Historical Magazine* 68, no. 3 (1973). Cohen's financial success is the more remarkable in that he was politically active as a Jew. He lobbied for the passage of the State Assembly Act that became known as "the Jew Bill." It passed in 1825; for the first time, Jewish men in Maryland with the necessary property qualifications had the right to vote and hold political office. Cohen himself was immediately elected to the City Council, serving with such elite men as James Carroll, Jr. He took a leading role in organizing the new public schools, acting as secretary treasurer of the committee. For a fine study of his community, see Richard Brilliant, *Facing the New World: Jewish Portraits in Colonial and Federal America.*

34. MHS, MS 57, Baltimore Chamber of Commerce Record Books (1820–1831).

35. MHS, MS 57, Minutes of the Chamber of Commerce Meetings, September 29, 1829. The organization continued to exist, however, and at the end of the decade still boasted sixty members. It remained active as a body of petitioners: they wrote the federal government to demand convoys to the Caribbean to protect their ships against pirates, to press for uniform debt collection laws in each state, and to urge the building of a link to the Pacific through Panama.

36. Courtland, "Reminiscences," pp. 5–8. *Baltimore Gazette and Daily Advertiser,* April 2, 1830. Because of the social function of the institutions, the students at the different schools tended to come from different segments of the elite. Although families that had traditionally been either landowners or import-export merchants or merchant-millers now had more diffuse roles and varied their in-

vestments considerably, there was still a line—albeit a blurry one—between families who lived primarily on their plantations and those centered in Baltimore. Often the country families, who did not expect that there would be a future need for such tight cooperation, sent their children further afield. Girls might go to Madame Grelaud's in Philadelphia, for example. Boys might go to Mount Saint Mary's, halfway between Baltimore and Washington. This school prided itself on being more academically rigorous than Baltimore's schools for elite boys, but there is no evidence that this was actually the case. The administration may have made such statements as an advertising technique: in fact the line between "landowners' children" and "merchants' children" was not hard and fast, and the urban and rural schools often competed for the same students. Saint Mary's and the Baltimore Academy both advertised on the same page of the same newspaper.

37. MHS, MS 1849, Hollingsworth Letter, Lydia Hollingsworth to Ruth Tobin, May 10, 1811; MS 1788, Spafford Family Papers, Samuel Spafford to his mother [Ann Spafford], n.d. 1822.

38. G. Hamilton Mowbray, ed., "Lonely in South America: Two Baltimoreans Write Home, 1828–29," *Maryland Historical Magazine* 85, no. 1 (1990): 75.

39. MHS, MS 1706, John Stump Papers, H. Whitely to Mary Alicia Mitchell, February 6, 1833.

40. MHS, MS 1706, John Stump Papers, Mary Alicia's school books, ca. 1830–1833.

41. Herman Kroos, "Financial Institutions," in *The Growth of the Seaport Cities, 1790–1825*, ed. David Gilchrist.

42. MHS, MS 1653, Dorsey Papers, Richard Dorsey to Thomas Biddle, October 23, 1839.

43. Richard Dorsey, Jacob Cohen, and several others did this. BCA, RG 32, City Register, 5% City Stock Ledger (1828–1838).

44. BCA, RG 32, City Register, City Stock Ledgers, 1830–1840. *Baltimore Gazette and Daily Advertiser*, January 14 (quotation), April 2, August 5, 1830, etc. MHS, MS 75, Baltimore Fire Insurance Company record books and policies (1808–1876).

45. Representatives in the state government largely agreed with local merchants on this issue. The State Assembly passed very few laws that could be construed as encouraging to manufactures. Their subsidies for transportation projects might be considered an exception, but these were primarily designed to increase agricultural exports. Mary Jane Dowd, "The State in the Maryland Economy, 1776–1807," *Maryland Historical Magazine* 57, no. 2 (1962).

46. MHS, MS 1849, Hollingsworth Letters, May 10, 1811. Such "pleasure jaunts" to mechanical sights continued to be commonly recorded in diaries and letters.

47. MHS, MS 1653, Dorsey Papers, Charles Goldsborough to Richard Dorsey, June 28, 1833. This problem was becoming particularly tricky in Maryland, for while most farmers did not have enough "hands" to process their own textiles and were turning toward mechanized plants, slaveowners whose labor forces had grown too large for the depleted soils were searching for methods of employing "their people" and kept their plantations entirely self-sufficient. See Richard Dunn, "After Tobacco: The Slave Labor Pattern on a Large Chesapeake Grain-and-Livestock Plantation in the Early Nineteenth Century."

48. Kenneth Sokoloff has demonstrated that these early manufactories were substantially more efficient than traditional shops, not at first due to mechanization, but rather to this division of labor. Sokoloff, "Was the Transition from the Artisanal Shop to the Nonmechanized Factory Associated with Gains in Efficiency?: Evidence from the U.S. Manufacturing Censuses of 1820 and 1850," *Explorations in Economic History* 21 (1984). BCA, RG 16, City Council Correspondence, document 475, January 1830. Winterthur Museum and Library, *Commercial Directory for the Union* (Baltimore: Joshua Shaw, 1823) and *The Manufacturer's Book of Wages and Work People's Companion* (Baltimore: James Morgan, 1825).

49. Dowd, "The State in the Maryland Economy." Dowd and others have tended to assume that the debate occurred between different types of elite investors and that artisans themselves did not participate much as speakers. The evidence in Baltimore indicates otherwise, as discussed in the following paragraphs.

50. BCA, RG 16, City Council Correspondence, document 476 (1827).

51. BCA, RG 16, City Council Correspondence, document 477 (1827).

52. BCA, RG 16, City Council Correspondence, document 479 (1827).

53. BCA, RG 16, City Council Correspondence, document 490 (1827). It is not clear from their statement whether they were importing the footwear from New England factories. They could have been selling Baltimore-made goods: local boot and shoe manufactories advertised themselves to retailers in the newspapers. See *Baltimore Gazette and Daily Advertiser*, July 2, 1830, for example.

54. BCA, RG 16, City Council Correspondence, document 488 (1827).

55. BCA, RG 16, City Council Correspondence, document 491 (1827). Certain merchant councilmen did continue to exercise their power over individuals. When Marcus Wolf, a butcher, asked to expand to a slaughterhouse, a banker and lawyer on the committee turned him down flat in three days. Other examples followed in the succeeding years. William Gist, who purified leads in his shop, was suddenly required to raise a much higher chimney or pay a fine of $10.00 per week starting immediately. David Sterret, a master dyer, found that bricks could be made out of the mud on his property, and he bought a kiln. He would have done better to curry more friendship among his neighbors, most of whom were craftsmen themselves; they complained to the council, and Sterret and other citi-

zens were forbidden to burn bricks within 400 yards of houses unless they already had an establishment doing so. B C A , RG 16, City Council Correspondence, documents 452 and 810 (1827); documents 421, 485, and 486 (1830).

56. *Baltimore Gazette and Daily Advertiser,* September 2 and October 1, 1830. De la Sagra, *Cinq mois,* June 17, 1835. M H S , MS 1131, Moses Hyde Diary, refers to Francis Hyde actually working in the factory; MS 1129, George Williams Business Papers (merchant's bills and papers including fire insurance documents). T. Stephen Whitman, "Industrial Slavery at the Margin: The Maryland Chemical Works," *Journal of Southern History* 59, no. 1 (1993).

57. *Baltimore Gazette and Daily Advertiser,* August 5, 1830.

58. B C A , RG 32, City Register, Summaries of the Annual Budgets, 1823–1830.

59. This is evidenced not only in the council's regular funding of the payment of the debt, but also in the careful calculations and plans that the Committee of Ways and Means made to ensure that the city would have money available to pay not only interest but also principal within the scheduled time frame. Jacob Cohen, James Carroll, Jr., and Fielding Lucas were active members of this committee. See B C A , RG 16, City Council Correspondence, document 787, February 1, 1830.

60. B C A , RG 41, Reports and Returns, document 1224, January 1, 1827. Browne, *Baltimore,* p. 112 (quotation). For a complete discussion, see J. H. Hollander, *The Financial History of Baltimore.*

61. B C A , RG 41, Reports and Returns, City Dog Tax, documents 1224 and 1264 (1827); RG 16, City Council Correspondence, document 412 (1827) (quotation) and 488 (1830).

62. B C A , RG 16, City Council Correspondence, document 628, January 28, 1830; document 509, February 5, 1830; documents 545 and 546, February 11 and 12, 1830; document 794, February 16, 1830.

63. B C A , RG 16, City Council Correspondence, document 882, March 15, 1830.

64. Wealthy merchants directed these meetings, although the middling sorts apparently participated. In the Fell's Point area, Archibald Kerr chaired. See B C A , RG 16, City Council Correspondence, document 630, March 31, 1830.

65. The Maryland Assembly momentarily considered augmenting the supply of coerced laborers in 1825 by hiring out prisoners to private employers, but they rejected the idea (and it did not resurface until after the Civil War). See Marvin Gettleman, "The Maryland Penitentiary in the Age of Tocqueville, 1828–1842," *Maryland Historical Magazine* 56, no. 3 (1961): 289. The city did not even use such workers for basic public maintenance tasks. The health commissioners reported that the main streets still stank because they had not been given enough funds "to employ a sufficient number of hands." See B C A , RG 16, City Council Correspondence, document 563, December 31, 1830.

66. *Baltimore Gazette and Daily Advertiser*, August 5, 1830. Phillips, *Freedom's Port*, Chapter 2; and Whitman, *Price of Freedom*, Chapter 4.

67. MHS, MS 1849, Hollingsworth Letters, February 8, 1815.

68. *Baltimore Gazette and Daily Advertiser*, May 1, 1830.

69. For an example of the violent punishments, see the account of the terrible death of a leader of a community of runaway slaves in Guiana, *Baltimore Gazette and Daily Advertiser*, January 14, 1830. The letters on the possible rebellion in Baltimore are preserved at the BCA, RG 9, Mayor's Office, document 463, 1831. MHS, MS 1131, Moses Hyde Diary, October 17, 1831.

70. BCA, RG 19, S9, Health Department, House of Industry (1817–1823), letters and proposed regulations.

71. BCA, Reports of the Commissioners of the Schools, 1829, 1830, 1831.

72. Sherry Olson, *Baltimore: The Building of an American City*, pp. 99–101. Frank Cassell, *Merchant Congressman in the Young Republic: Samuel Smith of Maryland, 1752–1839*, pp. 257–266.

73. MHS, MS 1849, Hollingsworth Letters, December 10, 1835.

74. James Huston, "The American Revolutionaries, the Political Economy of Aristocracy, and the American Concept of the Distribution of Wealth, 1765–1900," *American Historical Review* 98, no. 4 (1993).

CHAPTER 5. The Quest of the "Personas Decentes"

1. AHG, EP/J, document 536 (1823).

2. AHG, EP/J, document 6216 (1827).

3. Terry, *Travels*, p. 70. BMG, vol. 104, Causas Criminales (1830–1832).

4. ANH/Q, Fondo Gobierno, box. 71, June 3, 1824.

5. ASM, Documentos Varios (1828), single unbound sheet listing members. BMG, vol. 136, Padrones of 1832.

6. AHG, EP/J, document 2084 (1835). This court case preserved workers' bills, which specified names and ranks of workers, along with their days and hours.

7. David Sowell, *The Early Colombian Labor Movement: Artisans and Politics in Bogotá, 1832–1919*. See also Alan Middleton, "Division and Cohesion in the Working Class: Artisans and Wage Laborers in Ecuador," *Latin American Studies* 14, no. 1 (1982).

8. AHG, EP/J, document 902 (1827).

9. BMG, vol. 87, December 22, 1829; vol. 93, November 17, 1831. In other cities the guilds were more useful to ordinary practitioners of a craft in helping

them make political demands: Sowell in *Early Colombian Labor* compares the situation in Bogotá to that in Mexico City.

10. AHG, EP/J, documents 678 (1822), 6153 (1824), and 2084 (1835).

11. Lawrence Clayton, *Caulkers and Carpenters in a New World: The Shipyards of Colonial Guayaquil*, p. 115. For a contemporary traveler's observations, see Stevenson, *Historical and Descriptive Narrative*, pp. 220–221.

12. Juan Salvat, ed., *Historia del Ecuador*, vol. 4, p. 215. Codaccioni, "*El Patriota*," p. 62. Actas de Cabildo, May 5, 1827. There is an explicit reference to the frenzied pace in the office in *El Patriota*, July 7, 1821.

13. *El Colombiano de Guayas*, June 14, 1828. Actas de Cabildo, July 29, 1828, and July 7, 1831. BMG, vol. 84, October 27, 1829. ABC, Fondo Jijón y Caamaño, 58:13 (February 1832) and 59:6 (March 1833).

14. BMG, vol. 136, Padrones of 1832, Parish of the Matriz. Fernando Jurado Noboa, "Demografía y trascendencia del grupo africano en el Guayaquil de 1738," in *El Negro en la historia*, ed. Rafael Savoia, p. 145. "Capitán Gabriel Murillo, cuarterón," was his ancestor. Abel Romeo Castillo, *La imprenta de Guayaquil independiente*, p. 18. For the beginning of the rewriting, see Francisco Campos, *Galería biográfica de hombres célebres ecuatorianos*, pp. 71–72; and Pedro Robles y Chambers, *Contribución para el estudio de la sociedad colonial de Guayaquil*, p. 167. The life of Fernando Sáenz, who was *maestro mayor* of the white ship carpenters for many years, illustrates the maximum degree of success and wealth that an artisan could ever hope to achieve. He had been born in Lima in the mid-eighteenth century and by the time of the Wars of Independence was a prominent master craftsman in his sixties. He was a likable man, popular among the carpenters, and respected for his advanced age. During the political struggle, he used his influence to whip up popular support for the *independentistas* in the shipyards and the port. While Guayaquil was a sovereign nation from 1820 to 1822, the grateful elites actually asked him to serve on the council, and he did. The elites did not accept him as one of themselves, however. They did not pay him more than before or invite him to make investments with them: a decade later he was only one tax bracket above the much younger Murillo. While the rest of the council members called each other by the title *don*, he remained *maestro*. See Cubitt, "La composición social."

15. There were only fifteen priests listed in the city at this time. Local Guayaquil historians have made much of the negative aspects of these priests' lives. I find that legal documents often do support this view of them. See AHG, document 466 (1826); and BMG, vol. 64, June 9, 1826, for two separate incidents in the same year. AHG, document 1418 (1823).

16. *El Colombiano de Guayas*, October 15, 1829. BMG, vol. 64, June 3, 1826 (quotation). Frank Safford has written about this issue in a near region: *The Ideal of the Practical: Colombia's Struggle to Form a Technical Elite*.

17. ABC, Fondo Jijón y Caamaño, 55:66. AHG, EP/J, document 678 (1822). BMG, vol. 84, November 19, 1829. Hall, *Extracts from a Journal*, pp. 105–106 (quotation). On the army men, see BMG, vol. 80, February 2, October 8, and November 29, 1828; vol. 131, n.d. 1832; vol. 135, summary charts for 1832.

18. The Archive of the Biblioteca Municipal de Guayaquil preserves records of the salaries in most government agencies for the late 1820s: the Tobacco Administration (vol. 62), the Alcabala and the Post Office (vol. 72), the Customs-house and the Treasury (vol. 85).

19. BMG, vol. 72, n.d. 1827. The BMG records were almost all physically produced by these clerks. Some pertain explicitly to the clerks' own role in the process. See, for example: vol. 62, September 13 and December 25, 1826; vol. 69, August 21, 1827; vol. 72, February 5, 1827; vol. 85, February 23, 1827.

20. BMG, vol. 63, July 17, 1826; vol. 82, June 2, 1828; vol. 90, August 14, 1829; vol. 92, November 3 and December 16, 1830. Manuel Quimper to the Intendente, BMG, vol. 86, April 29, 1829.

21. *El Ruiseñor*, September 18, 1828. BMG, vol. 92, November 24, 1831; vol. 110, January 12, March 26, and November 8, 1831.

22. Actas de Cabildo, February 1, 1828.

23. BMG, vol. 79, August 17, 1828; vol. 86, December 7, 1829. ASM, Particulares, letter from Dr. José María Murrieta (really a *flebotomista*), July 27, 1832. Actas de Cabildo, January 12, 1827, and January 29, 1828. *El Colombiano de Guayas*, January 7, 1830. Greater London Public Record Office, Foreign Office 144.2, July 1, 1830. BMG, vol. 84, December 23, 1829. *El Patriota de Guayaquil*, January 21, 1822. Fernando Jurado Noboa, "Clases sociales de la independencia: Indios y negros," *Cuadernos de Historia y Arqueología* 43 (1981): 96–100. Julio Estrada Ycaza, *El hospital de Guayaquil*, pp. 102–105.

24. *El Patriota de Guayaquil*, March 2, 1822. *El Chispero*, December 15, 1825. BMG, vol. 82, May 13, 1828; vol. 84, September 30, 1829; vol. 110, June 16, 1831.

25. BMG, vol. 71, n.d. 1827; vol. 77, April 22, 1828. PRO FO 145.1, February 8, 1826. BMG, vol. 90, August 7, 1829. *El Colombiano de Guayas*, December 31, 1829, and January 7, January 21, and May 13, 1830.

26. ASM, Representaciones (1836), July 11, 1836, and an undated sheet eight pages preceding.

27. *El Patriota de Guayaquil*, June 30, 1821, and May 18 and September 14, 1822.

28. AHG, EP/J, documents 500 (1827), 539 (1823), 598 (1823), 772 (1823), and 3498 (1825), among others. BMG, vol. 71, April 5, 1827.

29. AHG, EP/J, documents 619 (1823) and 766 (1823).

30. AHG, EP/J, document 599 (1823). Actas de Cabildo, December 3, 1827.

31. AHG, EP/J, document 6140 (1824). Actas de Cabildo, May 7 and August 24, 1827, January 8 and January 12, 1828, and July 7, 1831. BMG, vol. 135, August 2, 1832.

32. *El Patriota de Guayaquil*, August 17, 1822. AHG, document 415 (1822) (quotation). For women in Quito who made this same argument, see Christiana Borchart, "La imbecilidad del sexo: Pulperas y mercaderas quiteñas a fines del siglo XVIII," in *Historia de la mujer y la familia*, ed. J. Núñez.

33. AHG, EP/J, document 616 (1823).

34. AHG, EP/J, 678 (1823) and 3478 (1825). BMG, vol. 84, June 21, 1829.

35. *Suplemento al Patriota de Guayaquil*, July 13, 1822. There were no women in attendance.

36. *El Patriota de Guayaquil*, November 27, 1821, and July 20, 1822. The newspaper's subscription lists were also printed in the paper.

37. Actas de Cabildo, January 25, 1828, September 14, 1831, and December 29, 1831. (For a sample letter of response from a nominee, see BMG, vol. 122, March 4, 1831.) BMG, vol. 79, August 11, 1828: "... la relación de los pulperos y gente vagos que han faltado a todas las listas de los Domingos y Jueves y que han cojidos sus papeletas de matrícula para asegurarse de no ser tomado de leva y así han evitado todo servicio público."

38. *El Patriota de Guayaquil*, May 8, 1826. BMG, vol. 72, March 5 and March 11, 1828; vol. 100, December 3, 1830.

39. BMG, vol. 87, December 17, 1829. AHG, EP/J, document 3481 (1830).

40. ASM, Documentos Varios, January 10 and March 14, 1826. PRO FO, 145.1, February 8, 1826. Actas de Cabildo, May 25 and November 12, 1827.

41. *El Patriota de Guayaquil*, September 21, 1822. ANH/Q, Fondo Gobierno, vol. 79, Posted Rules of the school, 1836.

CHAPTER 6. The Quest of the Contributing Citizens

1. Douglass, *Autobiographies*, pp. 330–334.

2. On 1827, see Jeffrey Brackett, *The Negro in Maryland*, p. 209. On 1828, see Whitman, *Price of Freedom*, p. 156. For a discussion of carters' cohesiveness and pride in their citizenship during this period in a different city, see Graham Hodges, *New York City Cartmen, 1667–1850*.

3. BCA, RG 16, City Council Correspondence, document 424, n.d. 1827.

4. BCA, RG 16, City Council Correspondence, document 582, March 29, 1830.

5. BCA, RG 16, City Council Correspondence, document 446, February 5, 1827.

6. BCA, RG 16, City Council Correspondence, document 401, n.d. 1830.

7. For sample petitions, see BCA, RG 16, City Council Correspondence, documents 420, 515, 759, and 800 (1830). For an example dispute about Pennsylvania Avenue, see BCA, RG 16, City Council Correspondence, document 820, 1830.

8. MHS, MS 1706, Spafford Papers, August 4, 1827.

9. MHS, MS 1140, Murray Account Book, year end 1824.

10. The general picture comes from real estate advertisements in such newspapers as the *Baltimore Gazette and Daily Advertiser* and the plats drawn by the city commissioners, BCA, RG 3 (1827–1831). For specific examples, see Pickering, *Inquiries*, p. 32; and Douglass, *Autobiographies*, p. 74. For the reconstruction of Poe's neighborhood, see Mary Markey and Dean Krimmel, "Poe's Mystery House: The Search for Mechanics Row," *Maryland Historical Magazine* 86, no. 4 (1991).

11. David Whitson, pumpmaker, BCA, RG 9, Mayor's Correspondence, document 1039, June 16, 1830. Benjamin Edes, printer, BCA, RG 3, City Commissioners, document 174 in 1827, dated December 25, 1826. Ebeneezer Hubball, brassfounder, *Baltimore Gazette and Daily Advertiser*, August 5, 1830.

12. Steffen, *Mechanics*, p. 14.

13. Bowen, *Rambles*, pp. 42–52. Bowen quotes from contemporary newspapers. Other observers also recorded their memories of the parade.

14. Olson, *Baltimore*, p. 45. MHS, MS 1848, Papers of Barnard Labroquère, bills and court papers, 1813–1832.

15. BCA, RG 16, City Council Correspondence, documents 418 (quotation) and 419, March 1827.

16. Sources do not allow us to determine the exact figure, but the records of master artisans do not include a large number of journeymen or apprentices. According to Billy Smith, in late colonial Philadelphia, at least two out of five advanced, and probably more, even among shoemakers and tailors, who relied on more low-skill laborers than did other tradesmen. *The Lower Sort: Philadelphia's Laboring People, 1750–1800*, pp. 139–40. Steffen, in *Mechanics*, has argued that Baltimore's artisan trades had not at this point lost their similar colonial structure.

17. MHS, MS 1993, Diary of William Minifrie, January 7 and 10, 1828.

18. MHS, MS 1993, Diary of William Minifrie, July 20, August 3, September 9 and 13, and October 14, 1828.

19. Winterthur Rare Book Room, Haviland, *Practical Builder's Assistant*; and Peter Guillet, *The Timber Merchant's Guide*. The former covered everything from preventing a building from slipping down a slope to finishing a paint job, while the latter diagramed the uses to which differently shaped tree and branch formations could be put.

20. *Baltimore Gazette and Daily Advertiser,* March 1 and August 5, 1830. MHS, Labroquère Papers, MS 1848, May 5, 1832.

21. BCA, Washington Monument Records (1820–1830). Rebecca Clackner is an interesting figure. Like other widowed women, she took over her husband's business. By 1830 she was grossing hundreds of dollars a year in city contracts alone, working closely with the prominent Frederick Crey. See BCA, RG 41, Reports and Returns, Workmen's Bills, document collection 1525 (1827) and 1504 (1830); RG 16, City Council Correspondence, document 171, May 15, 1827.

22. BCA, RG 32, City Register, Ledger for 1826–1829. RG 41, Reports and Returns, sets 1504, 1506, and 1507, workers' bills, checks, and vouchers for 1830. Similar sets through the decade. RG 16, City Council Correspondence, documents 511, 516, 520, 522 (1827).

23. That is, if workers absconded with any city materials or if their work needed repairs in less than two years, they would be responsible for paying varying amounts up to $5,000.

24. BCA, RG 41, Reports and Returns, Bonds, documents 329–353 (1830). RG 3, City Commissioners, Correspondence, documents 151, 158, and 167 (May–June 1830); Ledger of Contracts (1833–1836); Ledger of Minutes of Meetings (1832). RG 16, City Council Correspondence, document 434, January 4, 1827; document 414, April 26, 1830.

25. M. V. Brewington, "The Chesapeake Bay Pilots," *Maryland Historical Magazine* 48, no. 2 (1953): 115, 122–124, 130. Brackett, *The Negro in Maryland,* pp. 206–207. MHS, MS 1993, William Minifrie's Journal, March 24, 1830; MS 1521, Thomas and Hugg Papers, ship log for January 1831.

26. MHS, MS 1521, Thomas & Hugg Papers, Jacob Hugg's undated letters from the 1820s and ship logs, especially for 1831.

27. MHS, Courtland, "Reminiscences," p. 4. Levasseur, *Lafayette in America,* p. 168. The merchant George Williams (the same man who invested in the soap manufactory) paid one James Gould $22.00 every six months to give his daughter lessons. Walter Hartridge, "The Refugees from the Island of St. Domingo in Maryland," *Maryland Historical Magazine* 38, no. 2 (1943): 110–111. *Baltimore Gazette and Daily Advertiser,* May 1, 1830.

28. BCA, Report of the School Commissioners to the City Council, 1829.

29. Leonard Curry, *The Free Black in Urban America: 1800–1850,* pp. 154–157. Bettye Gardner, "Antebellum Black Education in Baltimore," *Maryland Historical Magazine* 71, no. 3 (1976). *Baltimore Gazette and Daily Advertiser,* January 1, 1830 (quotation). The most complete study of the black middle class's achievements at this time is Phillips, *Freedom's Port,* Chapters 5 and 6.

30. Graham, *Baltimore,* pp. 63–79. Douglass, *Autobiographies,* p. 225. Phillips, *Freedom's Port,* p. 232 (quotation).

31. *Baltimore Gazette and Daily Advertiser,* October 1 and December 24, 1830. Lucas and Latrobe, *Picture of Baltimore.* Pickering, *Inquiries,* p. 19. BCA, RG 16, City Council Correspondence, document 821, January 12, 1830.

32. BCA, RG 16, City Council Ordinance No. 36, 1828. RG 32, City Register, Ledger for 1826–1829. RG 16, City Council Correspondence, document 458, January 27, 1830. RG 41, Reports and Returns, document 1399, January 5, 1828.

33. BCA, RG 41, Reports and Returns, Bonds, document 332 (1830). RG 16, City Council Correspondence, documents 519 and 758, March 5 and 15, 1830.

34. BCA, RG 41, Reports and Returns, Pay Stubs, documents 1077–1080; and Bailiffs' Reports, documents 1081–1292 (1830). RG 16, City Council Correspondence, documents 409, 655, and 656 (1827) and document 419 (1830).

35. BCA, RG 16, City Council Correspondence, documents 471 and 472 (1827) (quotation); document 540, February 21, 1827; document 594, February 8, 1830. RG 9, Mayor's Correspondence, document 998, November 13, 1830.

36. *Baltimore Gazette and Daily Advertiser,* February 13, 1830. BCA, RG 16, City Council Correspondence, document 570, December 31, 1830. For a similar comment about the value of such employees, see MHS, Rare Book Room, "Report of the Directors of the Penitentiary," December 1829.

37. MSA, City Court Ledger for 1826, Holders of Ordinary Licenses. BCA, RG 41, Reports and Returns, Ordinary Licenses, document 1358 (1827); RG 42, Market Records, Receipts for Fell's Point (1830). On women's dairy stalls in connection with their agricultural business, see Joan Jensen, *Loosening the Bonds: Mid-Atlantic Farm Women, 1750–1850.*

38. BCA, RG 16, City Council Correspondence, documents 470 and 531 (1827).

39. Pickering, *Inquiries,* pp. 27–32. BCA, RG 16, City Council Correspondence, document 416 (1830). *Baltimore Gazette and Daily Advertiser,* May 1, July 2, and December 1, 1830.

40. For a few examples, see *Baltimore Gazette and Daily Advertiser,* January 14, February 1, April 2, May 1, and October 1, 1830. Kemble Butler, *Journal,* pp. 73, 81–82. See also Power, *Impressions,* pp. 140–141.

41. *Baltimore Gazette and Daily Advertiser,* February 1, April 12, and September 2, 1830. Similar notices appear in every issue. Wright's book was advertised throughout January 1830. In his journal the carpenter William Minifrie mentioned going to hear her twice.

42. Coke, *Subaltern's Furlough.* BCA, RG 16, City Council Correspondence, document 410, January 11, 1830. For sample ads, see *Baltimore Gazette and Daily Advertiser,* February 1, February 13, and March 1, 1830.

43. BCA, RG 16 S 10, Jefferson's Funeral Procession, printed program, 1826.

Pickering, *Inquiries*, p. 26. Several of the foreign travelers commented on the American love of military pomp and volunteer brigades.

44. MHS, MS 856, Records of the Union Fire Company, 1824–1832, minutes of the meetings of November 4, 1828 (quotation), and February 10, 1832. BCA, RG 16, City Council Correspondence, document 448, January 22, 1830. The Independent Fire Company cited therein was not the only one with expensive equipment. For a collection of companies' reports on their holdings, see RG 41, Reports and Returns, Fire Companies, documents 1269–1275 (1827). The First Baltimore Hose member listing appears in the *Baltimore Gazette and Daily Advertiser*, February 1, 1830. Steffen, *Mechanics*, treats the early politicization of Baltimore's artisans through such mutual aid societies. Fields, *Slavery and Freedom*, discusses the latent hostility embedded in them that breaks into increased violence against others later in the century.

45. Isaac Fein, *The Making of an American Jewish Community: The History of Baltimore Jewry from 1173 to 1920*, pp. 47–48. Jorg Echternkamp, "Emerging Ethnicity: The German Experience in Antebellum Baltimore," *Maryland Historical Magazine* 86 (1991). For the history of "the Jew Bill," see E. Milton Altfeld, *The Jew's Struggle for Religious and Civil Liberty in Maryland*.

46. Curry, *The Free Black*, pp. 199–202. Olson, *Baltimore*, pp. 94–95. Lucas and Latrobe, *Picture of Baltimore* (quotation).

47. Jacob Frey, *Reminiscences of Baltimore*, p. 47. BCA, Reports of the Commissioners of Schools for 1830 and 1831. The schools were less successful in extremely poor sections of the city: see Chapter 8 for further discussion.

48. For sample advertisements, see *Baltimore Republican*, August 2 and September 6, 1827; *Baltimore Gazette and Daily Advertiser*, May 1, June 1, and September 2, 1830; *American and Commercial Daily Advertiser*, January 2–7, 1834.

49. BCA, RG 16, City Council Correspondence, document 567 (1827).

50. Jerome Randolph Garitee, "Private Enterprise and Public Spirit: Baltimore Privateering in the War of 1812." MHS, MS 2055, Grafflin Papers (1808–1820).

51. The best discussion of the birth of the Mechanics' Bank is Steffen, *Mechanics*, pp. 191–208. For reports on the bank's situation in the 1830s, see Lucas and Latrobe, *Picture of Baltimore*, Charles Varle, *A Complete View of Baltimore*, and any other commercial directory of the city. For typical published bank reports, policies, and advertisements, see the *American and Commercial Daily Advertiser*, January 3, 1834. See Olson, *Baltimore*, p. 95, on popular use of the banks, and pp. 99–101, on popular participation in the riots.

52. For city stock sales, see BCA, RG 32, City Register, City Stock Records. MSA, Baltimore County, Wills and Estate Inventories, 1830. In 1830 nonelite figures are 29 percent of the total number of investors who die; further research among the estate inventories of other years is still needed.

53. MHS, "The [Third through Eleventh] Report of the Young Men's Bible Society of the State of Maryland," 1823–1830. The only reference to religious pamphlets that I found in all my reading of common people's documents was in a competing and hostile pamphlet printed in November 1821 called "A Warning to the Citizens of Baltimore." A copy is housed in the MHS Rare Book Room. For the number of churchgoers, see Bilhartz, *Urban Religion*.

54. *El Chispero*, December 8, 1825.

CHAPTER 7. Working on Dead Man's Rock

1. BMG, vol. 73, February 3, March 16, and March 21, 1827: " . . . cargando sobre mí una inmensa odiocidad."

2. BMG, vol. 68, March 3, 1827.

3. In early 1827 other men and women were already gathering near the mountain of Chilintomo, north of the city near the town of Babahoyo. They were Indians who had lost their land in legal disputes, runaway slaves, military deserters, and other "fugitives from justice" who built their own community on the mountain and fought off government troops as they approached. In fact, when the Peruvian invasion Bolívar so dreaded did come, they strategically sided with the foreigners and took offensive action rather than merely defensive. It was almost impossible to catch them, for a rebel could become an ordinary citizen in the blink of an eye. When government troops finally cornered a group whom they were certain were rebels, the captured men managed to convince the army that they were only ignorant, terrified local bumpkins who had made the mistake of going to the mountains in search of wood, mud, and stone to construct houses for their poor families. Yet only two weeks later, apparently after watching these men, the army managed to catch Juan Solis, the recognized leader of all the rebels. BMG, vol. 77, October 15, 1828; vol. 84, November 28, 1829; vol. 90, December 15, 1829. For a more complete discussion, see Jorge Núñez, "Las luchas campesinas en la costa en el siglo XIX," in *Segundo encuentro de historia y realidad económica y social del Ecuador*, vol. 1, p. 276. There were many other incidents of rural banditry and rural revolt, sometimes blending indistinguishably. As one of his early presidential orders, Bolívar authorized the execution of a group of known highwaymen in the area, just as soon as they could be caught (*El Patriota de Guayaquil*, October 19, 1822), and in 1826 a horrible robbery and rape occurred in a house on the island of Santay, near Guayaquil. The perpetrators wielded machetes and said sarcastically that they were there "de comición del Sr. Libertador" (AHG, EP/J, document 6156: "by order of the Liberator [Simón Bolívar]"). In January 1829 a group of "facciosos" (factious types) robbed the house of the mayor and tax collector of the town of Daule and then publicly distributed the goods they found inside (BMG, vol. 86, February 1829).

4. AHG, EP/J, document 536 (1823): "Un tejedor de sombreros y peón jornalero en cualquiera obra."

5. The Colombian and then Ecuadorian government changed tactics several times in the process of abolishing tribute payment. It was forbidden on the coast in order to encourage the growth of wage labor, but then reinstated and finally gradually reduced. For a complete discussion, see Mark Van Aken, "The Lingering Death of Indian Tribute in Ecuador," *Hispanic American Historical Review* 61, no. 3 (1981).

6. Frank Salomon, "Shamanism and Politics in Late Colonial Ecuador," *American Ethnologist* 10, no. 3 (1983).

7. BMG, vol. 80, September 22, 1828.

8. *El Patriota de Guayaquil*, January 26, 1822. BMG, vol. 70, September 15, 1828; vol. 112, January n.d. 1831; vol. 132, February 11, 1831.

9. AFL, Report of the Ministry of the Interior for 1833. Most of the complaints I found were directed at Hispanic officials; in most areas there would usually have been indigenous officials working simultaneously, but with less power. For interesting cases from El Morro, see BMG, vol. 67, July 26, 1826; vol. 91, April 4, 1830; vol. 122, April 16, 1830.

10. AHG, EP/J, document 6147 (1824). BMG, vol. 63, February 20–27, 1826.

11. *El Patriota de Guayaquil*, June 2 and 30, 1821. BMG, vol. 67, March 7, 1827 (quotation). Richard Spruce, *Notes of a Botanist on the Amazon and Andes . . . during the Years 1849–1864*, pp. 296–297.

12. BMG, vol. 80, October 24, 1828; vol. 90, March 30, 1829 (quotation); vol. 91, April 12, 1830 (quotation). The word "remit" was most commonly used.

13. ABC, Fondo Jijón y Caamaño, 53:85 (December 1827). BMG, vol. 79, August–September 1828; vol. 96, n.d. 1830; vol. 101, November 4, 1830; vol. 108, March 26, 1831.

14. BMG, vol. 101, November 4, 1830; vol. 108, March 26, 1831; vol. 93, April 5, 1831; vol. 128, January 10, 1832; vol. 135, March 4, 1832 (quotation). AFL, Report of the Ministry of the Interior for 1833. *La Opinión*, October 9, 1839.

15. AHG, EP/J, document 158 (1789), document 585 (1817), document 898 (1830), document 6240 (1830). For a detailed study of this subject in the city of Quito, see Martin Minchom, "Socio-racial Status and Mobility: The Declarations of Mestizo," in *The People of Quito, 1690–1810*.

16. BMG, vol. 90, June 10, 1829; vol. 86, December 30, 1829; vol. 102, February 17, 1830; vol. 129, n.d. 1832.

17. AHG, EP/J, document 5996 (1826): "Llegó a mis Oydos la dulce voz de la Patria y deseando yo ser uno de sus soldados tanto por sacudir el yugo de la Opre-

sión General como por liberarme de la esclavitud en que me allaba, corri veloz a presentarme a las tropas libertadores . . ."

18. AHG, document 769 (1823).

19. AHG, EP/J, document 6205 (1826): ". . . el deseo de Livertad [*sic*] que todo esclavo tiene . . ." For a similar comment, see AHG, EP/J, document 3471 (1830).

20. Many travelers noticed this trend during this period and for years afterward. Stevenson, *Historical and Descriptive Narrative*, p. 201. Spruce, *Notes of a Botanist*, p. 301 (quotation). Pfeiffer, *A Lady's Second Journey*, pp. 337, 361. For statistical studies, see Hamerly, *Historia social*, pp. 91–92; and Mills, "Economía y sociedad," pp. 152–156.

21. ASM, Particulares (1831–36), March 5, April 11, May 21, and July 2, 1830. AHG, document 1454 (1822).

22. Julio Tobar Donoso, "La abolición de la esclavitud en el Ecuador," *Boletín de la Académia Nacional de Historia* 39, no. 93 (Quito, 1959). Fazio, *Ideología de la emancipación*, pp. 105–115. Townsend, "En busca de la libertad," pp. 73–85.

23. AHG, EP/J, document 6145 (1824): "Tuve a bien ponerlos para fondo en el banco de manumisión, según la costumbre, y bajo la seguridad que podían ofrecer a los esclavos las disposiciones del Excelentísimo Sr. Libertador. Casi he contribuido con la mitad de mi valor, y después que nada he conseguido, veo que el dicho banco se halla destituido."

24. "Expediente sobre establecimiento de un sistema mutualista o cooperativo voluntario entre los esclavos para su liberación con la intervención de una Junta de Manumisión" (Guayaquil, July 14, 1822), printed in *La Revista del Archivo Histórico del Guayas* 5 (June 1974): 115–124. AHG, EP/J, documents 609 (1823) and 6145 (1824). BMG, vol. 71, n.d. 1827; vol. 61, January 1826. *El Patriota de Guayaquil*, January 6, 1827. After this, probate records make various references to the tax to be directed toward the bank, but according to bank records in 1830, far more cases were "pending" than "paid" (BMG, vol. 98, n.d. 1830).

25. AHG, EP/J, documents 6196 (1826), 672 (1831), and 501 (1830).

26. AHG, EP/J, documents 698 (1822), 769 (1823), 784 (1823), and 1484 (1822) provide excellent examples among dozens of cases.

27. BMG, vol. 71, April 5, 1827.

28. AHG, EP/J, document 3461 (1830). See Chapter 3 for a discussion of the elite predilection for coerced labor.

29. BMG, vol. 62, February 4 and November 25, 1826. MHS, MS 314, "Journal of John Dubois on a Cruise of the U.S.S. *Potomac*, 1831–1834." Actas de Cabildo, June 15, 1831. See also Actas, July 14 and November 9, 1831.

30. Terry, *Travels*, p. 59. Onffroy de Thoron, *Amérique Equatoriale*, p. 327. *El Patriota de Guayaquil*, October 19, 1822. ABC, Fondo Jijón y Caamaño, 55:76

(1829). BMG, vol. 108, April 13, 1830 (quotation); vol. 112, May 1831; vol. 118, June 7, 1831.

31. AHG, EP/J, document 769 (1823).

32. AHG, EP/J, document 2082 (1835).

33. AHG, EP/J, document 3493 (1835–1837). For cases offering more information on the lives of common carpenters, see AHG, EP/J, documents 2084 (1835) and 678 (1822).

34. *El Patriota de Guayaquil*, May 13, 1822. *El Colombiano*, December 31, 1829. Actas de Cabildo for July 1827.

35. BMG, vol. 135, March 7, 1832. ASM, unlabeled city finance record book for 1832.

36. BMG, vol. 81, n.d. 1828; vol. 85, n.d., September 15, and October 3, 1829; vol. 92, July 17 and 20, 1830.

37. Actas de Cabildo, June 16, 1831. ASM, unlabeled city finance record book for 1832; and Representaciones, July 4, 1836.

38. AHG, EP/J, documents 3472 (1832), 468 (1830), 1004 (1828), 500 (1827), 766 (1823), and 678 (1822). Terry, *Travels*, pp. 75–79. *El Colombiano de Guayas*, November 26, 1829, and January 28, 1830. BMG, vol. 100, October 14, 1830.

39. ABC, Fondo Jijón y Caamaño, 52 : 141 (1826). BMG, vol. 73, March 8, 1827; vol. 104, Causas Criminales (1834). AHG, EP/J, documents 549 (1823), 536 (1823), and 771 (1823).

40. AHG, EP/J, document 754 (1823). Actas de Cabildo, April 29, 1828. BMG, vol. 130, February 26, 1832.

41. AHG, EP/J, documents 6218 (1827) and 6157 (1826). BMG, vol. 113, April 27, 1831.

42. For examples, see AHG, EP/J, documents 3461 (1830), 3532 (1825), 6205 (1826), and 6217 (1827).

43. Actas de Cabildo, October 13, 1828. ABC, Fondo Jijón y Caamaño, 55 : 66 (1828).

44. AHG, EP/J, documents 979 (1822) and 3459 (1830). BMG, vol. 62, November 9, 1826; vol. 83, September 26, 1828; vol. 87, December 11, 1829; vol. 91, March 23, 1830; vol. 112, September 29, 1831; vol. 111, November 7, 1831.

45. ASM, Documentos Varios, April 27, 1826. BMG, vol. 63, November 2, 1826; vol. 103, August 12, 1830; vol. 118, January 17, 1831; vol. 109, September 17 and October 11, 1831; vol. 110, October 3, 1831; vol. 135, March 15, 1832; vol. 133, December 14, 1832.

46. ANH/Q, Fondo Gobierno, vol. 78, 16-V-1833. AHG, EP/J, document 6166 (1826–1838).

47. Stevenson, *Historical and Descriptive Narrative*, p. 259. Pfeiffer, *A Lady's Second Journey*, pp. 358 (quotation), 373. BMG, vol. 85, February 28 and May 31, 1829; vol. 135, June 9, 1832. ANH/A Hacienda, Libro 188 (1828).

48. Henry Wood's letter in *British Consular Reports*, ed. Humphreys, p. 250. AHG, EP/J, document 678 (1822). The Flores letter is located in BMG, vol. 102, February 25, 1830. Ship and court records involving British sailors are common. See, for example, BMG, vol. 79, October 23, 1828; vol. 121, April 19, 1831; vol. 135, September 12, 1832.

49. AHG, EP/J, document 1198 (1826).

50. BMG, vol. 82, July 14, 1828. Stevenson, *Historical and Descriptive Narrative*, p. 211. ASM, Representaciones, September 12, 1836. AHG, EP/J, document 415 (1822). The BMG collection contains extensive government correspondence about unauthorized *aguardiente* production and its suppression.

51. BMG, vol. 100, December 3, 1830. AFL, Report of the Ministry of the Interior for 1833.

52. BMG, vol. 110, January 4, 1831.

53. Hamerly (*Historia social*, p. 186) cites the example of a frustrated teacher in 1813 who got only five students.

54. Actas de Cabildo, December 31, 1831.

55. BMG, vol. 133, December 21, 1833. Van Aken, *King of the Night*, p. 59. I have found six such government orders issued in Guayaquil between 1822 and 1833.

56. BMG, vol. 103, January 6, 1830. This man was from Yaguachi, but poor men from Guayaquil also petitioned frequently to be excused from performing the service, usually to no avail.

57. Van Aken, *King of the Night*, pp. 54–55. ABC, British Consular Report for 1834–1835, pp. 30–32; Fondo Jijón y Caamaño, 52:137 (1826) and 54:77 (1828). BMG, vol. 67, January 8 and December 22, 1827; vol. 86, April 29, 1829; vol. 89, January 31, 1829; vol. 101, August 7, 1829. For the hostile discussion of the soldiers see *La Balanza* and *La Opinión* in 1839. I do not mean to repudiate entirely the traditional notion that the military offered a sort of "escape valve" for ambitious sons from poor families. The usefulness of the army in enhancing a soldier's sense of self seems to have varied dramatically from region to region. Benjamin Vinson III has demonstrated, for example, that the free-colored militia in late colonial Mexico actually helped to create the identity of being free-colored as well as being an inspiration to the community's people of color in general to demand rights they believed should be theirs, even including tribute relief. See "Creating Racial Identities: The Free-Colored Militia in Colonial Mexico," paper presented at the 1998 meeting of the Latin American Studies Association in Chicago.

58. AHG, EP/J, documents 3561 (1825), 886 (1826), 2067 (1828), and 888 (1829). BMG, vol. 80, January 26 and March 7, 1828.

59. Stanley, *Six Weeks*, pp. 61–62.

CHAPTER 8. "To Become the Unfortunate Tenants of Your Alms House"

1. MHS, MS 1866.1, Baltimore Almshouse Admission and Discharge Book, 1813–1826. For further information on the Almshouse, see Douglas G. Carrol and Blanche D. Coll, "The Baltimore Almshouse: An Early History," *Maryland Historical Magazine* 66, no. 2 (1971); Katherine Harvey, "Practicing Medicine at the Baltimore Almshouse, 1828–1850," *Maryland Historical Magazine* 74, no. 3 (1979).

2. This was later enacted into law: BCA, RG 16, City Council Proceedings, Ordinance Number 11, 1829.

3. De la Sagra, *Cinq mois*, June 20, 1835.

4. The first statistic is based on calculations using the information in the Admission and Discharge Book. The second comes from the BCA, RG 41, Reports and Returns, document 1454, Report of the Trustees of the Poor for 1827.

5. Of the children in the house when Margaret was there, 17 percent of the parentless later died, as did 15 percent of those with parents. Baltimore Almshouse Admission and Discharge Book, 1813–1826.

6. MSA, Baltimore County, Orphans Court, Indentures, January–February 1826. The "rule of Three" refers to the study of ratios, that is, "If a dozen eggs cost five cents, how much will six eggs cost?"

7. MHS, MS 1866.1, Baltimore Almshouse Admission and Discharge Book.

8. Ramón de la Sagra (*Cinq mois*) and various city officials visited the Almshouse. BCA, RG 41, Reports and Returns, document 1454, Report of the Trustees of the Poor, 1827; and RG 19, Health Department, documents 330 and 344, Reports of the Health Commissioners, 1826.

9. Travelers commented on the numbers of prostitutes working near the wharves of Fell's Point, although only two women in the house while Margaret was there publicly stated that they were prostitutes (Admission and Discharge Book).

10. BCA, RG 19, Health Department, Report of the Health Commissioners for 1826.

11. BCA, RG 19, Health Department, Report of the Health Commissioners for 1826; RG 16, City Council Correspondence, document 543, n.d. 1830, and document 566, January 12, 1827; RG 9, Mayor's Office, document 1040, January 9, 1827 (quotation).

12. BCA, RG 19, Health Department, documents 333 and 334 (1827). See also Olson, *Baltimore*, p. 91.

13. These numbers marked the end of one trend and the beginning of another. Leonard Curry, who relies on numbers published by the City Council, says that by the 1830s blacks represented a *higher* proportion in the Almshouse than they did in the city as a whole (*The Free Black*, p. 123). The black community was by then facing greater poverty, as documented by Phillips in *Freedom's Port* and Whitman in *Price of Freedom*.

14. BCA, RG 19, Health Department, document 350, 1827. Similar incidents suggest to some historians that the lives of the lower orders of Baltimore were in fact generally blighted at this time, to a greater extent than I would infer. See, for example, Seth Rockman, "Working for Wages in Early Republican Baltimore."

15. Graham, *Baltimore*, p. 25. For the achievements of blacks in this era, see Ira Berlin, "The Revolution in Black Life," in *The American Revolution: Explorations in the History of American Radicalism*, ed. Alfred F. Young.

16. BCA, RG 16, City Council Correspondence, document 438, February 12, 1827. There were frequent complaints about blacks "congregating" until in 1838 a 10 P.M. curfew was actually imposed.

17. MHS, MS 1653, Richard Dorsey Papers, Richard Dorsey to Mr. Goldsborough, February 19, 1840.

18. Phillips calls this the "urban mélange." To these three groups, he adds black sailors as well as people who had come from Saint-Domingue at the time of the Revolution, either as the property of fleeing whites or as fleeing mulattoes (*Freedom's Port*, Chapter 3).

19. *Baltimore Gazette and Daily Advertiser*, February 13, July 2, and October 1, 1830. *American and Commercial Daily Advertiser*, January 3, 1834.

20. BCA, RG 16, City Council Correspondence, document 655, February 19, 1827.

21. BCA, RG 16, City Council Proceedings, Resolution 70 (1830) and Resolution 3 (1831).

22. MSA, Baltimore County, Certificates of Freedom, 1825–1828 and 1830–1831. After 1831 it became especially important to register as having been free for years and then to pay an annual fee, for after that date a newly emancipated person was technically required to leave the state. See Brackett, *The Negro in Maryland*, p. 166.

23. *A Narrative of the Life of Reverend Noah Davis, a Colored Man, Written by Himself, at the Age of Fifty-four*, pp. 26–28 and 42. This part of the book recalls the period of the 1830s, although even as he wrote the author was still engaged in trying to buy his last two children. He hoped the sale of the book would help. Fields (*Slavery and Freedom*), Phillips (*Freedom's Port*), and especially Whitman

(*Price of Freedom*) treat the extraordinary success of Baltimore's slaves in gaining their own freedom and the extent to which the process drained them of resources.

24. Coke, *Subaltern's Furlough*, p. 1. BCA, RG 16, City Council Correspondence, document 564, December 26, 1830.

25. MSA, Baltimore City Court, Naturalization Record (1827–1851). Fields, *Slavery and Freedom*, p. 44. Steffen, *Mechanics*, pp. 6–7. Jean Baker, *The Politics of Continuity: Maryland Political Parties from 1858 to 1870*, p. 12. MHS, Papers of Bernard Labroquère, MS 1848, bills and receipts, 1820s. In the same period, on her Maryland plantation, Rosalie Calvert gave special attention to their indentured German gardener and his wife (*Mistress of Riversdale*, p. 343).

26. Systematic studies support the anecdotal evidence. The earlier migration from Europe was fed by wealthier countries than that of the exodus later in the century. For a summary of the literature, see John Bodnar, *The Transplanted: A History of Immigrants in Urban America*. Pickering, *Inquiries*, MHS, MS 1993, Diary of William Minifrie.

27. BCA, RG 16, City Council Correspondence, documents 447 and 475, January 1827; and City Council Proceedings, Ordinance Number 22 (1828). RG 9, Mayor's Office, document 1007, April 18, 1827. RG 41, Reports and Returns, Workmen's Bills, 1827–1831. Frey, *Reminiscences*, p. 48.

28. Steffen in *Mechanics* analyzes the statistics for the period immediately preceding this study. In the 1820s, although the number of Almshouse residents increased year by year, it only kept pace with the general increase of the city's population. The period of the dramatic expansion of the class of destitute industrial poor was to come later.

29. BCA, RG 3, City Commissioners, document 132, February 4, 1830, and document 144, February 13, 1830; RG 16, City Council Correspondence, document 516, n.d. 1827; RG 41, Reports and Returns, Workmen's Bills, documents 1525, 1827, and 1504, 1830. MHS, MS 1778, Spafford Family Papers, personal account notebook, 1831–1832, and tenants' notebook, 1832–1835. Pickering, *Inquiries*, p. 20.

30. BCA, RG 16, City Council Correspondence, document 831, n.d. 1830, and City Council Proceedings, Resolution No. 7 (1830) and Ordinance No. 1 (extra session, 1830) and Resolution No. 13 (1831).

31. BCA, RG 3, City Commissioners, document 180, April 28, 1827; RG 9, Mayor's Office, document 1001, 1827, and documents 1035–1045, 1830; RG 16, City Council Correspondence, document 527, February 8, 1827; RG 41, Reports and Returns, Pay Receipts, document 1507, December 31, 1829.

32. BCA, RG 16, City Council Correspondence, document 517, February 9, 1830; RG 41, Reports and Returns, document 1214, 1827, and 1296, 1830. For a fascinating study of the chimneysweeps of New York, see Paul Gilje and Howard

B. Rock, " 'Sweep O! Sweep O!': African American Chimney Sweeps and Citizenship in the New Nation," *William and Mary Quarterly* 51, no. 3 (1994).

33. MHS, MS 1706, John Stump Papers, April 19, 1823. MS 1521, Thomas and Hugg Papers, Captain Hugg's ship log, January 1831. Phillips, *Freedom's Port*, pp. 79–80. See also Peter Linebaugh and Marcus Rediker, "The Many Headed Hydra: Sailors, Slaves and the Atlantic Working Class in the Eighteenth Century," in *Jack Tar in History*, ed. Colin Howell and Richard Twomey.

34. Kemble Butler, *Journal*, p. 76 (quotation). Steffen, *Mechanics*, pp. 29–30. MSA, Baltimore County, Orphans Court, Indentures, 1827–1830. T. Stephen Whitman, "Industrial Slavery at the Margin: The Maryland Chemical Works," *Journal of Southern History* 59, no. 1 (1993).

35. BCA, RG 41, Reports and Returns, Report of the Directors of the Penitentiary, December 1829 (quotation). Steffen, *Mechanics*, pp. 45–46. Lynda Fuller Clendenning, "The Early Textile Industry in Maryland, 1810–1850," *Maryland Historical Magazine* 87, no. 3 (1992).

36. MHS, MS 1131, Moses Hyde Diary, January 27, 1832.

37. Royall, *Sketches*, p. 196.

38. BCA, RG 42, Market Records, Huckster licenses, 1830; RG 41, Reports and Returns, Bailiff's Reports, document 1430, 1830; RG 16, City Council Correspondence, document 406, March 14, 1827 and document 459, n.d. 1830. Duncan, *Travels*, pp. 230, 246 (quotation).

39. BCA, RG 41, Reports and Returns, Bailiff's Reports, documents 1360–1365, 1827, and document 1257, 1830.

40. BCA, RG 16, City Council Correspondence, document 426, May 17, 1827.

41. BCA, RG 16, City Council Correspondence, document 484, 1827.

42. BCA, RG 9, Mayor's Office, document 995, April 24, 1830; RG 16, City Council Proceedings, Ordinance No. 31, 1831; RG 41, Reports and Returns, Bailiff's Reports, document 1365, 1827. Joseph Pickering was told (*Inquiries*, p. 27) that "nine pins" had been outlawed, so people had begun playing "ten pins" instead. Apparently, the City Council decided not to fight the tide: the new license fee of 1831 applied to nine or ten pins.

43. BCA, RG 19, Health Department, Report of the Health Officer, document 342, January 23, 1826.

44. The following analysis comes from the records of the MSA, Baltimore City Court, Criminal Docket, 1826. A more cursory examination was also given to the records of the year 1828. See also Olson, *Baltimore*, p. 93, for similar results for the year 1831.

45. BCA, RG 16, City Council Correspondence, document 496, April 5, 1830. MHS, MS 1677, John H. B. Latrobe Diaries, summer 1824.

46. Royall, *Sketches*, pp. 194–195. B C A, RG 16, City Council Correspondence, document 570, December 31, 1830.

47. De la Sagra, *Cinq mois*, June 20, 1835. Duncan, *Travels*, p. 233. *Baltimore Republican*, September 27, 1827. *Baltimore Gazette and Daily Advertiser*, January 1, 1830 (and every week for the next several years). See also Gettleman, "The Maryland Penitentiary."

48. M H S, Rare Book Room, Report of the Directors of the Maryland Penitentiary, December 1825. B C A, RG 32, City Register, Ledger for 1826–1829, listings for 1826 and 1828. M S A, Baltimore City Court, Criminal Docket, John Brown case #654, June 1826, and notations added to the record later; and Baltimore City Court, Minutes, Account of Sales of Negroes Sentenced to Transportation, June 1826. See also Brackett, *The Negro in Maryland*, pp. 227–228. (The law was revived after 1835.)

49. B C A, RG 16, City Council Correspondence, document 571, March 8, 1830, and document 570, December 31, 1830. Royall, *Sketches*, p. 194 (quotation). M S A, Baltimore City Court, Criminal Docket, John Pearson, case #484, June 1826.

50. M H S, Minutes of the Meetings of the Trustees of the Poor for 1833.

51. M S A, Baltimore City Jail, Civil Docket; and Baltimore County Court, Insolvency Docket, 1827. (Anne Royall commented specifically on women debtors in the Baltimore prison in *Sketches*, p. 97.) This paragraph touches on complex issues: I am indebted to Bruce Mann and James Pearson for clarification of the major themes.

52. *Baltimore Gazette and Daily Advertiser*, March 15, 1830. *American and Commercial Daily Advertiser*, January 2, 1834.

53. M H S, Rare Book Room, Meetings of the Trustees of McKim's School for Poor Youths, 1821–1826. There were similar complaints on the part of the commissioners of the new public schools.

54. M S A, Baltimore County Orphans Court, Indentures, 1827–1830. M H S, MS 1866.1, Baltimore Almshouse Admission and Discharge Book, 1813–1826.

55. Douglass, *Autobiographies*, pp. 336–337. The newspapers of the early 1830s indicate a marked change in this regard. These examples are from the *Baltimore Gazette and Daily Advertiser*, February 13, April 2, October 1, and December 1, 1830. Fields (*Slavery and Freedom*), Phillips (*Freedom's Port*), and Whitman (*Price of Freedom*) document the increasing percentages of free black unskilled laborers as well as the growing attacks on them.

Conclusion

1. Bernal Díaz de Castillo, *The Conquest of New Spain*, p. 413.

2. A F L, Report of the Ministry of the Interior.

3. "A Farewell Exhortation to the Church and People of Dorchester in New England," quoted in Perry Miller, *The New England Mind from Colony to Province*, p. 4.

4. Adelman, *Colonial Legacies*, p. xi.

5. *The Brenner Debate*, ed. Aston and Philpin, p. 46.

6. Emmanuel, *Unequal Exchange*, p. xxxiv.

7. Although many conservative economists and most financial analysts have traditionally resisted this concept, preferring to find reasons for the accumulation of capital among certain individuals, the starkness of today's international realities is forcing some to reconsider. See "Latin America: The Fire Next Time," *New York Times*, January 23, 1999, commentary excerpted from *Business Week*.

BIBLIOGRAPHY

Archives Consulted

England

PRO   Public Record Office, Kew
          FO Foreign Office

Ecuador

ABC   Archivo del Banco Central, Quito
          Consular Reports
          Jijón y Caamaño

AFL   Archivo de la Función Legislativa, Quito
          Ministerios

AHG   Archivo Histórico del Guayas
          Actas de Cabildo de Guayaquil
          EP/J Escribano Público: Juicios

ANH/A Archivo Nacional de Historia, Núcleo del Azuay, Cuenca
          Administración
          Haciendas

ANH/Q   Archivo Nacional de Historia, Quito
         Gobierno
         Haciendas

ASM   Archivo de la Secretaría Municipal, Guayaquil
         Documentos Varios
         Particulares
         Representaciones

BMG   Biblioteca Municipal de Guayaquil
         Archivo Histórico
         Volumeres 40–153
         Colección Carlos Rolando
         Escrituras
         Folletos

United States

BCA   Baltimore City Archives
         RG 3. City Commissioners
         RG 4. Property Tax Records
         RG 9. Mayor's Office
         RG 16. City Council
         RG 19. Health Department
         RG 31. Department of Education
         RG 32. City Register
         RG 39. Harbor Records
         RG 41. Reports and Returns
         RG 42. Market Records

EPL   Enoch Pratt Free Library, Baltimore
         Census, 1830
         Maryland Room Newspapers

MHS   Maryland Historical Society, Baltimore
         Manuscripts Collection
         Rare Book Room, Pamphlets

MSA   Maryland State Archives, Annapolis
         Baltimore City Court
         Baltimore City Justice of the Peace
         Baltimore City Register of Wills
         Baltimore City Superior Court
         Baltimore City and County Commission of Insolvent Debtors
         Baltimore City and County Jail
         Baltimore City and County Trustees of the Poor

PFL   Princeton University Firestone Library Special Collections
       Iturbe e Iraeta Collection

Published Primary Sources

Ecuador

Newspapers

La Balanza	*El Ecuatoriano del Guayas*
El Chanduy	*9 de Octubre*
El Chispero	*La Opinión*
El Colombiano	*El Patriota de Guayaquil*
El Colombiano del Guayas	*El Ruiseñor*
El Correo	

Books

Avendaño, Joaquín de. *Recuerdos de mis viajes: Primer viaje a América—Ecuador.*
    El Museo Universal. Vol. 5. Madrid, 1861.
Campos, Francisco. *Galería biográfica de hombres célebres ecuatorianos.* Guayaquil:
    Imprenta "El Telégrafo," 1885.
Díaz de Castillo, Bernal. *The Conquest of New Spain.* New York: Penguin, 1967.
Hall, Basil. *Extracts from a Journal Written on the Coasts of Chili, Peru and Mexico.*
    London: Hurst, Robinson & Co., 1824.
Hallo, Wilson, ed. *Imágenes del Ecuador del siglo XIX: Juan Agustín Guerrero,*
    1818–1880. Quito: Ediciones del Sol, 1981.
Hassaurek, Friederich. *Four Years among Spanish Americans.* New York: Hurd &
    Houghton, 1868.
Humphreys, R. A., ed. *British Consular Reports on the Trade and Politics of Latin*
    America, 1824–1826. London: Royal Historical Society, 1940.
Laviana Cuetos, María Luisa, ed. *Francisco de Requena y su descripción de Guayaquil.*
    Seville: Escuela de Estudios Hispano-Americanos, 1984.
Mörner, Magnus, ed. *Informes sobre los estados sudamericanos en los años de 1837 y*
    1838. Stockholm: Library and Institute of Ibero-American Studies, 1962.
National Archives of the United States. *Despatches from the United States Consuls*
    in Guayaquil, 1826–1906. Microfilm. Roll 1. Washington, D.C.: National
    Archives and Records Service.
Onffroy de Thoron, Enrique. *Amérique Equatoriale: Son histoire pittoresque et poli-*
    tique. Paris: Jules Renouard, 1866.
Orton, James. *The Andes and the Amazon; or, Across the Continent of South America.*
    New York: Harper, 1870.
Pfeiffer, Ida. *A Lady's Second Journey round the World.* London: Longman, 1855.

291

Spruce, Richard. *Notes of a Botanist on the Amazon and Andes . . . during the Years 1849–1864.* London: Macmillan, 1908.

Stanley, Edward, Earl of Derby. *Six Weeks in South America.* London: privately printed, 1850.

Stevenson, William Bennet. *A Historical and Descriptive Narrative of Twenty Years' Residence in South America.* London: Hurst Robinson, 1825.

Terry, Adrian. *Travels in the Equatorial Regions of South America in 1832.* Hartford, Conn.: Cooke & Co., 1834.

A View of South America and Mexico by a Citizen of the United States. New York: Published for Subscribers, 1827.

Villamil, José. "Reseña de los acontecimientos políticos y militares de la Provincia de Guayaquil, desde 1813 hasta 1824." Reprinted in *La independencia de Guayaquil,* edited by Abel Romeo Castillo. Guayaquil: Banco Central del Ecuador, 1983.

United States

Newspapers

American and Commercial Daily Advertiser
Baltimore Gazette and Daily Advertiser
Baltimore Minerva and Emerald
[Baltimore] Monument
Baltimore Price Current
Baltimore Republican
Baltimore Weekly Gazette
Commercial Chronicle and Daily Marylander

Books

Baltimore Directory. Baltimore: R. J. Matchett, 1827.

Billings, Warren, ed. *The Old Dominion in the Seventeenth Century: A Documentary History of Virginia, 1606–1689.* Chapel Hill: University of North Carolina, 1975.

Bowen, Ele. *Rambles in the Path of the Steam-Horse.* Philadelphia: William Bromwell & William White Smith, 1855.

Callcott, Margaret, ed. *Mistress of Riversdale: The Plantation Letters of Rosalie Stier Calvert, 1795–1821.* Baltimore: Johns Hopkins University Press, 1991.

Coke, Edward. *A Subaltern's Furlough: Descriptive Scenes in Various Parts of the United States, Upper and Lower Canada . . . during the Summer and Autumn of 1832.* London: Saunders & Otley, 1833.

Commercial Directory for the Union. Philadelphia: J. C. Kayser & Co., 1823.

Davis, Noah. *A Narrative of the Life of Reverend Noah Davis, a Colored Man, Written by Himself, at the Age of Fifty-four.* Baltimore: John F. Weishampel, ca. 1858.

De Roos, Frederick Fitzgerald. *Personal Narrative of Travels in the United States and Canada in 1826.* London: William Harrison Ainsworth, 1827.

Douglass, Frederick. *My Bondage and My Freedom.* New York: Miller, Orton & Mulligan, 1855. Reprinted in *Frederick Douglass: Autobiographies.* New York: Library of America, 1994.

Duncan, John M. *Travels through Part of the United States and Canada in 1818 and 1819.* New York: W. B. Gilley, 1823.

Frey, Jacob. *Reminiscences of Baltimore.* Baltimore: Maryland Book Concerns, 1893.

Gray, Ralph, and Gerald Hartdagen. "A Glimpse of Baltimore Society in 1827: Letters by Henry D. Gilpin." *Maryland Historical Magazine* 69, no. 3 (1974): 269–270.

Guillet, Peter. *The Timber Merchant's Guide.* Baltimore: James Longrove, 1823.

Hall, Basil. *Travels in North America in the Years 1827 and 1828.* 2 vols. London: Simkin & Marshall, 1829.

Hamilton, Thomas. *Men and Manners in America.* London: William Blackwood, 1843.

Haviland, John. *Practical Builder's Assistant.* Baltimore: Fielding Lucas, 1830.

Hone, Philip. *The Diary of Philip Hone, 1828–1851.* Edited by B. Tuckman. New York: privately printed, 1889.

Kemble Butler, Frances. *Journal, in Two Volumes.* Philadelphia: Carey, Lea & Blanchard, 1835.

Latrobe, Charles. *The Rambler in North America.* London: Seeley & Burnside, ca. 1835.

Levasseur, Auguste. *Lafayette in America in 1824 and 1825.* Philadelphia: Carey & Lea, 1829.

Lucas, Fielding, and John Latrobe. *Picture of Baltimore.* Baltimore: Fielding Lucas, 1832.

Morgan, James. *The Manufacturer's Book of Wages and Work People's Companion.* Baltimore: James Morgan, 1825.

Mowbray, G. Hamilton, ed. "Lonely in South America: Two Baltimoreans Write Home, 1828–29." *Maryland Historical Magazine* 85, no. 1 (1990): 73–76.

Pickering, Joseph. *Inquiries of an Emigrant: Being the Narrative of an English Farmer from the Year 1824 to 1830.* London: Effingham Wilson, 1832.

Power, Tyrone. *Impressions of America during the Years 1833, 1834 and 1835.* London: Richard Bentley, 1836.

Royall, Anne. *The Black Book.* Washington, D.C.: privately printed, 1828.

———. *Sketches of History, Life and Manners, in the United States.* New Haven: privately printed, 1826.

Sagra, Ramón de la. *Cinq mois aux Etats-Unis de l'Amérique du Nord.* Paris: F. G. Levrault, 1837.

Shaw, Joshua. *U.S. Directory for the Use of Travellers and Merchants.* Philadelphia: James Maxwell, 1822.
Stuart, James. *Three Years in North America.* 2 vols. New York: n.p., 1833.
Tudor, Henry. *Narrative of a Tour in North America in a Series of Letters Written in the Years 1831–1832.* London: privately printed, 1834.
Varle, Charles. *A Complete View of Baltimore.* Baltimore: Samuel Young, 1833.
Wright, Frances. *Views of Society and Manners in America.* New York: Longman Hurst, 1821.

Secondary Sources

Adelman, Jeremy, ed. *Colonial Legacies: The Problem of Persistence in Latin American History.* New York: Routledge, 1999.
Aguirre, Carlos. "Mapping Lima's Morals: The Construction of the 'Criminal Classes' in Late Nineteenth Century Peru." Paper presented at the Latin American Studies Association, Chicago, September 1998.
Akerson, Louise. *American Indians in the Baltimore Area.* Baltimore: Center for Urban Archaeology, 1990.
———. *Baltimore's Material Culture.* Baltimore: Center for Urban Archaeology, 1990.
Alchon, Suzanne. *Native Society and Disease in Colonial Ecuador.* Cambridge: Cambridge University Press, 1991.
Altfeld, E. Milton. *The Jew's Struggle for Religious and Civil Liberty in Maryland.* New York: Da Capo Press, 1970.
Altman, Ida. "Emigrants and Society: An Approach to the Background of Colonial Spanish America." *Comparative Studies in Society and History* 30, no. 1 (1988): 170–190.
Andrade, Roberto. *Historia del Ecuador.* Guayaquil: Reed & Reed, 1934.
Andrien, Kenneth J. *The Kingdom of Quito, 1690–1830: The State and Regional Development.* Cambridge: Cambridge University Press, 1995.
———. "The State and Dependency in Late Colonial and Early Republican Ecuador." In *The Political Economy of Spanish America in the Age of Revolution, 1750–1850,* edited by K. Andrien and L. Johnson. Albuquerque: University of New Mexico Press, 1994.
Andrien, Kenneth J., and Rolena Adorno, eds. *Transatlantic Encounters: Europeans and Andeans in the Sixteenth Century.* Berkeley: University of California Press, 1992.
Appleby, Joyce. *Capitalism and a New Social Order: The Republican Vision of the 1790s.* New York: New York University Press, 1984.
———. *Liberalism and Republicanism in the Historical Imagination.* Cambridge, Mass.: Harvard University Press, 1992.
———. "Republicanism in Old and New Contexts." *William and Mary Quarterly* 43, no. 3 (1986): 20–34.

Arrom, Silvia M. *The Women of Mexico City, 1790–1857.* Stanford: Stanford University Press, 1985.

Arrom, Silvia M., and Servando Ortoll, eds. *Riots in the Cities: Popular Politics and the Urban Poor in Latin America, 1765–1910.* Wilmington, Del.: Scholarly Resources, 1996.

Assadourian, Carlos Sempat. *El sistema de la economía colonial: Mercado interno, regiones y espacio económico.* Lima: Instituto de Estudios Peruanos, 1982.

Aston, T. H., and C. H. E. Philpin, eds. *The Brenner Debate: Agrarian Class Structure and Economic Development in Pre-industrial Europe.* Cambridge: Cambridge University Press, 1985.

Ayala Mora, Enrique. *El Bolivarianismo en el Ecuador.* Quito: Corporación Editora Nacional, 1991.

———. *Historia, compromiso y política: Ensayos sobre historiografía ecuatoriana.* Quito: Planeta Letraviva, 1989.

———, ed. *Libro del Sesquicentenario IV, Economía, Ecuador: 1830–1980.* Quito: Corporación Editora Nacional, 1983.

———, ed. *Nueva historia del Ecuador.* 15 vols. Quito: Grijalbo, 1983.

Baker, Jean. *The Politics of Continuity: Maryland Political Parties from 1858 to 1870.* Baltimore: Johns Hopkins University Press, 1973.

Banning, Lance. "Jeffersonian Ideology Revisited: Liberal and Classical Ideas in the New American Republic." *William and Mary Quarterly* 43, no. 3 (1986): 3–19.

Bedini, Silvio. *The Life of Benjamin Banneker.* New York: Charles Scribner's Sons, 1972.

Bergquist, Charles. *Labor and the Course of American Democracy: U.S. History in Latin American Perspective.* New York: Verso, 1996.

———. *Labor in Latin America: Comparative Essays on Chile, Argentina, Venezuela and Colombia.* Stanford: Stanford University Press, 1986.

Berlin, Ira. "The Revolution in Black Life." In *The American Revolution: Explorations in the History of American Radicalism,* ed. Alfred F. Young. De Kalb: Northern Illinois Press, 1976.

Bilhartz, Terry. *Urban Religion and the Second Great Awakening: Church and Society in Early National Baltimore.* Cranbury, N.J.: Associated University Presses, 1986.

Bodnar, John. *The Transplanted: A History of Immigrants in Urban America.* Bloomington: Indiana University Press, 1985.

Bonilla, Heraclio, ed. *Los Andes en la encrucijada: Indios, comunidades y estado en el siglo XIX.* Quito: Ediciones Libri Mundi, 1991.

Borchart, Christiana. "La imbecilidad del sexo: Pulperas y mercaderas quiteñas a fines del siglo XVIII." In *Historia de la mujer y la familia,* edited by J. Núñez. Quito: Editora Nacional, 1991.

Borja, Doris León. "Prehistoria de la costa ecuatoriana." *Anuario de Estudios Americanos* 21 (1964): 381–436.

Borja, Doris León, and Adam Szászdi. "El comercio del cacao de Guayaquil." *Revista de Historia de América* 57 (1964): 1–50.

Bornholdt, Laura. *Baltimore and Early Pan-Americanism.* Smith College Series in History, no. 15. Northampton, Mass.: Smith College, 1949.

Bowser, Frederick. "Colonial Spanish America." In *Neither Slave Nor Free: The Freedmen of African Descent in the Slave Societies of the New World*, edited by D. Cohen and J. Greene. Baltimore: Johns Hopkins University Press, 1972.

Boydston, Jeanne. *Home and Work: Housework, Wages and the Ideology of Labor in the Early Republic.* New York: Oxford University Press, 1990.

Boyer, Richard. *Lives of the Bigamists: Marriage, Family and Community in Colonial Mexico.* Albuquerque: University of New Mexico Press, 1995.

Boyer, Richard, and Keith Davies. "Urbanization in Nineteenth-Century Latin America: Statistics and Sources." Supplement to *The Statistical Abstract of Latin America*. Los Angeles: Latin American Center, 1973.

Brackett, Jeffrey. *The Negro in Maryland.* Baltimore: Johns Hopkins University Press, 1889.

Brenner, Y. S., Hartmut Kaelble, and Mark Thomas, eds. *Income Distribution in Historical Perspective.* Cambridge: Cambridge University Press, 1991.

Brewington, M. V. "The Chesapeake Bay Pilots." *Maryland Historical Magazine* 48, no. 2 (1953): 109–133.

Brilliant, Richard. *Facing the New World: Jewish Portraits in Colonial and Federal America.* New York: Prestel, 1997.

Bromley, Rosemary, and R. J. Bromley. "The Debate on Sunday Markets in Nineteenth-Century Ecuador." *Journal of Latin American Studies* 7, no. 1 (1975): 85–108.

Browne, Gary Larson. *Baltimore in the Nation, 1789–1861.* Chapel Hill: University of North Carolina Press, 1980.

Bruchey, Stuart Weems. *Enterprise: The Dynamic Economy of a Free People.* Cambridge, Mass.: Harvard University Press, 1990.

———. *Robert Oliver: Merchant of Baltimore, 1783–1819.* Baltimore: Johns Hopkins University Press, 1956.

———. *The Roots of American Economic Growth, 1607–1861: An Essay on Social Causation.* New York: Harper & Row, 1965.

———. "Success and Failure Factors: American Merchants in Foreign Trade in the Eighteenth and Early Nineteenth Centuries." *Business History Review* 32, no. 3 (1958): 272–292.

Bulmer-Thomas, Victor. *The Economic History of Latin America since Independence.* Cambridge: Cambridge University Press, 1994.

Bushnell, David. "The Development of the Press in Gran Colombia." *Hispanic American Historical Review* 31, no. 1 (1950): 432–452.

———. "Independence of Spanish South America." In *Cambridge History of Latin America*, vol. 3. 10 vols. Cambridge: Cambridge University Press, 1985.

Campbell, Leon. *The Military and Society in Colonial Peru, 1750–1810.* Philadelphia: American Philosophical Society, 1978.

Carbo, Luis Alberto. *Historia monetaria y cambiaria del Ecuador.* Quito: Banco Central, 1978.

Cardoso, Fernando Enrique, and Enzo Faletto. *Dependency and Development in Latin America.* Berkeley: University of California Press, 1979.

Carr, Lois Green, Philip D. Morgan, and Jean B. Russo, eds. *Colonial Chesapeake Society.* Chapel Hill: University of North Carolina Press, 1968.

Carrol, Douglas G., and Blanche D. Coll. "The Baltimore Almshouse: An Early History." *Maryland Historical Magazine* 66, no. 2 (1971): 135–152.

Cassell, Frank. *Merchant Congressman in the Young Republic: Samuel Smith of Maryland, 1752–1839.* Madison: University of Wisconsin Press, 1971.

Castillo, Abel Romeo. *La imprenta de Guayaquil independiente.* Guayaquil: Banco Central, 1982.

Chaves, María Eugenia. *María Chiquinquirá Díaz, una esclava del siglo XVIII: Acerca de las identidades de amo y esclavo en el puerto colonial de Guayaquil.* Guayaquil: Archivo Histórico del Guayas, 1998.

Chavez Franco, Manuel. *Crónicas del Guayaquil antiguo.* Guayaquil: Talleres Municipales, 1930.

Cherpak, Evelyn. "The Participation of Women in the Independence Movement in Gran Colombia, 1780–1830." In *Latin American Women: Historical Perspectives,* edited by Asunción Lavrin. Westport, Conn.: Greenwood Press, 1978.

Childs, St. Julien Ravenal. "Cavaliers and Burghers in the Carolina Low County." In *Historiography and Urbanization,* edited by E. Goldman. Baltimore: Johns Hopkins University Press, 1941.

Chiriboga, Manuel. "Ciudad y campo en la costa durante el período cacaotero." In *Las ciudades en la historia,* edited by E. Kingman Garces. Quito: Centro de Investigaciones CIUDAD, 1989.

———. *Jornaleros y grandes propietarios en 135 años de exportación cacaotera.* Quito: Consejo Provincial de Pichincha, 1980.

Clayton, Lawrence. *Caulkers and Carpenters in a New World: The Shipyards of Colonial Guayaquil.* Papers in International Studies in Latin America, no. 8. Ohio University: Center for International Studies, 1980.

———. "Local Initiative and Finance in Defense of the Viceroyalty of Peru: The Development of Self-Reliance." *Hispanic American Historical Review* 54, no. 2 (1974): 284–304.

Clayton, Ralph. *Black Baltimore, 1820–1870.* Bowie, Md.: Heritage Books, 1987.

Clemens, Paul. *The Atlantic Economy and Colonial Maryland's Eastern Shore: From Tobacco to Grain.* Ithaca: Cornell University Press, 1980.

Clemens, Paul, and Lucy Simler. "Rural Labor and the Farm Household in Chester County, Pennsylvania, 1750–1820." In *Work and Labor in Early America,* edited by S. Innes. Chapel Hill: University of North Carolina Press, 1988.

Clendenning, Lynda Fuller. "The Early Textile Industry in Maryland, 1810–1850." *Maryland Historical Magazine* 87, no. 3 (1992): 251–266.

Coatsworth, John. "Obstacles to Economic Growth in Nineteenth-Century Mexico." *American Historical Review* 83, no. 1 (1978): 80–100.

Cochran, Thomas. *The Puerto Rican Businessman: A Study in Cultural Change.* Philadelphia: University of Pennsylvania Press, 1959.

———. *200 Years of American Business.* New York: Basic Books, 1977.

Codaccioni, Olivia. "*El Patriota de Guayaquil, 1821–1822:* Instrument et miroir de l'imaginaire politique guayaquilène." Master's thesis, Department of History at the Sorbonne, Paris, 1994.

Conniff, Michael. "Guayaquil through Independence: Urban Development in a Colonial System." *Americas* 33, no. 3 (1977): 385–400.

Contreras, Carlos. *El sector exportador de una economía colonial: La costa del Ecuador, 1760–1830.* Quito: Abya-Yala, 1990.

Cook, Alexandra Parma, and Noble David Cook. *Good Faith and Truthful Ignorance: A Case of Transatlantic Bigamy.* Durham: Duke University Press, 1991.

Cortes Conde, Roberto, and Stanley Stein, eds. *Latin America: A Guide to Economic History, 1830–1930.* Berkeley: University of California Press, 1977.

Cronon, William. *Changes in the Land: Indians, Colonists and the Ecology of New England.* New York: Hill & Wang, 1983.

Crowley, J. E. *This Sheba, Self: The Conceptualization of Economic Life in Eighteenth-Century America.* Baltimore: Johns Hopkins University Press, 1974.

Cubitt, David. "La anexión de la provincia de Guayaquil, 1822: Estudios del estilo político bolivariano." *Revista del Archivo Histórico del Guayas* 13 (1978): 7–30.

———. "La composición social de una elite hispanoamericana a la independencia: Guayaquil en 1820." *Revista de Historia de América* 94 (1982): 7–31.

———. "El nacionalismo económico en la post-independencia del Ecuador: El Código de Comercio de Guayaquil de 1821–1825." *Revista Ecuatoriana de Historia Económica* 1, no. 2 (1987): 131–152.

Curry, Leonard. *The Free Black in Urban America, 1800–1850.* Chicago: University of Chicago Press, 1981.

Cushner, Nicholas. *Farm and Factory: The Jesuits and the Development of Agrarian Capitalism in Colonial Quito, 1600–1767.* Albany: State University of New York, 1982.

Dawson, Frank. *The First Latin American Debt Crisis: The City of London and the 1822–25 Loan Bubble.* New Haven: Yale University Press, 1990.

Demelas, Marie Danielle, and Yves Saint-Geours. *Jerusalén y Babylonia: Religión y política en el Ecuador, 1780–1880.* Quito: Corporación Editora Nacional, 1988.

———. *La vie quotidienne en Amérique de Sud au temps de Bolivar, 1809–1836.* Paris: Hachette, 1987.

Destruge, Camilo. *Album biográfico ecuatoriano*. 2 vols. Guayaquil: Banco Central, 1984.

———. *Historia de la prensa de Guayaquil*. Quito: Tipográfica y Encuadernación Salesianas, 1924.

———. *Historia de la Revolución de Octubre y campaña libertadora*. Guayaquil: Banco Central, 1982. Reprinted from first edition of 1920.

Dirks, Nicholas, Geoff Eley, and Sherry Ortner, eds. *Culture/Power/History: A Reader in Contemporary Social Theory*. Princeton: Princeton University Press, 1994.

Dowd, Mary Jane. "The State in the Maryland Economy, 1776–1807." *Maryland Historical Magazine* 57, nos. 2 and 3 (1962): 90–133, 229–253.

Dueñas de Anhalzer, Carmen. *Soberanía e insurrección en Manabí*. Quito: Abya-Yala, 1991.

Dunn, Richard. "After Tobacco: The Slave Labor Pattern on a Large Chesapeake Grain-and-Livestock Plantation in the Early Nineteenth Century." Paper presented to the McNeil Center for Early American Studies, Philadelphia, September 11, 1998.

Earle, Carville, and Ronald Hoffman. "Staple Crops and Urban Development in the Eighteenth-Century South." *Perspectives in American History* 10 (1976): 7–78.

Echternkamp, Jorg. "Emerging Ethnicity: The German Experience in Antebellum Baltimore." *Maryland Historical Magazine* 86 (1991): 1–22.

Egnal, Marc. *Divergent Paths: How Culture and Institutions Have Shaped North American Growth*. New York: Oxford University Press, 1996.

Eisenstadt, S. N., ed. *The Protestant Ethic and Modernization: A Comparative View*. New York: Basic Books, 1968.

Elliot, John H. "The Role of the State in British and Spanish Colonial America." Paper presented at the Philadelphia Center for Early American Studies, May 12, 1989.

Emmanuel, Arghiri. *Unequal Exchange: A Study of the Imperialism of Trade*. New York: Monthly Review Press, 1972.

Engerman, Stanley L., and Kenneth L. Sokoloff. "Factor Endowments, Institutions, and Differential Paths of Growth among New World Economies: A View from Economic Historians of the United States." In *How Latin America Fell Behind: Essays on the Economic Histories of Brazil and Mexico, 1800–1914*, edited by S. Haber. Stanford: Stanford University Press, 1997.

Estrada, Jenny. *Mujeres de Guayaquil*. Guayaquil: Banco Central, 1984.

Estrada Ycaza, Julio. *Los bancos del siglo XIX*. Guayaquil: Archivo Histórico del Guayas, 1976.

———. "El comercio de armas en la guerra de independencia: La Compañía Muñoz-Henderson en 1820–1821." *Revista del Archivo Histórico del Guayas* 16 (1979): 29–59.

———. *La fundación de Guayaquil*. Guayaquil: Archivo Histórico del Guayas, 1974.

———. *Guía histórica de Guayaquil: Notas de un viaje de cuatro siglos*. Guayaquil: Banco del Progreso, 1995.

———. *El hospital de Guayaquil*. Guayaquil: Archivo Histórico del Guayas, 1972.

———. *La lucha de Guayaquil por el estado de Quito*. 2 vols. Guayaquil: Banco Central, 1984.

———. *El puerto de Guayaquil*. 2 vols. Guayaquil: Archivo Histórico del Guayas, 1972.

———. *Regionalismo y migración*. Guayaquil: Archivo Histórico del Guayas, 1977.

Ezell, John. "The Church Took a Chance." *Maryland Historical Magazine* 43, no. 4 (1948): 266–279.

Fausz, J. Frederick. "Merging and Emerging Worlds: Anglo-Indian Interest Groups and the Development of the Seventeenth-Century Chesapeake." In *Colonial Chesapeake Society*, edited by Lois Green Carr, Philip D. Morgan, and Jean B. Russo. Chapel Hill: University of North Carolina Press, 1988.

Fazio Fernández, Mariano. *El Guayaquil colombiano, 1822–1830*. Guayaquil: Banco Central: 1988.

———. *Ideología de la emancipación guayaquileña*. Guayaquil: Banco Central, 1987.

Fein, Isaac. *The Making of an American Jewish Community: The History of Baltimore Jewry from 1773 to 1920*. Philadelphia: Jewish Publication Society of America, 1971.

Fields, Barbara Jeanne. *Slavery and Freedom on the Middle Ground: Maryland during the Nineteenth Century*. New Haven: Yale University Press, 1985.

Fillól, Tomás. *Social Factors in Economic Development: The Argentine Case*. Cambridge: MIT Press, 1961.

Frank, Andre Gunder. *Capitalism and Underdevelopment in Latin America: Historical Studies of Chile and Brazil*. New York: Monthly Review Press, 1969.

Frey, Sylvia. *Water from the Rock: Black Resistance in a Revolutionary Age*. Princeton: Princeton University Press, 1991.

Fuentealba, Gerardo. "La sociedad indígena en las primeras décadas de la República: Continuidades coloniales y cambios republicanos." In *Nueva historia del Ecuador*, edited by E. Ayala, vol. 8. 15 vols. Quito: Grijalbo, 1983.

Galenson, David. "Labor Market Behavior in Colonial America: Servitude, Slavery and Free Labor." In *Markets in History: Economic Studies of the Past*, edited by D. Galenson. Cambridge: Cambridge University Press, 1989.

———. *White Servitude in Colonial America: An Economic Analysis*. Cambridge: Cambridge University Press, 1981.

Gardner, Bettye. "Antebellum Black Education in Baltimore." *Maryland Historical Magazine* 71, no. 3 (1976): 360–366.

Garitee, Jerome Randolph. "Private Enterprise and Public Spirit: Baltimore Privateering in the War of 1812." Ph.D. dissertation, Department of History, American University, Washington, D.C., 1973.

Genovese, Eugene. "The Slave States of North America." In *Neither Slave Nor Free: The Freedmen of African Descent in the Slave Societies of the New World*, edited by D. Cohen and J. Greene. Baltimore: Johns Hopkins University Press, 1972.

Gettleman, Marvin. "The Maryland Penitentiary in the Age of Tocqueville, 1828–1842." *Maryland Historical Magazine* 56, no. 3 (1961): 269–290.

Gibson, Charles. *Spain in America*. New York: Harper & Row, 1966.

Gilchrist, David, ed. *The Growth of the Seaport Cities, 1790–1825*. Charlottesville: University Press of Virginia, 1967.

Gilje, Paul, and Howard B. Rock. " 'Sweep O! Sweep O!': African American Chimney Sweeps and Citizenship in the New Nation." *William and Mary Quarterly* 51, no. 3 (1994): 507–538.

Glade, William. *The Latin American Economies: A Study of Their Institutional Evolution*. New York: American Book Company, 1969.

Gootenberg, Paul. "Beleaguered Liberals: The Failed First Generation of Free Traders in Peru." In *Guiding the Invisible Hand: Economic Liberalism and the State in Latin American History*, edited by J. Love and N. Jacobsen. New York: Praeger, 1988.

———. *Imagining Development: Economic Ideas in Peru's "Fictitious Prosperity" of Guano, 1840–1880*. Berkeley: University of California Press, 1993.

———. "Population and Ethnicity in Early Republican Peru: Some Revisions." *Latin American Research Review* 26, no. 3 (1991): 109–157.

———. "The Social Origins of Protectionism and Free Trade in Nineteenth-Century Lima." *Journal of Latin American Studies* 14, no. 2 (1982): 329–358.

Graham, Leroy. *Baltimore: The Nineteenth Century Black Capital*. New York: University Press of America, 1982.

Griffin, Charles. "Privateering in Baltimore during the Spanish American Wars of Independence." *Maryland Historical Magazine* 35, no. 1 (1940): 1–25.

Guevara, Dario. *Vicente Rocafuerte y la educación pública en el Ecuador*. Quito: Editora Nacional, 1965.

Haber, Stephen, ed. *How Latin America Fell Behind: Essays on the Economic Histories of Brazil and Mexico, 1800–1914*. Stanford: Stanford University Press, 1997.

Hahn, Steven, and Jonathan Prude, eds. *The Countryside in the Age of Capitalist Transformation*. Chapel Hill: University of North Carolina Press, 1985.

Halperín Donghi, Tulio. *The Aftermath of Revolution in Latin America*. New York: Harper & Row, 1973.

Hamerly, Michael. *Historia social y económica de la antigua provincia de Guayaquil, 1763–1842*. Guayaquil: Archivo Histórico del Guayas, 1975.

———. "Inter-American Notes: Archives of Guayaquil, Historical Archives and Private Collections." *Americas* 39, no. 1 (1983): 107–116.

————. "Quantifying the Nineteenth Century: The Ministry Reports and Gazettes of Ecuador as Quantitative Sources." *Latin American Research Review* 13, no. 1 (1978): 138–156.

Handelsman, Michael. *Amazonas y artistas: Un estudio de la prosa de la mujer ecuatoriana.* 2 vols. Guayaquil: Casa de la Cultura Ecuatoriana, 1978.

Harrison, Lawrence. *Underdevelopment Is a State of Mind: The Latin American Case.* London: Madison Books, 1985.

Hartridge, Walter. "The Refugees from the Island of St. Domingo in Maryland." *Maryland Historical Magazine* 38, no. 2 (1943): 110–111.

Hartz, Louis, ed. *The Founding of New Societies: Studies in the History of the United States, Latin America, South Africa, Canada and Australia.* New York: Harcourt, Brace & World, 1964.

Harvey, Katherine. "Practicing Medicine at the Baltimore Almshouse, 1828–1850." *Maryland Historical Magazine* 74, no. 3 (1979): 223–236.

Haskell, Thomas, and Richard F. Teichgraever III, eds. *The Culture of the Market: Historical Essays.* Cambridge: Cambridge University Press, 1993.

Heilbroner, Robert. *The Making of Economic Society.* Englewood Cliffs, N.J.: Prentice-Hall, 1980.

Hemming, John. *The Conquest of the Incas.* New York: Harcourt Brace & Co., 1970.

Henretta, James. "Families and Farms: Mentalité in Pre-industrial America." *William and Mary Quarterly* 35, no. 3 (1978): 3–32.

Herzog, Tamar. *Los ministros de la Audiencia de Quito, 1650–1750.* Quito: Libri Mundi, 1995.

Hewitt, Nancy. *Women's Activism and Social Change: Rochester, New York, 1822–1872.* Ithaca: Cornell University Press, 1984.

Hirschman, Albert. *Rival Views of Market Society and Other Recent Essays.* New York: Viking, 1986.

————. *The Strategy of Economic Development.* New Haven: Yale University Press, 1958.

Hodges, Graham. *New York City Cartmen, 1667–1850.* New York: New York University Press, 1986.

Hoffman, Ronald, et al., eds. *The Economy of Early America: The Revolutionary Period, 1763–1790.* Charlottesville: University Press of Virginia, 1988.

Hollander, J. H. *The Financial History of Baltimore.* Baltimore: Johns Hopkins University Press, 1899.

Horn, James. *Adapting to a New World: English Society in the Seventeenth-Century Chesapeake.* Chapel Hill: University of North Carolina Press, 1994.

Horwitz, Morton. *The Transformation of American Law, 1780–1860.* Cambridge, Mass.: Harvard University Press, 1977.

Huerta, Pedro José. "Las cofradías guayaquileñas." *Cuadernos de Historia y Arqueología* 3, no. 9 (1953): 167–210.

————. *Guayaquil en 1842: Rocafuerte y la fiebre amarilla.* Guayaquil: Imprenta de la Universidad, 1947.

Humphreys, R. H. "British Merchants and South American Independence." In *Proceedings of the British Academy*, vol. 51. London: Oxford University Press, 1965.

Hunefeldt, Christine. *Paying the Price of Freedom: Family and Labor among Lima's Slaves, 1800–1854*. Berkeley: University of California Press, 1994.

Hungerford, Edward. *The Story of the Baltimore & Ohio Railroad, 1827–1927*. New York: Putnam, 1928.

Hurtado, Osvaldo. *Political Power in Ecuador*. Albuquerque: University of New Mexico Press, 1980.

Huston, James. "The American Revolutionaries, the Political Economy of Aristocracy, and the American Concept of the Distribution of Wealth, 1765–1900." *American Historical Review* 98, no. 4 (1993): 1079–1115.

Ibarra, Alicia. *Los indígenas y el estado en el Ecuador*. Quito: Abya-Yala, 1987.

Innes, Stephen. *Creating the Commonwealth: The Economic Culture of Puritan New England*. New York: Norton, 1995.

———, ed. *Work and Labor in Early America*. Chapel Hill: University of North Carolina Press, 1988.

James, Alfred. "Sidelights on the Founding of the B & O Railroad." *Maryland Historical Magazine* 48, no. 4 (1953): 267–309.

Jara, Alvaro, and John J. TePaske. *The Royal Treasuries of the Spanish Empire in America, Volume 4: Eighteenth-Century Ecuador*. Durham: Duke University Press, 1990.

Jennings, Francis. *Invasion of America: Indians, Colonialism and the Cant of Conquest*. New York: Norton, 1976.

Jensen, Joan. *Loosening the Bonds: Mid-Atlantic Farm Women, 1750–1850*. New Haven: Yale University Press, 1986.

Johnson, Paul E. *A Shopkeeper's Millennium: Society and Revivals in Rochester, New York, 1815–1837*. New York: Hill & Wang, 1978.

Jones, Alice Hanson. *The Wealth of a Nation to Be: The American Colonies on the Eve of the American Revolution*. New York: Columbia University Press, 1980.

Joseph, Gilbert, and Mark Szuchman, eds. *I Saw a City Invincible: Urban Portraits of Latin America*. Wilmington, Del.: Scholarly Resources, 1996.

Jurado Noboa, Fernando. "Clases sociales de la independencia: Indios y negros." *Cuadernos de Historia y Arqueología* 43 (1981): 96–100.

———. "Demografía y trascendencia del grupo africano en el Guayaquil de 1738." In *El Negro en la historia*, ed. Raphael Savoia. Quito: Centro Cultural Afro-Ecuatoriano, 1990.

Kemp, Tom. *Historical Patterns of Industrialization*. London: Longman, 1978.

Kindleberger, Charles, and Guido de Tella, eds. *Economics in the Long View: Essays in Honor of W. W. Rostow*. New York: New York University Press, 1982.

Kingman, Eduardo Garces, ed. *Ciudades de los Andes: Visión histórica y contemporánea*. Quito: Centro de Investigaciones CIUDAD, 1992.

Kinsbruner, Jay. *Independence in Spanish America: Civil Wars, Revolutions and Underdevelopment.* Albuquerque: University of New Mexico Press, 1994.

Knight, Franklin, and Peggy Liss, eds. *Atlantic Port Cities: Economy, Culture and Society in the Atlantic World.* Knoxville: University of Tennessee Press, 1991.

Kolko, Gabriel. "Max Weber on America: Theory and Evidence." *History and Theory* 1, no. 3 (1961): 243–260.

Kroos, Herman. "Financial Institutions." In *The Growth of the Seaport Cities, 1790–1825,* ed. David Gilchrist. Charlottesville: University Press of Virginia, 1967.

Kulikoff, Alan. *Tobacco and Slaves: The Development of Southern Cultures in the Chesapeake, 1680–1800.* Chapel Hill: University of North Carolina, 1986.

———. "The Transition to Capitalism in Rural America." *William and Mary Quarterly* 46, no. 3 (1989): 120–144.

———. "Was the American Revolution a Bourgeois Revolution?" Paper presented to the Philadelphia Center for Early American Studies, April 6, 1990.

Kupperman, Karen Ordahl. *Providence Island, 1630–1641: The Other Puritan Colony.* Cambridge: Cambridge University Press, 1993.

Laclau, Ernesto. "Feudalism and Capitalism in Latin America." *New Left Review* 67 (May–June 1971). Reprinted in *Politics and Ideology in Marxist Cultural Theory.* London: Humanities Press, 1977.

Landes, David S. *The Wealth and Poverty of Nations: Why Some Are So Rich and Some So Poor.* New York: Norton, 1998.

Lang, James. *Conquest and Commerce: Spain and England in the Americas.* New York: Academic Press, 1975.

Larkin, Jack. *The Reshaping of Everyday Life, 1790–1840.* New York: Harper & Row, 1988.

Larson, Brooke, and Olivia Harris, eds. *Ethnicity, Markets and Migration in the Andes: At the Crossroads of History and Anthropology.* Durham: Duke University Press, 1995.

Laviana Cuetos, María Luisa. *Guayaquil en el siglo XVIII: Recursos naturales y desarrollo económico.* Seville: Escuela de Estudios Hispano-Americanos de Sevilla, 1987.

Lebsock, Suzanne. *The Free Women of Petersburg: Status and Culture in a Southern Town.* New York: Norton, 1985.

Lindstrom, Diane. *The Economic Development of the Philadelphia Region, 1810–1850.* Ithaca: Cornell University Press, 1978.

Linebaugh, Peter, and Marcus Rediker. "The Many Headed Hydra: Sailors, Slaves and the Atlantic Working Class in the Eighteenth Century." In *Jack Tar in History,* ed. Colin Howell and Richard Twomey. Fredericton, New Brunswick: Acadiensis Press, 1991.

Liss, Peggy. *Atlantic Empires: The Network of Trade and Revolution, 1713–1826.* Baltimore: Johns Hopkins University Press, 1983.

Livingood, James W. *The Philadelphia-Baltimore Trade Rivalry, 1780–1860*. Harrisburg: Pennsylvania Historical and Museum Commission, 1947.

Luce, W. Ray. "The Cohen Brothers of Baltimore: From Lotteries to Banking." *Maryland Historical Magazine* 68, no. 3 (1973): 288–308.

Maiguaischca, Juan. "El desplazamiento regional y la burguesía en el Ecuador, 1760–1860." In *Segundo encuentro de historia y realidad económica y social del Ecuador*, vol. 1. 3 vols. Cuenca: Instituto de Investigaciones Sociales, 1978.

Mallon, Florencia. *The Defense of Community in Peru's Central Highlands: Peasant Struggle and Capitalist Transition, 1860–1940*. Princeton: Princeton University Press, 1982.

Markey, Mary, and Dean Krimmel. "Poe's Mystery House: The Search for Mechanics Row." *Maryland Historical Magazine* 86, no. 4 (1991): 387–395.

Marshall, Gordon. *In Search of the Spirit of Capitalism: An Essay on Max Weber's Protestant Ethic Thesis*. New York: Columbia University Press, 1982.

Masur, Gerhard. *Simón Bolívar*. Albuquerque: University of New Mexico Press, 1969.

McCusker, John J. *Money and Exchange in Europe and America, 1600–1775: A Handbook*. Chapel Hill: University of North Carolina, 1978.

McCusker, John J., and Russell R. Menard. *The Economy of British America: 1607–1789*. Chapel Hill: University of North Carolina Press, 1985.

Menard, Russell. "British Migration to the Chesapeake Colonies in the Seventeenth Century." In *Colonial Chesapeake Society*, edited by L. Carr, P. Morgan, and J. Russo. Chapel Hill: University of North Carolina Press, 1988.

Middleton, Alan. "Division and Cohesion in the Working Class: Artisans and Wage Laborers in Ecuador." *Latin American Studies* 14, no. 1 (1982): 171–194.

Miller, Henry. "An Archaeological Perspective on the Evolution of Diet in the Colonial Chesapeake." In *Colonial Chesapeake Society*, edited by L. Carr, P. Morgan, and J. Russo. Chapel Hill: University of North Carolina Press, 1988.

Miller, Perry. *The New England Mind from Colony to Province*. Cambridge, Mass.: Harvard University, 1953.

Mills, Nick D. "Economía y sociedad en el período de la independencia (1780–1845): Retrato de un país atomizado." In *Nueva historia del Ecuador*, edited by E. Ayala, vol. 6. 15 vols. Quito: Grijalbo, 1983.

Minchom, Martin. *The People of Quito, 1690–1810: Change and Unrest in the Underclass*. Boulder: Westview Press, 1994.

Mino Grijalva, Manuel. *La economía colonial: Relaciones socio-económicas de la Real Audiencia de Quito*. Quito: Corporación Editora Nacional, 1984.

Molina, Ivan. *Costa Rica 1800–1850: El legado colonial y la génesis del capitalismo*. San José: Universidad de Costa Rica, 1991.

Moncada, José. "De la independencia al auge exortador." In *Ecuador: Pasado y presente*, edited by L. Mejía. Quito: Editorial El Duende, 1991.

Moreno Yánez, Segundo. "Formaciones políticas tribales y señoríos étnicos." In

Nueva historia del Ecuador, edited by E. Ayala, vol. 2. 15 vols. Quito: Grijalbo, 1983.

———. *Sublevaciones indígenas en la Audiencia de Quito desde comienzos del siglo XVIII hasta fines de la colonia*. Quito: PUCE, 1976.

Morgan, Edmund. *American Slavery, American Freedom: The Ordeal of Colonial Virginia*. New York: Norton, 1975.

Mörner, Magnus. *The Andean Past: Land, Society and Conflicts*. New York: Columbia University Press, 1985.

———. "Economic Factors and Stratification in Colonial Spanish America with Special Regard to Elites." *Hispanic American Historical Review* 63, no. 2 (1963): 335–369.

Morse, Richard. "The Heritage of Latin America." In *The Founding of New Societies*, ed. Louis Hartz. New York: Harcourt, Brace & World, 1964.

Muller, Edward K. "Spatial Order before Industrialization: Baltimore's Central District, 1833–1860." In *Working Papers from the Regional Economic History Center*, edited by G. Porter and W. H. Mulligan. Wilmington: Eleutherian Mills-Hagley Foundation, 1981.

Muller, Edward K., and Paul A. Groves. "The Emergence of Industrial Districts in Mid–Nineteenth Century Baltimore." *Geographical Review* 69, no. 2 (1979): 159–178.

Muñoz, Alberto. *Orígenes de la nacionalidad ecuatoriana*. Quito: Corporación Editora Nacional, 1984.

Murphy, R. C. "The Earliest Spanish Advances Southward from Panama along the West Coast of South America." *Hispanic American Historical Review* 21 (1941): 2–28.

Murra, John V. *The Economic Organization of the Inca State*. Greenwich, Conn.: JAI Press, 1955.

———. "Historic Tribes of Ecuador." In *Handbook of South American Indians*, vol. 2, edited by J. H. Steward. Smithsonian Bureau of American Ethnology Bulletin 143. Washington, D.C.: Smithsonian, 1946.

Newman, Simon. *Parades and Politics of the Street: Festive Culture in the Early American Republic*. Philadelphia: University of Pennsylvania, 1997.

Newson, Linda. *Life and Death in Early Colonial Ecuador*. Norman: University of Oklahoma Press, 1995.

North, Douglass. *The Economic Growth of the United States, 1790–1860*. New York: Norton, 1961.

———. *Institutions, Institutional Change and Economic Performance*. Cambridge: Cambridge University Press, 1990.

Núñez, Jorge. "Las luchas campesinas en la costa en el siglo XIX." In *Segundo encuentro de historia y realidad económica y social del Ecuador*, vol. 1. 3 vols. Cuenca: Instituto de Investigaciones Sociales, 1978.

Oberem, Udo. "Notas y documentos sobre los miembros de la familia del Inca Atahualpa en el siglo XVI." In *Contribución a la etnohistoria ecuatoriana*, edited by U. Oberem and S. Moreno. Otavalo: Editorial Rivadeneira, 1981.

Olson, Sherry. *Baltimore: The Building of an American City*. Baltimore: Johns Hopkins University Press, 1980.

Ortiz de la Tabla Ducasse, Javier. "El obraje colonial ecuatoriano: Aproximación a su estudio." *Revista de Indias* 149–150 (1977): 471–541.

Osaki, Amy. "A 'Truly Feminine Employment': Sewing and the Early Nineteenth Century Woman." *Winterthur Portfolio* 23, no. 4 (1988): 225–241.

O'Sullivan, John, and Edward F. Keuchel. *American Economic History: From Abundance to Constraint*. New York: Markus Wiener Publishing, 1989.

Padilla, Washington. *La iglesia y los dioses modernos: Historia del protestantismo en el Ecuador*. Quito: Corporación Editora Nacional, 1989.

Palomeque, Silvia. *Cuenca en el siglo XIX: La articulación de una región*. Quito: Abya-Yala, 1990.

Pancake, John. *Samuel Smith and the Politics of Business, 1752–1839*. Montgomery: University of Alabama Press, 1972.

Papenfuse, Edward C. *In Pursuit of Profit: The Annapolis Merchants in the Era of the American Revolution, 1763–1805*. Baltimore: Johns Hopkins University Press, 1975.

Paredes, Willington. "Economía y sociedad en la costa: Siglo XIX." In *Nueva historia del Ecuador*, edited by E. Ayala, vol. 7. 15 vols. Quito: Grijalbo, 1983.

Paredes, Willington, and Hugo Arias. "Crisis colonial y proceso de independencia en el Ecuador." In *Segundo encuentro de historia y realidad económica y social del Ecuador*, vol. 1. 3 vols. Cuenca: Instituto de Investigaciones Sociales, 1978.

Parsons, James J., and Roy Shlemon. "Mapping and Dating the Prehistoric Raised Fields of the Guayas Basin, Ecuador." In *Pre-Hispanic Agricultural Fields in the Andean Region*, edited by W. M. Deneven, K. Mathewson, and G. Knapp. British Archaeological Reports 359 (ii). London: Oxford University, 1987.

Paz, Octavio. *The Labyrinth of Solitude and Other Writings*. New York: Grove Press, 1985.

Pérez Pimentel, Rodolfo. *Nuestro Guayaquil antiguo*. Guayaquil: Editorial El Sol, 1987.

Phelan, John Leddy. *The Kingdom of Quito in the Seventeenth Century: Bureaucratic Politics in the Spanish Empire*. Madison: University of Wisconsin Press, 1967.

Phillips, Christopher. *Freedom's Port: The African American Community of Baltimore, 1790–1860*. Chicago: University of Illinois Press, 1997.

Phillips, Kevin P. *The Cousins' Wars: Religion, Politics and the Triumph of Anglo-America*. New York: Basic Books, 1999.

Pike, Frederick. *The United States and the Andean Republics: Peru, Bolivia and Ecuador.* Cambridge, Mass.: Harvard University Press, 1977.

Pineo, Ronn. "Misery and Death in the Pearl of the Pacific: Health Care in Guayaquil, Ecuador, 1870–1925." *Hispanic American Historical Review* 70, no. 4 (1990): 609–638.

———. *Social and Economic Reform in Ecuador: Life and Work in Guayaquil.* Gainesville: University Press of Florida, 1996.

Platt, D. C. M. *Latin America and British Trade, 1806–1914.* London: Adam & Charles Black, 1972.

Powers, Karen. *Andean Journeys: Migration, Ethnogenesis, and the State in Colonial Quito.* Albuquerque: University of New Mexico Press, 1995.

Pred, Allan. *Urban Growth and the Circulation of Information: The United States System of Cities, 1790–1840.* Cambridge, Mass.: Harvard University Press, 1973.

Price, Jacob. *Capital and Credit in British Overseas Trade: The View from the Chesapeake, 1700–1776.* Cambridge, Mass.: Harvard University Press, 1980.

———. "Economic Function and the Growth of American Port Towns in the Eighteenth Century." *Perspectives in American History* 8 (1974): 123–186.

Proano, Leonidas. "La iglesia y los sectores populares, 1830–1980." In *Política y sociedad, Ecuador 1830–1980,* edited by L. Mora. Quito: Corporación Editora Nacional, 1980.

Prude, Jonathan. *The Coming of Industrial Order: Town and Factory Life in Rural Massachusetts, 1810–1860.* Cambridge: Cambridge University Press, 1983.

Quintero, Rafael. "El carácter de la estructura institucional de representación política en el estado ecuatoriano del siglo XIX." In *Segundo encuentro de historia y realidad económica y social del Ecuador,* vol. 1. 3 vols. Cuenca: Instituto de Investigaciones Sociales, 1978.

Quintero, Rafael, and Erika Silva. *Ecuador: Nación en ciernas.* 3 vols. Quito: Abya-Yala, 1991.

Rama, Angel. *La ciudad letrada.* Hanover, N.H.: Ediciones del Norte, 1984.

Ribadeneria, Edmundo, ed. "Simposio sobre el Ecuador en 1830: Ideología, economía, y política." *Cultura: Revista del Banco Central del Ecuador* 6 (1980).

Robles y Chambers, Pedro. *Contribución para el estudio de la sociedad colonial de Guayaquil.* Guayaquil: Imprenta de la Reforma, 1938.

———. "Los Luzárraga." *Cuadernos de Historia y Arqueología* 44 (1982): 76–78.

Rockman, Seth. "Working for Wages in Early Republican Baltimore: Unskilled Labor and the Blurring of Slavery and Freedom." Ph.D. dissertation, Department of History, University of California at Davis, 1999.

Rodriguez, Linda Alexander. *The Search for Public Policy: Regional Politics and Government Finances in Ecuador, 1830–1940.* Berkeley: University of California Press, 1985.

Rodríguez, Mario. *La revolución americana de 1776 y el mundo hispánico.* Madrid: Editorial Tecnos, 1976.

Rolando, Carlos. *Crónica del periodismo en el Ecuador.* Quito: Tipográfica de la Sociedad Filantrópica, 1947.

Romero, José Luís. *Latinoamerica: Las ciudades y las ideas.* Buenos Aires: Siglo Veintiuno Editores, 1976.

Rountree, Helen. *Pocahontas's People: The Powhatan Indians of Virginia through Four Centuries.* Norman: University of Oklahoma Press, 1990.

Safford, Frank. *The Ideal of the Practical: Colombia's Struggle to Form a Technical Elite.* Austin: University of Texas Press, 1975.

———. "Race, Integration and Progress: Elite Attitudes and the Indian in Colombia, 1750–1870." *Hispanic American Historical Review* 71, no. 1 (1991): 1–34.

Sahlins, Marshall. *Culture and Practical Reason.* Chicago: University of Chicago Press, 1976.

———. *Stone Age Economics.* Chicago: Aldine-Atherton, 1972.

Salomon, Frank. *Native Lords of Quito in the Age of the Incas.* Cambridge: Cambridge University Press, 1986.

———. "A North Andean Status Trader Complex under Inka Rule." *Ethnohistory* 34, no. 1 (1987): 63–77.

———. "Shamanism and Politics in Late Colonial Ecuador." *American Ethnologist* 10, no. 3 (1983): 413–427.

Salvat, Juan, ed. *Historia del Ecuador.* 10 vols. Quito: Salvat Editores, 1981.

Salvucci, Richard, ed. *Latin America and the World Economy: Dependency and Beyond.* Toronto: D. C. Heath & Company, 1996.

Saurat, Gilette. *Bolívar: El libertador.* Bogotá: Editorial Oveja Negra, 1987.

Savoia, Rafael, ed. *El negro en la historia.* Quito: Centro Cultural Afro-Ecuatoriano, 1990.

Schaedel, Richard, Jorge Hardoy, and Nora Kinzer, eds. *Urbanization in the Americas from Its Beginnings to the Present.* Paris: Mouton Publishers, 1978.

Scharf, J. Thomas. *The Chronicles of Baltimore.* Baltimore: Turnbull Brothers, 1874.

———. *History of Baltimore City and County.* Philadelphia: Louis H. Everts, 1881.

Schlesinger, Arthur M., Jr. *The Age of Jackson.* Boston: Little, Brown & Company, 1947.

Schodt, David. *Ecuador: An Andean Enigma.* London: Westview Place, 1987.

Scobie, James R. *Secondary Cities of Argentina.* Edited and completed by Samuel L. Baily. New York: Oxford University Press.

Seligson, Mitchell. *Peasants of Costa Rica and the Development of Agrarian Capitalism.* Madison: University of Wisconsin Press, 1980.

Sellers, Charles. *The Market Revolution: Jacksonian America, 1815–1846.* New York: Oxford University Press, 1991.

Semmes, Raphael. *Baltimore as Seen by Visitors, 1783–1860.* Baltimore: Maryland Historical Society, 1953.

Sheller, Tina. "Freemen, Servants and Slaves: Artisans and the Craft Structure of Revolutionary Baltimore Town." In *American Artisans: Crafting Social Identity, 1750–1850*, edited by P. Gilje, R. Asher, and H. Rock. Baltimore: Johns Hopkins University Press, 1995.

Silver, Rollo. *The Baltimore Book Trade, 1800–1825*. New York: New York Public Library, 1953.

Silverblatt, Irene. *Moon, Sun and Witches: Gender Ideologies and Class in Inca and Spanish Peru*. Princeton: Princeton University Press, 1987.

Skocpol, Theda, and Somers, Margaret. "The Uses of Comparative History in Macrosocial Inquiry." *Comparative Studies in Society and History* (1980): 174–197.

Smith, Billy. *The Lower Sort: Philadelphia's Laboring People, 1750–1800*. Ithaca: Cornell University Press, 1990.

Socolow, Susan. *The Merchants of Buenos Aires: Family and Commerce*. Cambridge: Cambridge University Press, 1978.

Sokoloff, Kenneth. "Was the Transition from the Artisanal Shop to the Non-mechanized Factory Associated with Gains in Efficiency: Evidence from the U.S. Manufacturing Census of 1820 and 1850." *Explorations in Economic History* 21 (1984): 351–382.

Sowell, David. *The Early Colombian Labor Movement: Artisans and Politics in Bogotá, 1832–1919*. Philadelphia: Temple University Press, 1992.

Spindler, Frank M. *Nineteenth-Century Ecuador: A Historical Introduction*. Fairfax, Va.: George Mason University Press, 1987.

Steffen, Charles. *From Gentlemen to Townsmen: The Gentry of Baltimore County, 1660–1776*. Lexington: University Press of Kentucky, 1993.

———. *The Mechanics of Baltimore: Workers and Politics in the Age of Revolution, 1763–1812*. Chicago: University of Illinois Press, 1984.

———. "Who Owns the Waterfront? Property Relations in Fell's Point, Baltimore, 1783." *Urbanism, Past and Present* 8, no. 1 (1983): 12–17.

Stein, Stanley, and Barbara Stein. *The Colonial Heritage of Latin America: Essays on Economic Dependence in Perspective*. New York: Oxford University Press, 1970.

Steinfeld, Robert. *The Invention of Free Labor: The Employment Relation in English and American Law and Culture, 1350–1870*. Durham: University of North Carolina Press, 1991.

Stern, Steve J. "Feudalism, Capitalism, and the World System in the Perspective of Latin America and the Caribbean." *American Historical Review* 93 (1988): 829–872.

———. *Peru's Indian Peoples and the Challenge of Spanish Conquest: Huamanga to 1640*. Madison: University of Wisconsin Press, 1982.

Sundquist, Eric, ed. *Frederick Douglass: New Literary and Historical Essays*. Cambridge: Cambridge University Press, 1990.

Sunkel, Osvaldo, ed. *Development from Within: Toward a Neostructuralist Approach for Latin America*. London: Lynne Rienner, 1993.

Taylor, Alan. "The Early Republic's Supernatural Economy: Treasure Seeking in the American Northeast, 1780–1830." *American Quarterly* 38, no. 1 (1986): 6–34.

Taylor, William B. "Between Global Process and Local Knowledge: An Inquiry into Early Latin American Social History, 1500–1900." In *Reliving the Past: The Worlds of Social History*, edited by O. Zunz. Chapel Hill: University of North Carolina Press, 1985.

Temin, Peter. "Is It Kosher to Talk about Culture?" *Journal of Economic History* 57, no. 2 (1997): 267–287.

————. *The Jacksonian Economy*. New York: Norton, 1969.

Teran, Rosemarie. "Censos, capellanías y elites: Aspectos sociales del crédito en Quito colonial." *Procesos: Revista Ecuatoriana de Historia* 1, no. 2 (1991): 23–48.

Thernstrom, Stephen, and Richard Sennet, eds. *Nineteenth-Century Cities: Essays in the New Urban History*. New Haven: Yale University Press, 1969.

Tobar Donoso, Julio. "La abolición de la esclavitud en el Ecuador." *Boletín de la Académia Nacional de Historia* 39, no. 93 (1959): 5–30.

Townsend, Camilla. "En busca de la libertad: Los esfuerzos de los esclavos guayaquileños por garantizar su independencia después de la independencia." *Procesos: Revista Ecuatoriana de Historia* 4, no. 1 (1993): 73–86.

————. " 'Half My Body Free, the Other Half Enslaved': The Politics of the Slaves of Guayaquil at the End of the Colonial Era." *Colonial Latin American Review* 7, no. 1 (1998): 105–128.

————. "Story without Words: Women and the Creation of a Mestizo People in Guayaquil, 1820–1835." *Latin American Perspectives* 24, no. 4 (1997): 50–68.

Tyrer, Robson Brynes. *Historia demográfica y económica de la Audiencia de Quito*. Quito: Banco Central del Ecuador, 1988.

Tyrrell, Ian. "American Exceptionalism in an Age of International History." *American Historical Review* 96, no. 4 (1991): 1031–1055.

Ulrich, Laurel Tatcher. "Cloth, Clothing and Early American Social History." *Dress* 18 (1991): 39–48.

Urton, Gary. "Foreword." In *The Development of the Inca State*, by Brian S. Bauer. Austin: University of Texas Press, 1992.

Van Aken, Mark. *King of the Night: Juan José Flores and Ecuador, 1824–1864*. Berkeley: University of California Press, 1989.

————. "The Lingering Death of Indian Tribute in Ecuador." *Hispanic American Historical Review* 61, no. 3 (1981): 429–59.

Van Young, Eric. "Islands in the Storm: Quiet Cities and Violent Countryside in the Mexican Independence Era." *Past and Present* 118 (1988): 130–155.

Vega Ugalde, Silvia. *Ecuador: Crisis políticas y el estado en los inicios de la República*. Quito: Abya-Yala, 1992.

Vinson, Benjamin III. "Las compañías milicianas de pardos y morenos en la

Nueva España, un aporte para su estudio." In *Población y estructura urbana en México, siglos XVIII y XIX*, edited by C. Blázquez, C. Contreras, and S. Pérez. Xalapa, Veracruz: Universidad Veracruzana, 1996.

Wade, Richard. *Slavery in the Cities: The South, 1820–1860*. New York: Oxford University Press, 1964.

Watts, Stephen. *The Republic Reborn: War and the Making of Liberal America*. Baltimore: Johns Hopkins University Press, 1987.

Weber, Max. *The Protestant Ethic and the Spirit of Capitalism*. New York: Charles Scribner, 1958. Reprinted from the first English edition of 1930.

Weinman, Lois Johnson. "Ecuador and Cacao: Domestic Responses to the Boom Collapse Monoexport Cycle." Ph.D. dissertation, Department of History, University of California at Los Angeles, 1970.

Whitman, T. Stephen. "Industrial Slavery at the Margin: The Maryland Chemical Works." *Journal of Southern History* 59, no. 1 (1993): 31–62.

———. *The Price of Freedom: Slavery and Manumission in Baltimore and Early National Maryland*. Lexington: University Press of Kentucky, 1997.

Wilentz, Sean. *Chants Democratic: New York and the Rise of the American Working Class, 1788–1850*. New York: Oxford University Press, 1984.

Wiles, Dawn Ann. "Land Transportation within Ecuador, 1822–1954." Ph.D. dissertation, Latin American Studies Institute, Louisiana State University and Agricultural and Mechanical College, 1971.

Wood, Gordon. "Ideology and the Origins of Liberal America." *William and Mary Quarterly* 44, no. 3 (1987): 628–640.

Wright, Gavin. *The Political Economy of the Cotton South: Households, Markets and Wealth in the Nineteenth Century*. New York: Norton, 1978.

INDEX

African Americans. *See* Blacks in Baltimore; Blacks in Guayaquil; Race; Slaves and slavery in Baltimore; Slaves and slavery in Guayaquil

Agriculture: and Baltimore, 65, 117; and Ecuador, 233; and Guayaquil, 28, 29, 66; of Maryland, 62; and New England, 234

Apprenticeship in Baltimore: and artisans, 159, 160, 177; and blacks, 228, 230; and class relations, 41; and immigrants, 36; and merchants, 114, 124, 132; and poor, 206–207, 210, 216, 227, 230, 235; and slaves, 33, 63

Apprenticeship in Guayaquil, 230, 235

Arteta, María Manuela, 189, 194

Artisans of Baltimore: and banks, 173; and immigrants, 215; and manufactories, 13, 118, 120–121, 163, 178, 268–269n.55; memoirs of, 15; and middling sectors, 158–163, 177; and poor, 159, 216, 217, 227; and statistics, 66; and women, 159, 162, 275n.21

Artisans of Guayaquil: and civic involvement, 149; and class relations, 27, 139, 141–142, 152, 271n.14; and locations of shops, 26; and manufactories, 13, 149, 178; and merchants, 88, 133; and middling sector, 138–142, 177; and poor, 194–195; and statistics, 66

Bailey, Frederick. *See* Douglass, Frederick

Baltimore, Maryland: and British trade, 62; census of, 15, 246n.24; churches of, 37, 38–39, 44; and conquest, 53–58; daily life compared to Guayaquil, 13–15, 16, 19; as failed city, 47; founding of, 58; Indians of, 41, 45, 58, 125; literacy in, 43, 170; map of, *48*; and Market Street,

37–38; neighborhoods of, 35–39; occupational profile of, 65, 66; population of, 17, 33, 65, 246n.24; and public health, 39–40; shipping industry of, 33–34, 43, 65; status of, 58; structural similarities to Guayaquil, 16–17; and time period of study, 17–18; and trade, 105–109, 129. *See also* Elites of Baltimore; Middling sectors of Baltimore; Poverty/poor in Baltimore

Baltimore & Ohio Railroad, 41, 104, 107, 121

Banks and banking: and Baltimore, 110–112, 116, 127, 130, 131, 133, 173–174; and economy, 2; and Guayaquil, 83–84, 94, 130, 131, 191

Bergquist, Charles, 9–10

Blacks in Baltimore: and artisans, 159, 217; and banks, 174; and civic involvement, 165–166, 171–172; and class relations, 36–37, 42; and crime, 223; and education, 165–166, 227; and entrepreneurs, 168; free blacks, 35, 37, 41, 43, 124, 132, 154–155, 166, 178, 211–214, 224, 228–229; and merchants, 125; and poor, 37, 207, 211–214, 220, 222, 225–226, 229, 230; and professionals, 163; and social advancement, 228–229

Blacks in Guayaquil: and artisans, 140; free blacks, 138, 184, 189–193, 229; and poor, 27, 29; and shipyards, 25; and zambos, 29

Bolaños, José María, 201–202

Bolívar, Simón: and Baltimore elites, 125; and credit, 84, 94; and Guayaquil, 149; and independence, 59, 72; and slavery, 191; and taxation, 183

Breck, Captain, 105–106

Brenner, Robert, 239, 244n.11

Cacao: and Baltimore, 105; and Indians, 185; and merchants, 79, 87, 90, 130; and Mexico, 59, 77, 79; and school budgets, 85; and slavery, 29, 190; and Spain, 52, 61–62, 75; and trade, 16, 24, 28, 59, 61
Calvert, Caroline, 108, 130
Calvert, Cecil, Second Lord Baltimore, 55
Calvert, George, First Lord Baltimore, 55–56
Campusano, Alejandro, 189, 191
Caribbean, 34, 56, 63, 105, 108
Catholicism, 6, 38, 55, 102, 165, 175
Chamber of Commerce, 112–113
Chapman, John, 117, 120
Chile, 24, 49, 61
Clackner, Rebecca, 162, 275 n.21
Class relations: and Baltimore, 36–37, 41–42, 43, 157, 177; and culture, 10–11; and dependency theory, 5; and discretionary income, 239; and Guayaquil, 26–27, 29, 32–33, 45, 71–72, 139, 141–142, 145, 152–153, 177, 237, 271 n.14; and Spain, 12; and wealth, 9–10
Coerced labor: and Baltimore elites, 124, 132, 133, 269 n.65; Baltimore/Guayaquil comparison, 235; and class relations, 11; and economic culture, 3; and Great Britain, 12; and Guayaquil poor, 193; and production, 9. See also Slaves and slavery in Baltimore; Slaves and slavery in Guayaquil
Cofradías, 30
Cohen, Jacob, 111–112, 126, 171, 266 n.33
Coke, Edward, 214, 215
Colegio San Ignacio Loyola, 85–86, 146, 152
Colombia, 59, 60, 77, 95, 183
Consumption patterns: and Baltimore, 103, 225–226; and British colonists, 57; and discretionary income, 45, 178, 200, 239; and economy, 2; and Guayaquil, 200–201; Guayaquil compared to Baltimore, 44–45, 129, 231; and slavery, 9
Contrast of context model, 16
Costa Rica, 7, 12, 243 n.7
Credit networks, 3, 83–84, 94. See also Banks and banking
Crime: and Baltimore, 37, 110–111, 167, 216, 223–226, 230, 235; and Guayaquil, 31, 197–199, 203–204, 230, 235
Culturalists, 2–3
Culture: and class relations, 10–11; and

daily life, 16; definition of, 2, 4; and economic assumptions, 238; and economic development, 7–8; and elites, 10–11; and exclusion, 236; and labor/capital mobility, 239–240; and race, 4, 236; and Weberian dichotomy, 234–235; and work attitudes, 9, 10, 239. See also Economic culture
Dallam, Francis, 166–167
Day laborers in Baltimore: and class relations, 41; and elites, 124, 125; and free blacks, 229; and immigrants, 36–37, 215; and industrialization, 178, 216; and poor, 216–226, 230, 235; statistics on, 65, 66; and whites, 154
Day laborers in Guayaquil: and artisans, 140; and class relations, 29; and Ecuadoran suffrage, 150; and education, 152; and free blacks, 190; and poor, 193–200, 203, 230, 235; statistics on, 65, 66; and taxation, 183
De la Cruz Andrade, María, 80–81
De la Cruz, Mariano, 71, 97, 99, 184–185, 188–189, 204
Dependency theory, 5, 8–9
Díaz de Castillo, Bernal, 233, 234
Diseases, 31–32, 35, 39, 52
Dorsey, Richard, 109, 116
Douglass, Frederick: ambitions of, 1, 231; as Bailey, 242 n.4; and Baltimore, xiv–xv, 18, 33–43, 101; and Baltimore poor, 210, 211, 229; and civic involvement, 176; and education, 127; and literacy, 34; and opportunity, 46, 231, 240; and race, 154, 228, 237
Drinot, Tomás, 80–81
Economic culture: assumptions about, 234; Baltimore/Guayaquil comparison, 234–236; comparative studies of, 5–13; and daily life, 2, 13; and international trade access, 17; meaning of, 3, 4, 8, 13; relevance of, 1; transformation in, 12; and work attitudes, 4, 6, 13. See also Elites of Baltimore; Elites of Guayaquil; Middling sectors of Baltimore; Middling sectors of Guayaquil; Poverty/poor in Baltimore; Poverty/poor in Guayaquil
Economies: attitudes affecting, 2; comparatives studies of, 5–13; economic development, 3, 6, 7–8, 60–61, 179; and eco-

nomic historians, 2, 5, 10, 239; economic theories, 3, 5; of New World, 5–13, 244n.12

Ecuador: and cacao trade, 61–62; and cloth production, 59; and Gran Colombia, 60, 61, 77; Indians of, 49; presidency of, 17; and suffrage, 150; and taxation, 92

Education in Baltimore: and artisans, 159, 162, 178; and civic involvement, 172; and elites, 126, 235, 266–267n.36; and merchants, 113, 115, 126–127, 132; and middling sectors, 172–173; and poor, 208, 210, 216, 226–227, 228, 235; and professionals, 163, 164–165, 177

Education in Guayaquil: and elites, 86–87; and labor, 99; and merchants, 85–86, 132, 236; and middling sectors, 151–152, 153, 179, 201; and poor, 152, 201–202, 235; and professionals, 146–147

Egnal, Marc, 7–8

Elites of Baltimore: and agriculture, 117; and Almshouse, 126; and coerced labor, 124, 132, 133, 269n.65; and education, 266–267n.36; and exclusion, 237–238; Guayaquil elites compared with, 18–19, 128–133, 235; health maintenance, 39–40; and manufacturing class, 63; and poor, 103, 125–128, 133, 230; and professionals, 164. See also Merchants of Baltimore

Elites of Guayaquil: Baltimore elites compared with, 18–19, 128–133, 235; and civic involvement, 71–77, 79, 82, 84–85, 91, 150–151, 152; and class relations, 27, 32–33, 71–72, 152; and exclusion, 237–238; and independence, 71–76, 189; and Indians, 96–97; and poor, 194, 197, 201, 230; and professionals, 146; and taxation, 94–95, 184. See also Merchants of Guayaquil

Emmanuel, Arghiri, 239, 244–245n.12

Engerman, Stanley, 10, 11

Enlightenment, 133, 189

Entertainment in Baltimore: and artisans, 178; and class relations, 42; and consumption patterns, 44; and elites, 102; and entrepreneurs, 168–170; and poor, 222–223

Entertainment in Guayaquil: and consumption patterns, 44–45; and entrepreneurs, 148–149; and poor, 30, 197, 200–201

Entrepreneurship: and Baltimore, 168–170, 177–178; and culture, 10; and economic development, 8; and Guayaquil, 44, 147–149, 152, 177–178, 236

Europe and Europeans: and Baltimore labor, 124; and Baltimore merchants, 106, 118; and Baltimore trade, 62, 63; British colonists compared to, 57; colonial behavior of, 2, 12, 245n.20; and economic development of, 8; and Guayaquil trade, 61; and international trade, 9; northern and southern differences in, 11; and tobacco, 56. See also specific countries

Exceptionalism, 236–238

Fell's Point, and blacks, 166; conditions of, 33, 35–37; and consumption patterns, 44; and education, 126; and elites' charity, 39; and Jews, 171; and manufactories, 119; and middling ranks, 155, 168, 173; and poor, 217, 218, 228, 229; and slavery, 66; and taxation, 123

Flores, Juan José, 60, 90, 95, 200

France, 63, 80–81, 215

French Canada, 7–8

Galápagos Islands, 24, 82, 199

Garaicoa, Ana, 74, 75, 81, 130

Garostiza, José, 189, 194

Gran Colombia, 59–61, 65, 74, 76–77, 92, 94–95

Great Britain: and Baltimore, 33, 62–64, 106, 112, 116, 120, 131, 158, 215; colonial behavior of, 12, 53–58, 245n.20; economic development of, 8; and Guayaquil, 25, 53, 61–62, 73, 80, 87–92, 143, 260n.38; and work ethic, 11

Guayaquil, Ecuador: and Baltimore merchants, 105; churches of, 15, 26, 29–30, 44, 246n.24; and conquest, 47–53; daily life compared to Baltimore, 13–15, 16, 19; and entrepreneurship, 44, 147–149, 152, 177–178, 236; and exclusion patterns, 236, 237–238; and festivals, 30–31; and independence, 17, 59–60, 73–76; Indians' migration to, xiii–xiv, xv, 15, 23, 28–29, 31, 185, 188; map of, 22; neighborhoods of, 24–27, 28; occupational profile of, 65, 66; population of, 17, 65, 246n.24; potential of, 47; status of, 58; structural similarities to Balti-

Guayaquil, Ecuador (*continued*)
more, 16–17; and time period of study,
17–18; and trade, 16, 23–25, 28, 59, 61–
62, 73, 78–82, 129. *See also* Elites of
Guayaquil; Indians of Guayaquil; Middling sectors of Guayaquil; Poverty/
poor in Guayaquil

Hall, Basil, 71–72, 87
Harrison, Lawrence, 7, 243 n.7
Havana, Cuba, 17, 105
Hebrew Congregation, 171
Hetzler, John, 217
Hollingsworth, Levi, 109, 112, 116
Hollingsworth, Lydia, 100, 102, 107, 127–
129, 237
Hollingsworth family, 109, 114, 125
Hudson, David, 167–168
Hugg, Jacob, 163–164

Icaza, Juan Francisco de, 77, 91
Icaza, Martín de, 77, 79, 80, 89, 130
Icaza family, 82, 86
Immigrants, and Baltimore, 33, 36–37,
214–216
Indians of Baltimore, 41, 45, 58, 125
Indians of Guayaquil: and artisans, 139; and
class relations, 29, 153; and education,
99, 152; and elites, 71, 79, 96–97, 98;
migration to Guayaquil, xiii–xiv, xv, 15,
23, 28–29, 31, 185, 188; and poor, 184–
189, 229; and social banditry, 184,
278 n.3; and taxes, 151, 179, 186, 187,
188, 202; and trade, 24, 25; and tributes,
29, 53, 59, 92, 94, 96, 183–187, 233,
279 n.5
Indians of South America: Indians of
United States compared to, 54; Latin
American colonists' dominance of, 10,
11–12, 245 n.16; and Spanish conquest,
49–53, 185; and tributes, 11, 49–53
Indians of United States, 11, 13, 54–55, 57,
238
Industrialization: and Baltimore, 129, 178,
216; and consumption patterns, 239;
and Ecuador, 233; and wealth distribution, 5
Infrastructure in Baltimore: and employment, 33; Guayaquil compared to, 13,
45; and lotteries, 111; and merchants,
64–65, 104, 106, 116, 122, 132, 235–
236; and middling sectors, 156; and

property owners, 36; and taxes, 106–
107, 123–124, 178–179; and transportation, 41
Infrastructure in Guayaquil: Baltimore
compared to, 13, 45; and culture, 239;
and lotteries, 26; and merchants, 94–95,
132, 235–236; and middling sectors,
151, 153, 179; and poor, 32
Internal trade: and Baltimore, 40, 64, 106;
and Guayaquil, 61, 78–79; and production, 6; and taxation, 59; and wealth distribution, 5. *See also* International trade;
Trade
International trade: and Baltimore, 34, 65,
106; Baltimore/Guayaquil comparison,
128–129; and dependency theory, 5, 8–
9; and economic historians, 2; and
economic relationships, 18; and Ecuador, 61–62; geographic access to, 17;
and Guayaquil, 78–82, 88–91, 129, 130;
and internal relations of production, 9,
244 n.11. *See also* Internal trade; Trade
Iraeta, Francisco de, 79, 80

Jefferson, Thomas, 74, 170
Jews in Baltimore, 111–112, 126, 171,
266 n.33

Labor: and Baltimore manufactories, 118,
120; Baltimore merchants' relationship
with, 124–128, 132, 235; and Baltimore
middling sectors, 154, 176; and class
relations, 9, 11; and conceptions of
workers, 2, 13, 45, 237; and economic
culture, 6; Guayaquil merchants' relationship with, 95–99, 132, 235; and
Guayaquil middling sectors, 176;
mobility of, 239; and race, 4. *See also*
Coerced labor; Work attitudes; Work
ethic
Labroquère, Bernard, 159, 161, 177
Laclau, Ernesto, 8–9
Latin America: and colonial dominance of
Indians, 10, 11, 245 n.16; and international trade, 5, 17; and production, 8–9;
and Protestant ideals, 7; and resources,
10; United States compared to, 1, 10, 12
Long, Robert Carey, 159, 161
Lotteries, 26, 43, 74, 111–112, 116, 168
Luke, Elizabeth, 174, 176
Luzárraga, Manuel Antonio, 81, 82, 83–84,
86

Macrocausal studies, 16, 246n.23
Magdalena, María, xiii–xiv, 23, 28–29, 185
Manufactories of Baltimore: and artisans, 118, 120–121, 163, 178, 268–269n.55; and conceptions of workers, 45; and day laborers, 219–220; limitations of, 17; and merchants, 104, 112–113, 117–121, 131, 163, 178, 235, 267n.45, 268–269n.55; and neighborhoods, 37–38
Manufactories of Guayaquil: and artisans, 13, 149, 178; and conceptions of workers, 45; and entrepreneurs, 149; limitations of, 17; and merchants, 88, 91–92, 131, 235
Manumission Fund, 95
Market Revolution, 12
Marxism, 8, 243n.11
Maryland: agriculture of, 62; and Baltimore professionals, 163; and British colonists, 56, 57–58; and Catholicism, 38; and education, 126; and immigrants, 33, 215; lotteries of, 111; resources of, 234; and taxation, 122–123
Materialists, 2–3, 8, 11
Mather, Cotton, 233–234
McDonald, Alexander, 162–163
Mechanics' Bank, 173, 174
Merchants' Guild, 84–85, 94
Merchants of Baltimore: and daily practices, 109–115, 131; and intermarriage, 108, 129; and investment strategies, 116–121, 131, 173; and manufactories, 104, 112–113, 117–121, 131, 163, 178, 235, 267n.45, 268–269n.55; and political status, 103–105, 106, 121; and relationship with labor, 124–128, 132, 133; and taxation, 121–124, 132, 133; and trade networks, 105–109, 129
Merchants of Guayaquil: and civic involvement, 76–77; and crime, 198; and daily practices, 82–87, 131; and entrepreneurs, 147; and government monopoly, 91–92, 131, 261n.49; and independence from Spain, 76, 77; and investment strategies, 87–92, 131, 260–261n.47; and manufactories, 88, 91–92, 131, 235; and newspaper subscriptions, 75; and poor, 201; and races, 29; and relationship with labor, 95–99, 132, 133; and taxation, 76–77, 79, 92–95, 132, 256–257n.15, 262n.54; and trade networks, 78–82, 129

Mexico, 59, 61, 77, 79, 80
Middling sectors of Baltimore: and banking, 110; and civic involvement, 154–157, 166, 170–175, 176; and class relations, 157, 177; and culture, 235; and entrepreneurship, 168–170, 177–178; Guayaquil compared with, 18–19, 175–179; and investments, 173; and professionals, 66, 163–168, 177; and race relations, 154–155. See also Artisans of Baltimore
Middling sectors of Guayaquil: Baltimore compared with, 18–19, 175–179; and civic involvement, 149–153, 176; and class relations, 177; and culture, 235; and entrepreneurs, 44, 147–149, 152, 177–178, 236; and personas decentes, 137–138; and professionals, 66, 142–147, 149, 152, 177. See also Artisans of Guayaquil
Minifrie, William, 159–161, 175, 177, 215
Mitchell, Mary Alicia, 115, 130
Moale, Charles, 100–101
Murillo, Manuel Ignacio, 140–142, 152, 153, 175–176, 177
Mutual aid groups, 30, 171–172
Mutual Security fire insurance company, 83–84

National character, 7, 243n.6
Native Americans. See Indians of Baltimore; Indians of Guayaquil; Indians of South America; Indians of United States
New England, 7–8, 13, 234
New World economies, 5–13, 244n.12
Nicaragua, 7, 12, 243n.7

Oliver, Robert, 104–105, 108–109, 112, 120, 265n.23
Ortega, José, 79–80

Panama, 25, 50–51, 61
Peale, Rubens, 169–170
Peru: and Colombia, 183; and Guayaquil trade, 24, 25, 61, 254n.39; and independence from Spain, 60, 75; and Pflücker, 90; and Spanish conquest, 49, 51, 185
Pflücker, Charles (Carlos), 89–90
Pizarro, Francisco, 50–51
Poe, Edgar Allan, 157

Poverty: and British colonists, 56, 57; and dependency theory, 5; and economic culture, 1–2, 3; of majority, 10. *See also* Wealth

Poverty/poor in Baltimore: and alcohol, 200–211; and Almshouse, 205–211, 224–225, 226, 227–228, 230; and artisans, 159, 216, 217, 227; and banks, 174; and blacks, 37, 207, 211–214, 220, 222, 225–226, 229, 230; and consumption patterns, 225; and day laborers, 216–226, 230, 235; and elites, 103, 125–128, 133, 230; and entrepreneurs, 168; Guayaquil compared with, 1–2, 18–19, 33, 229–232, 237; and middling sectors, 172; and social advancement, 226–229; and taxation, 121, 122, 123, 209–210

Poverty/poor in Guayaquil: and army service, 202, 282 n.57; Baltimore compared with, 1–2, 18–19, 33, 229–232, 237; and cacao trade, 62; and consumption patterns, 200–201; and day laborers, 193–200, 203, 230, 235; and diseases, 31; and education, 152, 201–202, 235; and elite, 99, 132; and free blacks, 189–193; and hospitals, 32; and Indians of Guayaquil, 184–189, 229; and middling sector, 138; and social advancement, 201–204; and taxation, 183, 201, 203

Power: and Baltimore elites, 129; and dependency theory, 5, 8; and human relationships, 4, 11; and labor costs, 239; and materialists, 3

Production: and British colonists, 57; and demand, 238, 239; and economic culture, 5–6; internal relations of, 6, 8–9, 243–244 n.11, 244–245 n.12

Professional services: and Baltimore, 66, 163–168, 177; and Guayaquil, 66, 142–147, 149, 152, 177

Protectionism, 6

Protestantism: and Baltimore, 102, 104, 109, 165, 175; and work ethic, 6–7, 8

Puerto Rico, 7, 34

Puritans, 11, 12, 13, 234

Race: and Baltimore, 36, 45–46, 154, 228, 237; and British colonists, 58; and culture, 4, 236; and Guayaquil, 29, 45, 237; and relationships between racial groups, 4, 9–10, 13; and zambos, 29, 139, 140, 152, 188, 202. *See also* Blacks in Balti-

more; Blacks in Guayaquil; Whites in Baltimore; Whites in Guayaquil

Rationality: and Baltimore, 131, 133, 178; Baltimore/Guayaquil comparison, 43–44; and culture, 239; and economic culture, 6, 7; and economy, 2; and Guayaquil, 92, 131, 133, 178, 238; and Weber, 6

Relationships between humans, 4, 9, 11, 242 n.2

Religion in Baltimore: and artisans, 160, 161; and churches, 37, 38–39, 44; and elites, 101–102, 109; Guayaquil compared to, 44, 235; and merchants, 109, 131; and middling sectors, 175–176; and neighborhoods, 38–39; and poor, 208; and professionals, 163; and Protestantism, 102, 104, 109, 165, 175

Religion in Guayaquil: Baltimore compared to, 44, 235; and churches, 15, 26, 29–30, 44, 246 n.24; and merchants, 82–83, 131; and middling sectors, 142, 175–176; and poor, 29–30; and taxation, 92

Resources: and economic historians, 10; and Guayaquil merchants, 259–260 n.38; Indians as, 233; of Maryland, 234; and materialists, 3; sharing of, 240

Rico Rocafuerte, María Francisca, 81, 86

Robinet, William, 77, 88

Rocafuerte, Francisca, 81, 86

Rocafuerte, Vicente, 17, 60, 90

Roca, Vicente Ramón: Baltimore elites compared to, 128–129; and civic involvement, 73, 77, 82; and credit, 84; and crime, 71, 99; and day laborers, 194; and poor, 197, 237; and taxes, 95, 183–184, 203; and trade, 89, 105

Samaniego family, 91, 92

San Ignacio de Loyola, 146

Santa Ana Hill, 27, 28, 31

Santos, Manuel, 91, 92

Second Great Awakening, 109, 175

Simmonds, William, 53

Slaves and slavery in Baltimore: and education, 228; and elites, 101; and free blacks, 224; limitations on, 40–41, 43; and manufactories, 219; memoirs of, 15; and merchants, 108, 124–125, 132; and opportunity, xiv–xv; and poor, 211–213, 230, 232; population of, 17, 33, 45, 63; and public auction, 35; and statistics, 66

Slaves and slavery in Guayaquil: and artisans, 139, 141; and cacao, 62, 190; and class relations, 29; and consumption patterns, 200; and entrepreneurs, 149; and hospitals, 32; and independence, 189, 190; and merchants, 95–96, 97; and middling sector, 138; population of, 17, 66; and Spanish conquest, 51, 53; and taxation, 184
Small, Jacob, 104, 122–123, 177
Smith, John, 11, 54
Sociedad Económica de Amigos del País, 84
Sokoloff, Kenneth, 10, 11
South America: and Baltimore, 34, 108, 164; and Great Britain, 61, 88; and independence from Spain, 59, 64; and women's education, 86. See also Indians of South America
Spafford, Samuel, 114, 157
Spain: and cacao trade, 59; and class relations, 12; and conquest, 9, 47, 49–53, 185, 245 n.16; feudalism of, 55; and Great Britain, 53–54; and Guayaquil artisans, 139; and Guayaquil Indians, 25; and Guayaquil merchants, 80, 129–130; and Guayaquil poor, 33; independence from, xiii, 59–60, 73–76, 105; and slavery, 95; and taxation, 52, 59; and work ethic, 11, 234
Stern, Steve, 9, 244 n.12
Structuralists, 2–3
Stump, John, 107–108
Stump, Samuel, 107–108
Stump family, 106, 107, 115

Taxation in Baltimore: and infrastructure, 106–107, 123–124, 178–179; and merchants, 121–124, 132, 133; and middling sectors, 155; and poor, 121, 122, 123, 209–210; and professionals, 166–167; and wealth distribution, 67
Taxation in Guayaquil: extent of, 28; and merchants, 76–77, 79, 92–95, 132, 256–257 n.15, 262 n.54; and middling sectors, 151; and poor, 183, 201, 203; and wealth distribution, 67
Tertulias, 73–74, 82
Tobacco, 55–56, 58, 62, 65, 92
Tobar, Luis, 193–194
Trade: and Baltimore, 105–109, 129; and economic culture, 5–6; and economic historians, 2; and Guayaquil, 16, 23–25,

28, 59, 61–62, 73, 78–82, 129; and Indians, 49; and poverty of majority, 10; and trade/commerce occupations, 66. See also Internal trade; International trade
Tyson, Thomas, 105–106, 130
Tyson family, 106, 125

Union Female Society, 171–172, 174
United States: antiaristocratic tradition in, 132–133; foreign policy of, 7; and free blacks, 211; and Great Britain, 131; and Guayaquil merchants, 87, 89–90, 92; and Guayaquil trade, 25, 61; Indians of, 11, 13, 54–55, 57, 238; and international trade, 5; Latin America compared to, 1, 10, 12; and Protestantism, 6–7; slavery in, 238

Vejarano, Jacinto, 79–80
Venezuela, 60, 80
Villamil, José, 74, 77, 81–82, 91–92, 130
Virginia, 55, 57

Wallerstein, Immanuel, 9, 244 n.12
War of 1812, 42, 63–64, 125, 173
Watkins, William, 166
Wealth: and Baltimore, 67, 123; and colonists, 10, 57; distribution of, 9, 66–68, 239, 240, 288 n.7; and domestic market, 5; and independence from Spain, 60; and materialists, 3; of United States, 1
Weber, Max: and economic culture, 6, 12–13, 236; and Harrison, 243 n.7; and Landes, 8; and work attitudes, 234
Whites in Baltimore: and civic involvement, 171; and crime, 223; and day laborers, 154; and education, 127, 165, 227, 228; and free blacks, 178, 211–212; and poor, 225–226; and professionals, 163, 166; and slaves, 212–213
Whites in Guayaquil: and artisans, 140; and class relations, 29; and professionals, 143; and slavery, 95; and taxes, 151
Women in Baltimore: and artisans, 159, 162, 275 n.21; and banks, 174; and civic involvement, 171–172; and education, 228; and elites, 102–103, 130; and entrepreneurs, 168–169; and manufactories, 219–220; and merchants, 107, 108, 114–115; and poor, 209, 220–221, 222, 226, 227; and professionals, 165; and work opportunities, 36–37

Women in Guayaquil: and day laborers, 29, 193; and elites, 72, 73–74, 75, 80, 81, 86–87, 130, 257–258n.23; and entrepreneurs, 147–148; and free blacks, 190, 192; and hospitals, 32; and Indians, 186; and poor, 195, 196, 197, 203; and taxes, 183; and wages, 98; and work opportunities, 29

Work attitudes: Baltimore/Guayaquil comparison, 45, 179; and culture, 9, 10, 239; and economic culture, 4, 6, 13; and Weber, 234

Work ethic: Baltimore/Guayaquil comparison, 44, 133, 231; and culture, 10; and economy, 2; and Protestantism, 6–7, 8; and Spain, 11, 234

Yagual, Ana: ambitions of, 1; documentary evidence on, 14–15; and elites, 71; and entertainment, 197; and exclusion, 237; and impressions of Guayaguil, 18; and middling sectors, 177, 204; and migration to Guayaquil, xiii–xiv, xv, 23, 28–29; outcome of, 240

Zambos, 29, 139, 140, 152, 188, 202